D1328463

American Passage

THE COMMUNICATIONS FRONTIER
IN EARLY NEW ENGLAND

KATHERINE GRANDJEAN

Harvard University Press

Cambridge, Massachusetts
London, England
2015

Copyright © 2015 by Katherine Grandjean
All rights reserved
Printed in the United States of America

Library of Congress Cataloging-in-Publication Data

Grandjean, Katherine, 1977–
    American passage : the communications frontier in early New England / Katherine Grandjean.
        pages cm
    Includes bibliographical references and index.
    ISBN 978-0-674-28991-8
    1. New England—History—Colonial period, ca. 1600-1775. 2. New England—Social
    life and customs—To 1775. 3. New England—Social conditions—17th century.
    4. Communication—Social aspects—New England—History—17th century. 5. Social
    networks—New England—History—17th century. 6. Information behavior—New
    England—History—17th century. 7. Frontier and pioneer life—New England. I. Title.
    F7.G736 2015
    974'.01—dc23   2014014452

For my parents

Contents

. . . All these upwhirled aloft
Fly o'er the backside of the world far off
Into a limbo large and broad, since called
The Paradise of Fools, to few unknown
Long after, now unpeopled, and untrod;
All this dark globe the Fiend found as he passed,
And long he wandered, till at last a gleam
Of dawning light turned thitherward in haste
His traveled steps . . .

—John Milton, *Paradise Lost*

Every place whereon the soles of your feet shall
tread shall be yours.

—Deuteronomy 11:24

Footprints

New England, 1638

It happened in the woods, north of Narragansett. Four English servants lost their bearings. They had been on their way to New Netherland—and freedom. But on making their escape, "they went not the ordinarie way, but shaped such a course as they thought to avoyd the pursue of any." Avoiding familiar terrain had a price. Somewhere in "the way that lyeth between the Bay of Massachusetts and the Narrigansetts," the trees and the brooks and the leaves underfoot began to blur together. They were lost. Now half-starved and desperate, they paused along an unfamiliar riverbank and rested.[1]

Twelve miles to the south, news of the lost party reached Roger Williams. A "native, passing through us, brought me word," he later wrote. Narragansett travelers had noticed the "famished" men who had encamped at the Pawcatuck River, and may even have talked to them. A Narragansett messenger was apparently able to tell Williams how long the party had been lost ("five days") and how far they had wandered ("into our path but six miles"). Williams promptly sent provisions. The next morning, when the refreshed wanderers appeared at his doorstep, he learned who the men were: "one Arthur Peach of Plymouth, an Irishman, John Barnes, his man, and two others come from Pascataquack, traveling to Qunnihticut." While they ate breakfast, Williams quickly penned some letters for them to carry to Connecticut and went about finding them a guide for their travels.

Not long after the men had gone (with Williams's missives in hand), darker news arrived at Williams's door. A Native man, carrying cloth and wampum from Massachusetts Bay, had been found "groaning in the path," bloody and near death. He had been stabbed "through the leg and the belly with one thrust." What Williams heard next must have turned his stomach. Who had slain him, the Narragansetts had asked the dying man. He answered, "four Englishmen." Hearing this, the Indians had gone to look for the killers at Pawtucket. But alas, "Arthur and his company" had hastily "got on hose and shoes and departed in the night."[2] That very morning, it appeared, Williams had unknowingly fed the murderers and happily sent them off with full bellies, a guide, and a packet of his own letters.

This was New England in the summer of 1638: not New England at all, really, but a scattered collection of English hamlets. It was easy to get lost by straying too far from the "ordinarie way." Arthur Peach and his fellow runaways had fallen into the gap between Massachusetts Bay and Connecticut. They had simply wandered into the wrong path—one that channeled straight into Narragansett. Though it was a well-beaten route, it was virtually unknown to most Englishmen. (In fact, the location of the murder would eventually present a quandary, when it came to doling out punishments to Peach's gang, since "no English had jurisdiction in the place."[3])

Early New England was little more than a spotty patchwork of settlement. In the late 1630s, it was perhaps at its spottiest. The English settlements had just begun to expand, truly. In only a few short years, the near-bursting Massachusetts Bay had spun off several new colonies, none particularly nearby. Connecticut was settled in the mid-1630s, Providence in 1636, and New Haven in 1638. William Pynchon trekked westward to found Agawam, later Springfield, in 1636. By water, these places were separated by long, arduous boat trips; by land, lengthy and unfamiliar stretches of woodland. Between the colonies lay huge pockets of uncertainties, deterring all but the most intrepid of travelers. Even the most dauntless of Englishmen had only a tenuous command of the great, yawning spaces between colonies. In 1648, Roger Williams hinted at how the English felt about this geography, when he described his fellow colonists as "poore grashoppers, hopping and skipping from branch to twig" in a "vale of teares."[4] Peach's men had simply found themselves lost, in mid-hop.

Williams himself, unwitting host to the fugitives, had only recently struck out into this "vale of tears." And he, too, had been avoiding capture. If Arthur Peach leads us into the gaps between New England's early plantations, Roger Williams's story tells how such gulfs had lately opened up. Colonizing the northeast should have been fairly harmonious, since those who were settling New England in the 1630s were a relatively homogeneous group. By and large, they were 'Puritans' (the somewhat pejorative term used in England to describe Protestants who were especially zealous about purging the Church of England of its lingering vestiges of Catholicism). In England their beliefs had cohered well. But in the New World, English Puritanism began to fracture under the weight of its own rigidity.

Roger Williams fell into one of those cracks. On arriving in Massachusetts Bay in the early 1630s, he had quickly drawn the ire of the colony's leaders. His preaching in Salem had challenged magistrates' authority and eventually earned him banishment from Massachusetts Bay. Only two years before Peach's party stumbled southward, Williams himself was chased from the colony. In January 1636, disapproving leaders voted to exile the rogue minister back to England "by a shippe then readye to departe." But Williams refused to be "shipped." When a pinnace was dispatched to collect him, Williams's would-be captors "fonde, he had been gone 3: dayes before, but whither, they could not learne."[5] In fact, he had turned away from the shore and fled inland, instead, into an icy Narragansett winter.

Williams's trek may have taken him down the same southwestward winding, Narragansett-bound trail used by Peach. Virtually all that connected the colonies, by land, was a labyrinthine system of Indian pathways—what the English writer William Wood called the "strange labyrinth of unbeaten bushy ways in the woody wilderness."[6] English travelers were woefully unequipped to understand this "labyrinth," actually an elaborate network of trails, some narrow and some broad, all wending toward significant Algonquian places. Inexperienced wayfarers could be bitten by their own overconfidence. On one journey, Wood and some fellow travelers had lost their way along a trail that they adjudged "too broad for an Indian path (which seldom is broader than a cart's rut)." Their instincts proved faulty: The trail they were following was, in fact, an Indian path. The "daily concourse of Indians from the Narragansetts who traded for shoes, wearing them homewards," Wood explained, "had made this Indian tract like an English walk and had reared up great sticks against trees and marked the rest with their hatchets in the English fashion, which begat in us a security of our wrong way to be right."[7] Even when they looked for markings made "in the English fashion," Wood suggested, sojourners could easily be led astray.

Such deceptive markings may have also seduced Arthur Peach and his fellow men toward Narragansett. The path into which Peach's runaways "fell" was probably a trail running roughly west from Plymouth through various Wampanoag and Narragansett places: Titicut, Cohannet, Misquamsqueece (where the murder occurred), Seekonk, and, finally, Pawtucket falls. Just to the south lay Roger Williams's small foothold at the headwaters of Narragansett Bay, a place he called Providence. The path apparently saw little English traffic. As "a means of communication," one historian notes wryly, "the Indian path only may have reminded the Separatists at Plymouth and the religious dissenters in Providence of the great distance existing between them."[8] That "great distance" did indeed complicate communication with other English plantations. When Peach and his men arrived in Providence, Williams was eager to seize the opportunity. Passing news along was never easy. That Williams so hastily scribbled a few lines for delivery in Connecticut, and handed them over to perfect strangers, is not terribly surprising. Most long-distance news traveled this way in early New England: by whatever means were available, and never with regularity. Though by his own account he frequently welcomed Native sojourners, passing colonists were much more of a rarity. Williams would have been only too thrilled to greet English passers-by on their way to Connecticut.

But Arthur Peach's men never went to Connecticut, and neither did Williams's letters. Instead they headed southeast, toward the ocean. Ironically, the fugitives used Williams's correspondence as a kind of pass, as they moved through Narragansett. When the Narragansett sachem Miantonomi demanded to know their business, they simply held up the packet. "[T]they showed Miantunnomu letters to Aquedenick, (which were mine to Qunnihtiqut,)," Williams later fumed, "and so to Aquedenick they past." Once there, the men likely hoped to board a boat to New Netherland, the Dutch colony that lay two hundred miles to the west and well out of the reach of English authorities. But on Aquidneck Island the spree ended. When a messenger Williams had sent "pursuing after them" learned of the men's passage to the island, Williams promptly "sent information of them" to the English there.[9] The information moved quickly through Narragansett messengers. English news may have moved clumsily over land, but Indian transmission was swift. The four men—Arthur Peach, Thomas Jackson, Richard Stinnings, and Daniel Cross—were captured.

If Arthur Peach proved a poor pilot for his fellow runaways, he nonetheless makes a perfect guide into early New England. The New England of Arthur Peach was a dangerous realm, a place still largely unfamiliar to Englishmen. Its colonies were growing wildly; Massachusetts Bay was all but overflowing, as thousands of English transplants arrived at its doorstep. New settlements had begun to sprout wherever these migrants found marsh and floodplain to their liking. But English colonists, like Peach himself, had little command of this geography. In its features, in its landmarks, and, most of all, as defined by the people who traversed it, the northeastern landscape remained, for decades, decidedly Algonquian. English transplants struggled mightily to master Indian travel routes, like those that had baffled Arthur Peach, and, ultimately, to forge their own. How that struggle unfolded is a fundamental part of the story of English colonialism.[10]

With these things in mind, this book offers a retelling of how New England was settled. In many ways, the following pages revisit a very old story: the meeting of peoples in early America. It is a story that demands telling, again and again. A story that we are oddly compelled to keep telling ourselves, as if—perhaps once—the outcome might be different. Historians have told this story many times, in many different ways. But the principal actors are almost always the same: sailors, soldiers, pilgrims, and Indians. In the late fifteenth century, Europe began shedding small convoys of explorers and adventurers, soon followed by colonists. These seedlings of colonization grew into great taproots of power and eventually all but overwhelmed Native America. There is good reason to keep plumbing the depths of this story. For the western world, at least, the meeting of Europe and the Americas was one of the most momentous developments in human history. It is this same drama that I am interested in, though I see it in different terms. Rather than envisioning the history of English colonization as a series of settlements being planted in American soil, I see it as something more fluid, more fragile, more animated. I see it as a web of communications.[11]

Early America was a busy tangle of travelers, couriers, sailors, and riders—a mess of motion. But this bustle is generally not what we picture. What we see, instead, is usually fairly stationary. No corner of English

America suffers more, in this sense, than early New England. In textbooks, and in the mind's eye, we see the early northeast from a bird's-eye view. Our mental image of the English colonies owes, in great part, to the printed maps of the early modern period, which, in a great leap of imagination, rose high above the land to offer sweeping vistas of colonial power—even where their creators knew very little about the actual land depicted.[12] Take, for instance, the one printed here. This, the water-colored creation of English cartographer John Seller, is something like how we generally envision early "New England": as a fixed block of territory, labeled boastfully in great block letters. By their very nature, the maps that hover over New England are relentlessly static; they offer, only, a collection of insistent boundary lines, colonies fixed into place, Native villages pinned into position. But human beings are hardly so obedient. What we rarely see lurking behind these maps, and what they cannot capture, is something far more capricious: early America's human landscape. Missing from most maps, it seems, are the very footprints of early American history.

We know surprisingly little about how news and people traveled in earliest America. Although historians have ably plotted later developments in colonial communication, they have left the seventeenth century largely unexplored.[13] Scholars can perhaps be forgiven for assuming there was not much to study. Earliest America published no newspapers. Not until 1704, when the newly appointed Boston postmaster commenced printing early America's first recurring newspaper, would readers be able to glean news from a "public print." Nor did postal service exist. It is true, then, that news often lumbered in these early years. Most information passed privately, orally and through leaders. Correspondence crawled, sometimes taking weeks to reach its destination. But this backward image does not begin to capture the complexity of early America's channels of communication.

Descriptions of early New England tend to conjure images of orderly, insular Puritan towns, with Indians and others pushed to society's edges.[14] But the reality was much messier. Early New England was not simply a patchwork of walled-off pastures and plots. It had an alternate, *human* geography, as well—a geography of letters, travelers, rumors, and movement. This book recreates that buzzing scene. It reconstructs an unseen world of communications during the earliest years of English colonization, from about the 1630s to the 1710s. Using diaries, travel literature, almanacs, court records, war narratives, and the thousands of English letters that have

John Seller, "A Mapp of New England," ca. 1675. Hand-colored engraving. *(Courtesy of New York Public Library)*

survived the intervening centuries, it is possible to build a portrait of long-distance networks snaking through the countryside. With that portrait in view, the settling of New England, it turns out, looks different. No longer do the colonies seem to be such steady bastions of English strength, nor comprised of the secure and quiet villages of popular imagination. The English quest to control the northeast, in fact, entailed a great struggle to control the flow of people and news.

Travel and communications, in fact, provide uncannily strong barometers of power. Who could travel where, who controlled the routes winding through the woods, who dictated what news might be sent—These things tell as much about power and geographic authority as any deed or document.[15] Historians may not have conceived of communication as a critical piece of the English colonial project. But colonists and kings, alike, did. They understood: Gaining control of New England was not solely a matter of consuming territory, of transforming woods into farms. It also meant mastering the lines of communication.[16] Colonial travelers coursing through the landscape did as much as any transfer of land to claim and define the region as English. Following them, over the years, reveals a new dimension of contest and conquest in the northeast. With their bodies, with their very feet, colonists marked the bounds of English New England.

"Every place whereon the soles of your feet shall tread shall be yours," promises a verse in Deuteronomy. And so it was. Though not, perhaps, quite so easily as we might imagine.

II.

New England. The very name is an act of arrogance, of hubris. It was coined not by the region's first colonists but by England's infamous adventurer John Smith, who first explored the climes north of Virginia in 1614. Smith was a prolific writer and a tireless promoter of colonization. His boosting of the realm that he called, rather presumptuously, "New England" did not go unheard. When English separatists—those we know as "the Pilgrims"— looked to settle in America in 1620, they used Smith's map. (Smith himself was willing to act as a guide, but preferring simply to consult his writings instead, they refused his offer of service.) Even in this decision, however, lurks a bit of irony: When the Pilgrims arrived on the east coast, they sailed astray. In fact, they had not even intended to land at Cape Cod; they had had the Hudson River in mind, but a series of errors and misfortunes landed them on the Massachusetts coast instead. There, the *Mayflower* nearly wrecked amidst the treacherous shoals that lay just off the coast.[17] The land proved no more welcoming than the sea. When a scouting party stepped ashore at "First Encounter" beach, they were promptly peppered with arrows by fearful Nauset Indians.

Despite Smith's determination to christen it a "New England," then, this northern realm proved cold, unfamiliar, and rather intimidating to its first colonists. One among them, William Bradford, later remembered the December 1620 landing thusly:

> And for the season it was winter, and they that know the winters of that cun-
> trie know them to be sharp & violent, & subjecte to cruell & feirce stormes,
> deangerous to travill to known places, much more to serch an unknown

coast. Besids, what could they see but a hidious & desolate wildernes, full of wild beasts & willd men? and what multituds ther might be of them they knew not. Nether could they, as it were, goe up to the tope of Pisgah, to vew from this willdernes a more goodly cuntrie to feed their hops; for which way soever they turnd their eys (save upward to the heavens) they could have litle solace or content in respecte of any outward objects. For sumer being done, all things stand upon them with a wetherbeaten face; and the whole countrie, full of woods & thickets, represented a wild & savage heiw.[18]

Later readers have tended to adjudge this description of such a "hidious & desolate wildernes" overblown. Still, not all of this rhetoric was exaggeration. Even after the Pilgrims selected a place in which to settle, they were slow to explore the surrounding countryside. And when they did, they often got lost. Bradford's characterization of both the land and its people as "wild & savage" betrays a certain prejudice. But his befuddlement also underscores the absurdity of calling such a place "New England."

For much of the seventeenth century, what we call *New England* was little more than a few isolated pockets of plantings. This was not a contiguous landscape. Even the title "New England" is something of a hopeful fiction, since neither its territory nor its identity had yet hardened into a solid whole. Too tight a focus on Massachusetts Bay—admittedly, the "capital" of the region in these years—threatens to lull us into imagining New England as a closed, contiguous society where Englishmen reigned supreme from early on. But look to the north, and there are the French—a constant worry for English colonists. Look to the west: Mohawks. Iroquoia. Scan southward, and there flows Long Island Sound. The Narragansetts, the Dutch, New Netherland. Within and among English settlements: Pequots, Mohegans, Nipmucks, and others, all there. Colonists may have imagined New England as a unit as early as the 1630s, but geographically, it was merely an archipelago of scattered, English islands in a vast, Indian sea. Not only at the margins of New England but in the interior, in the vast gaps of land between plantations, English control did not exist. It was an idea, not reality.

The early northeast was the meeting place of a varied lot. Populating the borderlands of Lower New England, in the early seventeenth century, was a motley cast of characters. Its first people, of course, were the many groups of Algonquians who had long called the region home. Estimates of the Native population vary widely. But, before contact with Europeans introduced the diseases that swept through Native villages with devastating impact, as many as 140,000 Algonquians may have lived in the place later called "New England."[19] Of these thousands, the greatest part was concentrated in southern New England. These coastal Algonquians are the Native characters who mostly populate the story that follows.

"Algonquian" is a linguistic descriptor. Northeastern Algonquians were part of a language group that ranged as far north as the edges of Huronia (the Great Lakes region) and as far south as Carolina. (To the west lived great numbers of Iroquoian speakers, including the much-feared Mohawks, the scourge of eastern Algonquians.) But shared language did not necessarily translate into shared perspective or political alliance. Although Algonquians were probably far more interconnected than the historical record can truly reflect, there were important political and cultural distinctions among them. The Indians who lived in the northeast—Nipmucks, Pocumtucks, Narragansetts, Pequots, Massachusetts, Mohegans, Wampanoags, Abenakis— shared cultural connections, but, much like Europeans, they lived in a world of shifting allegiances and complex political relationships, built both on kinship and on tribute. Political leadership, among Algonquians, was rather more diffuse than in Europe; there was no "king" among Indians, despite the haste of some later Englishmen to crown various Native men as such. But there were indeed leaders, called "sachems," and—again, like Europeans—Native groups sometimes harbored bitter and festering rivalries, as well.[20]

The arrival of Europeans aggravated some of those rivalries. Well before the Pilgrims landed, local Algonquians had known Europeans, passing fishermen and traders, mostly. (The Nausets attacked the 1620 scouting party partly because they had seen their kin taken captive by an earlier ship.) Narragansetts had first encountered Europeans at least a century earlier, when explorer Giovanni da Verrazano coasted into their bay. "We formed a great friendship with them," he wrote.[21] By 1638, when Arthur Peach wandered into their country, the Narragansetts were fully plunged into a new world. Trade with Europeans enriched some Indians, but it also bred competition among them, and the Narragansetts were gaining new enemies as well as friends. Alliances wobbled. (The man Arthur Peach killed, Penowayanquis, was not a Narragansett; he was a Nipmuck, who was working for them. A few decades later, Penowayanquis's people would try to shake off Narragansett dominance by casting their lot with Massachusetts Bay.)

What further complicated these relationships, in the early seventeenth century, was the arrival of Dutchmen. In the 1610s, the Dutch built a permanent trading post on the Hudson River; by the mid-1620s, they had purchased Manhattan Island. Though they sent a smattering of colonists to plant permanently, the Dutch were more interested in trade than in land. "New Netherland," therefore, never grew in quite the same manner as did the English colonies. Even at its peak, it probably claimed no more than a few thousand colonists. But, to all living in the region, the Dutch were quite obviously present. When the first English arrived in the 1620s, in other words, they set roots in a place that was already busy with non-English characters. To those alighting on the crust of coastline along Long Island Sound, the Dutch presence would have been especially apparent. There, English colonists would have regularly spied Dutch ships docked in nearby coves, handing off duffel and knives and other such items to Indian traders.[22]

Among these people, and through the many in-between places of the northeast, there was a lively and mutable march of goods and things, pulsating, always, across space. Words and letters, like people, traversed the region's hazy and pretended boundaries. There was, in early New England, a "communications frontier." Although it is not a perfect abbreviation, that phrase captures the two chief concerns of this book: the movement of people, goods, and information (communications) across a region of intercultural contact (frontier). *Frontier* is a loaded word, with a fraught history. I use it in the sense of describing a realm of intercultural exchange and competition, in which no one group is able to exercise dominance over another.[23] If that definition applies to certain physical places in the early northeast, it also applies to the slippery realm of information, talk, and rumors. Collecting news was critical, in this confused world. But it was also difficult to do reliably.

The stories that follow evoke the English pursuit of dominance in this place, along this frontier. Because, to its first colonists, much of the northeast was unfamiliar marchland, colonial exchange was often at the mercy of Algonquians. It sometimes depended on Algonquians. For much of the century, in fact, English communications blurred with Dutch and Algonquian networks. Even when it was meant solely for English eyes, news did not pass solely through English hands. Try to follow it, and you will be pulled swiftly outward from English towns into Indian pathways, over land and into the water, down into the holds of Dutch ships. Algonquian and Dutch characters were very present, and very involved, in the English world of talk and letters. Particularly outside of Massachusetts Bay, early New England was a polyglot place, a babel of languages and cultures, anything but assuredly *English*.

But the latter part of the seventeenth century witnessed a quiet revolution in English communications. The second half of the book registers these changes. Partly, they were fueled by a drive to bring goods to market. A spike in the availability of horses (bred, mostly, for export to the West Indies), for instance, sent English travelers into interior pathways with new abandon. But English efforts to control the communications frontier also happened by design. Some of these moves, like the first attempt at postal service in the 1670s, were prompted by the King. These shifts in English communication have not been recognized by historians. But they were significant to early New England's history. In surprising ways, history turned on the flow of news. English efforts to improve communications triggered new problems, even as they enabled the colonies to become more secure. All of this had profound implications, too, for the northeast's Native people.

The story does not end, however, with a neat and tidy English conquest of the communications frontier. Not quite. In the late seventeenth and early eighteenth centuries, it is true, easier English communications fell into place. Roads were forged, and posts traveled them more regularly. A newspaper began trumpeting stories throughout the region. Printing presses grew busy, multiplied. But the story isn't quite so simple. As it happened, these were also the very years during which imperial wars flared along New England's northern borderlands and a new menace emerged: French and Indian raids began to thrash, repeatedly, the outermost English settlements. Although most New Englanders did not experience this violence, they heard and read about it—at length. The book thus concludes with an ironic twist, of sorts: Better-established communication was not, entirely, a blessing. New England's own communications network, in a sense, turned on itself. The press, in particular, brought the horrors of war to all parts of the region.

I chose to write about New England, in part, because the sources are frankly unparalleled. Thousands of letters, court records, diaries, and other narratives capture, in sometimes stunning detail, the flow of people and things. At the heart of this study is a database of nearly 3,000 letters, drawn from the Winthrop Family Papers, through which I track couriers and travelers across the region.[24] But these records are, of course, not perfect. They reflect, mostly, the concerns of elite English writers. Particularly bothersome is how often they fail to capture the experiences—not to mention the humanly passions, the everyday joys and troubles—of Native people. I have wherever possible tried to plumb the perspectives of Native, as well as English, characters. Where their faces remain stubbornly shadowed, I respect silences in the record—though, as with other mysteries left unresolved in the historical record, I sometimes resort to speculation, or to searching aloud for possible answers. There is much to be uncovered about this passage of American history. But there are some things we can never know with absolute certainty.

On the whole, this narrative does not substantially rewrite the chronology of early American history. It does, however, offer a new angle on what happened—and how. Changes in travel and communications worked both to tie the English colonies closer together and to broadcast English control of the region. This story, I believe, foreshadows broader—and more studied—'communications revolutions' that later echoed across the continent. Ultimately, it contributes to a new view of early America as a living, moving landscape. It poses this question: Does the walking trail, perhaps, tell as much as the fence?[25]

IV.

What precisely had happened along that trail to Narragansett, in 1638, emerged eventually. The man Arthur Peach had killed was Penowayanquis, a Nipmuck trader. Penowayanquis had been on his way back from trading in Massachusetts Bay, with "cloth & beads aboute him," when he crossed paths with the four fugitives. The men had spotted him crouched at the edge of a swamp, "a little way out of the path." They recognized him; they "had meett him the day before," in Massachusetts. Penowayanquis knew the Englishmen, as well. He knew they had seen him "in the bay [with] his beads." They saw his beads again, now, and to Arthur Peach those beads were a tempting booty, one that could pay for the rest of his journey. He whispered to his comrades, *I'll rob and kill the Indian.* The other men balked. Surely this was a bad idea. But Peach grew obstinate. He would do it.[26]

Peach called out to Penowayanquis. He held up a pipe and beckoned the man to come drink tobacco. Penowayanquis came, perhaps warily, and sat with Peach's men. When he reached for the pipe, Peach drew his sword and slashed the man "through the leg into the belly." Bleeding, Penowayanquis clambered to get away. Peach lunged at him, again, but missed. Penowayanquis found his footing and began to run, but the men followed. Badly wounded and robbed, Penowayanquis finally slipped into a swamp, where the Englishmen "lost him quite." The crunch of their footsteps slowly faded. When night fell, hoping that "some passenger might help him," he crawled into the path and collapsed. Narragansetts found him soon thereafter, languishing and bloody but able to tell what had transpired.[27]

Arthur Peach got his due punishment in the end. He and his cohorts (save Daniel Cross, who escaped, rather improbably, and was never recaptured) were hanged for their misdeeds in mid-September 1638. But his story only begins to evoke the darkness overhanging early New England. It only begins to suggest the contested nature of New England's pathways, of its thorny landscape. Well before Arthur Peach had set out on his reckless way, Englishmen had begun to awaken to the problem of sending news and things across vast stretches of unmastered space. Two years before Arthur Peach blundered into the woods, a different Englishman, one who also likely thought himself in command of the route that stretched before him, encountered a problem in his path. It was 1636, summer, over the dusky waters of Long Island Sound. We start there.

I

"the Ocean of Troubles and Trials wherein we saile"

Now strike your sailes ye jolly Mariners,
For we be come unto a quiet rode,
Where we must land some of our passengers,
And light this wearie vessell of her lode.
Here she a while may make her safe abode,
Till she repairéd have her tackles spent,
And wants supplide. And then againe abroad
On the long voyage whereto she is bent:
Well may she speede and fairely finish her intent.
 —Edmund Spenser, from *The Faerie Queene,* Book I, Canto XII

Comishoónhom?   *Goe you by water?*
 —Roger Williams, *A Key into the Language of America* (1643)

JOHN OLDHAM DIED in his boat. In sticky midsummer 1636, a thick heat hovering over Long Island Sound, the English trader was found dead. His corpse was discovered entangled in the netting of his pinnace, afloat off the northern tip of Block Island. Sailing by, fellow trader John Gallop spied the vessel moving erratically and quickly realized something was amiss. Gallop's crew first spotted "an old seyne" dangling from the boat and only later "perceived a dead body under it, with the head cut off." That the body was

Oldham's was not immediately obvious. The hapless trader was "starke naked" and "his head clefte to the braynes." When the boat was discovered, Indians were still aboard, apparently in the midst of cutting off his hands and feet. After forcing the Native men from the pinnace (tossing some overboard with their hands tied, thereby precluding any swimming), Gallop took up the "bloody head and . . . knew it to be Mr. Oldham's." "[A]h Brother Oldham, it is thee," he said. "I am resolved to avenge thy blood." He then reverently slipped the body into the sea.[1]

It was barely sixteen years since the first English settlers had stepped, rather cautiously, onto the beaches of Cape Cod. New England was, in many ways, flourishing. It was welcoming numberless new migrants, the greatest part of them clustered at Massachusetts Bay. The Bay Colony had its origins at the Shawmut Peninsula, soon recast as "Boston," but by 1636 thousands of recent English arrivals had spilled over into the adjacent countryside. They flew further, too, as crowding and quarrels, mostly theological, forced fractures among them. One of these fractures in the community of saints had sent Roger Williams fleeing southward into exile in Narragansett. Another inspired a migration westward, and inland, to found new settlements on the Connecticut River. There, migrants from Massachusetts Bay staked out a crook of land just below the falls of the Connecticut (what would later become the colony of that same name). Meanwhile, another group of Bay men built a fort at the river's mouth. All of them jostled for control of this tempting western intervale.

The wider English Atlantic, in the 1630s, was roiling. Tens of thousands of Englishmen were pouring out of England and landing in various beachside and island colonies. They were, collectively, creating an empire.[2] New England, in many respects, was not like those other places. It seemed to grope its way toward stability faster than other parts of the English colonial world, where men competed ruthlessly and starved and died. Migrants to New England were exceptional. Mostly, they were like-minded and religious and committed to community, and they shuffled aboard ships with small children and spouses and some means, whereas migrants who went elsewhere, overwhelmingly, were indentured young men. Compared to those other places, New England looks strong and secure; better fed and more orderly, for instance, than its chaotic stepsibling, the Chesapeake.[3] But in some regards, it may not have been so different. Here, too, the struggle toward stability pushed Englishmen to do brutal and desperate things. Despite its gestures toward expansion, the New England of 1636 was still a world of uncertainties. It rested on tenuous footholds and white knuckles. That became clear when John Oldham's body surfaced in July.

No one knows quite why John Oldham died. He was a seasoned trader, one that must have seemed unlikely to meet his death at the hands of Indians. Had he angered his trading partners by brokering some bad deal? Had he gotten drunk and violated some important custom of exchange?[4] What led to the murder will likely never be known. What followed in the wake of his death, though, is far less of a mystery. Somehow, the discovery of John Oldham's body triggered a series of events that flared into New England's first Indian war. The Pequot War—named for its eventual losers—lasted roughly from 1636 to 1638. War is, in fact, a lofty word for what occurred over these years. The conflict is better understood as a series of bloody raids and surprise attacks: traders killed, corn burned, captives taken. Eventually the violence escalated toward a wholesale assault on the Pequot people. The war reached its gruesome apex with the burning of Mystic Fort, where, in May 1637, hundreds of Pequots perished in a single morning. This would be the bloodiest episode that the newly-planted New England colonies had yet known.[5]

How this came about is not easy to tell. Although colonial writers nearly always cited that macabre scene in Long Island Sound—Oldham's demise— as a chief "ground of the Pequente warr which followed," that explanation seems, somehow, unsatisfactory.[6] The death of a grizzled English trader, in short, hardly seems sufficient explanation for the horrors that followed. But John Oldham's death came during a precarious moment in the colonies. There was not enough to eat. There was very bad weather. A great hurricane blasted through the colonies in 1635, destroying much of that year's harvest. Crops and cattle failed. At the same time, waves of new migrants put sudden stresses on New England's ability to provide for itself. In this perfect storm of calamities, the newer colonies were hit particularly hard. What made their situation so dire was the very fact that they were so far removed from the economic and social hub of Massachusetts Bay. Communications between colonies were fragile and often unreliable. Not only was widespread scarcity gripping New England in 1636; it was also difficult to get goods to the people who most needed them. Here lies the menace that colonists must have perceived in Oldham's loss. In the mid-1630s, only a precious few coastal traders connected the far-flung colonies of earliest New England. One of them was John Oldham.

Nothing can justify the war's injustices. No explanation, despite historians' compulsion to somehow explain the inexplicable, satisfies entirely.

But, with the war's true backdrop in view, it becomes easier to see how a few dead, bloated traders could have taken on a particularly fearful meaning. These people, after all, were the ones who brought supplies, letters, food, and news. Without them, Connecticut and the other outlying colonies had no lifeline back to Massachusetts. They had little hope of survival. With menacing clarity, the Pequot War lay bare the vulnerabilities borne by English expansion and the resulting holes in the English landscape.

I.

It is hardly a secret that many of the earliest English colonies struggled with hunger. Roanoke suffered when Algonquian neighbors refused aid; Bermuda went hungry in the 1610s, after rats dispatched by a Spanish ship devoured the island's supplies; Barbados and Providence Island were similarly strained in the 1630s. Early Jamestown endured a "starving time" so severe that some of its inhabitants were driven to cannibalism, even unearthing corpses that had been claimed by the colony's double curse of famine and disease. To some, the inability of England's first colonists to feed themselves appears almost baffling, inexplicable.[7] Part of the problem, clearly, was that many expected to be fed by Indians, who were to provide food in exchange for English trade goods. The English in Virginia, for instance, brought great sheets of copper that they cut into pendants and jewelry and gave to the Powhatans, often in return for corn. But Native people could only afford to feed so many English—Powhatan told John Smith that he thought corn "more pretious" than copper, for "he could eate his corne, but not his copper"—and they did not like to be bullied into it. Moreover, the Powhatans' repeated protests that they had insufficient corn to spare might have been, simply, true. Recent clues drawn from tree rings and other environmental evidence suggest that the Chesapeake Indians, too, might have been experiencing hard times brought on by record drought and cold.[8] In the end, tensions over foodstuffs sparked a great deal of violence between the English and Indians of Virginia, including the massacre of 1622, in which Opechancanough's men rose up to slay nearly 400 English colonists, in some cases after first sitting down to breakfast with them.

Yet New England's story was different. Except, perhaps, for the miserable and deadly first winter suffered by the Pilgrims in 1620 (an ill-timed landing that sent William Bradford's wife, intentionally or not, over the side of the *Mayflower*), early New England has been viewed as largely exempt from such trauma.[9] If some of its first migrants battled scurvy, none, it must be said, were desperate enough to eat "powdered wife."[10] There were, none-theless, early lessons in hunger's propensity to beget violence. In the early 1620s a starving outpost of men at Wessagusset, most of them indentured servants sponsored by London merchant Thomas Weston, had resorted to filching corn from the nearby Massachusetts Indians. Predictably, this thievery earned the ire of the "Salvagis," who "seemed to be good freinds with us while they feared us," Phinehas Pratt later wrote, "but when they see famin prevall, they begun to insult." In the depths of winter 1622–1623, a breathless Pratt sprinted to Plymouth to beg for help in defending against the Massachusetts, who were allegedly plotting "to kill all Einglish people." (Pratt ran the entire thirty miles between Wessagusset and Plymouth, fret-ting all the way about the "ffoot steps" he had left in the snow.) Plymouth, in turn, sent north an expedition under Captain Miles Standish, who slew several of the Massachusett sachems and returned with Wituwamet's head.[11] Even some Englishmen thought this a rather inauspicious beginning to English relations with nearby Natives. (On hearing of the killings John Robinson, an advisor and former minister to the Plymouth English, famously proclaimed, "oh! how happy a thing had it been, if you had con-verted some, before you had killed any.")[12]

In the mid-1630s the specter of hunger returned to New England with a vengeance. The years immediately preceding the Pequot War were hungry ones for English colonists—and perhaps for Native people, as well. Scarcity rode in on a wave of punishing weather. Late summer 1635 brought a pounding hurricane, "a mighty storme of wind & raine" the likes of which "none living in these parts, either English or Indeans, ever saw." The great hurricane of 1635, as it became known, smashed boats, overturned homes, and swept away much that had been planted. Calling it "strang & fearfull to behould," Plymouth's William Bradford likened the storm to "those Hauricanes and Tuffons that writers make mention of in the Indeas." He described a dizzying swath of destruction: blown-over houses, missing roofs, trees uprooted by the thousands, and a twenty-foot storm surge. "[S]ignes and marks of it," Bradford thought, "will remaine this 100. years." At Narragansett a fourteen-foot flood reportedly drowned eight fleeing Indians as they scrambled to climb trees. Where it did not destroy people and their homes, the tempest certainly threatened crops. "It threw down all the Corn to the ground, which never rose more," Nathaniel Morton wrote.[13] Extreme frost and snow followed in early winter.[14]

Environmental punishments exacted an especially heavy toll on the fledgling Connecticut settlements, which had been planted barely a month before the hurricane struck. So difficult was the ensuing winter that some in Connecticut, starving, chose to return to Massachusetts. During the winter of 1635, the *Rebecka* delivered a group of about "70: men & woemen" back to the Bay Colony. But even these poor folks encountered trouble. Seeking relief after some expected provisions had failed to arrive at Connecticut, they had hastily clambered aboard. Unfortunately, the *Rebecka* promptly ran aground. As its crew struggled to free the boat from sandbars, some of the passengers reportedly succumbed to starvation. Spring, unfortunately, brought little relief. The "greatest parte" of the cattle that had been brought to Connecticut prior to winter, John Winthrop noted in April 1636, had been lost to the season's punishments (though some were miraculously able to survive, even "without any haye"). Winthrop estimated these losses at "neere 2000li: worth of Cattle." English families were thus "putt to great streightes for want of provision," reduced, even, to eating "Acornes."[15]

But if the pattern was most acute in Connecticut, it was evident elsewhere, as well. In February 1636 John Winthrop noted the "great scarcitye of Corne" in Massachusetts Bay. That same month, colonists were heartened when the *Rebecka* sailed into the bay carrying thousands of potatoes, lemons and oranges, "which were a great releife to our people" (although the ship, disappointingly, had already offloaded its corn in the West Indies). Months later, food was still in short supply. In April 1636, Massachusetts allowed its more remote towns to participate by proxy in that year's court of election, due to the "scarcity of victualls" in the country.[16] Meanwhile, in a struggling English fort at the mouth of the Connecticut, Lieutenant Lion Gardiner worried that he was like to be "starved," for Indian corn grew very expensive and he had little of it. "[S]eeing in peace you are like to be famished," he asked himself, "what will or can be done if war?"[17]

Aggravating these shortfalls was the fact that New England was in the midst of an unwieldy expansion. While the woes of New England's colonists hardly compared to the horrors known elsewhere, they did, nonetheless, experience some rather sharp growing pains. In Virginia, famine resulted largely from the fact that the Chesapeake was for so long a death trap, in which countless numbers died and those left behind were either too weak or too listless to grow any food. New England's plight was just the opposite: Nearly all of its migrants arrived in a great rush, in only a few short years during the 1630s. And almost none died. In a sense the northern colonies suffered from their own successes.[18] What spurred shortages, perhaps as much as the storms that soaked the harvest, was the endless tide of new arrivals from England. The 1630s witnessed a "great migration," in which roughly 14,000–21,000 new colonists voyaged to New England.[19] But the pace of that migration was not evenly spread over the decade; in fact, the year 1634 witnessed a "steep increase" in the number of migrants, a surge that did not abate until decade's end. Historian Robert Charles Anderson has identified no less than 1,300 individuals and families arriving just in the years 1634–1635, "amounting probably to twenty percent or more of the entire Great Migration." Roughly 2,000 to 2,500 people reached New English shores in 1634 alone.[20]

All these additional mouths necessarily placed untenable demands on New England's food supply. That the Great Migration exerted such a strain is rarely now remembered, but contemporary writers drew the link repeatedly. One account, William Wood's *New England's Prospect,* suggests that the colonies were feeling hunger pangs caused by the migration as early as 1633. Though his object was to paint New England in a bright and promotional light, Wood, writing in 1633, conceded that, "of late time there hath been great want." He blamed the "many hundreds" who, departing England, brought with them few or no provisions, "which made things [in New England] both dear and scant."[21] What likely exacerbated the problem was the timing of these migrations. Most migrants left England in early spring, in hopes of encountering pleasant weather during their transatlantic voyage, and arrived in summer—too late to help plant, but just in time to make a run on the year's harvests.[22] Several more years of record migration only made the problem worse. In 1636, Edward Trelawny noted the problem in a letter to his brother in England. "The country at present is sick in a general want of provisions, by reason of the multiplicity of people that came this year and relying wholly on it," he wrote, before pleading for "all sorts of provisions and cattle."[23]

If, in the seasons just preceding the war, the colonies were rather pinched, were the region's Native people equally straitened? Hadn't the same storms and frost also preyed upon *their* cornfields? Answering that question is difficult—much harder than gauging English distress, given how little testimony affords a view into Native communities in these years. But it makes sense, at least, to wonder. Although it is doubtful that the region's Indians were undergoing any kind of dire hunger, they had probably known want recently, as well. That Native people's harvests were also falling short is suggested by a trip made by John Oldham to trade with the Narragansetts in November of 1634: "the Indians had promised him 1000: bz. [bushels]," John Winthrop reported, "but their store fell out lesse then they expected."[24] The great hurricane of 1635—a tempest that roundly "spoiled the maize harvest," according to English testament—must have taken a long-term toll.[25] An additional problem in procuring corn was that there were simply fewer people to plant it. Indians across the northeast were experiencing a demographic catastrophe entirely opposite that of the English. For decades plagues had raged through Native villages, most recently in 1633–1634. In January 1634, an English visitor to the Connecticut River reported that smallpox had ravaged Native settlements "as farr as any Indian plantation was knowne to the west & muche people dead of it."[26] Although it is not clear how deeply the Pequots themselves were affected by this "great mortalitie," it surely claimed untold numbers of the subordinate bands who paid tribute to them. They had also recently lost the allegiance of several tributary groups, defectors to Narragansett protection, who may have been supplying the Pequots with a heavy tribute in corn for years.[27] Gone went this supply, as well. It thus stands to reason that the Pequots, if not Native people generally, were experiencing some of the same hardships.

But their troubles may not have been quite as acute. Native people were better prepared, in many ways, to handle scarcity. Certainly they would have had trouble warding off the damages of a major hurricane, but northeastern Indians did have some strategies with which to cope with lesser environmental challenges. To protect food stores, for instance, Algonquians built deep storage pits of earth and tree bark—ideal for shielding vegetables from frost and rain.[28] The Indian diet was also mercifully diverse: the Pequots and their neighbors were accustomed to eating a prodigious array of different foods—squashes, melons, berries, beans, roots and nuts, turkeys and other wild game, fish, clams, crabs and lobster. Should any one of these food sources fail, in other words, others would likely be available.[29] English newcomers, by contrast, may have suffered for their inflexibility in adhering rigidly to Old World dietary custom. Colonists mostly attempted to replicate "traditional English fare," eating meat stews accompanied by breads, cakes or puddings. Some small amounts of vegetables and garden crops brightened the summer diet, and butter and cheese supplemented some meals—especially in late summer and fall. But, in the winter, colonists were relegated to eating mainly salted meat from the autumn slaughter, and to relying on pease porridge. Spring, in general, was the hungriest season of the year, as families transitioned from dwindling stored supplies to fresh. The principal food on which colonists relied throughout the year—the backbone of the English diet—was grain, the very fodder that would eventually take center stage in the Pequot War.[30] Of this, English records make clear, Native people had more; and yet there was simply not enough, in the mid-1630s, to go around.

II.

For the English at least, the Pequot War began with the deaths of several traders. Oldham's death became the most notorious incident, but it was not the first. It recalled other attacks, including one that had happened two years earlier, in 1634. That summer, another trader—Captain John Stone—had been slain, apparently by Pequot tributaries, near the mouth of the Connecticut River. He had hired (or perhaps coerced) these Indians "to go as Pilots" with two of his crewmen toward the Dutch colonies. But before the cohort had departed, the two Englishmen "were both Murdered by their Indian Guides." Stone, "asleep in his Cabbin," was slain next, followed by the rest of his crew—seven men, in all. The Indian pilots, according to a later account, then heedlessly "plundered what they pleased and sunk the Bark."[31] Much more recently, yet another English trader had fallen prey to Indians on the shores of Long Island. Only a month before Oldham was found, William Hammond shipwrecked in the Sound. Though seven with him drowned, Hammond and another "escaped on shore," but were subsequently "killed by the Indians."[32]

When colonists took up their pens to explain the coming of the war, nearly all pointed first to these incidents. John Mason opened the preamble to his *Brief History* of the war with the scene of Stone's crew being "Murdered," while John Underhill cited the "taking away the life of one Master John Oldham" as a critical spark. William Bradford, too, identified Oldham's death as "one ground of the Pequente warr."[33] (Even Lion Gardiner, an English soldier initially unenthused by the prospect of war, backhandedly acknowledged John Stone's death as a premise. "[I]f they will now make war for a Virginian"—Stone—"and expose us to the Indians,"

Gardiner thought, about the Bay Colony's leaders, "they, I say, they love the Virginians better than us.")[34] There is no doubt that, in the wake of Oldham's death, the colonies stirred hastily toward war: Barely a month after Oldham perished, soldiers from Massachusetts and Connecticut ran roughshod over both Block Island and Pequot villages.

Why a few such episodes escalated into Indian war, however, remains one of the riddles of early American history. If the English reaction to Stone's and Oldham's deaths was extreme, it seems difficult to believe that it had anything to do with the particular persons killed. Stone had been something of a ne'er-do-well, a "freebooter" and a rascal.[35] And John Oldham, too, had a colorful past. Although he had lately become somewhat respected in elite circles, he had gained a reputation as a troublemaker years earlier in Plymouth. In 1624, he and another colonist, John Lyford, had been suspected of sending ill news back to England. So determined were Plymouth authorities to prove these transgressions that they had sent a shallop out to chase after a ship already well on its way to England, newly stuffed with colonists' letters. Lyford's, as feared, were found to be "larg" and "full of slanders." Oldham's letters were deemed less offensive, partly because they were harder to read ("he was so bad a scribe as his hand was scarce legible," William Bradford later sniped). But, when he discovered that his letters had been snatched and read, Oldham flew into a fury. Eventually, he was ordered "expeld" from Plymouth, whose musketeers each gave him a "thump on the brich" before he was "conveied to the water side, wher a boat was ready to cary him away."[36]

But water, unfortunately, was never kind to John Oldham. Soon after his expulsion from Plymouth, it brought him to his knees. During a winter voyage to Virginia, a year later, the bark in which he was traveling fell into some "danger." Oldham and the other passengers, fearing their lives, were thus prompted to "begine to examine their consciences and confess such sins as did most burthen them." It was in this moment, according to William Bradford, that Oldham repented for the "wrongs and hurt" he had caused at Plymouth and "prayed God to forgive him, and made vowes that, if the Lord spard his life, he would become otherwise." The story redeemed John Oldham, at least in Bradford's eyes, and he was welcomed back to visit and to do business at Plymouth. But, of course, the Virginia voyage was not the worst of Oldham's troubles. His ultimate waterborne catastrophe still lay ahead. It came, as we have seen, in the summer of 1636. "This his death," Bradford recounted mournfully, "was one ground of the Pequente warr which followed."[37]

That these men were hardly eminent citizens has left some historians suspicious of the fact that English leaders would provoke a war simply to avenge their deaths. It is easier to imagine, instead, that Englishmen conveniently seized upon these "relatively minor incidents" to justify attacking one of the more formidable Native groups nearby.[38] For the Pequots were, indeed, powerful. Situated along the northern shore of Long Island Sound, mostly to the east of the Pequot (later Thames) River, they had recently enjoyed a period of great power coinciding with the advent of Native-European trade. The waters that eventually claimed Oldham's body lay at the nexus of complex trading spheres, where Dutch, English, and Native interests overlapped, and, though they had recently fallen out with Dutch traders, the Pequots largely dictated trade terms in the region. Living along a coast whose shores brimmed with quahog shells, they enjoyed a great measure of control over the making and trading of wampum—the white and purple beads so prized by Dutch and Indian traders. The Pequots' relative power in this trading world undoubtedly made them special targets for English economic jealousy. It seems possible, then, that the English-driven escalation of violence was attributable to plainly economic motives, a bold and transparent grab at Pequot wealth and territory.

Well before Oldham's body sunk below the surf, the Pequots were in a desperate struggle to maintain power in these trading circles. In 1633, hoping to preserve their exclusive trading relationship with the Dutch, they had killed some Narragansetts who were traveling the path to a Dutch trading house. The Pequots paid dearly for this. Naturally, they angered the Narragansetts (who later fought against them with the English). But they also angered the Dutch, who promptly captured (and killed) the Pequot sachem, Tatobem. When war came, it was predicated on these nasty breaches over trade. (The Pequots claimed, for instance, to have killed John Stone in 1634 because they had mistaken him for a Dutchman.)[39] It is possible, too, that John Oldham was murdered for getting too close to the Pequots. He was killed by Block Islanders, tributary to the Narragansetts. (After interviewing one of the Indians involved in Oldham's death, John Winthrop wrote that Oldham had been attacked "because he went to make pease & trade with the Pekodes last yeare."[40]) Certainly the Pequot War was, in some respects, an "economic contest."[41] But to read the war's origins as so much high-level jousting over trade overlooks the more fundamentally troubling lessons that its prelude held for the English.

One of the first things to strike the reader, in combing through English renderings of the war, is how much of it happened on the water. That John Oldham died at sail is appropriate. The Pequot War was, in many ways, a water war. Water rushes through contemporary accounts of it with all the restless immediacy of waves lapping impatiently at Oldham's pinnace. In a 1637 letter, with the war crashing in around him, Roger Williams bemoaned the "Ocean of Troubles and Trialls wherein we saile."[42] It was a fitting turn of phrase. Although the violence eventually moved onto land, its early episodes unfolded in the marshes and channels of Long Island Sound. Its first English victims were traders, killed in their own boats. Contemporary observers painstakingly chronicled these incidents, adorning their accounts with many a watery metaphor. In his tale of the war's dangers to colonists, Edward Johnson, for his part, imagined the Almighty "plunging them in a gulph of miseries, that they may swim for their lives through the Ocean of his Mercies, and land themselves safe in the armes of his compassion."[43] How easily English writers availed themselves of such language attests to the omnipresence of water in the lives of New Englanders, and to their utter dependence on it. Virtually everyone and everything traveled by water in the 1630s, especially over long distances, and therein lies something of a clue. The fates of Stone and Oldham smarted, in great part, because they called into question English charge over colonial waters—something that had seemed relatively assured. In the 1630s colonists did not yet have command of, and did not pretend to control, land routes through New England. But with the deaths of a few mariners, the English learned that they were not even safe on the waterways. It was a difficult pill to swallow for a people who prided themselves on maritime prowess.

The English were a seafaring people. They hailed from an island kingdom, and each had spent a period of woozy weeks at sea in order to reach New England. But in the colonies, even more than in England itself, the ocean was a fact of life. Earliest New England was a world of water, so oriented toward the sea and riverways that among the key officials in Providence were its "water-bailies."[44] Straightaway on arriving in the New World, colonists set about building boats. New England's first great vessel was the *Blessing of the Bay,* finished in 1631, and several others followed. Soon, a swarm of "pinks, pinnaces, ketches, schooners, lighters, shallops, sloops and periaguas" were plying colonial shores. River crossers could expect to use great, flat-bottomed ferries that were generally large enough to carry man and beast, alike.[45] Some travelers would sooner stay home than be without a boat. In 1631, Salem-based John Endecott regretted that he could not attend court at Boston, after he had "put to sea" and been driven back ashore.[46] To look toward the water was an impulse that was deeply ingrained in English culture, and one that colonists carried to the New World. New England's collective gaze was trained outward, toward the boundless blue.

Colonists expected to do much of their traveling, even locally, by water. For most, the vehicle of choice was the canoe. Visitors to the colonies could not help but comment on the abundance of these coastal craft. Arriving in the 1630s, William Wood was struck by the number of canoes he saw in Salem, where "every household [had] a water horse or two."[47] Quick, light, and relatively cheap, these briskly multiplied. Canoes were so prevalent, in fact, that several plantations felt compelled to regulate their use. In the 1640s, fearing the proliferation of shoddy "cannowes"—"some made by the English, some bought of the Indians"—New Haven leaders required every canoe in town both inspected and marked.[48] In Pequot, snatching a stray canoe from the riverbank was so easy that in 1649 town leaders imposed a five-shilling penalty for filching "any canoow that shall be founde fastened with an rope," whether tethered "to a stake or a stone," set "aground," or left "riding in the water."[49]

Indians were watermen, too. Canoes were an Indian technology, often purchased from Indian builders. Early entries of farmer Thomas Minor's diary, for instance, find him contracting with his Indian neighbors to build canoes for him, usually for about twenty shillings apiece. "I bought the new canoow," he wrote triumphantly in May 1655, following an agreement with Sabiantwosucke. Later, he "agreed" with Pequot sachem Harmon Garret about another. One could never have too many canoes, it seems, as they were easily pilfered, apt to float away, and prone to sinking. (Minor spent November 23, 1657, "looking [for] the canoow," and in April 1658, he "suncke the Canoows" while carting hay home from Goodman Burrows' lot.) Canoes came in several shapes and sizes, some big, some small, some fashioned from bark and rosin, others dug out from great logs. The most common, and the sort Thomas Minor probably purchased, were the smaller, lighter variety. William Wood called them "cockling fly-boats, wherein an Englishman can scarce sit without a fearful tottering," though Indian boatmen would "venture to sea" in them with nary a thought.[50]

But coastal Indians also had great canoes, comparable to English shallops. John Josselyn called them *"Birchen-pinnaces."*[51] Formed from the great, hollowed out trunks of oaks, pines, sycamores, and other trees, these took Native mariners well out to sea. Propelled by oars (and, occasionally, by sails that the Narragansetts called *sepákehig*), some of these craft were as much as fifty feet long and could carry dozens of men. In the 1630s Indian seamen were more experienced at negotiating the winds, tides and sandbars of the New England coast, and they were often enlisted as pilots on English boats. (When he died, John Oldham had with him two Narragansett men, who were probably guiding his course.) Although English writers liked to think that Native people were less equipped as seamen, Indians were as comfortable in New English waters as any Englishman, if not more so.[52]

Although Englishmen preferred it, traveling by water was often risky. Coastal shoals forced mariners to navigate cautiously "among terrible hazards." Sudden storms, surging tides, and the shifting "maze of ledges, great rocks, and sandbars" that lay beneath coastal waters made sailing a tricky proposition.[53] In the first years of settlement, plenty tested the waters and quickly found themselves blown off course. Some wrecked, amidst Boston Harbor's many islands. Early entries of John Winthrop's *Journal* contain at least as many stories of hapless sea-goers as of those who went astray by land—perhaps a measure of their haste to push off, rather than set out on foot. A particularly harrowing fate, for instance, met Richard Garrard, who in December 1630 took off toward Plymouth in a shallop, "against the advise of his freindes." Garrard's boat lost its anchor and began taking in freezing water. When the shallop finally drifted toward land on Cape Cod, some of the passengers' legs were so "frozen into the Ice [that] they were forced to be cutt out." After spending a frigid night in the "open ayre," two of the party went overland toward Plymouth for help. They supposed the colony was a few miles away; it was, in actuality, fifty miles off. Indians eventually helped these wanderers home, but Garrard himself perished from exposure before aid arrived. So solidly was the ground frozen that the others could not even bury his body. Such misfortunes schooled the English in the dangers of coast-wise travel.[54]

Some men were more at home in this coastal "wilderness" than others. A cohort of coastal traders had emerged, by the mid-1630s, upon which New England utterly depended. The role that men like Oldham played in connecting the English colonies can be glimpsed in Pequot War–era correspondence. Letters make plain that in the 1630s communications were fragile, waterborne, and rested on the backs of just a few seamen. Those carrying letters between Massachusetts and Connecticut, for instance, were a select few English shipmasters and traders: John Oldham, John Throckmorton, John Hodges, Joseph Tilly, and John Gallop. Bostonian John Winthrop relied on these important figures to send messages to his son, John Winthrop, Jr., isolated in the fort at the mouth of the Connecticut River, and his letters reflect that the exchange was almost wholly water-bound. Ships and seamen sail through Winthrop's script, looping back and forth along the coast: "Sonne, I wrote unto you by the Rebecka . . . ," he wrote, before taking another opportunity to send "by mr. Oldhams Pinace." The "Blessing," the "Wrenne," the "Bacheler": all came and went.[55]

All of these voyages, it should be said, were not easy. Even under the best of circumstances, navigating New England's coastal geography could be tricky. Early on, travel and communications between Connecticut and Massachusetts Bay proved nettlesome, as frequent shipwrecks and other calamities vexed intercolonial carriers. Weather took its toll on boats, much as it did on crops and cattle. In October 1635, two shallops "goeinge laden with goodes to Conectec[o]t" were dashed against Brown's Island; all aboard drowned. The following month, a pinnace returning from Connecticut to the bay was "cast awaye in manemett Baye." Its crew wandered for ten lonely days through "extreame Colde, & deepe snowe." In October 1637, another furious storm claimed one more coasting vessel. "The Wren, a small pinnace, coming from Connecticut," recorded John Winthrop, "was taken in a N.E. storm, and . . . wrecked." Her crew survived, if only to see pieces of the pinnace pulled out to sea.[56]

Land travel was little better. It was also far less common. Although traces of those traveling the one hundred miles between Massachusetts Bay and Connecticut are spotty, for these years, it is clear that few did.[57] Massachusetts men had first learned of a trail to Connecticut's rapids in 1631, when Wahginnicut, a Connecticut sachem, had informed them that his home was "not above 5: dayes journey from us by lande." Not until 1633 is there a record of any Englishman traveling that way, and then, it was the infamous John Oldham. Oldham and three others "went over land to Conectecott to trade" and "lodged at Indian townes all [the] waye." When colonists began to consider planting on the distant river, a few years later, many went by land. Still, hints persist that the overland route was a difficult one. More than a few taking it "lost themselves & endured muche miserye." Some arrived safely, "after a teadious & difficult journye." But others, like the group returning to

Massachusetts in November 1635, became lost and even drowned; their the trek took an interminable "10: dayes." Even the stories of uneventful journeys seem somehow disbelieving. "This month one went by land to <u>Conectecott</u> & returned safe," John Winthrop noted, in January 1636.[58]

Imagine the alarm of Englishmen, then, when coastal traders began to fall victim to Indian attacks. Even before Oldham's death, rumors had circulated of Pequot intentions to attack English barks. In late June 1636, trader Jonathan Brewster sent warning down the Connecticut River of a close call experienced by one of his vessels. He had heard belatedly (and perhaps inaccurately) that Pequots had recently "purposed to cutt off our Barke, after shee had done trading with them." Only a "fayre wynd," spiriting the English traders away more quickly than expected, had saved them from the "80 men in Canoes" reportedly en route to attack. The men, Brewster reported with relief, had thus unknowingly "escaped the danger." But Brewster heard further rumors of the Pequots' hostile intent toward "both . . . English and natives" along the Connecticut. "Sir . . . give notice to bootes as they passe up and downe," he wrote to John Winthrop, Jr., at Saybrook, "not to be too secure."[59]

But several sailors soon proved "too secure." After another trader's shallop was attacked and lost on its way downriver, the man in charge of Saybrook Fort, Lion Gardiner, moved to limit river runs to those who were armed. He insisted that "no boat or bark should pass the fort, but that they come to anchor first, that I might see whether they were armed and manned sufficiently." But in October 1636, to Gardiner's dismay, master Joseph Tilley disregarded this advice and soon met his fate on a riverbank that Gardiner later dubbed, smugly, "Tille's folly." Now more than ever, Gardiner was determined to monitor and, if necessary, to halt boat traffic along the river. "I thinke it would be good if no vessels may be suffred to come," he wrote shortly after Tilley's death, except those that were suitably armed. All men should be "charg'd not to goe ashore." Hundreds of Indians, patrolling the riverbanks, "shoote at our Pinaces as they goe up and downe."[60]

If the English read these deaths as attacks on their superiority as a seafaring people, they can hardly be blamed. Native assailants were careful to drive this lesson home. Pequots flouted English control of the waterways by using English seamen and their boats as fearsome billboards. Consider, first, how they used Joseph Tilley's body to send a message to the English at Saybrook. After seizing him, his captors "carried him alive over the river in our sight," Gardiner shuddered. After killing several English at Wethersfield in winter 1637, Pequots sailed down the Connecticut, past Saybrook, in mock "barks" with sails fashioned from the dead's clothing. The exhibition hit its mark. As one witness later described, the Pequots "put poles in their canoes, as we put masts in our boats, and upon them hung our English men's and women's shirts and smocks, instead of sails, and in way of bravado came along in sight of us as we stood upon Seybrooke fort." Another unwelcome effigy floated by Saybrook in June 1637. That month Cobbin Beets' shallop was attacked, while on its way downriver, and was subsequently discovered "ruinated." The following day, "one of the slane menn came drivinge [i.e., drifting] by saybrooke, stuck with 3 or 4 arrows."[61] For good reason, English witnesses read these exchanges of violence as markedly waterborne.

But the significance of water, in the war, was more than metaphorical, and the deaths of these coastal traders threatened more than merely English seafaring pride. What trussed New England together, quite simply, were its waterways and the men who sailed them. The wheel of New England's economy turned on these men, to be sure, but the colonies depended on them in even more basic ways.[62] Even in bountiful times, coastal traders were often the ones to procure and provide food. Newer settlements, in particular, often looked to add to their own meager harvests by trading with more established English towns or, frequently, with Indians. Men like John Oldham, therefore, had a special role to play in trucking precious goods to places in need. Both Plymouth and Massachusetts had relied on purchases of Indian corn, the latter using Oldham himself as an intermediary. As a trader he had brokered for corn, when necessary, from Indian neighbors. On at least one occasion, he had helped feed Massachusetts Bay, where, in 1634, the *Rebecka* unloaded "500: bz. of Corne given to mr Jo: Oldham" by the Narragansetts.[63] And after his death, in fact, the Connecticut government's first concern was with Oldham's stock of corn. Even as they dealt with escalating tensions with the Pequots, magistrates carefully appointed men to "looke to & prserve the Corne of Mr. Olda & . . . bringe an Accompt the next Cort what quantitie there is of it."[64]

Another trader's downfall is perhaps more revealing, even, than Oldham's. Although less remembered, the fate of William Hammond also hints at the crucial role of traders, especially in times of crisis. Only a month before Oldham was found, Hammond, on his way to Virginia, had shipwrecked in the Sound. He and a companion had "escaped on shore," but were subsequently killed by Natives. What made Hammond's fate so grievous was that it scuttled a crucial voyage: When he died, the coaster had been on his way to

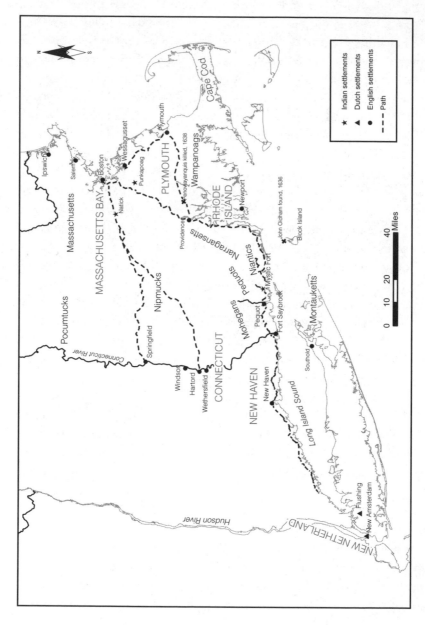

Southern New England, 1630s–1650s

Virginia—his boat loaded with everything he could "make and borrowe"—
to trade for "Corne." He had been engaged, in other words, in an important
journey seeking food for the hungry northern English. Historians rarely, if
ever, cast Hammond's death as a factor in the coming of the Pequot War, but
Massachusetts Bay considered it a serious grievance against the Pequots.[65]
With English hunger restored to view, the fearful meaning of these deaths
becomes easier to grasp. These men, after all, were the ones who brought letters, news, provisions, and food. The lesson English observers surely drew, in
watching such events unfold, was this one: Because the violence threatened
those who carried goods between English colonies, it threatened all.

Some, of course, were more vulnerable than others. Especially so were
the newer colonies—those huddled along the Connecticut River. These
souls, especially, were at pains to communicate with other English, from
whom they were separated by a chancy overland trek or a weeklong boat
trip. In fact, the lonely predicament of the Connecticut settlements goes far
in explaining how the murders of a few traders—even traders with arguably
sordid pasts—could have triggered such a tremendous overreaction. Begun
barely a year before John Oldham's death, the Connecticut plantations were
in a precarious way in 1636. They had endured the ferocious weather and
hunger pangs afflicting most of New England, but not very well. Conditions
at Saybrook, downriver, were no better. Servants in the fort lodged a written
complaint that they were insufficiently clothed and fed. Bread, breakfast,
and beer had all been "taken away," they protested, leaving them nothing to
eat but "peass porig."[66] But the hunger extended beyond the fort's lower
ranks. When a shipmaster failed to bring him corn in May 1636, John
Winthrop, Jr., pled to his father in writing to be "supplied by the first shipping that arrive with any store of provisions." "I see noe meanes to be supplied heere," he grumbled.[67] Only two months later, John Oldham was
discovered dead. And here was the problem: scarcity in Connecticut was
amplified by even small hiccups in English shipping. These fledgling villages relied on ties to markets in Massachusetts Bay for survival. Particularly
for Connecticut colonists, the loss of John Oldham made real the possibility
of being cut off from other Englishmen. Oldham's killing was offensive not
merely because it was done at the hands of Indians. It also robbed grain
from the mouths of English colonists.

One wonders, in fact, whether robbing food from colonists was precisely
the point. Had the "Corne of Mr. Olda" had something to do with his death?

Although the evidence will likely never be conclusive, both the timing and context are telling. John Oldham died in July, just about the time when local Native groups would have been readying themselves for the Green Corn feasts, an annual celebration of immature summer corn. It was also a moment in which the English colonies were experiencing the height of scarcity. Had Oldham tried to bully some Block Islanders into sparing some corn, thus inviting retaliation? Or had they, alternatively, looked to remedy their own hardships with a rash grab at Oldham's goods? Plunder, in some sense, was a factor: When Oldham's pinnace was discovered, a canoe "full of Indians & goodes" was in the midst of rowing hastily away.[68] But even if the tug-of-war over food had little to do with Oldham's fate, it had everything to do with what followed—not least because the episode presented a new reason, and new opportunities, for the hungry English to seize food from Natives. In what followed Oldham's downfall, it became clear just how desperate were a few lonely men in Connecticut to lay their hands on a bit of Indian corn.

III.

Corn was central to the waging of the Pequot War. Some English clamored for Indian corn, while others burned and destroyed it with abandon. Corn was everywhere stolen, fired, or dug up. In the records surrounding the war, English interest in corn is palpable. War narratives show almost a bald obsession with it. To witness Englishmen razing Indian cornfields may not seem especially notable; it was a favorite strategy for crippling Native enemies throughout early American history.[69] But, once one comprehends the environmental difficulties that had plagued New England in these years, the records that capture the unfolding of the Pequot War assume a somewhat different countenance. The recurrent mentions of corn begin to appear in telling relief. Did distress over this important staple play a role in pushing both English and Native characters toward war in 1636? When the English and their Mohegan and Narragansetts allies had finally crushed the Pequots in 1637, it is worth pausing to remember that among the principal spoils they shared was grain—the Pequots' corn. Corn may not have been merely coincidental to the fighting of the Pequot War. Eagerness for provisions pushed some English into a desperate and belligerent stance. It led them to make hasty decisions that contributed to the coming of the war.

That corn should take center stage in the march toward war is perhaps unsurprising. It was a prized commodity among both the English and

Indians. Corn was the one food, in fact, on which both peoples depended tremendously. By "corn," what the English truly meant was "Indian corn," or *maize*. Maize was not a part of the English diet, prior to colonization—in early modern England, the word "corn" would have referred to virtually any grain—but it was embraced almost instantly by English colonists. Indian corn was hearty and easy to grow, whereas English grains required more coaxing and more labor before they would thrive. When efforts to plant wheat and other traditional English crops faltered, colonists converted quickly, and maize soon became a staple food for both people and livestock. It would not be too much to say that corn consumption fueled the settlement of the English colonies.[70] Corn was also fundamental to Native culture. Indians ate corn in many ways—dried, ground, boiled, baked into bread, or "whole like beans, eating three or four corns with a mouthful of fish or flesh," as William Wood reported in 1633. On hunts, while traveling, or during war, Indian men ate *nókehick,* parched corn mixed with water for a quick and easy meal. Corn was also celebrated in a variety of rituals and ceremonies, including the "green corn" celebrations that many Native groups staged around the mid- to late-summer growth of immature, new corn.[71] Corn was such a precious resource in early New England that it sometimes functioned as kind of currency. Colonists were occasionally allowed to pay taxes in bushels of corn, and both Natives and English alike used it to pay off debts.

The English military reaction to John Oldham's death, by no accident, revolved around Indian corn. Early actions taken against both the Block Islanders and the Pequots—the actions that finally provoked full-scale warfare—were what essentially amounted to corn raids. To avenge the death of John Oldham, in August 1636 Massachusetts dispatched a force of men under John Endecott to Block Island to raid and punish its inhabitants— Oldham's reputed killers. Endecott's men, to their disappointment, met with few Indians on the island. What they did find, however, were "great heaps of pleasant corn ready shelled," which—only after realizing they were "not able to bring it away"—they promptly burned. Failing to find many people, Endecott's men took out their frustrations on the Block Islanders' crops. The wanton destruction that they unleashed on the island was extensive; John Underhill, party to the expedition, remembered spending nearly two days pillaging the island. When they discovered a village "where was much corn," the soldiers took out their weapons and cut it all down, as if doing battle with the stiff, defenseless stalks.[72] If English colonists did not have enough to eat, the soldiers ensured, neither would the island's Indians.

Not all Englishmen, however, were ready to engage in such rampant waste, no matter how fervently they resented what "great heaps" of corn the Indians possessed. If Massachusetts' men had the luxury of punishing Block Island by devastating its food supply, those in Connecticut did not. Not surprisingly, given their need for provisions, some in Connecticut disagreed with Endecott's tactics. Perhaps revealing the disparity in how ill-fed were Connecticut colonists versus those in Massachusetts, military men differed over how to handle Indian stores of corn. Bay militiamen were rather quick with flame, while those garrisoned at Saybrook hoped to salvage the corn for themselves.[73] The man in charge at Saybrook, Lion Gardiner, for one, was not pleased with Massachusetts Bay's reckless instigation of Indian war. Saybrook was "famished" even in peace, he warned, and war would be disastrous, sure to divorce Saybrook from access to its meager cornfields. Thus, when he heard that Endecott's force also planned to visit Pequot and to demand answer for the still-unresolved killing of John Stone, Gardiner— at least according to his own claims—objected strenuously.[74]

But it was Gardiner's own empty belly that helped ignite the Pequot War. The best evidence that English desire for corn tipped the colonies toward war, in fact, comes from the pen of Lion Gardiner. Gardiner had been concerned about the specter of hunger well before the war. Preparing to build Saybrook Fort in 1636, he had warned Massachusetts' magistrates of the danger in attending to fortifications before provisions. "I said it was Capt. Hunger that threatened them most," Gardiner later wrote.[75] When it was clear that his protests against Endecott's expedition would do nothing, therefore, he decided to be pragmatic. Gardiner saw in the escalating tensions with the Pequots an opportunity to secure some much-needed sustenance. He thought of the Pequots' piles of corn, "gathered" and "ready to put into their barns," and suggested the English soldiers raid the harvested grain. "Sirs, Seeing you will go," he begged Endecott's men, "I pray you, if you don't load your Barks with Pequots, load them with corn, for . . . both you and we have need of it." Gardiner's haste to procure Pequot corn extended even to providing vessels and bags in which to carry it ("I will send my shallop . . . to go with you, [and] you may load your barks with corn," he offered breathlessly. "But they said they had no bags to load them with, then said I, here is three dozen of new bags, you shall have thirty of them, and my shallop to carry them"). Gardiner even suggested an elaborate system for guarding the corn and carrying it to the waterside.[76]

It was the resulting rampage at Pequot that ultimately provoked war. Even if they had not endured quite the same hardships, Pequot men and women were surely in no mood to share. Imagine their horror, then, when English soldiers arrived in August 1636 and began plundering rampantly. When Endecott's men disembarked at Pequot after raiding Block Island, they threatened swiftly to "march through the country, and spoil your corn" if given no satisfaction for the murder of John Stone. Satisfaction eluding them (a short, perhaps perfunctory, parley went nowhere), Endecott's soldiers went about laying waste to Pequot much as they had done at Block Island. When they spied Pequots hurriedly burying corn and other items, the English made it their mission to dig up even these hidden stores. Gardiner's men, in the meantime, rushed to scoop as much corn as possible into their sacks (though they were attacked as they scurried back to their boats). Burned, trampled, or stolen, hordes of corn were destroyed.[77] Corn raiding was not the sole offense committed by the English, while there, nor is it the only key to explaining Pequot anger. But the decision to plunder ruthlessly helped set New England on the course to war with the Pequots. The Indians could not sit idly by as Gardiner's henchmen snatched grain by the sackful.[78] That they understood Gardiner's men to be key offenders during the raid is patently clear from their immediate reaction. Pequot vengeance came to Saybrook in the form of a siege: supplies were cut off, as the Indians harassed the fort and pilfered its livestock. They also retaliated in kind, for what Gardiner's men had done: they attacked Saybrook's pitiable cornfield.[79]

Unfortunately for the English, stealing Indian corn solved very little. After the raids on Block Island and Pequot, Gardiner's men did, in fact, return to Saybrook with a "pretty quantity of corn." ("I was glad of the corn," Gardiner remembered vividly.)[80] But whatever relief Gardiner felt that August was painfully short-lived. As the weather turned again toward winter, cattle and corn were once more costly and scarce. "Cattle were grown to high rates;—[and] Corn was now at 5s. the bushel," John Winthrop recorded, before adding, immediately thereafter, "Things went not well at Connecticut. Their cattle did, many of them, cast their young, as they had done the year before."[81] By November, Saybrook was once again desperate for "victualls." When a ketch passed by, carrying corn from the nearby

Narragansetts, Gardiner hurriedly commandeered some of its booty. "I have tacken one hondard buchils of it," he explained, "becaus I do not know whethar we shall have anie relief or not."[82] Connecticut's hunger problem still had not abated when Pequot retaliation reached the river towns, in an attack on Wethersfield in February 1637. Even as Connecticut soldiers prepared to march on Pequot, in response, Captain John Mason felt the gnawing in his empty stomach. "Our Commons were very short," he wrote, "there being a general scarcity throughout the Colony of all sorts of Provision." As they boarded the boat for Pequot, the Reverend Thomas Hooker said a few words to the soldiers. Hooker prayed that the Pequots *"should be Bread for us*. And thus when the Lord turned the Captivity of his People, and turned the Wheel upon their Enemies . . . then was our Mouth filled with Laughter, and our Tongues with Singing."[83]

No surviving account of the war casts the conflict as having been fought, in any way, for corn. Nowhere, in ink, did any Englishman admit any such thing. But given the "scarcity of victuals" vexing New England, raiding Native corn—as well as punishing Indians—was clearly all too tempting to both English leaders and ordinary souls in 1636. Perhaps Oldham's death was, after all, merely an "excuse" for what terrors came later. But in the matrix of causality, in the calculus that unfolded in English minds, hunger certainly played a role. We should not underestimate the yearning, particularly on the part of Connecticut colonists, to have their mouths "filled." Reading English provocation of the war as having simply been about trade, then, misses some of the desperation—and contingency—that lay behind colonists' belligerence. It misses the privation that pushed Lion Gardiner's hand in 1636. New England was not, in the end, so different from other English colonies. This was a story that unfurled itself countless times, in many other dark corners of the English empire. When in 1625 George Percy wrote his *Trewe Relacyon* of Jamestown's now famous starving time, he prefaced it with a feeble reminder that "If we Trewly Consider the diversety of miseries mutenies and famishmentts w[hi]ch have attended upon discoveries and plantacyons in theis our moderne Tymes, we shall nott fynde our plantacyon in Virginia to have Suffered aloane."[84] He may have been more right than we have yet understood.

In May 1637, the Pequot War reached its climax in a grisly spectacle of fire and death. At dawn on the twenty-sixth, English soldiers surprised the Pequots slumbering at Mystic Fort. Captain John Mason's forces—fresh from praying that the Pequots might be "bread for us"—had with them "little refreshment." Some on the march had fainted and were given sips of liquor to revive them.[85] The plan, Mason later wrote, was to kill the Pequots and then raid their supplies. "We had formerly concluded to destroy them by the Sword and save the Plunder," he remembered. But when it became clear that this tactic would not work, Mason arrived at a new plan: "We must Burn them." He acted quickly. Mohegan and Narragansett allies to the English formed a loop around the fort, preventing escape, as Mason and other English soldiers took burning wood from within the Pequots' own wigwams and set fire to all inside. Hundreds of Pequots burned alive.[86]

The enormity of this event is almost blinding. So numerous were the deaths, that morning, that Captain John Underhill—present at the burning—later empathized with the unseasoned English militiamen who were unaccustomed to seeing such carnage. "Great and doleful was the bloody sight," he wrote, "to the view of young soldiers that never had been in war, to see so many souls lie gasping on the ground."[87] Trying to grasp the whole of the war's story, while looking backward through the Mystic massacre, is not unlike gazing downward, through water, at the bottom of a pond: much is distorted. After this one morning, the Pequots were all but broken. Captivity, slavery, and death followed for most that had survived. The gravity of English actions, on May 26, 1637, thus makes it difficult to avoid viewing the Pequot War as a great and brutal display of English strength.[88] It was not. What happened in the war, to the contrary, was as much the result of English desperation.

Meanwhile, as the war drew to a close in 1637, some English looked eagerly toward a brighter, less hungry future. In his account of the conflict, Philip Vincent grafted an impossibly happy ending onto the narrative, complete with corn aplenty. "Corn and cattle are wonderfully increased," he reported buoyantly, so much so that colonists sometimes even had enough "to spare to new comers." Lush fields of planted grain now greeted these new arrivals, gushed Vincent: indeed they "never saw such a field of four hundred acres of all sorts of English grain, as they saw at Winter-towne."[89] His descriptions may not have been entirely fanciful. There was some relief: in July 1637 the English shared Pequot corn stores with their Narragansett allies.[90] And though 1638 greeted New Englanders with a notably severe winter and a spring so cold that the corn seed "rotted in the ground" (not to mention an April snowstorm featuring "flakes as great as shillings"), John Winthrop reported that the year's harvest happily yielded "corn beyond expectation" in Massachusetts.[91] Things were not quite as hopeful in

Connecticut. Dearth struck again in 1638, forcing colonists to beg corn from the Pocumtucks to their north. It is probably not a coincidence, furthermore, that harvesttime found Mason making yet another visit to Pequot, ostensibly to punish the Pequots who had begun to resettle there. In effect it was another corn raid: the Connecticut militia planned to "supplant them, by burning their Wigwams, and *bringing away their Corn.*" While there the English spent the day filling their bark with corn, "whereof there was Plenty, it being their time of Harvest."[92] At last, and once more at Pequots' expense, Connecticut filled its rumbling belly. Its colonists ate well that year.

IV.

War faded; trade continued. All was not dire. By mid-1638, the first published accounts of the Pequot War were already circulating in England. Scouring the land of Pequots in a way the war itself had not done, these tracts beckoned new migrants to American shores. Captain John Underhill's "Newes from America" took time out from its first-hand narration of the war to describe a litany of places "that as yet have very few or no Inhabitants": *Queenapoick, Hudson's River, Long Island, Naransett Bay, Pequet.*[93] Would-be migrants were listening. As the violence of the Pequot War sputtered to a close, the "great migration" accelerated. In the summer of 1638 alone, twenty ships dumped "at least three thousand persons" onto the shores of Massachusetts Bay, so overfilling the colony that the newcomers were "forced to look out new plantations."[94] To the south, in the meantime, Pequot slept. North from there lay Mohegan, its steaming pits rich with oyster. Eastward, Narragansett seethed. And south, across the channel, "Lange Eylandt" stretched westward to New Netherland—New Netherland, where Arthur Peach's party had been headed before taking a wrong turn. This landscape was not static. It buzzed and moved and lurched in all directions.

The war did not leave in its wake an entirely peaceful New England.[95] For both English and Algonquians, the Pequot War had sown lower New England with new and unknown dangers. Some colonists worried about that. As early as May 1637 Roger Williams fretted that the war's upheavals threatened the already fragile connections among colonies. "[I]f there [was to] be any more land travel to Qunnihticutt," he wrote to Massachusetts Bay, the colony would have to come to some sort of agreement with the

Wunnashowatuckoogs, an inland group rumored to be "confederates with and a refuge to the Pequts." Failing that, Williams knew, there would be no "hope of a safe passage to Qunnihticut by land." But warnings also came from Indians themselves. In one tense moment, for instance, a Narragansett man advised English messengers to Mohegan to turn back, for "he knew they should have no guides" and would "be destroyed in the woods as they travelled." Following the Peach murder in 1638, Indians similarly admonished that the English "be carefull on the high wayes."[96]

Lingering dangers stemmed somewhat from new and bitter rivalries between Native groups. With the Pequots all but broken, a new enmity had exploded between the erstwhile allies of the English in the war—the Mohegans and the Narragansetts. After the war, Englishmen scrambled to quash this feud. In fact, the Treaty of Hartford—the document drafted to "end" the Pequot War, in September 1638—was a desperate attempt by the Connecticut English to quell the enmity between Miantonomi's Narragansetts and Uncas's Mohegans. Arrangements leading up to the summit had begun nearly a year earlier. At least since the previous February, the magistrates in Connecticut had hoped to arrange a meeting between Miantonomi and Uncas, and they were eager to host. In Providence, seventy miles east of the Connecticut villages, Roger Williams also worked to arrange a meeting between the "Averse Sachims." If only Uncas would "touch in at the Nanhiggonset mouth," Williams offered, he could get Miantonomi "aboord" and begin negotiations.[97]

What made the Englishmen so anxious to secure an agreement between the two sachems is not, at first, entirely obvious. It was not simply an impulse to bring the Indian groups under English control, not some generalized move to "establish English hegemony," not even, in fact, a maneuver toward English colonization of Pequot.[98] There was something else. Roger Williams hinted at it, in a letter to John Winthrop. A "peace is much to be desired betweene the Monahig: and Nanhiggon," he wrote, if only "for keeping a passage open betweene yourselves and Qunnihticut by natives."[99] Keeping a passage open. This was one reason why peace between the Mohegans and Narragansetts was critical: The ability of the English to communicate with other plantations depended on it. (When Williams accompanied Miantonomi on his trek to Hartford in 1638 to sign the treaty, they found the way, which ran through Mohegan and Pequot country, very dangerous. Assassins lay in wait. The Narragansetts "had word of neere 700. Enemies in the way, yet generally they all resolved that it was a shame to feare and goe back," recalled Williams.[100]) Roger Williams knew firsthand: If Miantonomi could not pass safely between Narragansett and Connecticut, neither could English letters.

Amidst the turmoil of the Pequot War, an odd pattern had emerged. One of Massachusetts Bay's greatest sources of information about the war's events, ironically, was the exiled Roger Williams. In 1637 Williams was newly ensconced on the western shore of Narragansett Bay, about midway between Boston and the chief Pequot settlements. In Providence, he was closer to the war, and, settled snugly up against Narragansett country, he had better information. Although Williams witnessed none of the war's violence, Narragansett informants kept him well apprised of what was happening just to the west. Presented with any bit of news, suspect or not, he hastily forwarded it to Boston.[101] Williams was clever. Though exiled from Massachusetts, he made himself indispensable to Indian affairs and to war preparations. In reporting all "Newes and Tidings" of the Pequot War, he slyly positioned himself as a kind of war correspondent; a keeper of news for which, he knew, Massachusetts men would be clamoring. He was careful to highlight his own diligent reportage: "Sir, In the morning I wrote by John Throckmorton, what I heard and thought in generall," he scribbled, in one letter. That afternoon, he sent further "Varietie and Plentie and Strangenes of Newes and Tidings, I hope true."[102] *I hope true.* Williams's information was not always correct. But he did his best to gauge its accuracy, and his script is pitted with tentative language. As if writing newsletters, he dutifully forwarded all "reports" and "Intelligence" gathered, despite his uncertainties.[103]

Many of these reports, it turns out, traveled in the hands of Natives. Though Williams sent some letters with Englishmen, an overwhelming majority was carried by Indians. Williams's reliance on Native letter bearers grew from his diplomacy. As his letters show, he helped to arrange the alliance of the Narragansetts and the English against the Pequots, and in taking up that charge, he began speeding news back to Boston via Narragansett messengers. This was only natural, and it was convenient. Native people, after all, were the sources of virtually all of his information, and the ones best prepared to carry it through the largely unknown terrain between Providence and Boston. Comments within the correspondence bear testament to his increasing reliance on Indian messengers. "Sir, I have presumed to send this Nahigonsick man, to attend your pleasure concerning the Pequts," he wrote, in one letter. Forwarding another piece of intelligence, Williams attested that the importance of the news had "forced me to send, and speedily, on purpose, by a native."[104]

But Williams was not alone. Others involved in the war also leaned on Indian couriers. On May 23, 1637, just prior to the horrors that would unfold at Mystic Fort, Captain Daniel Patrick scrawled a hasty update to the governor in Boston, in which he promised, "if possible," to "send constant word of our proceedings." 'Constant word' was perhaps optimistic, but in June he did manage to send a letter describing recent violence around Saybrook—via an Indian. (Patrick's postscript betrays the bearer as Native: "a Coate and a pare of shoes the Indeane is to have," he nudged, prompting Winthrop to pay for the letter's carriage.) Plymouth, too, learned of the slaughter at Mystic from an Indian messenger. Meanwhile, as news trickled northward from the sites of the war, Indians also carried letters in the reverse direction: In August, the Massachusetts governor himself sent an Algonquian man "with letters to Pequt."[105] In a time when sending news was critical, but potentially dangerous, English leaders had discovered the advantages of hiring Indians to convey their letters. The spoils of war, it seems, included a new way to send news.

The stakes in all of this were greater than one might think. The founders of New England had always known that the fate of their heady experiment hinged on community. It hinged on cohesion. Aboard the *Arbella* in 1630, well before his fleet of colonists had even landed in Massachusetts Bay, John Winthrop had penned a lay sermon expressing exactly that. He had composed the speech, which he called "A Modell of Christian Charity," during the salty, chill Atlantic crossing; perhaps because, after weeks of tossing about at sea, he sensed that the passengers' faith was flagging. In grand terms, Winthrop reminded them of their special covenant with God, their duty to create a perfect, godly society—a model for the world. "[W]ee must Consider," Winthrop famously intoned, "that wee shall be as a City upon a Hill, the eies of all people are uppon us." Failure would be profound. It would bring mockery, disgrace, and God's wrath. If his hearers worried about their ability to meet such a charge, Winthrop assured them that he knew the way to success. "Now the onely way to avoyde this shipwracke," he explained, was to "rejoyce together, mourne together, labour, and suffer together," even be "knit together . . . as one man," as "members of the same

body." Christian love would bind this "body" together, much like "the sinewes and other ligaments of a naturall body."[106]

Winthrop did not put his vision of Christian community in geographic
terms, though he did acknowledge that distance must not be allowed to
undermine it. ("[T]hough wee were absent from eache other many miles," he
wrote, "and had our imploymentes as farre distant, yet we ought to account
our selves knitt together by this bond of love.") But what happened in the
years after Winthrop stepped off the *Arbella* proved that distance was more
of a threat than perhaps he had anticipated. When he'd thought of planting
his "Citty upon a Hill" in the New World, he probably had not imagined so
many of his brethren ambling off beyond the city's bounds, as it were, and
into the wandering wood, only to be lost amidst a maze of Indian footpaths.
"Noe body can be perfect which wants its propper ligamentes," he had
written in 1630.[107] But what if the "ligamentes" were Indian?

2

A Messenger Comes

Aumáumuwaw, Páuasha. *A messenger comes.*
   —Roger Williams, *A Key into the Language of America* (1643)

LATE WINTER, 1648: John Winthrop was gravely ill. Along with its expected cold and gloom, winter had visited him with chills and a persistent fever that left him "very low." He had lain abed for weeks, plagued by a nasty "coffe," too weak even to lift his pen. In letters, son Adam Winthrop kept others apprised of his father's flagging condition, even as he watched in agony as the man grew "weaker then ever I knew him."[1] Death came just as winter ended: On March 26, 1649, in a small, chilled room in Boston, the sixty-one-year-old founding governor of Massachusetts breathed his last. At his death the men at his bedside cast about for quills: the news must be spread. With the Reverend John Wilson serving as scribe, they huddled in the parlor and composed a letter alerting Winthrop's son, John, Jr., to his father's death. They then faced the quandary of how to send the missive. Though Adam Winthrop had remained at his father's side in past weeks, his brother John lived much further away, one hundred miles south of Boston, by land, in the old Pequot country. How to reach him? Perhaps no ship was ready; perhaps ice blocks lingered in the harbor, after a frigid stretch. Or maybe they judged sending by water too slow. A ship rounding Cape Cod could take seven days, not quick enough to summon the younger Winthrop to his father's funeral. The message written, the men handed it, instead, to a man they judged a "Trustie and Swift messenger": an Indian named Nahawton.[2]

Early New England is by now well known for its love of letters. Of all the colonists flung out among the various reaches of England's burgeoning empire, probably none were quite as enamored of letters, and letters in every sense of the word: not just the missives sent by distant correspondents, or the characters of stiff print, set into books, but, simply, the very idea of reading and writing. Being the hotter sort of Protestants, most of them, New England's colonists believed in the importance of being able to read scripture. The northern colonies were thus quite literate. The first printing press creaked into motion at Cambridge, Massachusetts, in 1639 (although virtually all that it published before 1660 were "government-related publications, the annual almanac, a local translation of the Psalms, a few short catechisms, and not much else unless a subsidy was provided").[3] But scribal communication, if less known, was far more common. Before he died John Winthrop himself consumed countless quires of paper. He filled them to bursting with thoughts composed in his spidery hand—sometimes in an impenetrable secretary script, sometimes in a more welcoming and rounded italic, sometimes both in the same document.[4] He wrote hundreds of letters, to a bewildering cast of recipients. Yet, however heavily colonists relied on letters, sending was rarely easy. For nearly a half century after England's first weary pilgrims stepped ashore at Plymouth, no postal service existed. In the colonies, the English love affair with letter writing confronted the cruel difficulties of delivery.

How letters circulated is something of a mystery. While historians have avidly plumbed letters' content, they have seldom asked how these early mails were delivered.[5] This is odd, if only because there is no lack of evidence. Thousands of seventeenth-century letters survive, each containing echoes of the many couriers who once crossed New England. Some of the best evidence of how letters traveled, in fact, comes from the very people who sent Nahawton on his way: the Winthrops. Between the 1630s and the 1670s, the Winthrops generated and collected a staggering number of letters. Counting only those that circulated within the Americas, nearly three thousand survive. The sheer breadth of this collection makes it an unparalleled portal into colonial communications. It is, of course, not without biases. The Winthrop family ranked highly among New England's founders. But if the Winthrops were elite, many of their correspondents were not. They exchanged countless letters with ordinary, even barely literate, people. They also drew correspondence from all over the colonial world. In short, their letters offer the best available portrait of scribal New England in the seventeenth century—the best existing evidence of how letters circulated, and where.[6]

Many, apparently, traveled in the hands of Indians. That Winthrop's attendants chose to use an Indian courier was not, in fact, unusual. Indian messengers surface regularly in the Winthrops' correspondence; Nahawton is one of hundreds mentioned. Rarely is there more than a passing reference, but their presence is clear. "Your kinde lines I receaved by Mascanomet," noted John Endecott, in a 1639 letter. Other writers likewise informed John Winthrop that they had "received a letter lately from you by Nippumsint," or had sent a letter by "Will, my servant," a "native." Not all couriers were mentioned by name. Some English correspondents only noted obliquely that they had sent or received mail "by an Indian messendger." Others pled with the Winthrops to "send an Indian over" or to "procure some Indian to bring your note."[7] Anecdotal evidence of this pattern, in other words, is readily apparent. "I must request you to send your letter to Rich: Collicuts," went a typical request from Roger Williams in 1638, "that so a native may convey it."[8] Nahawton was far from alone.[9]

Nahawton was not a servant. He was a leader. He thought he had something to gain by carrying that letter. As messengers go, he was a good choice. He was a Massachusett man, from the Blue Hills (not far from Boston), and already a steadfast friend to the English. He had worked as a guide, piloting them through places unknown. He had even experimented with Christianity, after the Reverend John Eliot, in the 1640s, began preaching to Massachusett Indians. (In 1648, when Nahawton heard Cutshamekin's wife speaking of "worldly matters" on the Sabbath, he intervened to stop her.) A few years later he helped settle Punkapoag, a settlement of Christian Indians, of which he was "Chief Ruler." He loved his "Country" and its people, with whom he could be lax: "He is more loved than feared," John Eliot thought. The English loved him, too. "*Nabanton* is a sober good man," wrote one, "and a true friend to the English ever since our Comming." Almost certainly he was paid, in 1649, to carry the letter. But his doing so was symptomatic, too, of a greater decision: to befriend the English leaders of Massachusetts.[10]

Nahawton's friendship, and the friendship of those like him, was valuable. The English hold on the northeast, in these years, was fragile. Only a thin and brittle web of communications connected the English settlements. For decades much of interior New England—the woody spaces between colonies—remained alien to Englishmen. For that reason, correspondents in search of couriers often turned to those who better understood, and often controlled, the terrain: Indians. Men bent on writing letters had to have a way to send them, and the anemic trickle of English travelers and coastal seamen sometimes would not suffice. Indians, possessed of their own means of sending news, provided a convenient solution. The pattern is not limited to the Winthrop letters. Native people served frequently as couriers, carriers, and messengers: They formed a human web of words and letters, connecting even the English hubs of New England. Early New England's communications depended, sometimes desperately, on Indians.

I.

Imagine an English letter: a small, paper object, containing a message. It is folded, and, if it has far to go, it is likely sealed. Red wax, or, more rarely, black, stamps its flap shut. Open it: curls of purplish-black characters looping across paper, pulpy and rough. If you can read, you'll know its contents. It may ask for soap, or report the news of a great fire consuming London. It may deliver a warning or a plea for help. Each has its own tale to impart, even if "badly written," crumpled, "slurred," or "rinsed with sea water."[11]

Early American letters were conjured from various Old and New World materials, most obtained wherever possible. Shortly after the younger John Winthrop moved to Pequot, for instance, his father sent him a recipe for cooking ink—a careful process of dissolving, adding, bruising, boiling, and cooling.[12] Although ink could be bought, most colonists likely brewed their own. One method called for ink makers to combine soot or charcoal with gum arabic (added to help the ink cling to paper) and then to stir the mixture into a solvent, such as water, vinegar, or wine. Ink was also made from oak galls ("Galles," to the elder Winthrop): parasitic growths left by wasps and other insects on the bark of oak trees. The galls were ground up, combined with copperas or ferrous sulphate, mixed into a solvent, and then left to rest. The Winthrops' recipe was an amalgam of these techniques: a perfect brew of gum arabic ("Gumme"), gallic acids, and copperas—all cooked over a fire.[13]

But if ink could easily be boiled and brewed in a posnet, other materials were harder to find. Pens were made from bird quills, some of them plucked from turkeys.[14] Although these were perhaps readily available in the colonies, correspondents like William Pynchon—who declared tersely, in 1636, "I have no good pen"—were quick to bemoan the quality of their quills. Far more often, however, writers complained of their lack of paper, which had to be imported and was thus rather scarce. Papermaking was an arduous process; cloth fibers were mixed in great vats of water, then sifted out, pressed, treated with animal fats or alum, and finally sanded. In general, paper was produced neither in England nor in the colonies. Much of the paper used by English correspondents on both sides of the Atlantic came, in fact, from Holland.[15]

Pen and ink were useless, of course, without paper. Some commented on its dearth forthrightly, as when Roger Williams cut off a characteristically windy missive with the rather premature conclusion: "Sr. I want paper . . . Yors. R.W."[16] Others simply crowded their script onto impossibly small slips of paper. (Most letters penned in England contained a feast of blank space: they were formed by folding a sheet in half to create four pages, of which only the first was "used." Colonists had no such luxury. Their letters were more irregularly shaped, more congested with script, and more likely to show evidence of ripping and cutting, to make use of excess.)[17] A final element of many English letters—though not all—was wax. This, too, usually came from Europe. Sealing wax, almost always red, was sold in sticks that could be melted easily over the flap of a folded letter. Sealing a letter may have been something of a luxury in early New England, reserved solely for messages demanding secrecy. More than a few correspondents thought better of writing freely, if short of wax. "I want Wax to seale," Roger Williams mused, once, "otherwayes I would have exprest something which I reserve till another season."[18]

Caught without any of these requisite letter-writing materials, some felt themselves bitten by the loneliness of early New England's remoter parts. Winter, especially, could be cruel and isolating. "Sir, I pray you send me some sealing wax, if there be any to be had with you," Jonathan Brewster scribbled, in a January 1657 letter from his trading post near Mohegan. "We heare not any newes here from forrain parts," the trader lamented. "If you doe, I pray you," came the final plea, "imparte it." Without wax, he could not write; without letters, he had few ties to the world beyond the Pequot river.[19] Brewster's predicament was not unique. Communication was often broken up by New England's social geography, as the great unknown spaces between colonies barred easy exchange. Outside of Boston, the chief market, many felt challenged by the difficulties of collecting news. Yet none questioned the pressing need to correspond, want of wax or no. Letter writing was a way of making New England whole, of conquering space.[20]

R. Bellingham, John Cotton, John Wilson, and John Clark to John Winthrop, Jr., 26 March 1649. This is the letter that was carried by Nahawton, informing the younger Winthrop of his father's death. Original manuscript from the Winthrop Family Papers. (Courtesy of the Massachusetts Historical Society)

From its earliest moments, New England was built on letters. Alongside its fledgling world of print existed a world of couriers and scribes, inkpots and quills. This was an intensely scribal culture. Written communication helped to bind together the region's scattered English communities, clinging to the far side of an ocean. Although not all could write, most could coax a neighbor, or a minister, to transcribe a letter. Even the barely literate were apt to act as scribes, prompting complaints that too many records were written in "false English, so that no man can scarcely read or make sense of them."[21] If their "scripts" were not always polished, colonists nonetheless relied tremendously on correspondence, for all occasions. They used letters to send simple greetings, to do business, to seek medical advice, to handle diplomatic crises, and, most critically, to convey bits of news.[22]

As New England expanded in the 1640s, correspondence became a critical means of connecting its many outposts. Colonial leaders recognized early that New England's defense, as well as its identity, hinged on letters. Foremost on their minds, when they founded the United Colonies of New England in 1643, was this problem of communicating across strange, even hostile territory. "We are further dispersed upon the Sea Coasts and Rivers then was at first intended," they explained in the preamble to their Articles of Confederation, "so that we cannot ... wth convenience communicate in one Govment and Jurisdiccon." What complicated the problem, beyond simple distance and unfamiliarity with the land, was that the colonies were frankly surrounded by a bewildering web of Indian villages and peoples—not to mention a smattering of Dutch posts and French forts. "We live encompassed," writers added, "wth people of sevall Nations and strang languages," some of whom had already proven a threat to New England's "posteritie."[23]

But if leaders worried about rousing distant brethren from their beds amidst an attack, others corresponded with far more commonplace concerns in mind. Families, too, leaned on letters. From Ipswich, thirty miles removed from her parents in Boston, a pregnant Mary Winthrop Dudley used letters to pester her stepmother for a myriad of household goods. Over the winter of 1635–1636, she penned plaintive missives bemoaning her want of cloth, of fruit, of thread, even of a faithful maidservant. She first complained of troubles with her maid in March, and by April declared her desire that she be sent a new servant girl. She wrote, too, of her need for "cloutes," "sheetes," and "pillow-beeres," sugar and "sope," and finally, a "childs chaire"—"for I can get none made heear." Her stepmother failing to answer many of these demands, Mary eased her tone by late spring. "[D]welling so farre from the bay," she wrote sheepishly, "makes me the oftener troublesome to you."[24]

One senses that Mary Winthrop Dudley reached rather quickly for her pen, whether in pursuit of "fine thred" or, simply, soap. But that is not surprising. The literate English, after all, were accustomed to writing letters. Corresponding was becoming far more prevalent among them, in this very period. The act of writing letters, of course, has a much longer history. It is an ancient practice: Correspondence has been plucked from the ruins of Mesopotamia, dating back four thousand years. Long before Europeans reached the Americas, expanding empires had been pressed to find means of sending messages over long distances. Facing their own problems of communication, the Romans famously created the *cursus publicus,* a relay system of couriers and carriages designed to speed messages along thousands of miles of imperial roads. But only in the early modern period did the letter become, for the English at least, the principal "material medium, *tout court,* of . . . social exchange."[25]

Shared considerations shaped English letter writing, whether it was done in Europe or the Americas. The early modern letter was governed by certain conventions, and, not surprisingly, colonial correspondents borrowed much from English custom. Most epistles were terribly formulaic. Shuffle through any collection, and you are apt to trip on hopelessly tired tropes. Few writers could resist mentioning their epistolary "debt" to the addressee, or apologizing for their "hasty scribblings." A typical letter was addressed, opposite the seal, with appropriate deference ("To our honoured Governor and his much esteemd freind Mr. Winthrop" went one oft-repeated model), though such careful language was liable to crumble away in the heat of emergency. Further instructions might follow, including specific direction as to where the recipient might be found. "[A]t his howse in Boston," one writer beseeched, "present theise."[26]

Such directives conjure a ghostly figure: the letter's bearer. Letters must be delivered, after all, and here was one respect in which New England correspondents were forced to seek out new ways and means. No one, of course, would have expected perfectly efficient delivery. Despite the letter's ascent in English culture, postal service was not well established, even in England.[27] Even the royal posts sometimes lagged. Under James I, one letter spent an impossibly long nine days in transit from London to Scotland, despite an inscription that spurred its bearer to ride "For life, for life."[28] (In England, writers sometimes drew gallows on their letters, to nudge "partially literate" carriers to ride for their lives.)[29] Thus, it must be said, English migrants to America did not necessarily bring with them the expectation of regular delivery of letters. Still, colonial correspondents faced challenges unknown in England, where couriers traveled well-trod post roads and deposited mail at familiar landmarks such as the "sign of the white horse." If postal service was spotty and inefficient in England, nothing even resembling such a system existed in the colonies.

As early as 1638, colonists appealed to England to establish a colonial post office, but to no avail. Without a post, correspondents were forced to seize whatever opportunity presented, and these came few and far between. In 1652, one Massachusetts writer voiced the frustration of countless others in lamenting the persistent "uncertenty of when, and how, to convey lettres."[30] Those who did find a way worried, nonetheless, about their missives. They had good reason. Surviving letters bear ample testament of those that never "came to hand." Careless couriers dropped or misplaced letters all too often. In 1673 Amos Richardson encountered a courier, frantically searching, on the path between Rhode Island and Connecticut. Having lost an important piece of official correspondence, he had wisely "gon Back to seeke It."[31] Not until the 1670s would postal service even be attempted in the northeast. Before then, no postal carrier awaited colonists' letters; no horn heralded his coming; no rider came to scoop up their scrawlings in his satchel. Who, then, carried letters?

Discovering who carried mail is not terribly difficult. Many letters name their own carriers, while others can be traced through evidence from later correspondence.[32] The vast majority of letter bearers, it must be said, remain anonymous: Of 2,856 letters ferried between the Winthrops and their correspondents between the 1630s and the 1670s, only 443 (or about 16 percent) can be linked to a particular courier. Still, that is a substantial number, enough to suggest broader patterns. The Winthrops' letters conjure an eclectic array of couriers, most of them—as might be expected—chosen by happenstance ("I wrote to you about a weeke since by a neighbour of mine, yet having so fitt opportunity by this bearer . . .") or because they were part of New England's cohort of watermen ("The inclosed letters were sent hither last weeke to be conveyed to you and we have now an oportunity of a vessell of providence . . .").[33] But the letters also contain glimpses of something else: a marked reliance on Indians. They reflect a hidden geography of Native travelers, weaving across the northeast with English news in hand. Nahawton, who sped the letter bearing news of John Winthrop's death to his son in 1649, is one of well over one hundred Native messengers mentioned in letters dated between 1635 and 1675. In fact, the Winthrops' letters imply, one in five letters traveled with an Indian. Yet in particular situations, and along certain corridors, their role was far greater.

American Natives had probably borne written messages for Europeans virtually since the dawn of colonization. English records find Indians carrying letters at least as early as 1627. That year, a ship wrecked off the coast of Cape Cod, and, spying a cluster of approaching canoes, its passengers were relieved to hear several Indians "speake English unto them, . . . and [offer] that they would bring them to the English houses, or carry their letters." Indeed, after bestowing gifts on their rescuers, the English "sente 2. men and a letter" to Plymouth. (They soon received aid.) If these Indians seemed remarkably familiar with the notion of carrying messages for Europeans, they may have learned the practice from the Dutch. Later in 1627, in fact, letters from the Dutch plantations arrived at Plymouth—also borne by Indians. Like those who had discovered the marooned passengers at Cape Cod, these Natives had also apparently "offered ther service to cary letters unto you."[34]

But regular mentions of Native people carrying correspondence do not arise until the late 1630s, when, amidst the turmoil of the Pequot War, Roger Williams comprehended the necessity of sending news, quickly and safely, over significant distances. The first such courier to be mentioned by name is Assotemuit, a Narragansett man who brought one of Roger Williams' letters to Boston in July 1637. And just like that, others followed: Yotaash, Juanemo, "Panaquanike Indian," and various other Algonquians, named and unnamed, all in a flurry. By the spring of 1638, the Pequot War dying down, Williams had sent so many letters with Indians that he felt free to comment on their shortcomings as couriers. "Tis true I may hire an Indian," he wrote, "yet not alwayes, nor sure, for these 2 things I have found in them: sometimes long keeping of a letter: 2ndly if a feare take them that the Letter concernes themselves they suppresse it."[35]

If the pattern sprang from the upheavals of the late 1630s, it quickly grew. Over the next forty years, a good many of New England's letters would pass through Indian hands. Diarist Thomas Minor recorded a number of instances when he paid them to act as couriers, both locally and over longer distances. "[N]oosacke The Indean was sent to the bay & had fiftie shillings," he wrote in January 1662. Local Indians brought letters from his son John ("I recived a leter by sonnamooten from John") and then returned his reply ("I sent . . . to john by Secoggisbus squa"). More locally, Minor also paid them to carry goods: In October 1664, he "sent Eight bushells of Corne to Cary by pyatungus."[36] But these arrangements were not always as informal as with Cary Latham's corn. Indians also carried letters as part of official English business. Connecticut and Rhode Island colonies, for instance, sometimes used Indian couriers to deliver their correspondence. Notwithstanding it had dispatched at least one urgent letter via "an Indian [named] Quinomp," Rhode Island later huffed that the Connecticut General Court had sent an important missive "by an Indian." Did New England's leaders hesitate to consign official letters to the care of Algonquians? Perhaps. But by the 1650s, the pattern was widespread and familiar. Pequots confirmed this fact in 1655, when they told Ninigret's men that they were often recruited "to carry letters or burthens abroad wher the English should have occasion to send them."[37]

They seem to have been recruited, moreover, to carry the most pressing of news. Early New England's letters generally traveled one of two ways: "by opportunity" or "by express." Letters sent by opportunity, as the phrasing suggests, went with any soul who happened to be traveling along the desired route. These letters often languished, waiting to be taken by some rare way-farer or sea captain. Once on their way, such letters also made frequent stopovers, planned or unexpected, before arriving at the intended destina-tion. Most letters went this way. A goodly number, in fact, were composed only upon hearing of some plum "opportunity" to correspond. Colonists rushed to write, even as their prospective messengers waited impatiently. "I durst not lose this opportunity," Edward Winslow scrawled hastily, in May 1637; but, "being called on to seale," he was forced to cut short his missive. Hence correspondents' hurried apologies for their abortive writings. "This oportunity is but very suddaine by one that passed through the towne," John Winthrop, Jr. wrote mournfully, in one letter, "therefore I have scarce tyme to write." "[T]he messenger cals for my letter and I must breake off," went another familiar refrain.[38]

Some letters, however, could not await such intermittent carriage. Urgent messages required more express delivery. Because New England's writers commented so frequently on the disjointed ways in which their letters trav-eled, we can see the distinction—both in their minds and on the ground. One friend, for instance, beseeched John Winthrop, Jr., to forward his letter "so soone as opportunity," but insisted that "there is no occasion for an

Expresse messenger."[39] Others made the opposite plea. "I pray Sr.," implored one, "hasten away the letter . . . with a messenger on Purpose and that in the most spedyest manner."[40] Expresses traveled directly (and, ideally, in the "most spedyest manner"), much as a royal post would have done in England. In the colonies, however, "Expresse messengers" were often Indians. Much mail could wait. But when the information was important and perishable, Indians were enlisted. Colonists tended to turn to Indian couriers in their most vulnerable moments. These messages were pressing, penned in times of exigency.

Illness and death, for instance, pressed more than a few desperate New Englanders to seek out an "Indian barer." The pattern is most visible in the letters of John Winthrop, Jr., who fancied himself something of a specialist in medicine and was thus inundated with pleas for medical advice.[41] People wrote to John Winthrop, Jr., for all kinds of reasons, from all sorts of places. But before his own death in 1676, he received some four hundred or so letters detailing the various ailments of his English neighbors. One writer averred that his fellow Englishmen regarded Winthrop "not only as a Civil Governor but head of a great Hospital, wherein from all parts we are comming with our Complaints unto you for help and health."[42] Many of these "Complaints" arrived in the hands of Algonquian messengers. "I have . . . hyred this Indian to be the bearer of these lines," the Reverend John Davenport, ailing and fearful, penned nervously in 1653, "and pray you to returne by him your advise."[43] Others expressed more frankly their sense of urgency. His wife dying, Richard Smith dispatched a message to Winthrop pleading for any medicine that might preserve her life. "Sir I have sent this indyan to you to gett sumething of you for my wiufe, she being exceding ile," he wrote. "[P]raye dispach the indyan baicke with all spede."[44]

Other circumstances also called for express messengers. A rush to collect debts, or pipe staves, or even livestock, could move a trader to "send an Indian purposly."[45] More often, urgent news concerned war or some other impending threat. Upon hearing that "many thousands" of Mohawks were headed toward Narragansett in the mid-1640s, for instance, a Dorchester man sent a warning letter "by an Indian" to nearby colonists. (The rumor, it turned out, was spurious.) And when a Dutch fleet captured New York in 1673, Rhode Island men hastily dispatched an "Ingin mesenger" to collect news of the "duches prosedings." Because quick delivery was imperative in these situations, speed is a recurrent theme of such letters. "Sir this Indian is hyerd of purpose to understand your mind fully," read the postscript to one letter. "I pray dispatch him backe with a speedy answer."[46] This language is repeated in countless letters. Such an appeal signaled, with some firmness, that the matter at hand deserved the recipient's immediate attention.

It also meant that some type of payment was involved. Ordinary letters could be sent with merchants or travelers, who were often happy to forward mail for only a token acknowledgement.[47] But colonists who needed to send urgent news were sometimes forced to pay for the privilege.[48] Often, that meant hiring an Indian. This detail, in fact, tells something about the phenomenon of Indian letter bearing. Although some couriers were undeniably servants to the English (several letters reference the bearer as "my native servant" or "Your Indean"), many were not. The cost, for those in dire straits, could be considerable. "[I]f you doe your businesse by Indians you will find it deerer then to send an Englishman," William Pynchon instructed one of his correspondents in 1644, after a courier named "Ta-mag-gut" delivered the man's desperate plea for cheese and butter. (Sending Ta-mag-gut unfortunately did the writer no good. Pynchon coldly informed him, "whereas you write for butter and cheese it is not to be had.")[49]

Those anxious to receive returns from the Winthrops eagerly promised to pay for Indian expresses. Jonathan Brewster twice offered to "contente" the messenger, if only John Winthrop, Jr., would send "worde . . . by an Indian." When his daughter was afflicted with a palsy, Richard Odell similarly offered to "satisfy" an Indian messenger for his "paynes," if necessary. Another father, fretting over his child's jaundice, also wanted to receive Winthrop's immediate advice, via a Native messenger. "I will please him for his journey," the man pledged.[50] In winter 1660, when the pestilence raging through New Haven took hold of John Davenport's son, the minister pled for a quick return by a hired Indian courier. "Sir you see our need of a speedy answer, if it were possible, by some winged messenger," he wrote. "[I]f an Indian could bring it sooner . . . I will pay him for his paines whatever you please to promise."[51]

How these writers "pleased" their Indian couriers is more difficult to judge. Early on, Indians were paid in trade goods, like the "Coate and . . . pare of shoes" that Daniel Patrick's courier was promised upon delivering the soldier's letter to Boston. Assotemuit, who carried Roger Williams' July 1637 letter, was also to be paid in cloth: "[F]orget not," Williams reminded John Winthrop, "to reward this messenger with a Coate." Williams also promised his couriers various other goods, including pairs of breeches and even awl blades. On at least one occasion, he and John Winthrop, Jr., split the cost of "postage": Williams granted the "Bag cariers" six awl blades to take the letters as far as "Nenekunats," or about halfway to their final stopping point. He expected Winthrop, the recipient, to pay the other half. "[P]ay 6 more to him that brings them to you," he charged.[52]

One other circumstance drew Indians, more often, into service: winter. Use of Native couriers was highest in the winter months, particularly January, February and March.[53] It was terribly difficult to send during winter. Boats were stilled in ice, paths buried, and whole towns "shutt up with snowe." Winter imprisoned colonists, its frigid wind a "cold messenger," bearer of "deep snows and bitter frost," "commanding every man to his house."[54] John Winthrop, Jr., probably echoed the sentiments of most colonists when he declared tersely, in November 1669, "[T]he season is over for travaile."[55] Trapped by "snow and frost," English correspondents sometimes found Native couriers their only recourse. During the brutal winter of 1664–1665, the younger John Winthrop needed to send an important message from Hartford to Narragansett, an overland distance of over eighty miles. But he knew that, after months of snowy weather, the "way hath beene blocked up and [is] not passable for man, or horse." His only option, he thought, was to hire an Indian messenger. "I send these by an Indian who takes his owne way in some place to get over," Winthrop wrote.[56]

But even when "great snows" had not blanketed the landscape, Native people had their "owne ways" of navigating New England. This is no small point. Indians made opportune messengers—the only messengers available, in many cases—because the routes they took were largely untraveled by colonists. Indians carried letters where Englishmen did not, or would not, go. Perhaps the greatest reason that Indians were so often employed as couriers was their vastly superior knowledge of New England's geography, a fact that English writers repeatedly affirmed. "[T]hey are so exquisitely skilled in all the body and bowels of the Countrey (by reason of their huntings)," gushed Roger Williams, "that I have often been guided twentie, thirtie, sometimes fortie miles through the woods, a streight course out of any path."[57]

That Indians could take a "streight course" between correspondents was precisely what made them attractive messengers, particularly in times of crisis. We might like to trail these Indian couriers as they traveled through the northeastern interior, punching down snow, underfoot. But, for the most part, we cannot. There is much about these transactions that we cannot know, and for good reason: English correspondents themselves had little familiarity with inland routes. Locked into viewing Indian messengers from the confines of English letters, we are trapped, motionless, at points of departure and arrival. With feet planted firmly in Boston, or Hartford, or Springfield, we can only gaze out, across the countryside, and imagine phantom paths—unknown and inaccessible to English writers.

II.

Of the many reasons why Indians made appealing couriers of sensitive information, one at first seems to leap out: they could not read. For most of the seventeenth century, and certainly before the late 1650s, nearly all Native people were illiterate in English.[58] Even those handling a letter, then, could rely on little more than suspicion and "feare" to discover whether its contents "concern[ed] themselves." Given Indians' inability to read, clandestine messages could be entrusted to them. This was a valuable recourse. Some writers went to great lengths to keep their letters "secret," even from those carrying them. One of John Winthrop, Jr.'s correspondents even resorted to sending a casement—a stencil-like sheet that, when laid over a letter, exposed only certain words and thus revealed the writer's true message. Others wrote in Latin, a measure that effectively shielded sensitive passages from all but the most studied of readers. In 1654 the Reverend James Fitch wrote to Winthrop for medical advice, on behalf of a neighbor suffering from an embarrassing "distemper." On concluding, he added a note in Latin: "*Modo hoc obsecro, ut si aliquid secreti scribas—latine scriberes.*" Winthrop would have had no problem translating: "Only I entreat this," Fitch had written, "that if you should write anything secret, may you write it in Latin."[59] Sending an Indian, too, churned up fewer concerns that the carrier might yield to curiosity and pry open one's letter. It offered the opportunity to write more freely—even about Indian-related matters. Unable to decode English script, Indian bearers sometimes unwittingly delivered information that doomed their own neighbors. When in 1639 Roger Williams sent to Boston a list of Pequots "to be killed," he included a telling note: "The messenger is ignorant of the matter and is satisfied," went his chill postscript.[60]

But to cast Indians as entirely illiterate is not quite right. They may have been unable to read English, but some Native traditions of reading and writing did exist. In the far northeast, Abenaki and Mi'kmaq people kept records on birch bark. In 1652, Father Gabriel Druillettes, a French missionary, watched in astonishment as Mi'kmaq students set his teachings down in writing. "Some of them wrote out their lessons in their own manner," he wrote. "They made use of a small piece of charcoal instead of a pen, and a piece of bark instead of paper . . . They carried this paper with them to study." These were individual ways of recording ideas, but they could be read and passed on.[61] The Jesuit missionary Sébastien Rale observed similarly that Abenakis shared information in pictographs "as well as we understand each other by our letters."[62] Further from New England, a wilder array of Indian literacies bloomed. The Mexica kept records on bark paper called *amatl*. Incans used *quipis*, strings knotted in particular sequences, to convey important messages. Even wampum, so often cast as currency by Europeans, was a medium of communication. For the Iroquois, belts and strings of wampum beads could carry recorded information.[63] If not in ways that were alphabetic, Indians nevertheless read, and they wrote.

In fact it was likely their knowledge of Native modes of communication, rather than their ignorance of English ones, that made Indian couriers so favorable. At contact, some Native Americans had communication systems that rivaled, or even surpassed, those in Europe. Many groups could send news across hundreds of miles. As early as the fourteenth century, the Inca of Peru had established a relay messenger system, not unlike Rome's *cursus publicus,* that covered roughly 2,500 miles of Incan "highways." Evidence suggests that the Iroquois also used relays. Their couriers covered the "Iroquois Trail," a 240-mile artery connecting the confederacy from eastern Mohawk territory to the western Seneca. Ethnographic and anthropological evidence from across North and South America has unearthed "courier-runner traditions" among various different groups.[64] Although Algonquians sometimes had quite local allegiances, they also maintained connections with other relatively distant groups.

Though far more difficult to reconstruct than, say, the tottering English postal system, northeastern Natives had demonstrably wide-ranging ties. Trade items, such as copper from the north, shells from the south, and even glass beads, attest to an unseen web of exchange.[65] New England's Native people were therefore well prepared to communicate over distances. Having observed the Narragansetts, Roger Williams described a relay system of messengers among them: "If it be in time of *warre,*" he wrote in 1643, "he that is a *Messenger* runs swiftly, and at every towne the *Messenger* comes, a fresh *Messenger* is sent."[66] Some couriers may have been messengers among Algonquians, long before being drafted to carry English news. Recall

Assotemuit, who sped Roger Williams's war-related letter to Boston in July 1637. Although Assotemuit dutifully served as a courier of Williams's "Newes and Tidings" that summer, he was first a messenger of the Narragansett sachems. To Williams, in fact, he came recommended by Narragansett leaders as a "noted" and "especiall Messenger."[67]

Native people were as eager for fresh news as were the English, and the evidence suggests that they were more efficient at spreading it. "Their desire of, and delight in newes, is great, as the Athenians, and all men, more or lesse," attested Williams. A messenger arriving with important news would, accordingly, summon villagers with "mutuall *hollowing*" and be brought to a "place of audience, where by this meanes is gathered a great confluence of people to entertaine the *newes*." Williams witnessed, on occasion, many Narragansetts convene in like fashion: "Their manner is upon any tidings to sit round, double or treble or more, as their numbers be; I have seene neer a thousand in a round," all of whom sat in "deepe silence" and devoted rapt "attention . . . to him that speaketh." Glances of more prosaic communications among Native people are elusive, but the very presence of such an intricate network of inland pathways suggests a complex web of interactions reaching rather extensively into the past. "It is admirable to see, what paths their naked hardned feet have made in the wildernesse," Williams wrote effusively.[68] Later observers echoed Williams in attesting that an Indian could "mark his courses as he runs more readily than most Travellers who steer by the Compass."[69]

Some of these descriptions exaggerate. In truth, Williams and others probably overstated Indian powers of navigation. Surely Native northeasterners lost their way, or were lured by a faulty fork in the path, on occasion. But in imagining Indians to be unfailingly swift and adroit travelers, colonists betrayed their own ignorance of the countryside. To be able to read that countryside was a kind of literacy in itself, a literacy possessed almost wholly by Indians. In this case, it was Englishmen who were illiterate.

III.

Roger Williams owned a compass. It was small and round and sturdy. It survives still, though its face is slightly rusted and the needle gone. Was it a comfort to him, as he fretted about "land travel to Qunnihticut"?[70] Did it help him find the way? In all of his colorful and voluminous writings, Williams mentions no compass. Placing it in his hands, even, is difficult. Though perhaps a feeble clue, Williams's compass nonetheless points us toward important questions: How did early colonial travelers approach the landscape? How did they find the way?[71] Not easily. In early New England, traveling over land often meant negotiating one's way through the dangers and discomforts of Indian places. It meant confronting the possibility of becoming lost and confused, even of starving. To say the least, these were unappealing prospects. Most preferred water transport instead, though it was both seasonal and slow, and water, of course, brought its own risks.

But for Englishmen, water was at least familiar. Land was another matter entirely. The perils of water passage probably paled against the unknowns of New England's interior. Historians have been quick to discount Puritans' complaints about the "howling wilderness" that nipped at their ankles, but some of this talk was rooted in real fears.[72] English colonists were the inheritors of ancient terrors that held the forest to be a menacing place. First-century Roman invaders had shuddered when faced with caliginous German forests. Medieval peasants feared the wild and mystical beasts that prowled beyond their villages.[73] These fears of the wilderness persisted into the early modern era. "Until well into the seventeenth century," writes landscape historian John Stilgoe, "peasants peered at the wilderness through the prism of bewilderment and chaos. Every sort of experience beyond the farthest field was distorted by the certainties attendant upon losing one's way."[74] In real ways, travel was circumscribed by fears of the unknown wilds.

Such fears were particularly powerful in the New World, which was far more forested than any realm of Europe. Though the wooded wilds remained an imagined province of all sorts of strange and frightful beings, England in fact had few woods of its own. Perhaps as early as the arrival of the Romans, English forests had been vastly reduced; by the Middle Ages, they had virtually disappeared.[75] (Narragansetts may not have been terribly far off in imagining that English colonists had left their homelands in search of firewood.[76]) Whatever trepidation was inspired in the earliest colonists by New England's impressive forests was likely tempered, it must be said, by a certain happiness at finding such ample reserves of fuel and timber for construction. "Here is good living for those that love good fires," cheered Francis Higginson in 1630. But with the English countryside all but denuded, early modern English men and women would have had little experience in probing their way through thick copses of woodland. How daunting it must have been, then, for William Bradford's lot to find, on arriving in 1620, that Cape Cod was positively "woodded to the brinke of the sea."[77]

Compass and sundial owned by Roger Williams. Brass, ca. 1630. Photograph number RHi X17 1147. *(Courtesy of the Rhode Island Historical Society)*

Although the earliest promotional literature painted New England as a bountiful garden, this characterization quickly gave way to harsher assessments. Once it had been planted, so to speak, the garden became something altogether different. In early histories of New England, like Edward Johnson's *Wonder-Working Providence of Sions Saviour in New England* (1654), the distress of traveling through the region's "Desart Wildernesse" emerged as a recurring theme. Johnson spent pages relating colonists' "difficulties traveling through unknowne woods, and through watery scrampes [swamps], . . . sometimes passing through the Thickets, where their hands are forced to make way for their bodies passage," and their feet to find secure footing amidst boggy muck. Johnson described brambled pathways where "the ragged Bushes scratch their legs fouly" and tore flesh, "if [it] be not otherwise well defended with Bootes, or Buskings."[78]

Certainly these tales worked well for Johnson's purposes. His account of wandering planters—"bewildred indeed"—was carefully crafted to hail the God-given mission of settling New England, despite all travails. (Johnson, for one, was sure that the "directing Providence of Christ" was better guidance in the wilderness than a thousand paths.) Hence his elaborate descriptions of how the English had triumphed over a wilderness determined to bloody their legs and to bewilder their minds. That Johnson's history bore a particular message, nonetheless, does not mean that it was fictitious. Real experiences lay behind his stories. His tale of a young servant "loosing her selfe in the Woods," for instance, bears a heavy resemblance to the very real "mayd servant of mr Skelton" who had spent days lost "in the woodes" between Salem and Saugus in the winter of 1632-1633. And behind Johnson's prickly brambles was many a colonist who found that, in his travels, he had "torne his legges muche."[79] The lost, beleaguered English traveler was not just a trope.[80]

Bewilderment was a true danger. Even those traveling between Boston and its outlying neighbors might find themselves lost. Every journey, certainly, was not threatening; as early as 1631 or so, John Winthrop enjoyed exploring the country surrounding Boston.[81] But early entries of Winthrop's *Journal* describe several parties who went astray while venturing among Massachusetts towns. In September of 1634, a man went missing between Dorchester and Wessagusset and "wandered in the woods & swampes 3: dayes & 2: nightes," before stumbling into Scituate. Months later, two Ipswich men lost their way whilst traveling "homewardes" from Boston. These two rambled through the countryside for six long days, until an Indian discovered them "allmoste sencelesse" from hunger and fatigue. Nighttime travel posed further challenges, as one man found while "travelling late" between Dorchester and Watertown in 1642. "[B]enighted . . . in a swamp about 10 of the clock," the frightened traveler cried out for "help, help." Hearers in Cambridge feared he was being tortured by Indians and sounded an alarm that swept as far north as Salem.[82]

Though confusing, New England's woods were not trackless. Well-worn paths lured travelers into the Indian interior. Early New England was etched with a matrix of complex trails and pathways, familiar to Indian wayfarers but often confusing to Englishmen. From the first, these paths guided English movements. Pilgrim scouts "struck into the Land" using the "little paths or tracts" that beckoned to them from beyond the beach. But these were difficult to follow, given their lack of familiar signposts. When Pilgrim searchers "followed certaine beaten pathes and tracts of the *Indians* into the Woods," they expected to find some "Towne, or houses." Instead, they found themselves meandering aimlessly through what seemed an unmarked maze. Colonists had begun to test some of these paths as early as the 1630s, but they were still terribly prone to getting lost. Even after English colonists gained some familiarity with using Indian trails, these routes remained nettlesome and confusing. Like William Wood's Plymouth-bound party in the 1630s, those who went between English settlements risked "being deluded by a misleading path."[83]

Easily seduced down the wrong path, long-distance travelers often required the aid of an Indian pilot. Native people played an enormous role in piloting colonial travelers through the wood. Acknowledging this, early writers heaped breathless praise on Indian guides.[84] "The wildernesse being so vast, it is a mercy," averred Roger Williams, "that for hire a man shall never want guides." For hire, indeed, a guide might also carry one's things, shepherd one over a roiling river, or even help a weary traveler find lodging. Reflecting the importance of these pilots, Williams's 1643 *Key into the Language of America* helpfully tutored English readers in the terms of arranging for such guidance: "Tou nishin méyi? *Where lies the way?*" "Kokotemíinnea méyi. *Shew me the way.*" "Kuttánnoonsh. *I will hire you.*" "Cummáuchanish. *I will conduct you.*" "Yò aûnta. *Let us goe that way.*" "Tounúckquaque yo wuchê. *How far from hence?*" "Maúchatea. *A guide.*" "Máuchase. *Be my guide.*"[85] Mindful, undoubtedly, of his own helpless wandering toward Narragansett, Williams noted, "I have heard of many *English* lost, and have oft been lost my selfe, and my selfe and others have often been found, and succoured by the *Indians.*"[86]

Colonial travelers had few other aids to guide them through the maze. Those lucky enough to own compasses (in all likelihood, an extremely small number) could use such handy instruments to point them in the right direction. Others used the sun. (William Wood attributed his own bewilderment to the "day being gloomy" and "our compasses at home." Phinehas Pratt likewise remembered of one journey, "The sonn being beclouded, I wandered, not knowing my way."[87]) Many resorted to such measures as finding higher ground, to get a better vantage on the countryside. A group of thatch cutters in early Plymouth, for instance, wandered too far off and spent a snowbound night, before climbing "an high Hill," from which they spotted "the two Iles in the Bay, and so that night got to the Plantation, being ready to faint with travaile."[88] Climbing a tree was also a useful method of reckoning. In the 1630s, a party of Indians found a confused African slave perched "in the top of a tree, looking out for his way which he had lost." After puzzling over this strange, treed figure, they helpfully led the "poor wandering blackamore" back to his master.[89]

But these were merely means of dead reckoning. Climbing a tree, or tilting a sundial skyward—such acts might give a general sense of direction, but they were little help in steering through particular paths, toward particular places. Of those paths and places, few maps existed. While mariners might consult sea charts or almanacs, overland travelers had nothing comparable to reference.[90] Maps of virtually any sort were wanting. Many of John Winthrop, Jr.'s European correspondents clamored for a "plott or mappe of N.E." One declared his greedy "desire," in 1632, "to know New England and all the new world." But these men were sorely disappointed. Perhaps Winthrop chuckled, on reading their pleas: Would that he had such a map! Of course, he did not. For years, cartographic knowledge of New England was rigidly confined to coastal areas. (When Winthrop finally did forward a map to a friend in England, it was a "Mapp of the Coast about Pequot.")[91]

But if maps were few, those providing guidance to land travelers were all but nonexistent. Maps of this era were not intended as travelers' guides. Most served, instead, to make grand proprietary claims over territory—territory that often remained largely unknown to those claiming it. And given English ignorance of the interior landscape (not to mention the relative backwardness of English cartography), these basic and half-blank charts would have offered little aid to travelers. Maps showing travel routes would not appear until the late seventeenth and early eighteenth centuries, when colonists began forging their own roads through New England. Even then, cartographers' sketches of New England's pathways were terribly rudimentary. To envision a wandering colonist, map in hand, is both unfair and inaccurate. Their ways of navigating New England were far less grand.

A better measure of how ordinary New Englanders approached the landscape, perhaps, lies in early descriptions of the region—verbal maps, of sorts. Visual maps they did not have; what they had, instead, were words. Visitors and colonists alike penned elaborate 'topographical descriptions' that ranged widely over New England's many hamlets, guiding their readers as if by hand.[92] In about 1650, the Reverend John Eliot wrote one such "breife topographicall description" that covered the waterfront, literally. Plodding through every English town then settled, Eliot offered up distances between each and described their positions along each compass point: "[N]orth-northeast from charlstowne .3. myles lyeth Malden," reads one passage, ". . . And .4. myles further on the same poynt lyeth Reading, where Mr Hoph is Pastor,—Northeast from Charlstowne about .7. myles lyeth lynn. which is upon the Sea cost within the Bay, there the great Iron workes are." Sweeping from Massachusetts Bay southward to Long Island Sound, Eliot went on, in like fashion, for pages.[93]

This amounts to a rather dry read. But it does tell something of how colonists viewed travel and geography: as a string of places and landmarks, with certain ministers and tales and "Iron workes" attached to each. Eliot's description was an itinerary of sorts, though even this sort of guide would have been of limited use to the everyday traveler. While Eliot did give some indication of which places were easily reached by water and which were more land-locked ("By streame southward lyeth Sudbury," he wrote, though Dedham lay "in land from Roxbury"), he proffered no description of travel routes.[94] Instead, Eliot's orientation was squarely toward perambulating coastal New England. Nowhere does he mention a path or a road. At 1650, it seems, inland ways were still largely unknown, unused, perhaps even unimportant, to most English colonists.

But not to all. At least one map survives to capture colonists' early attempts to chart these paths. In 1642 Massachusetts Bay hired Nathaniel Woodward and Solomon Saffery, a pair of sailors—as if sketching New England's hilly interior were the same as sounding its shores—to chart its boundary with Connecticut.[95] Such a boundary was merely a figment, at this point—an invisible line of latitude running through a nondescript "hilly country." But because it is the earliest surviving sketch to show pathways through interior New England, the map they made is worth pondering. While betraying unfamiliarity with the land between colonies, Woodward and Saffery's map does suggest how colonial people may have navigated that land. Along the trail between Boston and Springfield, they groped for distinguishing landmarks: "Blew hills," "Nipnat river," "Pine plains," "Thisle Swamps." Where they found a "little pond" or a "bad hole" in the path, they noted such features. Some landmarks—like the hulking "Wathuget hill"—were significant enough to be glimpsed and recorded, despite being far off the path. In 1642, only a select few colonists would have had any experience traversing these trails. But in the years to come, this was how colonists likely navigated: they looked for a pond, a brook, a familiar fording place, or a hill in the distance.

Smaller monuments also helped. Indians and English both marked pathways, for a host of reasons. Native travelers might leave a bent branch posted in the ground, to indicate the direction in which they had headed. They might strip the bark from a tree and mark it, with paint or notches, to indicate a successful war party.[96] Some also built permanent monuments along each path, as reminders of important events that had unfolded there. Native people

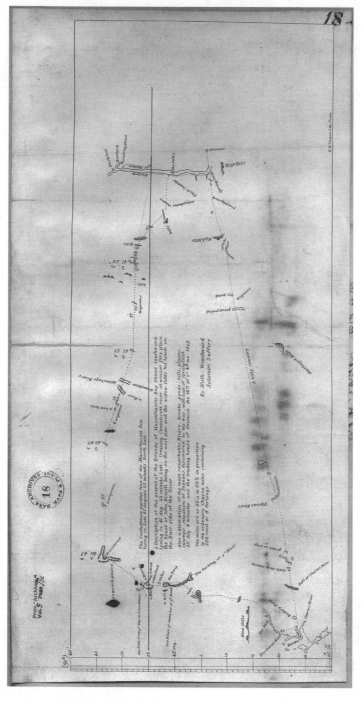

Sketched when Woodward and Saffery were charged with surveying the Massachusetts boundary in 1642, this is one of the earliest maps of interior New England. It also gives a sense of how Englishmen navigated, by looking for landmarks: "Blew Hills," a "little deep swamp," or a cluster of "wigwams." Third Series Maps, 35:18, Plan of southern boundary of Massachusetts–Connecticut line, made by Nathaniel Woodward and Solomon Saffery, dated June 14, 1642 [Lithograph copy]. SC1/series 50x. *(Courtesy of the Massachusetts Archives)*

remembered their past spatially: "Instead of records and chronicles," observed Edward Winslow, "they take this course. Where any remarkable act is done, in memory of it, either in the place, or by some pathway near adjoining, they make a round hole in the ground, about a foot deep, . . . which when others passing by behold, they inquire the cause and occasion of the same." Indians were careful to repair these monuments regularly, by scooping dirt from any holes that had been "filled or grown up by accident," thus keeping even the distant past "fresh in memory." Indian guides acquainted their English charges with some of these stories. If he could "understand his guide," Winslow related, an Englishman's "journey will be the less tedious, by reason of the many historical discourses [that] will be related unto him."[97]

English memory settled in certain spots, as well—John Eliot knew Hellgate as a place close to where "Ms Hutchinson lived and was slaine by the Indians," for instance—but colonists seldom erected monuments to commemorate such things. They were far more likely to leave markings of possession. If Indians left "messages emblazoned on trees," Englishmen carved characters into tree bark as a way of bounding property. Although property lines did not always intersect with pathways, landowners often marked property near a trail—simply because this was the place where the property line was most likely to be encountered. Notches, X's, letters, words, initials and other English markings slowly began to appear on New England's trees. Indians were well aware of the significance of these. In a 1659 ceremony, for instance, Quinebaug Indians watched as an oak tree, standing "neere the path," was marked on three sides to show English ownership. English surveyors used other signs as well, perhaps borrowing from Indian custom. In the path between Massachusetts and Plymouth, surveyors built huge heaps of stones and drove "a great marked stake" into the ground, in order to mark the border between colonies.[98]

All of this amounted to a kind of dialogue in the landscape—messages planted here and there, some clear and others open to interpretation. For years, Indians dictated the terms of this conversation in the wood. The intercolonial landscape was overwhelmed with Indian landmarks, punctuated with but a few English traces. Even Woodward and Saffery produced a map that cast an eye toward the "situation of Indians discovered by the waye," their anonymous wigwams squatting trailside. A 1645 travel diary kept by John Winthrop, Jr., makes the point even more forthrightly. It preserves, to some degree, the sights that would have met the English eye along some of the region's main routes. Though he passed through a few English oases—Thomas Ford's house in Windsor, Walter Palmer's at Seekonk—his landmarks were mostly Native ones. Leaving the English trading house at Cocumscussoc, Winthrop stepped in a trap "just in the path right ag[ains]t Pesicus fort." At "Niantiga," he passed another Indian fort, and toward Nameag, he alighted on a cluster of Indian "houses." He spied the homes of Wehasse and Wequashcook, trekked past "Tossaconawayes wigwam," and spent several nights with Indian hosts.[99] To any with a mind to travel, it was patently clear: The land spoke Algonquian.

Sojourners braving the interior without a guide could only hope for Indian hospitality and, with luck, shelter. One party traveling overland to Boston in November 1646, blindsided by a raging "Tempest," must have thought themselves improbably lucky when, "wandering in the night God brought them to an empty wigwam, where they founde 2 fires burninge, and wood ready for use."[100] Finding lodging was often troublesome. Many travelers relied on their guides to find hunting-lodges or friendly Native homes, where they might rest. Most reported Indians to be terrific hosts, "very hospitable." Lucky English travelers supped on "fat bear" and slept in warm wigwams.[101] For any looking to travel more than a few miles inland, this was the only alternative to heaping grass and branches into a makeshift blanket, as John Winthrop, Jr., did in 1645. English houses and ordinaries were few and far between. Traveling from Boston to Springfield, for instance, took several days, with no prospect of a tavern's warmth—or any English household—in between.[102]

But the reason to have an Indian guide, or, better yet, courier, went beyond simple convenience. It was often a matter of safety. With the slightest stir toward war, pathways became doubly dangerous. As Kieft's War raged in New Netherland, for instance, Indians killed an Englishman while "travilling" between Stamford and Unkaway, near the eastern fringe of the Dutch colonies. In response, nearby New Haven could only counsel "those that goe abroad in the woods or meddowes . . . to carry their armes with them."[103] Likewise, when Indian war threatened in 1647, Edward Hopkins wondered on behalf of his fellow commissioners "how safe itt may be for all the Indyans . . . to be acquainted with the direct tyme of our travelling through the Cuntrey."[104] Particularly during Indian scares, which flared up frequently, English colonists feared for their safety. During a typical panic in 1642, men complained of having "to travell with Convoyes from one plantation to another."[105] But even in times of relative peace, any journey could be risky.[106] New England's travel routes were liminal places, interstices between Indian and English territory. As such, they were often perilous. Fear, danger, bad weather, the likelihood of wandering off course—all of these conspired for years to keep colonists out of Native pathways.

Particularly when the distance was great, colonists clung to the coasts. At least until midcentury, the uncertainties of moving through unfamiliar territory kept long-distance voyagers largely confined to the water. Few traveled over land, in this early period, and those who did confronted conditions that were, at best, inconvenient, and, at worst, dangerous. Until they could seize on landmarks to help them through the weald, colonists were wont to avoid the samey woodland that lurked beyond their plots. What lay beyond was the province of unknown, unmet Indians. It was unfamiliar, unmapped, and to English eyes at least, almost wholly unmarked. One wonders how the newcomers began to find their way.

IV.

In 1649 Pequot Plantation, the place at which Nahawton was to deliver his letter to John Winthrop, Jr., was merely a cluster of English homes huddled unsteadily on the Pequot River. The families who had followed Winthrop to this remote outpost two or three years earlier had probably, by now, ceased living in wigwams and moved to proper lots. But it remained a small, somewhat isolated settlement, not yet the bustling harbor that the younger Winthrop envisioned.[107] New Haven lay fifty miles to the west, Providence fifty miles east, the Connecticut River towns fifty miles northwest. Overland routes between these places were all but unknown, and, in some cases, entirely untested. Pequot was the sort of spot to which an Indian was likeliest to carry letters: remote, to the English at least, and yet most directly reached via land. Among those carrying correspondence, Indians may never have been a majority. They held sway, though, over certain routes.

Indians carried letters to virtually all parts of the colonial northeast. But they played a bigger role along certain corridors.[108] If they carried letters in particular circumstances (heavy snow, urgent ailments), they also brought correspondence to and from particular places, generally those that lay on the western and southern fringes of New England, shouldering still-great numbers of Indians. Judging from the Winthrops' letters, Native messengers were most likely to be enlisted by correspondents from Narragansett, Springfield, and Providence. In those places, they carried fully 67 percent (37/55) of departing letters. Moderately often, Indian messengers were traveling from Connecticut, where they made up 16 percent (16/100) of identified bearers, New Haven (16 percent, or 6/38), Rhode Island (22 percent, or 4/18), and Pequot (32 percent, or 8/25). Less often, they departed from Massachusetts Bay, from whence they carried correspondence only about 13 percent (11/86) of the time.[109] The typical Indian messenger, then, carried letters from somewhere beyond Massachusetts Bay—likely from Narragansett, Springfield, Providence, or Pequot. These were frontier places, remote from the buzzing hub of Boston. So, geography mattered: Native bearers filled gulfs in the English traveled landscape.

Proving how particular letters traveled is difficult. Few hint whether they moved over water or land, much less reveal the route taken. Yet a close reading of couriers' names and identities is suggestive. Take, for example, the corridor traveled by Nahawton in 1649: Boston to Pequot. The Winthrop letters mention twenty-six couriers who bore letters between those two places during the 1640s and 1650s. Seventeen were English, and nine were Indians. While several of the Indians were unnamed (and therefore unidentifiable), those that can be tracked were associated with settlements along the pathways between Boston and Pequot. Nahawton, for instance, was connected to Punkapoag, a place about fifteen miles southwest of Boston in the direction of Pequot.[110] Others were also linked to Indian settlements between the two English places: Newcome (a Native man later associated with the Niantics), "Ninicrafts Indian," and "providenc Indian" all point to Native messengers who were associated with the arc of land through Narragansett. Of the seventeen English couriers, on the other hand, at least seven—or nearly half—can be identified as ship captains or owners.

Both in practice and in English minds, Indians seem to have ruled interior routes. By the time of Nahawton's journey in 1649, colonial correspondents had begun to associate Native couriers with quick overland delivery. "Send me word *over land by an Indian* to Duxborow," Jonathan Brewster tellingly implored, in 1648.[111] Whether Indian couriers were truly faster is not entirely clear.[112] At least one English writer was doubtful. In 1644, William Pynchon refused to send pork with a courier, fearing that "with carriage it will putrifie," since "Indians will often linger on such a jorney." But when the news was urgent, even a lingering Indian who knew the path to Boston was vastly preferable to an Englishman who might wander, unknowingly, off course.[113] Nahawton, for one, proved "Trustie." He did, in the end, reach Pequot, though how "swiftly"—and by what route—is not clear. He

Couriers Mentioned: Boston—Pequot Corridor, 1640s-1650s

Name	Letter

From Boston to Pequot

John Robinson	(Adam Winthrop to JWJ, 29 October 1646)
Wm: Cowley	(mentioned, JW to JWJ, 16 November 1646)
Capt. Malbon *	(JW to JWJ, 16 November 1646)
	-also JW to JWJ, 19 November 1646
Indians ^	(mentioned, JW to JWJ, 14 May 1647)
"Roxbury butcher"	(mentioned, JW to JWJ, 16 October 1648)
[Joseph Wise?]	
Mr. Throgmorton *	(Adam Winthrop to JWJ, 1 November 1648)
	-also Amos Richardson to JWJ, 10 November 1648
	-also mentioned, JW to JWJ, 3 February 1648/49
Unnamed Indian ^	(Amos Richardson to JWJ, 3 Feb 1648/49)
[possibly Newcom]	
Newcome ^	(JW to JWJ, 3 February 1648/49)
Mr. Morton	(Adam Winthrop to JWJ, 14 March 1648/49)
Nahawton ^	(John Wilson et al to JWJ, 26 March 1649)
Mihell Tainter,	(Adam Winthrop to JWJ, 3 June 1649)
shipmaster *	
Mr. Alford *	(Adam Winthrop to JWJ, 25 February 1650/51)
John Gallop *	(Amos Richardson to JWJ, 2 December 1652)
Unnamed Indian ^	(Edward Rawson to JWJ, 18 March 1652/53)
"Ninicrafts Indian" ^	(Amos Richardson to JWJ, 26 April 1653)
Amos Richardson *	(Thomas Broughton, merchant, to JWJ, 12 August 1654)
Codman	(mentioned, John Elderkin to JWJ, 14 March 1656/57)
Goodman Wellman	(mentioned, John Elderkin to JWJ, 14 March 1656/57)

From Pequot to Boston

"Willys"	(mentioned, JW to JWJ, 14 May 1647)
"your neighbor Lathropp"	(JW to JWJ, 3 & 26 July 1648)
Mr. Brewster *	(mentioned, JW to JWJ, 16 October 1648)
Goodman Trumbull	(mentioned, Amos Richardson to JWJ, 3 Feb 1648/49)
Newcome ^	(mentioned, JW to JWJ, 3 Feb 1648/49)
"providenc Indian" ^	(mentioned, Adam Winthrop to JWJ, 14 March 1648/49)
Joseph Wise	(mentioned, Adam Winthrop to JWJ, 27 November 1649)
Unnamed Indian ^	(mentioned, Thomas Broughton to JWJ, 12 August 1654)
Total Couriers = 26	

* = English shipmaster/owner
^ = Native bearer

disappears after leaving that cold parlor in Boston, letter in hand, and reappears only on arriving in Pequot, where he presumably found John Winthrop, Jr., somewhere amidst the thawing fields and scattered cattle. That the letter reached its intended destination is assured by John's own hasty notation, on its back—a reminder that the letter had served, sadly, as a summons to "my fathers funerall."[114] But that is perhaps all we can say about this particular delivery. Nahawton's trail is otherwise largely invisible.

V.

A messenger comes. Three words, and behind them: the silhouette of Roger Williams, exiled and alone. His quill pen, stained fingers, and brittle paper. Early American letters were fragile things, and in them, perhaps we should read the vulnerability of their writers, as well. Roger Williams, John Davenport, John Winthrop—Histories have turned these men into giants. If the Winthrops were powerful in their time, the writings they left behind have only magnified that power. That so many of the Winthrops' letters have stubbornly survived, these four hundred years, means that—even in death—these men dictate what tales historians may tell. But look beneath the fixed, immutable script. Undergirding these writings, however invisibly, were Indians. Their unknown journeys: The trails, the clearings, the water, the ground. The things they carried.

Nahawton surely knew what that letter said, in 1649, though he could not read it. Reading him, and those like him, is almost as hard. Nahawton was caught up in a changing world; he was, probably, scrambling to cope with that new world. His people had come under great pressures. To the Massachusetts, in 1649, the English appeared formidable enough to be dealt with carefully, even to be appeased. It would be easy to dismiss Nahawton as, simply, a servant, part of a broader appropriation of Indian knowledge and networks. The word "messenger," in English, sounds faintly servile. It sounds subordinate. But that reading misses the complexity of his transaction with the Englishmen at John Winthrop's deathbed. He thought he had something to gain from them; they needed him. At the level of individuals, history is sometimes blurrier. To a husband fearing his wife's death, no figure was more important than Bouldbackim or Cassacinamon, bearing red coral and medical advice. Turning over an urgent letter to an Indian, in such a moment, was an admission of vulnerability, of contingency. In a strange way, the very act of hiring an Indian bearer reveals a sense, among colonists, that Indians ruled the vast countryside beyond their doors.

Employing Indians as the chief carriers of precious information was a tricky business. In an age when Indian war was constantly feared and Algonquians were becoming more facile with communicating in English, it tempted disaster. (New Netherland's leaders received an unwelcome reminder of this danger in 1655, when the Indian couriers they had been using to send messages to Delaware exposed Dutch plans to attack New Sweden, nearly undermining the invasion.) While messengers were generally drawn from the ranks of servants or allies, they were nonetheless vulnerable to interception by rival Indians, a prospect which in 1659 forced Thomas Stanton to plead with restive Pocumtucks not to "hinder nor injur[e] nor detaine any Indian sent with letters by the English."[115] Despite the risks, however, the English stubbornly continued to use Indian couriers even during times of heightened tension. That was the case in 1648, when during one of the many crises with the Narragansetts, the Commissioners of the United Colonies "Rescaved a packat brought by two Indians," containing important letters from John Winthrop, Captain John Mason, Thomas Stanton, and others.[116]

Nahawton couldn't read that letter, but he knew what it said, and he knew it was important. If nothing else, Nahawton's tale serves as a stark reminder that Native people were sometimes surprisingly involved in the convoluted world of English communications. If they were frequent porters of letter-bound news, Indians participated even more fully in the chatter that rippled across the landscape. Native people were deeply entangled in the passage of news. This era would not end before striking some fear into the hearts of colonists who thought themselves in control of channels of communication. They were not. News was promiscuous, and its promiscuity was dangerous.

3

Native Tongues

Awaun mesh aunchemókau?   *Who brought this newes?*
   —Roger Williams, *A Key into the Language of America* (1643)

"What newes?"
   —Ninigret, to Indians around Manhattan, 1653

THE WATERS OF Long Island Sound, in January, were not hospitable. They were black and cold. They were sometimes choppy, pestered by bitter wind. But, in winter 1653, Ninigret went west, across the Sound. He went very far from home, his place on the edge of Narragansett country, near where the Pawcatuck River spilled into the Sound. This journey took him well over a hundred miles from there. It took him into Dutch territory. That was the point, but it was also the problem. If we could gaze down over the frigid waters flowing east of Manhattan, that January, we would see him, and his men, rowing mutely toward the island. Others were watching, too.

West of New England, in the 1650s, lay New Netherland.[1] It had been there all along, predating nearly all of the English colonies in the northeast. New Netherland's origins are most often placed in about 1609. Sailing on behalf of Holland that year, Henry Hudson explored the river that would later take his name (Dutch colonists called it, simply, the North River), before mutineers sent him drifting toward an icy death in the future Hudson Bay. Colonists did not follow immediately on the heels of Dutch explorers.

But in the 1620s, as Plymouth colonists built a village atop their "new found Golgotha," the Dutch famously purchased Manhattan Island from local Algonquians and set about channeling a flood of furs through their newly-claimed corner of North America.[2]

"Nieuw Nederlandt," the Dutch called it. Sloping shores, green and sandy, washed by the Atlantic's brilliant blue. In Dutch watercolors, New Netherland's inviting islands of settlement burst from the page. But they have faded, somewhat, into the background of early American history.[3] To be sure, the Dutch colonies were smaller: In population, New Netherland never truly rivaled New England; it was quickly dwarfed by the hordes of English migrants that poured into the northeast in the 1630s. As late as the 1650s, its motley collection of traders, soldiers, farmers and fortune seekers numbered only a few thousand. But the Dutch colonies shaped New England in significant ways. They were far from invisible. Without New Netherland in the picture, it is difficult to make sense of the fears that stalked New England, near constantly, in mid-century.

Ninigret's visit to Manhattan, to wit, birthed a panic. In early 1653, as the ice retreated along the shoreline and the spring thaw began, English ears began to pick up worrisome snippets of news. They heard that the Dutch were plotting with Indians to attack the English colonies. Some charged that Ninigret, one of the more determinedly independent sachems in the northeast, had voyaged to Manhattan that winter to conspire with the Dutch. When chatter turned to letters, and the letters reached Boston, New England leaders became alarmed. An emergency meeting of the United Colonies was arranged. Interpreters were alerted, witnesses tracked down, and Indians interviewed. Some came forward, with no prodding, to reveal the dangers facing New England's towns. Particularly in the western colonies (those nearest New Netherland), fear took hold.

Talk of Indian "plots" was nothing new. It was as much a fixture of the New England frontier as were the trade goods that passed from hand to hand. In the past decade, there had been frequent alarms. This time, however, something was different. Barely a year earlier, in July 1652, war had broken out between England and the Netherlands. At issue were the newly passed Navigation Acts of 1651, barring Dutch traders from English colonial ports. Trade was Dutch America's chief business, and Holland could hardly let such a measure stand. Word of war reached the colonies over the winter of 1653, just before Ninigret's mysterious visit to New Amsterdam. "In

England is open warrs with the Hollander," Amos Richardson reported to John Winthrop, Jr., in December. "[M]any fights and shipps taken of Each syde."[4] Ripples from this Atlantic rivalry, New Englanders knew, might well wash ashore in the colonies.

War with the Dutch lent new probability to the terrifying prospect of an Indian attack. Such fears were not groundless. Around the time of Ninigret's trip, English seamen captured a Dutch ship carrying a letter in which West India Company directors advised New Netherland's leaders to "make use of the Indians," should any trouble arise with the New English.[5] With the two powers doing battle at sea, English colonists fretted at home. At Pequot Plantation, ammunition was hurriedly gathered and scouts put on watch. Townsmen clamped down on the Indian trade, upriver; no one was to travel north to buy corn. Local people listened anxiously for the sound of three gunshots and a drum—the raising of an alarm.[6] Such was the atmosphere in New England, as rumors of a Dutch-Indian plot reached Boston.

This particular panic was one of many. It was only a single moment in a long, tangled history of colonial fear and intrigue, neither unexpected nor particularly unusual. Nor was it any kind of watershed. But it does provide an unmatched glimpse into the communications frontier between New England and New Netherland, at midcentury. In many ways, this was a world of slippery alliances and shifty characters—of "lyares and tale carryers," as some Pocumtucks dubbed untrustworthy Englishmen, in 1659.[7] Though the portrait is imperfect, faint outlines of those characters connecting the Dutch and English colonies are evident in records generated around the 1653 crisis. In various tongues Dutch sailors, English merchants and Native travelers boasted, shared stories, and swapped news. But shared language did not always lead to greater understanding. Possessed of enough pidgin to make clear their meaning, inhabitants of the frontier often spoke threateningly. What issued from these exchanges was not always good.

What happened in 1653 is captured in only a handful of documents, virtually all of them set down by English leaders. But the crisis forced some of the northeast's most obscure channels of communication into view. The vista is too good to pass up. Here is an opportunity—a command, really— to look beneath the high-level diplomacy, the carefully scripted letters, and the highly choreographed speech of interpreters. The frontier was more blurred than any of those things are capable of reflecting. For a brief moment, a rent opens in the record and offers a glimpse of what lay beneath. Sorting it all out means attempting to peel back layers of rumor, passed promiscuously through English, Dutch and Indian circles. News tended not to obey neat boundaries. Nor did the people who carried it.[8]

I.

On maps, New Netherland is sometimes separated from New England by bold, black lines, boundaries that appear inviolable and permanent. But these maps lie. In the seventeenth century, colonial borders were hazy and still very much in contention. Fugitives, merchants and migrants all crossed these imaginary lines with ease. Following these travelers, one wonders whether the English and Dutch colonies really merit such separate treatment. New England and New Netherland were, admittedly, different. In many ways, they developed quite separately. But trade and talk muddied the waters between them.[9]

In fact, the Dutch and English empires were heavily entangled at their fringes.[10] Many English colonists had extensive ties with the Dutch, both to their west and in Europe. Some had even lived in Holland. This was especially true of the Plymouth English, some of whom had spent years in the Low Countries and even learned to speak Dutch, before departing for the New World. Others had fought as soldiers in the Dutch service and had even taken Dutch wives. Along Long Island Sound, Dutch-English marriages were not uncommon. Several veterans of the Pequot War—John Underhill and Lion Gardiner, both of whom had lived in Holland and fought in the Dutch army, as well as Captain Daniel Patrick—were married to Dutch women. (John Winthrop thought Patrick's wife "a good Dutch woman and comely." She was also, however, the unfortunate victim— Winthrop noted in distaste—of Patrick's propensity for chasing other women.[11])

A frontier of goods and letters had opened between the English and Dutch colonies virtually as soon as each was planted. In 1627, the lonely settlers at Plymouth had been visited unexpectedly by "letters, and messengers from the Dutch-plantation." In case Plymouth's colonists were puzzled as to how the Dutch had discovered their whereabouts, one letter helpfully explained: Indians had told them. Drifting "farr northward," a Dutch

shallop had encountered Natives who eagerly spilled news of the English
newcomers. The Indians had informed the Dutch sailors that "they were
within halfe a days journey of your plantation, and offered ther service to
cary letters unto you," the letter related. "[T]herfore we could not forbear
to salute you with these few lines." Behind this cheerful greeting, of course,
lay evidence—perhaps unnerving to the English at Plymouth—of how
close and well informed were the Dutch. More letters, accompanied by
sugar, linens and other goods, arrived the following year.[12]

Letters and goods, words and things: These moved together, and both
were soon flowing. Trading contacts followed. Trade, perhaps more than
anything, tethered the English to their Dutch neighbors. Trading connections between the English and Dutch colonies remain somewhat uncharted,
but they were extensive.[13] Dutch and English merchants were competitors,
of course, often vying for the same furs and Native contacts. That English
and Dutch traders both had hands in this business meant that it was not
always harmonious. But New England traders also cooperated with the
Dutch, their circles often overlapping. In 1634, John Winthrop noted that
both Plymouth and Massachusetts Bay "had ofte trade with the dutche at
Hudsons River (called by them New netherlandes[)]," and he admired that
realm's "great trade of beaver."[14] Of the English colonies, Rhode Island, in
particular, traded heavily with New Netherland, while New Haven, too, fell
"into Manhattan's commercial orbit."[15] Hints of these trading relationships
echo through English letters.[16]

Some English men and women had even drifted into the Dutch borderlands for good. English colonists had begun filtering onto Long Island—
Dutch territory—as early as the 1640s. Within a decade, whole communities
of them quietly resided under Dutch authority: Hempstead, Gravesend,
Newtown. Many found the Dutch colonies appealing for the freedoms they
offered. Several families moved to New Netherland in pursuit of freedom of
worship. Both John Underhill and Daniel Patrick broke with their churches
in Massachusetts, before heading toward Dutch ground. (Underhill
"speaking the Dutch tongue and his wife a Dutch woman," John Winthrop
thought, the choice was not surprising.[17]) Some were pulled by a complex
vortex of economic and religious factors; trade could be as powerful an
incentive as religion. Manhattan was after all a lively port, promising riches
in beaver drawn from its northern and western hinterlands. Such promises
surely enticed the Hutchinsons, clan of the religious visionary Anne

Hutchinson (who was expelled from Massachusetts in 1638) but also one of Boston's greatest merchant families.[18] Her family had planted on Dutch soil by 1643.

Others in New England looked upon these border-crossers, it must be said, with some measure of suspicion. In his history *Of Plimoth Plantation,* William Bradford used a telling metaphor in describing Isaac Allerton, an English trader who eventually established a trading house on Manhattan. Allerton had lived in Holland, and with the other English pilgrims left Leiden for the *Mayflower* in 1620. But he was pushed out of Plymouth Colony in the 1640s, after being accused of questionable dealings in the colony's fur trade. Allerton, in Bradford's estimation, "plaid his owne game" in trading ventures. On Allerton's slippery dealings as a liaison among trading parties, Bradford wrote that he distrusted the trader for his ability to "swime, as it were, betweene both."[19]

But Allerton's ability to chart a course between worlds was terribly emblematic, as Bradford probably realized, of the greater communications frontier linking New England and New Netherland. With so many men "swimming" between the Dutch and English colonies, news flowed relatively easily. In great part, too, it traveled through the mouths and in the hands of Native people—the Algonquians living along the fringes of the Sound. Just as Indians had first carried Dutch letters to the weary souls at Plymouth, they often carried news—or spread it—in later years, as well. The need to re-imagine the midcentury Dutch-English borderlands is patently clear when one looks closely at communications, including even the most fleeting of spoken words. Although the tendency among some historians has been to treat Dutch and English histories as if sealed off from one another, they were not.

Stretches of thicketed woodland, it's true, genuinely divided much of Dutch and English America. But water was another thing. Sharing Long Island Sound, the English and Dutch colonies effectively sat cheek by jowl. In the mid-seventeenth century they were yoked together by a multitude of characters populating the periphery of Long Island Sound. Traders and travelers, riding the waves, knew few bounds. They took what they could, whence they could, and collectively raised a cacophony of trade jargons and pidgins. Try as they might, English and Dutch leaders could not control this babel. Word traveled swiftly and recklessly, in the sacks of Pequot runners or in the holds of Dutch sloops. Even if it was sometimes garbled.

II.

Ninigret was a daunting presence in early New England, perhaps the most important Native leader of his time. In a portrait thought, possibly, to be of him (which, if true, says something about his stature in seventeenth-century New England), he wears opulent bands of white and purple wampum. He clutches, in his right hand, a knife. He was not easily cowed. He signed documents with the figure of a war club.[20]

He rose, in his life, from sachem of a smaller Native group, the Niantics, to become one of the principal leaders of the greater, more potent Narragansetts. He had been born to elite Niantic parents, and was related to Canonicus, the great sachem of the Narragansetts, by blood and by marriage. Canonicus's death, in 1647, made way for Ninigret to lead more fully in Narragansett affairs. But Ninigret did not step lightly into that void. He angled, aggressively, for position in Native politics. He gathered allies. In the wake of the Pequot War, he worked to gain sway over Pequot captives and tributaries, sometimes by force. He challenged the Mohegans, who were also jockeying for power in this political maelstrom. (In recent years he and Uncas, the Mohegan sachem, had reportedly dodged mutual assassination attempts, by poison and sword.)[21] Visiting Manhattan was, at least in some way, part of this larger quest.

In recent years Ninigret had been harassed, ever more insistently, by the English (usually when they suspected him of plotting some unspecified "Evill" against colonists).[22] But, more frustratingly, they also meddled, repeatedly, in his dealings with other Indians. He resented their protection of the Mohegans and the Montauketts, whom Connecticut counted as allies, but he treated as enemies and subjects, respectively. He wanted to be able to raid the Montauketts, on Long Island, without English interference. "Why doe the English slight mee and respect the longe Islanders and the Mohegins?" Ninigret grumbled, months after the 1653 tumult. "Why doe they Inquire the ground of my warr against the long Islanders[?] did they not heare that the long Islanders Murthered mee a Man?"[23] When Ninigret loaded Dutch guns into his canoe in 1653, in fact, they may have been meant for use against the Montauketts, rather than the English. (He attacked them the following September.) Befriending the Dutch, for all these reasons, would have seemed sensible.

Native American Sachem, ca. 1700. Oil on canvas. This portrait was long believed to be of Ninigret, though it may in fact depict a Pequot man or another of his contemporaries. Photography by Erik Gould. *(Courtesy of the Museum of Art, Rhode Island School of Design)*

What met his eyes, that winter day, as he approached Manhattan's ice-fringed shores? Like New England, New Netherland was comprised of several far-flung forts and settlements, perched along various rivers. But at its heart lay New Amsterdam, at the southern tip of Manhattan Island (or, as the English often rendered it, "Monhadoes"). Through this port went a steady parade of furs and goods, some arriving from the furthest reaches of Iroquoia. The island sat uncomfortably close to several English towns. From Stamford, one Dutchman attested in the early 1650s, "one could travel now in a summer's day to the North River and back again, if one knows the Indian path."[24] But most did not come by land. Like Ninigret, Manhattan's visitors generally arrived by paddle or sail. From the water, they may have noticed first the buzz of sloops and shallops, the canoes and ferries hovering close by, and beyond them, on Manhattan's grassy eastern shores, a gallows, a loading hook, and rows of gabled houses and other wooden buildings. Toward the west loomed a windmill, its blades facing Pavonia. And, of course, there was the fort—Fort Amsterdam, a great hulking thing of wooden walls and earthen barriers, squat at the tip of the island.

That Ninigret came here, in the winter of 1652–1653, is certain. But the reason for his visit is much murkier. Later, he would claim that he had only gone to Manhattan to visit a French doctor about his ailing health. Others, however, had a darker read on the purpose of his voyage. Rumor had it, instead, that he had traveled there to meet with Dutch leaders—and to plan assaults on the English. Some reports had him cloistered for days with the Dutch governor and "other Sagamors" in a "close Rome," from which they stirred only to fetch a "cole of fier." They had made a "league," it was charged, sealed with a large gift of wampum and—more ominously—with guns, powder, and bullets. Others claimed that Ninigret had also traveled across the Hudson, to visit other Native communities and to recruit "Aide and assistance" in the plot.[25] Eventually, Ninigret himself admitted that he had tried to visit the Dutch governor. While there, he remembered, he had rapped "att the Gov[erno]rs dore." But, he said, he had not even been invited in from the winter cold.[26]

New Netherland's leader, in 1653, was Petrus Stuyvesant. Stuyvesant was a formidable character. In his only surviving portrait from life, he appears hardened, proud, stout. Dark, wide-set eyes meet the onlooker's gaze resolutely, betraying nothing. He wears armor. A former soldier, Stuyvesant had witnessed battles throughout the Dutch empire before being tapped, in 1647, as Director-General of New Netherland. Evidence of this experience was manifest in Stuyvesant's very body—not merely in his weather-beaten face, but also in his wooden leg, lavishly "embroidered with silver bands" and standing in where a Spanish cannonball had done its work, years earlier. No such combat had yet been necessary in his dealings with New

Peter Stuyvesant, attributed to Hendrick Couturier, ca. 1660. Oil on wood panel. Accession number 1909.2, negative number 6071. *(Collection of The New-York Historical Society)*

England. But managing the expanding English colonies had not been easy. Often saddled with untenable diplomatic duties, Stuyvesant had nonetheless proven himself equal to the task.[27]

Stuyvesant had good reason to want Ninigret's friendship. Relations between New Netherland and New England had never been particularly placid. Particularly at the highest levels, the tone of exchange could be contentious. Leaders were forever choking on several "chronic bones of contention": unreturned fugitives, contested boundaries, seized ships. Often, too, the English complained bitterly of Dutch traders' proclivity toward arming the region's Indians.[28] But with the outbreak of a hot war between England and the Dutch Republic, Stuyvesant understood, what had been intermittent sniping might easily flare into warfare. In several ways, he had already begun preparing for that possibility. What Ninigret might also have seen, had he stayed a bit longer, that winter, was a wall—or, rather, a wall being built. He might have passed slaves and other workers, headed north toward the *bouwerijs*. The wall they were making, in 1653, would eventually reach across the entire island, from east to west, sealing off New Amsterdam on its north side. This was yet another sign of the war—a sign that the Dutch relationship with New England was crumbling, even as this twelve-foot palisade grew stronger.

The Dutch had also had their share of Indian troubles. Only a few years earlier, Stuyvesant had taken leadership of New Netherland in the wake of a harrowing war with the Indians surrounding Manhattan. Kieft's War, as it became known, had begun in the early 1640s, sparked largely by an unwise decision by Stuyvesant's predecessor, Willem Kieft, to tax nearby Native people. Bitterness spun into violence, and the war that followed nearly turned New Netherland into "piles of ashes." Many fled, in terror, back to Holland. In September 1643, at the urging of Isaac Allerton (swimming, as ever, between his Dutch and English friends), New Netherland recruited renowned Indian fighter John Underhill to aid in its war. In early winter 1644, at Underhill's command, hundreds of Indians died in ghastly scenes of fire, snow and blood.[29] The following summer, war, at last, subsided into an uneasy peace. For his role in this calamity, however, Kieft lost his position as Director-General (and his life, when the ship carrying him back to Europe was dashed against reefs off the coast of Wales). Stuyvesant, in 1647, assumed control of a province badly crippled by Indian war. He needed allies.

Whatever his intentions in visiting Manhattan, Ninigret no doubt learned a great deal, while there—particularly about the ongoing Anglo-Dutch War. One of his men later said as much. During his journey to the westward, Ninigret asked an Indian there "*What newes?*" and received an intriguing answer: A ship had arrived "at the Monhatoes," the man told him, "and shee brought guns powder & c." There was further word, too, that the war would soon spread to the colonies. "[M]ore shipps," Ninigret heard, "were a cominge to fight with the English heere."[30] This last undoubtedly sent chills through the English interpreters who eventually heard it from Ninigret himself. If nothing else, the story proved that the Native people across the northeast—across hundreds of miles, even—were fully communicative, and that they might share news amongst themselves that was, to English ears at least, of potentially grave use.

But was there some great plan hatched, some deal struck, between Native and Dutch leaders? The answer to that question proves stubbornly elusive. Both Ninigret and Petrus Stuyvesant later offered vehement denials of any such plotting. "Ninicrat says that he have plotted no Evill nor wrought no Evill against the English," one man reported, after passing through Niantic country.[31] What is certain, however, is that the prospect of a Dutch-Native combination generated a remarkable amount of chatter in the spring of 1653. In the resulting frenzy of talk, suspicions eventually spread far beyond the lonely figure of Ninigret. The rumor took on a life of its own. So much so, in fact, that the looseness of tongues regarding the matter probably obscures the truth of what happened. We may never know what transpired in Manhattan, that winter. But we can know a good deal of what people said about it.

III.

Murmurs about Ninigret's travels crept into English letters early that spring. From various outcrops around the Sound, writers penned reports to John Winthrop, Jr. At first, these were merely afterthoughts, threaded into longer letters. In late February 1653, William Morton, keeper of Winthrop's livestock on Fishers Island, mentioned speaking to "a Duch man which brought Ninniwecraft from the Duch who came into the iland."[32] Some in Connecticut found the news unsettling. "Some Jealousies of the Dutch plotting with Nyn," John Mason wrote, in another spring letter. Such "Jealousies" escalated quickly. In Southhold, Long Island, Richard Odell and his neighbors grew unnerved. "Sir we heare a great rumor of an insurrection amongst the Indians," he wrote, in an undated letter, "but we have no certain inteligence."[33]

Some of the talk indeed came from dubious quarters. Much of the evidence against Ninigret, in fact, came to the English through the Mohegans—

bitter foes of the Narragansetts. The Mohegan sachem Uncas, a perennial enemy of the Narragansetts and ever the sly opportunist, squawked especially loudly of Ninigret's plotting. That fact has led some historians to dismiss the "plot" as a figment, cooked up by Uncas in an attempt to draw the English hammer down on the heads of his Narragansett enemies.[34] Uncas did, indeed, tell Connecticut men quite a tale. He claimed that, while wintering in Manhattan, Ninigret had exchanged gifts and wampum with the Dutch governor, before heading across the Hudson to conspire with Indians there, as well. As further proof of Ninigret's guilt, Uncas's scouts captured a Narragansett canoe on its way back from the Dutch colony, two of the passengers of which, on being turned over to the English, promptly—and predictably—"confessed the whole plott."[35] (They had special incentive: Uncas's men, Ninigret later complained, "bore holes in his mens breech[es] with allblades.")[36]

Uncas was clever. He knew that gossip was often as good as a gun. But in this case, he was not the only one talking. Others also stepped forward, some to warn and others to threaten. From New Haven, Long Island, Pequot, and Rhode Island, reports came flooding forth. Native people scattered throughout the Long Island Sound basin murmured that a blow was coming. Some contended that a Dutch fleet was en route and would soon raise a signal to trigger attacks on the English, with the Dutch invading "from theire ships" and Indians falling on English towns "by land."[37] From what they said, it became painfully clear that Indians throughout the northeast—Raritans, Munsees, Montauketts, Narragansetts, and Mohegans— were well aware of the ostensibly distant Anglo-Dutch war. It was clear, too, that the threat ran deeper than Uncas's loose tongue—deeper, even, than Ninigret's curious voyage.

Ninigret's journey caused quite a hubbub. This alone, however, was not sufficient ground for panic. In the wake of his travels, more troubling information began to surface, all along the frontier. (Perhaps it was only in light of this increasing chatter that Ninigret's trip began to seem suspicious.) While English colonists gossiped that Ninigret had sailed homeward in a "Duch sloop," Algonquian speakers began to whisper of a wider conspiracy. In Manhattan, English traders heard from local Indians that the Dutch had been furiously recruiting Native allies for attacks on the English. An English shipwright, who claimed to understand Indian speech "as well as most Duch men," also heard that Stuyvesant had been campaigning among

Algonquians. In Stamford, nine sagamores confessed voluntarily of Dutch efforts to shower them with "guns powder swords weapons wascoates and coats." In Rhode Island, meanwhile, word circulated that the Dutch had promised to trade with the Narragansetts at "halfe the prise" of English goods. Even some Dutchmen began to mutter tauntingly at the English sailors they encountered.[38]

Much of this hubbub was likely only talk. But the English took such talk almost as an assault in itself, as verbal shots fired. Traders in Rhode Island were tellingly alarmed in noting that "the Indians Discourse" had taken a dark turn. Narragansetts now spoke, they reported, "wholy in high comendation of the Duch with Disrespect to the English." Much of what the English heard about the purported danger, in fact, came from Indians themselves—including some who appeared to be friendly informants (like the "Indians of long Island" who brought "Newes of this Plott" to Englishmen there) as well as others who spoke with a sharper measure of "disrespect." The "Indians Round about for divers hundred of miles cercute," noted English leaders, "seeme to have drunk deep of an Intoxicating cupp att or from the Monhatoes against the English."[39]

Stuyvesant, for his part, did all he could to quash the rumor. Firstly, he wrote several conciliatory letters to New England. Shortly after learning of the war's outbreak, he had assured English leaders of his friendship. And once more, in early March 1653, with the ice breaking in the rivers around Manhattan, he took up his pen. By this point, rumors that he had hatched a plot with Narragansetts were already astir in New England. Perhaps aware of this, he assured New England's leaders that he meant to maintain friendship, that he had no plans to spread war to the New World. Rather, wrote Stuyvesant, he wished only for "friendly and peaceable Compossuers off any difference that May aryse in these parts, betwixt Our two nations."[40]

Stuyvesant was no fool; he knew the power of letters. Letters gave ballast to colonial relations. They quelled misunderstandings and eased complaints. Almost immediately upon stepping ashore as Director of New Netherland in 1647, in fact, Stuyvesant had been initiated into New England's network of "neighbourlie correspondencie." From their craggy perches along the Sound, Englishmen like Theophilus Eaton and John Winthrop, Jr., had hastily showered him with greetings—though the tone of their letters quickly soured, in squabbles over fugitives and captured ships, among other prizes. Still, Stuyvesant knew that letters were among his best weapons in managing the weight of the English colonies, looming to his east. Thus did he send his "friendly and peaceable" greeting, in late winter 1653.[41]

But even the way his letter traveled signals how little he controlled the movement of news through the borderlands. The letter left New Amsterdam in the fist of Symon Joosten, a Dutch shipmaster. But, after traveling across the Sound, it was passed at Pequot to a Native messenger. Though meant for express delivery to Boston (Stuyvesant had hoped the letter would be propelled northward "with all possible expedition"), the packet was much delayed. Along the way, something went awry. A month later, Stuyvesant had still received no return. In Manhattan, he stewed, waited. Sometime in early April, an English merchant turned up in Manhattan carrying Stuyvesant's long-awaited return mail—a cool, measured response from the Massachusetts governor, as well as John Winthrop, Jr.'s apology for the delay. Weather had upset the courier's return. The "messinger [an Indian]," Winthrop wrote, "was something retarded in his returne by reason of a deepe snow that fell as he was in his Journye backe."[42]

There are letters, and then there is talk. And if Native people moved European letters, they also moved information orally. Rumors of Stuyvesant's duplicity were already bubbling up from lower New England. Stuyvesant might write all he liked, but he could not stop the babble.

IV.

By late April 1653, the rumor was at full tilt. As commissioners of the United Colonies convened at Boston, bits of information hinting at some sort of Dutch-Indian menace continued to arrive from New England's fringes. Not all of it was plausible. Imaginations ran amok. Wild talk—like the rumor that Ninigret had returned from New Amsterdam with a mystical "wildfier" that would "kindle and burne any thinge"—simply took flight, spun out of anyone's control.[43] But commissioners were also confronted with more credible tales, from Manhattan, from Long Island, from New Haven, from Rhode Island. What William Bradford had always thought a "duble danger," for Connecticut especially—a threat from "both the Dutch and the Indeans"—seemed quite possibly to be converging on New England.[44]

At times like these, interpreters were called into service. English leaders naturally wanted to conduct their own investigation, to get to the bottom of things. A primary concern was to test the intentions of the Narragansetts, a strong group nestled in the very bowels of New England. Ninigret would have to be questioned. In such an instance a sort of ritualistic diplomacy churned into gear, usually dependent upon the careful maneuvering of interpreters—those deemed satisfactory go-betweens, generally possessed of some special cultural and linguistic knowledge. In the New England of the 1650s, there were few men considered expert in Algonquian languages. One of them was Thomas Stanton. When the rumor reached Thomas Stanton in the woods of Connecticut, he must have felt it was simply one more in what was becoming a rather regular series of alarms. He had been to Narragansett on diplomatic business too many times to count, in recent years. This day, the information came in the form of two breathless soldiers, hastily dispatched by the United Colonies to alert Stanton to the situation and to commandeer his help. They arrived bearing a message that needed to be read—and translated—to some of the Indians under suspicion. Stanton, once more, was pressed to serve as "able Interpreter" for New England. Within a day, he was headed for Niantic. Thus did Stanton find himself, in mid-April, riding east into the woods of Narragansett, armed with a message for the "chiefest" Narragansett sachems.[45]

Before we allow him to ride any further, meet Thomas Stanton. What can be said about him is surprisingly little, despite the renown he eventually achieved as New England's favorite emissary to the Indians. Ironically, he transferred far fewer of his own words onto paper than he did those of his Native counterparts.[46] He spoke their language with a singular ease—a talent that revealed itself during a 1636 incident in the swamp at Saybrook fort, in which Stanton impressed English superiors by negotiating with marauding Pequots in their own dialect.[47] No surviving document tells how he learned to speak Algonquian. But the skill brought him great advantage in his life. It won him a hefty salary in wampum and some powerful Indian contacts. Like so many others, Stanton was a trader as much as an interpreter. Just two years before the current crisis, he had built a trading house on the Pawcatuck River, in the borderlands between Pequot and Narragansett—the western fringe of Ninigret's Niantic lands. He had reportedly scouted the location during a diplomatic visit.[48]

So he would have well known the path to Narragansett. Arriving there, he unfurled a paper containing eleven queries, carefully scripted. All were variations on a theme: Were the Narragansetts conspiring with the Dutch "to fight against the English"?[49] After explaining that the colonies had reason to believe that such a "warr" was planned, Stanton was to read the questions to the sachems and then to record their answers. He did this, with little embellishment. What did he find in Narragansett, that April day? Was he suspicious? Was he fearful? Did the meeting take place at Ninigret's fort? Or further east along the Pequot-Narragansett path, perhaps at Richard Smith's Cocumscussoc trading house?[50] Stanton recorded none of this. All that he did write down—in a script nearly as cryptic as the man himself, archaic loops skittering hurriedly, unpunctuated, across the page—were the Indians' disembodied answers to his questions. But even Stanton's inert and stilted hand could not blunt the Narragansetts' dismay. It bursts through the confines of his transcription.

"Doe you thinke that wee are madd," Pessicus cried.

On this, Stanton may have repeated, in a carefully measured tone, a section of the message that he carried: "Wee have been and are very slowe to give creditt to what wee heare; or to engage in a warr against you," it read. Yet "wee thought it nessesarie upon the aforsaid Rumer to bee a little more vigilent then ordinary and to send our messengers . . . to understand the truth of these Reports."[51]

But Pessicus and Mixam insisted that they knew of "noe such plott." To ally with the Dutch would be foolish, they understood. For "how can the Duch shelter us," Pessicus exclaimed, "being soe Remote against the power of the English"?[52]

Ninigret, too, utterly denied making any pact with Stuyvesant. Of his much talked-of voyage to Manhattan, he repeatedly insisted that he had only gone in search of medicine. While there, he admitted, he had knocked innocently on the Dutch governor's "dore." But he had not been invited in. He had not even seen Stuyvesant, let alone made any "league" with him. Nor had he heard anyone else speak of such a thing. "I did never heare the Duch men say they would goe and fight against the English," he told Thomas Stanton. "Neither did I heare the Indians say they would Joyne with the Duch to fight against the English."[53]

At first, Ninigret mirrored Thomas Stanton's formal, diplomatic language ("You are kindly welcom to us and I kindly thanke the Sachems of the Massachusets . . ."). But with Stanton's repeated demands that Ninigret explain "what hath passed betwixt the Duch and you," careful ritual began to break down. Tiring of their questions, the sachem grew indignant. "[W]hat shall I answare these things over and over againe," he asked, exasperated. Did the English think him rash enough to gamble his people's lives for a few Dutch guns and promises? What good would a "few guns" do, he blurted, "when wee are dead"?[54]

Given the detail with which Stanton translated Ninigret's frustrations into the record (and it is quite striking), it is easy to forget that the sachem's words had had to pass through a rather formidable filter of language. Each vivid quote was, after all, Stanton's transliteration. However faithfully the interpreter recorded Ninigret's sentiments, the language barrier was significant; without it, Stanton's services would hardly have been necessary. Still, language may not have been quite as much of an obstruction as some historians have supposed. As important as it is to witness the circumspect exchange between Stanton and Ninigret, that exchange is ultimately somewhat misleading. Others talked far more freely.

Imagining Stanton's afternoon in Narragansett is not, ultimately, that helpful in any quest to understand the broader significance of 1653's episode. If anything, the scene draws our eyes away from the rumor's most basic lesson. The real significance of what happened in 1653 lies not in the relative *difficulty* of cross-cultural communication but, rather, in the relative *ease* of speaking across languages. To understand how easily news moved, at times, it helps to set aside the image of Thomas Stanton delivering his carefully circumscribed speech in Narragansett. Think of him, instead, as a trader. Now look south, from his Pawcatuck trading house, into the water. A host of exchanges—far less formal—were taking place there, along the Sound's reedy shores. Where trade brought the English, Dutch, and Algonquian worlds together, and where the water met the land, people talked—and not always in the same tongue.

V.

Recall the English shipwright who boasted, in New Amsterdam, that he could understand the Indian language "as well as most Duch men." Claims like his abounded, among those who spread the rumor. As English leaders sought to discover whether Stuyvesant and Ninigret truly were planning attacks, in 1653, they turned up a healthy crop of individuals who had absorbed bits of several languages. Servant Benjamin Crane told them that his Dutch mistress heard tell of the plot because she could "speake very

good Indian." Addam the Indian, too, "spake English very well," as he
spilled what he knew.[55] A Narragansett messenger spat threats—"in
Duch"—at a Boston man. Around Manhattan, Dutch speakers dropped
reminders of 1623's Amboyna Massacre, in which the Dutch at Ambon had
killed (and reputedly tortured) the English and Japanese living at the British
East India Company Factory. They warned their terrified English neighbors
that they would "shortly have an East India breakfast."[56] None of this was
lost in translation. If much about this story is muddy, one thing is perfectly
clear: The promiscuous sharing of Native, Dutch and English words acted,
in 1653, as an accelerant.

Tracing the rumor's origins, we arrive, always, at the fault lines of language. When Hutchinson, the English shipwright, related to fellow
Englishmen in Manhattan what local Indians had told him of the conspiracy, he made a telling comment. He said that Stuyvesant had miscalcu-
lated the ability of the English around New Netherland to communicate
with Indians. The Dutch, he sneered, had assumed—rather foolishly—that
Englishmen could not "understand the Indian toungue." But this was a
mistake. Hutchinson could understand as well as any Dutchman, he
boasted.[57] The news traveled through the mouths of people like him,
through places like Isaac Allerton's trading house in New Amsterdam.
Without doubt, it is difficult, at this distance, to recover the "privatt talkes"
and whispers that happened in the gloaming, in English hayfields and ship-
yards.[58] What does seem clear, nonetheless, is that news traveled fairly flu-
idly. News could jump the borders between New England, New Netherland,
Narragansett, and Mohegan; and once it had, its flow was not easily stopped
up. All of which raises the question: Who spoke what, in the colonial
northeast?[59]

English and Dutch speakers were often well able to understand one
another. Leaders, of course, kept interpreters close at hand. So frequent were
his occasions to deal with Englishmen that Petrus Stuyvesant even had an
English Secretary, George Baxter. And when Stuyvesant reverted to using
Dutch in his correspondence, in 1647, New Haven governor Theophilus
Eaton railed at him for failing to employ either English or Latin. Because
Stuyvesant had written in "Low Dutch, wherof I understand little," Eaton
griped, his letters would remain unread "till I meete with an interpreter."[60]
But for others, language presented far less of a hurdle. Having spent years in
Holland, many of the Plymouth English understood Dutch fairly well.

Though he called it a "strange & uncouth language," William Bradford, for instance, knew Dutch well enough to translate incoming letters from New Netherland and even to respond in Dutch (though he was compelled to beg pardon for "our rude and imperfecte writing in your language").[61] Perched along Dutch trading channels on the Rhode Island shoreline, Roger Williams was sufficiently proficient to practice his Dutch with England's Secretary of Foreign Tongues.[62] Traders, too, often knew some Dutch.[63]

The Dutch colonies themselves were something of a linguistic jumble. Looking to boost the population, the West India Company had actively invited settlers from all over Europe, and these arrivals added to the babel. In 1644, a visitor to New Netherland reported (perhaps with some exaggeration) that eighteen different languages were spoken there.[64] Counting Native languages, the colonies must indeed have been quite the confused collection of tongues. Although they were determined to converse with their Native trading partners, the Dutch experienced some difficulty in confronting Indian languages. "There is no Christian here who understands the language thoroughly," Dominie Johannes Megapolensis wrote of the Mohawk speech used around Rensselaerswyck in the 1640s. "Those who have lived here long can use a kind of jargon just sufficient to carry on trade with it, but they do not understand the fundamentals of the language."[65] In conversing with Indians, Dutch colonists faced a particularly complicated language front, since New Netherland rested on the fault line between the two major linguistic groups in the Native northeast: Iroquoian and Algonquian. Each of these was comprised of an even more florid collection of dialects and regional speech patterns, sometimes different enough to impede intelligibility. Still, some Dutchmen did learn to communicate with both Iroquoian and Algonquian speakers, at least well enough to trade— and usually "by long and continued intercourse and conversation with the Indians."[66]

But the thorniest and most elusive language front, perhaps, rested between Algonquians and English. Historians have never been sure just how much language exchange occurred between New England's natives and newcomers.[67] But most are not particularly sanguine about the ease of these early conversations. In looking at language, scholars have often privileged misunderstanding, which is probably only natural. Certainly, communication posed problems. Basic conversation, to be sure, proved a major stumbling block as Native and European people negotiated the twists and

turns of encounter. Roger Williams' translation of *Matnowawtawatémina*—
"Wee understand not each other"—was a literal one: the expression was
meant to convey that a story, or a bit of news, had been misunderstood.
This, Williams knew, was a common predicament. Language barriers, after
all, gave rise to a much-studied fixture of colonial life: the *interpreter*. The
very ubiquity of Thomas Stanton in the Indian affairs of early New
England—his name emblazoned on virtually every deed, treaty, deposition,
and translation—suggests the singularity of his skills. Roger Williams'
writings, too, bear testament to the scarcity of Englishmen who were so
deft with Indian dialects. "A stranger that can relate newes in their owne
language, they will stile him a *Manitióo*, a God," he wrote of the
Narragansetts.[68]

That the language encounter was riddled with misunderstandings is not
a matter of debate. Few Indians spoke a fluid English, and still fewer
Englishmen were at ease with Algonquian languages. But language exchange
was not an all-or-nothing affair. Where European and American tongues
met, they birthed jargons and pidgins that were more than sufficient, in
many cases, for conveying one's meaning. *Jargon*, a fairly rudimentary
hodgepodge of language, was often employed by traders who required only
"the absolute minimum of vocabulary" to conduct business. *Pidgin* forms of
Algonquian or English—that is, much simplified versions, "reducing . . .
native speech to its simplest elements"—had also begun to take root.[69]
Glimpses of these, however fleeting, are present in more than a few English
records. With varying degrees of mastery, evidence suggests, people all
along the New England frontier possessed some grasp of this blurred, hybrid
speech. Many were traders, naturally, but some understanding of Algonquian
seems to have spread even to English farmers, wives and children.

Early New England's *lingua franca* was probably a pidgin English, "liberally spiced with native words and locutions."[70] Indians were quicker to
adopt English speech than colonists were to try Algonquian. Partly, this was
because English leaders practiced "linguistic imperialism"; that is, in order
to "*help* England rule," they pressed Native people to learn English. Yet, to
a much larger extent, Indians' early attempts with the new language were
probably a matter of choice: they understood the advantages to be won with
English words, particularly for those eager to trade.[71] Some Algonquians
learned English speech before European settlement had even begun in New
England. At Plymouth, very early on, the Pilgrims famously met Samoset

and Squanto, both of whom already knew something of the English tongue. That was fortuitous, since even the most motivated of Plymouth colonists found the local Indian language "copious, large, and difficult."[72] A decade later, Massachusetts's colonists still knew little Algonquian. "Their language is hard to learn, few of the English being able to speak any of it, or capable of the right pronunciation," wrote William Wood, in the 1630s.[73]

A few Englishmen, nonetheless, determined to master an Indian language. "There are some Schollers amongst us," John Endecott observed in 1651, "who addict themselves to the study of the *Indian* Tongue."[74] Chief among these "Schollers," and the man to whom Endecott undoubtedly referred, was the Reverend John Eliot. Eliot, who had arrived in New England in 1631 and was soon after ordained minister at Roxbury, Massachusetts, was the Englishman most fervently engaged in converting Native people to Christianity. Spreading Christianity had been, from the first, an imagined goal of the English colonial project; the charter of the Massachusetts Bay Colony, in fact, called this mission the "principall Ende" of colonization. (As if to underline the point, the official seal of the colony featured a near-naked Indian man, pleading, "Come over and help us.") But little was done about it in the early decades of settlement. In the 1640s, amid rumblings that Massachusetts Bay was failing to fulfill the promises of its charter, Eliot was nominated to begin preaching to nearby Massachusett Indians. He understood intuitively that, to do so, he would have to speak their native tongue.[75]

It became his life's work. Eliot first learned the Massachusett language from a "pregnant witted" Montaukett man named Cockenoe, who "pretty well understood" English. (How well Cockenoe actually spoke Massachusett is hard to say. He was a captive of the Pequot War and had ended up a servant in Sergeant Richard Collicut's house in Dorchester, Massachusetts, perhaps because Collicut himself had captured him. But he was in fact a native of Long Island, where Native speech differed substantially from that further to the north.) "He was the first that I made use of to teach me words," Eliot later remembered.[76] Eliot soon knew quite a few Indian words, though his preaching in Massachusett, by his own admission, was awkward. Although his Native audiences could "picke up some knowledge by my broken expressions," he could see that his strained lecturing was not nearly as "effectuall" as the Indians' "owne expressions," spoken "in their owne tongue."[77] His auditory understanding of Algonquian speech also proceeded slowly. When he sought to record several Native conversion narratives in 1653 in hopes of gathering an Indian church, he still struggled to grasp the meaning of what was spoken. "Oft I was forced to inquire of my interpreter (who sat by me)," Eliot related, "because I did not perfectly understand some sentences."[78]

But John Eliot was not easily daunted. By the time grumblings about Ninigret's trip to Manhattan had begun circulating in 1653, Eliot was engaged in a missionary project that went well beyond merely preaching in the Massachusett tongue. Because Protestantism depended fundamentally on being able to read scripture, and to experience it intimately as the word of God, Eliot realized he would need not only to preach in the Indians' language, but to *print* Christian texts in it, as well. In 1653, this project was just getting underway. (In fact it was momentarily stalled, Eliot noted later, by the "jealousie too deeply apprehended," in 1653, that "even these praying *Indians* were in a conspiracy with others, and with the *Dutch,* to doe mischief to the *English.*" It was best, he figured, not to move forward "when the waters were so troubled."[79]) But Eliot had by then begun his most majestic piece of work, the translation of the entire English Bible into Massachusett. In 1655, he published a trial run of the Book of Genesis, and, after years more spent in laborious translation (with much help from Native collaborators), Eliot's so-called "Indian Bible" appeared in 1663. It took fully three years to print, not to mention a new press, an enormous amount of new type, a Native apprentice (who became known as "James Printer") and a journeyman printer sent from England to aid in the Bible's production. Staggering amounts of paper went into the Bible's first run of 1,000 copies, one of which was even presented to the English king, Charles II. Eliot also shepherded into print many other translated primers, catechisms and Christian tracts, which collectively became known as the "Indian library."

John Eliot's linguistic project was spectacular. It was glaring in its ambitions, unparalleled in scale. But, to some extent, Eliot's work in crossing the language divide has obscured other more accidental, and probably more common, types of exchange. In communicating to Indians a "sacred language about the holy things of God," Eliot's fellow missionaries thought, "Mr. *Eliot* excells any other of the *English.*" But, they admitted, there were other men who "in the *Indian* language about common matters excell him."[80] Common matters, though, as much as religion, defined the language encounter in early America. Even as Eliot sweated over his translations of Genesis, other colonists were learning—albeit less deliberately—to talk to Indians. Some could even comprehend when Native people spoke in their "American tongues."[81] If, early on, Indian dialects mostly mystified the English, they gained in familiarity. Algonquian speech persisted. Even those Indians who cannily, if slowly, experimented with English were not wholesale converts. They continued to speak Native languages, and in many cases obliged English traders and settlers to bend their own tongues toward Indian forms of expression.[82] Bits of pidgin Algonquian, in turn, crept into English speech and leaked into English documents. Probably no Englishman ever truly mastered an Algonquian language. Even much-heralded interpreters Thomas Stanton and Roger Williams likely spoke versions that were heavily larded, and perhaps distorted, with pidgin.[83] But particularly along the colonies' frontiers, there were English colonists who *understood* some Algonquian—even if in bits and pieces.

Evidence of this fact emerges most often in the places rimming Long Island Sound. In these marshy borderlands, English scribes caught the occasional bit of pidgin with their pens. Fragments of Algonquian were snatched out of the air and fixed onto paper. In October 1639, for instance, a New Haven clerk slipped the word *weregin* into a trial record. A Pequot man named Nepaupuck, suspected of having attacked Connecticut colonists during the war of 1637, had been imprisoned. After much questioning, New Haven men demanded a confession: "being asked if he would nott confess that he deserved to dye," the scribe recorded, "he answered, it is weregin."[84] *It is weregin.* No translation is offered, in the record. Was this a capitulation, an admission of guilt? Or a stubborn refusal to answer? In fact, it was the former. *Weregin* meant something like "it is good."[85] Nepaupuck had given in. Because the word was apparently plenty familiar to New Haveners, the scribe was not moved to translate. To all present, Nepaupuck's meaning was plain enough.[86]

In some lucky instances, you can almost hear people speaking to one another. When John Dyer was called to testify about Dutch merchant-captain Augustine Herriman (accused of selling guns to Indians on the Connecticut River), he related a full conversation, including pidgin words, untranslated. On a wet day, in spring 1651, he said, he had carried three Indians in his canoe. They had paddled together, toward Saybrook. Rounding the sandbar at the river's mouth, they spied several ships riding in the cove: merchant vessels, at least one of them Dutch. The canoe gliding closer, the Indian passengers asked Dyer "whether the Dutchman had any coates." He answered: *"tutta."* He did not know.[87] On this, one of the Indians stood up in the canoe, rocking it dangerously, and called to the vessel: "Way bee gon coates?" Indeed, there were coats, came the response, shouted in Dutch. Translating, Dyer told his Indian travelers, *"Nux."* Yes.[88]

Other Algonquian words also found their way into English talk and records. *Uncup* (alcohol, that frequent subject of Native criminal cases) spilled into court documents. In a July 1646 account, Pawquash, a Quinnipiac man, was captured speaking blasphemy: "Jesus Christ was mattamoy & naught, & his bones rotten," he spat, riling New Haven's rigid Puritans.[89] Pidgin English could be equally inflammatory. In 1654, Hester Ward related that an accused witch, Goodwife Staplyes, had accepted dangerous idols from an Indian man. The Indian, Ward revealed, had given Goody Staplyes "two litle things brighter then the light of the day, and told [her] they were Indian gods." "[I]f she would keepe them," he then promised, "she should be *so big rich, all one god."*[90] Snippets like these appear intermittently throughout seventeenth century records. Although it is hard to know how well Indians and English actually fathomed what was being said, people were certainly talking.

How many were talking? Among those making homes in the old Pequot country along Long Island Sound, a surprising number. Few colonists communicated as well as Thomas Stanton, but many were familiar with local Indian dialects. Take Thomas Minor, a farmer who moved into the coves bordering Ninigret's land in 1653, the year that brought news of the plot. Like so many residents of early southeastern Connecticut, Minor spoke some Algonquian and, on occasion, even dropped Indian phrases into his writing, without bothering to translate—a good indication that he used them frequently and comfortably. In December 1654, for instance, he noted that an Indian neighbor, Sabiantwosucke, had promised "to bring me six pecks of *nunip.*" If such word-borrowings seem superficial, Minor's diary also offers evidence of more extensive communication—and not always for trading purposes. On several occasions, the Indians he knew also brought news. "agedouhet Toald us that the Ketle was stolne as he heard," Minor reported cryptically, in one entry. And in another: "Wequach Cooke was fined 62. fathom for goeing to Coneticut to Complaine against Captaine Denison," he wrote, "as I was tould by an Indean Agedouset."[91]

Eavesdropping on these bits of conversation helps us understand how rumors could spread, in spite of language barriers. Talk of stolen kettles and fines levied was not idle gossip. Information was a kind of currency, and Minor was careful to record any scrap of news that might later become useful, particularly any story that he might need to recite in court. Although his diary does not reveal whether Minor and Agedouset conversed in Algonquian or English, they may have used a clipped mixture of both. Agedouset, an Eastern Pequot living close to Minor's farmland, had likely begun to speak English. Minor mentions him on several occasions, even noting the birth of Agedouset's daughter in 1665. In at least one instance, in 1649, Agedouset seems to have acted as a trading agent for Thomas Stanton, who tapped him to bring "goodes" and wampum to John Winthrop, Jr.[92] Living and working in close proximity to Englishmen, he likely learned to speak some of their language. But Minor, too, knew a bit of Algonquian. Even Grace Minor, his wife, was capable of understanding what Indians said: In 1650 an Indian woman was deposed "in the hearing of Thomas Minors wife who understandeth the language."[93]

Traders were perhaps the most avid students of Indian speech. By mid-century, to hear some colonial writers tell it, many traders—even their wives—had developed a rather sophisticated ear for Algonquian chatter. Some even claimed to be able to distinguish between the various *dialects* of Indian speech.[94] In 1645, for instance, a Narragansett man visited Providence, where, "feineing himself to be of Coneettacut," he "spake in that dyalect." The Indian's intent was to mask his identity, pretending to be a representative of Uncas. But because he "could not put of[f] the Narrohigganset tone," an English trader's wife ("who well understood the Indian language") was not fooled. Fooled or not, she was probably spooked. Speaking in his pretended Connecticut "dyalect," the man issued a warning: "English Messengers should not passe to the Mohegans," he said, "[for] he knew they should have no guides, but should be destroyed in the woods as they travelled."[95] Words might fail to cloak identity, but they were plenty effective in spreading fear.

In later years, as colonial and Algonquian landscapes converged, so, too, did their languages. Not only were more Indians speaking English, by the 1660s, but—through simple proximity—more English somewhat "understood" Indian speech.[96] An episode from the backcountry of New London attests to this blurring, as well as its effects. In 1669, a young English boy revealed that an Indian "conspiracy" was afoot, according to what he had heard near "Robines town," a Pequot settlement. Several Indians had warned the boy that the Pequots would have back a favored patch of land, even if "it should Cost them there bllood." One Indian woman unveiled further dimensions of the "seecrit": "[T]he Narrowgancets and the pequits and the mohegins & the mohakes," she whispered, "weare plotting to kill all the ingLish," as soon as the "greene indian corne was ripe." This "Inglishe boye," only twelve years old, understood what was said because he was "well versed in the Indian tung." Indeed, the Native woman had "Toulde itt him in Indian," before, he, in turn, "toulde itt his mother in Inglish." On demand, the boy was able to "peficktly relate . . . these things in Indian," well enough, at least, to satisfy "marshall Gilbert & Mr Stanton and sum other interpreters."[97] How well the boy truly spoke the "Indian tung" is doubtful. But at the very least, the story hints that in the hinterlands and hayfields of New England, more colonists than historians have yet acknowledged—children, even—absorbed some bits of Algonquian language.

To ignore the contexts of these exchanges, of course, would be foolish. Troublingly, colonists' claims to understanding the "Indian tung" came oftenest amidst attempts to prove some plot. English ears were most attuned, it seems, to those Indian tongues that spoke threateningly. But if witnesses' avowals that they "well understood" Algonquian were a bit convenient, they were also reassuring. Behind these claims stood Englishmen struggling to unthread evidence that was both unnerving and uncertain. Countless Indians stepped from the shadows to reveal plots, threats, and dangers. But, as with Goodwife Arnold's encounter with the man "feineing" Connecticut inflections, it was often difficult to gauge which of these informants meant to help and which to hurt. Some undoubtedly came forward out of earnest concern, and many likely revealed real threats. Others, though, seemed to relish sparking fear with simple talk. When charged with calling the Osborne boy "machet" and threatening to burn down the family's house, during the 1669 scare, Nawag-has, for one, simply "owned itt & Laughed."[98]

Terror was powerful, even if it was solely spoken. It is hard to avoid the impression that, much as colonists waged war with their pens, others did violence with their tongues. Did it matter whether these threats were real or imagined? Did it matter that bodily warfare did not erupt? Fears shuddered across New England, nonetheless. And when fear struck, as one Indian informant slyly put it in 1653, "the English were apte to beleive as children."[99]

VI.

Among Ninigret's emissaries to Boston, in 1653, was one who was well skilled in speaking threats, even across languages. His name is something of a puzzle. Commissioners called him "Newcome Mattuxes," perhaps a clue into his blended identity. In succeeding years, his name would surface in English documents rendered variously as "Mattakist," "Newcome," "Nucom," "Mattake," "Mattak," "Nucum," and "Muttuxxet," among other versions. Really, he had only two names, one favored by Englishmen and one by Indians, as demonstrated by later records which mention "Newcome or as the Indians call him Mattakist." He spoke some English, a skill he would later stretch as an interpreter for the Narragansetts.[100] And in 1653, amidst the plot crisis, it became clear that he also spoke some Dutch.

He had likely learned the language in his travels. In recent months, he had been quite mobile around the Long Island Sound basin. By the United Colonies leaders, he was identified as "somtimes of Road Island" (near the Narragansetts), though he had also "lived att south hoult" on Long Island. Glimpses of his activities around the Sound appear in other records, as well. Over the winter of 1648–1649, he had carried letters for the Winthrops living in Boston and Pequot.[101] In December 1652, he was "living . . . at Flushing in Newe-Netherland," where he collected skins for Ninigret.[102] In a few years, then, he had surfaced in a number of places. His name, too, may hint at his mobility. To the English, the word "new-come" described migrants who were newly arrived, as when William Wood distinguished between America's "new-come *English* Planters" and its "old Native Inhabitants." Was even Newcome's name a sort of pidgin-English nod to his travels?[103]

While in Boston, Newcome behaved in ways that ruffled English commissioners. If he had been sent to help clear the Narragansetts of suspicion, he only inflamed English fears. He confirmed the rumors of an imminent Dutch attack, saying that he had been told by an Indian at Southold that, "the Duch would come against the English" and "save the weemen and Children and guns for themselves." Newcome also made brazen threats, some delivered "in Duch." A Bostonian named John Lightfoot reported that Newcome "told him *in Duch* that the Duchmen would cutt of the English on long Island."[104] If the English read on Newcome's character is any indication, the spirit in which he spoke was not friendly. It verged, instead, on menacing. Infuriated by this "cuning and bould Narragansett

Indian," they subsequently barred him from Boston for giving such "offence." Commissioners coldly informed Ninigret that, "had the said Newcom not bine a Messinger sent by Ninnigrett hee should not have escaped without some punnishment."[105]

One lesson that emerged from Newcome's threats was that the Native people throughout the northeast were well informed about the ongoing Anglo-Dutch War. Given that knowledge, they were equipped to say things that made English listeners squirm. Even Ninigret had confessed to Thomas Stanton that, during his visit to some "Indian Wiggwames" near New Amsterdam, "there came som Indians that told mee there was a shipp come in from holland which did Report the English and the Duch were fighting together in theire owne countrey." What he said next must have made Stanton particularly uncomfortable: Other ships, Ninigret related, were also en route "to fight against the English heer," and when the fleet arrived, "there would bee a great blow given to the English." But this, the sachem then slyly added, "I had from the Indians and how true it is I can not tell."[106] What tone he took in relating this news is hard to say. But the subtle menace lurking behind Ninigret's words is hard to miss.

It was also a clever thing to say, for Ninigret knew very well that Indians did sometimes use rumors, lies, and trickery as political weapons. More than a few lies were lobbed against him by Native enemies, in his life. Indians, of course, were not the only ones who understood the political potency of threatening information. One finds, in sorting layers of testimony from 1653, that nearly all involved had something to gain. To those who spread it, the story had purpose. It does not take much, for instance, to discover Stuyvesant's enemies at work. Indians on western Long Island harbored plenty gripes against the Dutch, with whom they had recently fought a war. Another informant, "Mary Vandunkes," it happened, was the wife of Adriaen van der Donck, a Dutchman bent on ousting Stuyvesant (and the West India Company) from power. (When the 1653 crisis occurred, van der Donck was in fact abroad in the Netherlands making that very plea to the government.)[107] Ninigret had his personal detractors, too: Uncas, of course, but some of the Natives on eastern Long Island, also, hated him for his persistent raiding. Nor are English motives so plain to sort out. Among them, too, were many saber-rattlers, looking for grounds for war both with the Dutch and with Ninigret.

But people were also, simply, afraid. The northeast was an uncertain place; the Sound was unsound. What ruled, more than any single group, was fear. None exploited this fact more skillfully than Algonquian speakers. Nawag-has was not alone; there were many Native talkers who laughed at English fears. There were more, still, who whispered of alleged plots and conspiracies—and colonists clung to their every word. Anyone who spends time poring over seventeenth-century records will be confronted with hordes of these Native tale-tellers. In these years, the specter of Indian war stalked the English at virtually every turn. Colonial leaders spent much of the century navigating the threats, real or imagined, posed by their non-English neighbors. They cultivated alliances with Native leaders, like Uncas, simply to stay informed. But the warnings kept coming. That threatening information could be deployed against the English colonies, as well as Native enemies, was a lesson quickly grasped. For Native people leveraging against the growing heft of the English colonies, threatening speech could act as a weapon.

Much of the evidence of a plot, in 1653, came from Indians. Before it leapt into the English community and raced across the Sound, the rumor had originated with what Natives around Manhattan began revealing to their European neighbors. The most compelling information came directly from the mouths of Algonquians. At least in the English renderings of these "pressing Testimonies," hints arise that not all of these informants had the best of intentions. English hearers sensed that "the Indians Round about for divers hundred of miles cercute seeme to have drunk deep of an Intoxicating cupp . . . against the English."[108] Intentions, in the end, are terribly hard to prove. But perhaps some of these Native informants meant merely to terrify their colonial neighbors. Certainly some few seemed to enjoy issuing warnings. When an Indian woman near Wethersfield whispered that "the Dutch and Indians generally were confeaderated," perhaps at first she seemed brave and selfless. But then, ominously, she reminded Wethersfield men of their folly in ignoring her earlier warnings about the Pequot attack of April 1637. Townsmen, she warned, should "remember how deare theire Slighting of her former Informacon of the Pequatts coming upon the English [had] Cost them."[109]

To understand the power of such threatening talk, one need only glimpse the typical English reaction: panicked letters, emergency posts flying across the countryside, leaders summoned from their homes to assess the level of danger—and often, all based on the most ethereal of rumors. Concrete effects of such threats rippled through the colonies. In 1643, earlier fears concerning the "plottings of the Narigansets" to draw northeastern Indians "into a generall conspiracie against the English in all parts" had led directly to the formation of the United Colonies, the confederation that in 1653 scrambled to meet, to dispatch interpreters, and to discover Dutch and Indian intentions. (This earlier scare, too, had emerged from the "many dis-coveries and free-conffessions of sundrie Indians . . . from diverse places."[110]) Mere word of violence threw whole towns into paroxysms. When some Indians fired guns "within hearing" of English towns and others "came to the English & tould them the Indeans would fall upon them," in 1644, work and travel ground to a near-total halt. Watches commenced, both "night & day."[111] In 1653, likewise, colonists complained that, because of the steady flow of frightening reports, "the peace of the English through the whole countrey [was] desturbed," and that they were "weried with extreordinary watchings and wardings." Some abandoned their spring plantings.[112]

But even without such concrete disruptions, threats had grave effects. Perhaps the most dislocating, if intangible, imprint was left on the colonial psyche. Fear ran deep. However simple that point may be, talk, in the highly tense atmosphere of the early northeast, could translate into terror.

VII.

War did not come, in 1653. The "discovery of the plott," if in fact it was a plot, upset its progress. In the end, English fears came to nothing. Several English plantations on Long Island were evacuated and abandoned, but no wholesale attack occurred. No Dutch fleet descended on New England shores. The Dutch did not slay the English near Manhattan, nor did the Narragansetts make any move to "cut off" eastern English. No fighting broke out, largely because Massachusetts balked at going to war with the Dutch, for fear of "letting in of waters."[113] With all that might have washed ashore along the Sound, it was a fitting metaphor.

In May, three English agents journeyed to Manhattan to investigate further. An incredulous Petrus Stuyvesant listened as they invited him to participate in a sweeping inquest into the matter—on his turf. They were harshly rebuffed. But, determined to collect evidence of Stuyvesant's perfidy, they encamped at John Underhill's house in Flushing and interviewed witnesses there, instead. What they heard might not have been new—for weeks, information had been rolling in, and now they were mostly building a case—but it was unsettling. From Indian, Dutch and English residents alike came tales of Stuyvesant's efforts to build a sweeping alliance against the English. Addam the Indian claimed that Stuyvesant had personally traveled, that spring, to Fort Orange, to "Ackicksack" ("a great place of Indians"), and "from thence to Monnesick, thence to opingona thence to Warranoke," all "in his owne p[er]son." To Pocumtuck, said Addam, he had sent "baggs of Wampam," cloth, and arms. He had spent days in close consult with Ninigret and other sachems. Some of those sachems, meanwhile, stepped forward to corroborate this evidence. When one had resisted Stuyvesant's overtures, he had been given "a great kettle to bee silent."[114]

It was a compelling case. But, in the long run, not quite compelling enough. Some in New England were more ready to believe than others. With all of the testimony from the New Netherland frontier splayed out before them, the United Colonies commissioners—chiefly those of Massachusetts and Plymouth—shrank from taking action. (At least one Massachusetts official worried that the Indian information was flawed "for want of due Interpters.")[115] Though the evidence of Stuyvesant's campaign was of enough "waight to enduce us to beleeve the Reallitie therof," too few were convinced of the wisdom of declaring a war. So, the rumor hung, suspended, in anticlimax. By June, the episode had seemingly fizzled. Commissioners dispersed and headed homeward. "The newes from the Bay is (for the commisioners are returned home)," wrote Samuel Stone on June 12, 1653, "nulla salus bello, pacem te poscimus omnes. They have concluded, no warre."[116]

So war did not arrive. But it came terribly close. By the fall of 1653, months later, the chatter about Dutch designs on New England had swept ashore in old England, where it lurched grotesquely back to life. Stitching together inflammatory stories carried to Europe by New England merchants, a London printer published *The Second Part of the Tragedy of Amboyna,* outlining the feared plot of the Dutch "For the Total Ruining and Murthering of the English Colonies in New-England" and casting the episode as a sequel to 1623's murders of Englishmen at Ambon. It was pure propaganda. The pamphlet imagined the Dutch, ungrateful for John Underhill's efforts to save their colonies just a few years earlier, hiring several

Indian "Grand Princes" and filling their "Wigwambs" with weapons sent from Holland, "the Fountain of Treacheries."[117] (West India Company directors, who saw this as a bald attempt to stir up English hostility toward the Dutch at a time when the English government was broke and desperate for wartime contributions, called the tract "the most shameless and lying libel which the devil in hell could not have produced."[118]) Every sentence beat the drums for war. With this tract whipping up anti-Dutch sentiment in England, Lord Protector Oliver Cromwell—not one to shy from an excuse for conquest—resolved to send four warships to attack New Netherland. They left England in February 1654, carrying orders for the New England colonies to help expel the troublesome Dutch.

But Cromwell's plans were hobbled by a series of contingencies. First, wild weather blew his fleet off course and badly delayed its Atlantic crossing. When the ships finally arrived at Boston in May 1654, the men spilling out of them found that New Englanders were not uniformly ready to stir up the wrath of the Dutch. The English colonies ultimately agreed to raise men for an expedition against New Netherland (though Plymouth and Massachusetts, especially, were reluctant), an attack that might have toppled Stuyvesant. But before any forces were massed, word arrived in the colonies that England and the States had reached a peace. The Anglo-Dutch War was over; the moment had passed. If not for foot-dragging in some of the colonies, contemporaries thought, New Netherland might have been taken. Writing a few years later, Samuel Maverick blamed those in New England who were altogether too close to their Dutch neighbors. "Those of Plymouth being Mungrell Dutch," he sneered, "and some of the Grandees amongst them haveing a sweet trade with the Dutch," the eastern colonies "held out the dispute till it was to late[,] the peace being concluded."[119]

The "peace being concluded," the episode faded. What happened to those who had had prominent roles to play, in the drama? Most retreated into the murky communities of lower New England, surfacing from time to time in later years. Uncas remained an important figure in New England politics, settling into a pattern "of advancing his own ends by manipulating the English fear of Indian 'conspiracies.'"[120] Ninigret's relations with the English cooled considerably and remained turbulent for years. The next time Thomas Stanton came riding in, Ninigret was far less welcoming and tolerant.[121] In the summer of 1653, the ever-bellicose John Underhill staged a small rebellion, of sorts, against Dutch authority on Long Island.[122] It came to little. In 1672 he died, appropriately enough, at Oyster Bay, where the contested border between Dutch and English territory had once lain. Petrus Stuyvesant, in the meantime, presided over New Netherland until the year 1664, when an English fleet under Colonel Richard Nicolls sailed up to New Amsterdam and coolly demanded that the Dutch turn over their holdings. After a small tantrum, in which he dramatically tore up English appeals for his surrender, Stuyvesant relented. He died in 1672.

Had Stuyvesant and the Narragansetts launched a combined assault on the English in 1653, they might have rewritten New England's history. But was there truly such a "plot"? That seems unlikely. In the most probable scenario, Stuyvesant—acting, perhaps, on orders to "make use of the Indians"—had probably hoped to amass a defensive force of Indian allies, in case the Atlantic war should spread to the colonies. Certainly, he underestimated how quickly the news might spread, how swiftly it might be seized upon and distorted by those looking to cast his actions in a sinister light. Or, perhaps he minded little that the word got out. Terror, after all, is as effective a political weapon as any—and a particularly apt one for those outnumbered by the English. And what of Ninigret's winter visit to Manhattan, where, according to Addam the Indian, the sachem had spent "two daies in a close Rome" with Stuyvesant and "other Sagamors"? Was this only talk?

Maybe. Maybe all that mattered, though, was what a Native Long Islander named Ronnessock told Englishmen, that May. He did not say that attacks were surely planned. But he did attest that "the Duch said they would goe and *tell* the English that the Indians will come and cutt [them] of[f]."[123] Telling them, perhaps, was enough.

4

Post Haste

... Ere I was risen from the place that show'd
My duty kneeling, came there a reeking post,
Stew'd in his haste, half breathless, panting forth ...
—William Shakespeare, from *King Lear*

THE FIRST POST departed Manhattan on January 22, 1673. Packets in hand, he readied himself for the ride. It was a wet month. The postman must have struggled to keep his letters dry, as he slogged through the muck along the Great Trail to Boston. On the 24th, as he passed through Connecticut, a "great storme of rayne" roared overhead.[1] To the north, heavy snow fell. Somewhere near Hartford, he may have lodged overnight, his satchel stashed safely under the bed. That did not make the next day's travels any easier. For many of the 225 miles between New York and Boston his horse's hooves likely sank ever deeper into the mud. But no matter, it was a historic trek. The journey, if slow and wet, represented a new mastery of the terrain. Regular delivery of mail had begun, or so it appeared.

Manhattan, by 1673, was much changed. Most significantly, it was no longer Dutch. The island, as well as the rest of what had once been "New Netherland," now belonged to the English (though, of course, a goodly amount of Dutch men and women still resided there). In 1664, Petrus Stuyvesant—ever the thorn in New England's west side—had finally, and reluctantly, surrendered his realm to an English fleet. In a rage, he had initially torn up English demands for his capitulation, but ultimately yielded almost as soon as the confetti of shredded letters had settled at his feet. Although the surrender was bloodless, it took its toll on the embattled Stuyvesant. By 1672, surely sapped by this embarrassing episode, Stuyvesant was dead. He was buried at his bouwery on Manhattan.[2] *"Stir not the sand too much, for here lies Stuyvesant,"* memorialized a mourner, *"Who once commanded all that was New Netherland / And much against his will delivered it to foes. / If grief and sorrow any hearts do smite, his heart / Did die a thousand deaths, so lethal was the smart. / His first years were too sweet; his last, too full of woes."*[3] The English, in the meantime, wasted no time in renaming the province. In a blink, Stuyvesant's New Netherland was gone—captured, vanished. In its place, now, was "New Yorke upon the Island of the Manhatoes."[4]

Presiding over "New Yorke upon the Island of the Manhatoes," in the winter of 1672–1673, was Governor Francis Lovelace.[5] More, apparently, than many of his contemporaries, Lovelace understood the need for regular exchange among the northern colonies. Within New York, the governor had already taken steps to ease communications. As early as 1669, he had ordered roads built and new ferries readied for passengers.[6] But his most ambitious effort was 1673's postal experiment. From his perch within Fort James, the decaying hulk that had once belonged to the Dutch, Lovelace sketched the parameters of the New York-Boston post. He was its chief author. In December 1672, a proclamation appeared in New York, tacked to trees and perhaps nailed to the fort's splintered walls. It announced "a Post" that would "goe monthly from this City to Boston & back againe." Any who had "Letters or small portable Goods to bee conveyed to Hartford, Connecticut, Boston, or any other parts in the Road" were invited to consign them to the post. While these items awaited departure, the announcement promised, they would be kept safely in a "lockt Box" in the Secretary's office. Postage was to be paid in advance, "before the Bagg bee seald up." Delivery would begin in January.[7] In letters to New England, meanwhile, Lovelace excitedly promoted his plan—the "scheme I have drawn to promote a happy correspondence," as he phrased it.[8]

Lovelace had plenty of reasons to wish for such a "happy correspondence." He was openly displeased with the sluggishness of his dispatches from England, which, he complained, arrived as slowly as "the production of Ellephats, once almost in 2 yeares." ("[W]ee had as well crost Lethe, as the Athlantiq ocean," he griped.)[9] He had also been personally frustrated by the problems impeding colonial mails. Their unpredictability nettled him. When some of Lovelace's letters disappeared, in 1669, he lashed out against the courier. "[A] greater Rascall I never mett with," he wrote bitterly.[10] But, for reasons not entirely due to a lack of honest letter bearers, news had never flowed easily between New York and Massachusetts. On arriving as governor, Lovelace had been sorely disappointed by New Englanders' decided failure to shower him with warm, welcoming letters. Meeting, instead, with continued silence, Lovelace had gone so far as to offer Massachusetts's leaders a lesson in manners. It was "receiv'd Practice," he wrote frostily, "that when any Stranger enters himselfe into a Neighbourhood, the prsent Inhabitants (by the Rules of Urbanity) ought to Congratulate his Reception." Lovelace thought himself the victim of an epistolary snubbing. Nevertheless, he hoped, yet, for closer relations. Regular postal exchange, he thought, might be the "most compendious means to beget a mutual understanding" among the northern colonies.[11]

Lovelace was a loyal royalist, who had served as a colonel in the English civil war (and who, when it did not go well for his side, had gone into exile with Charles II). He may have erred in expecting much fanfare from Puritan New England.[12] But Lovelace had more immediate concerns, and these were painfully close to home. More than anything else, the post was a defensive measure. It emerged from a moment of imperial contest, with Lovelace fumbling for a way to collect news of "all public occurrences."[13] By 1672, England and Holland were once again at war. On hearing this news, Lovelace worried, rightly, that the Dutch might try to recapture New York. "If so," he wrote, "it will be high time for us to buckle on our armor, and to put ourselves into . . . a posture of defense." Confronted with the specter of a Dutch invasion, Lovelace could ill afford to remain isolated from New England. He needed the intelligence. Particularly valuable was the European news that so often docked, first, in Boston. His solution: a "constant post, which shall monthly pass between us."[14]

The postman's name was Mr. Hatfield. He traveled on horseback and probably carried a "Horne," as he had been instructed to do, though at first its blast may have puzzled—even startled—most townspeople, unaccustomed as they were to such a sound. He also brought with him a great "Port-Mantle," a few lonely letters stuffed into its maw. Among these were several penned by Francis Lovelace himself, in which he cheerfully announced Hatfield's arrival. "Dear Sir," he wrote buoyantly, in one letter, "I here presented you with two rarities,—a packet of the latest intelligence I could meet withal, and a post." Though the news he carried was fleeting and fresh, the post, by contrast, was to be permanent. Hatfield—a worthy man, "active, stout, and indefatigable," Lovelace added—would ride regularly between Boston and New York with a "fresh supply" of letters and news. With as much fanfare as any bleating horn, Lovelace's lavish script trumpeted the coming of a "constant Post" to the northeast.[15]

Hatfield's memory has largely been lost to history. Few studies recount his icy ride as the inaugural post-master. Perhaps this lacuna should come as no surprise. Most New Englanders alive, that winter, likely found the event unremarkable, if they were even aware of its unfolding. Certainly few knew the name of this solitary figure, carrying mail. Even John Winthrop, Jr., perpetuated the man's anonymity. Sending a letter with the post, he left a yawning pause where the man's name should have gone: "This," he wrote, "is by an oportunity of one   who cometh as a post fro N: Yorke to Boston." Still, in the same letter, Winthrop betrayed his sense that the settling of such a "constant Post" was significant. Perhaps with a touch of awe, he noted that, instead of traveling only when necessary, this post was to be permanent, a messenger that would go "all the yeare long" between Boston, Hartford, and New York.[16] It was a grand plan. Before Hatfield ventured forth from Manhattan, that winter of 1673, no regular, intercolonial postal service had ever been attempted.[17]

It didn't quite work, in the end. But it is a story that is well worth telling, nonetheless, if only for what it reveals of English intentions. Clumsy though it were, Hatfield's ride is significant, and its timing is telling. In the 1660s and 1670s, after decades of finding themselves at the mercy of the communications frontier, Englishmen began to make moves to control it. Some of these moves were imperial, pursued by the English king: The post, at least according to Francis Lovelace, was His Majesty's idea. It did not emerge organically out of colonists' clamoring for easier exchange of letters. It was the product, instead, of the newly restored monarch's grand vision for binding together his empire. Ultimately, it was the King's desire that "all his Subjects in their distinct Colonyes . . . enter into a strict Allyance and Correspondency," said Lovelace, that sent Hatfield on his way.[18]

But Hatfield's ride also coincided with earthier changes in the northeast. Already underway, by the time he set off from Manhattan (though it has been somewhat invisible to historians), was a quiet revolution in travel. In the latter part of the seventeenth century, colonists moved from a world almost wholly defined by water travel to one that looked increasingly to the interior. Roads were laid, and land was cleared. Canoes gave way, increasingly, to horses. In the course of a lifetime, travel changed considerably. While colonists at first fumbled to find their way, by about the 1660s they had moved toward a substantially greater command of the region's geography. And, moreover, they were far better equipped to traverse it. As much as the deeds that furiously professed to consume Indian land, intercolonial travel worked to remake New England into a signally English place.

I.

Early colonial writers did not employ the term "post." The word itself is almost wholly absent from their letters. Not until the mid-1660s, a few years prior to Hatfield's ride, does it even begin to appear in correspondence. But then, suddenly, "posts" seem to invade. A "letter by Post" arrives from the governor of Plymouth; another is hurried to Hartford "post haste," "without delay"; a witness to New York's fall is "post[ed] away" to spread the news; a man swears his intention to have "gonn post" to alert John Winthrop to his wife's illness, had she not belatedly revived. A few letters are even deposited at their destinations "post payd."[19] What did it mean to label a letter in this way? What, exactly, constituted a "post"? This is a trickier question than one might think. It is clear that colonists were not referring to steady, regular carriage of private letters; that was well in the future. But beyond that, their language can be confusing. *Post* was a slippery word. It could be a noun, a verb, an adverb. One could post a letter, or "ride post" to deliver one. A "post" might be the courier bearing news, or the news itself. All posts were not the same. Despite the rampant and sometimes cloudy use of the word, however, the word "post" usually meant something quite particular.

One of the connotations it bore was carriage of public, even royal, business. Most posts consisted of information that was sent urgently, and officially, on the country's account. In the colonies the beginning of official "posting," so called, coincided with the English takeover of New Netherland. The first to make any official gesture toward such a practice seems to have been Colonel Richard Nicolls, the very man who had sailed into Dutch waters and snatched Manhattan from a surly Petrus Stuyvesant. The first governor of New York after its capture, Nicolls saw straightaway that, where official correspondence was concerned, New Englanders' makeshift modes of sending simply would not do. He quickly decreed that "for the speedy dispatch of Letters of publicke concerne," any letter inscribed with his name (or that of any English governor) could be "Immediately dispatcht from Constable to Constable, who is to presse a horse and man, for such service at the rate of sixe pence per mile." Nicolls was most concerned about the prospect of the Dutch reappearing suddenly to reclaim the jewel that had once been Dutch Manhattan. His intent, he wrote, was "to strengthen this place the best I can against the threats or possibly the assaults of the W:I:Company or States."[20]

But the man who truly stood behind these early posts was not Richard Nicolls. It was the English king, Charles II. After years of civil war and upheaval, English subjects were just now becoming accustomed, again, to living under a king. In spring 1660, after a long stint of Puritan republicanism, England's monarchy had been restored. Plucked from exile in the Spanish Netherlands, Charles II had returned to England and had been treated to a hearty welcome as he toured the countryside on his way to London. Bonfires roared in the streets and ladies tossed flowers at the King's carriage.[21] When the cries of "God save the King" had faded, Charles II's accession to the throne brought about renewed efforts at imperial consolidation. This included careful attention to communications: It was during his reign that England saw the birth of truly public postal service. Royal posts had been dutifully flying across England since at least the sixteenth century, but it was only within recent decades—with the Restoration, especially—that the postal service had begun to carry private letters.[22]

With postal service came new attention to England's long-neglected roads. Traffic along the highways of the British Isles, "with goods carried by pack pony, cart, or on the backs of pedlars," had been swelling throughout the seventeenth century, so much so that England's few serviceable roads suffered mightily from the habitual damages of wheels, hooves and feet. Some in England were alarmed at the rising deluge of traffic. In 1672, John Cressett published a pamphlet, *The Grand Concern of England Explained in Several Proposals to Parliament,* that promoted the idea of stopping it. He proposed that "the Multitude of Stage-coaches and Caravans now travelling upon the Roads may all, or most of them, be suppressed." (Cressett fretted, among other things, that the increase in wagon travel was destructive to England's tradition of "good Horsemanship, a Thing so useful and commendable in a Gentleman" and that it would diminish the "Breed of Watermen, who are the Nursery for Seamen, and they the Bulwark of the Kingdom.")[23] But Parliament seems to have accepted England's waggoners as unavoidable new fixtures of English life. In the 1660s, for the first time in a century, the government took measures to maintain England's distressed roads. Beginning in 1662, England's shires were required to pay a tax providing for repair of highways. And in 1663 Parliament passed its first turnpike law, the faint signal of a new age in which road upkeep would be funded with tolls paid by travelers themselves.[24]

But the King himself began to contemplate roads in more majestic terms. In 1671 he even appointed a Royal Cosmographer, John Ogilby, who was charged with creating great maps of the King's possessions—including the first cartographic representations of England's highways. Only now, and largely thanks to the work of Ogilby, did maps begin to appear depicting roads. Though by 1671 there were six main post roads connecting London to various parts of the country, these routes had almost never been surveyed or mapped. In 1668, a few sheet maps appeared, showing the web of post roads. (One of them, Richard Carr's *A Description of al[l] the postroads in England,* was based on sketches by a postal official.)[25] But Ogilby's projects were far more grand. With royal direction to "have help in the affixing of sufficient Marks for the better Direction of Travellers, and Ascertaining the Distances from Stage to Stage in Our said Kingdom," he became the first cartographer since perhaps the 1250s to attempt a comprehensive pictorial itinerary of *all* English roads.[26] Within a year of being appointed, Ogilby was busily surveying roads, hurrying through the heaths and hedges of England to plot its byways.

In 1675, Ogilby produced *Britannia*—a stunning, 300-page atlas of all of England's major roads, as well as some of its lesser-known routes. The sheet map bound into *Britannia* not only showed many more roads than any other cartographer had done; it also spotlighted them, subordinating other features of the landscape.[27] One hundred lush, scrupulously detailed engravings followed. Ogilby sneered at the inaccuracy of previous *"Geographers,"* whose maps seemed to him "but so many *Guess-Plots*" and *"Perambulated Projections."* He had some reason to be smug. His plates of Britain's roads were to-scale and accompanied by prose descriptions of each itinerary. London to Aberistwith: "You come to a Descent sprinkled with Woods," then "enter *High-Wickham,* seated in a pleasant Vale, a large and Well-built Town, numbring near 200 Houses, with several good Inns . . ." The atlas even alerted travelers to "Backward Turnings," where one should avoid becoming disoriented.[28]

Just how practical these maps were for ordinary travelers is doubtful. A few readers may have cut selected sheets from the bulky book, presumably

In his grand atlas *Britannia,* John Ogilby included detailed itineraries for all of the major routes through England, as well as this ambitious map of the kingdom's roads. "A New Map of the Kingdom of England" from Ogilby, *Britannia* (London, 1675). *(© The British Library Board. Maps C.6.d.8 frontispiece [recto and verso])*

to take with them in their travels. But, however magnificent were Ogilby's sketches, they were likely mocked by the lowly coachmen and waggoners who knew the roads best. Portable versions of Ogilby's work, meanwhile, were not published for another forty years (though, almost immediately, *Britannia* inspired a flurry of cheaper and more practical pocket travel books, some of them using Ogilby's own calculations).[29] But *Britannia* was mostly symbolic. It expressed, in grand terms and bright paint, the King's imperial sensibilities. Its gorgeous *"Copper-sculps"* of *"Your Majesty's* High-Ways" were intended primarily to celebrate, as the book's dedication trumpeted, the power emanating *"from this Great* Emporium *and* Prime Center *of the Kingdom, Your Royal* Metropolis."[30]

These same sensibilities sent Hatfield on his way. Posting was begun, in the 1670s, not because of colonial necessity, but because of Charles II's imperial designs. At least one historian has contended that we should not think of postal service as having appeared relatively late in colonial history; rather, it is in some ways surprising that it was tried at all.[31] In the colonies, some efforts had been made previously to organize mail delivery. But these had been faltering and disjointed. As early as 1639 Massachusetts Bay had named its first "postmaster," Richard Fairbanks, who was to collect all ship letters arriving from England and to ensure that these mails reached their intended readers. (Little evidence suggests that this plan lasted, however.) In 1657, Virginia's House of Burgesses enlisted colonists' help in forwarding letters, by obliging every plantation owner to forward official messages. Historians have dubbed this plan the "Tobacco post," for the penalty incurred by failing to participate—one hogshead of tobacco.[32]

But serious talk of intercolonial posting did not begin until the 1660s, after the English conquest of New York. (Around the time that he seized New Netherland as his rightful prize, in fact, the Duke of York—the King's brother—had been granted the post office's profits. It was thus fitting that a colonial postal service might emerge from New York, his American province.[33]) Only then did some dare to imagine a more sweeping network of communications that would connect the English colonies by land. In a 1669 letter from England, Henry Oldenburg wondered aloud how Marylanders, for instance, might correspond with "other English, either towards Virginia or towards N. Engld." He proposed sending forth English colonists to settle intermittently, say, "at every 10. miles distance," along a great road reaching from Massachusetts to Virginia. Though Oldenburg's vision was still far off, it was not unthinkable. "How happy would it be," he mused, "if there were a Union of all our English colonies for free communecations."[34]

But American posting did not emerge simply out of England's imperial concerns. There are signs, too, that more homegrown changes were unfolding in the colonies. Letters suggest that delivery had begun to cluster more accidentally on certain 'nodes' in the colonial landscape. One such place was the trading house of merchant Alexander Bryan, at the water's edge in Milford, Connecticut.[35] On the coast about halfway between Hartford and Manhattan, and about sixty miles from each, Bryan was well positioned to forward letters. Beginning in the mid-1660s, a new concentration of mail converged on Bryan's knob of shoreline.[36] Positioning himself as a kind of early postmaster, he became a pivot of important news. He wrote what resemble early "news-letters," informing John Winthrop, Jr., of imperial events. By 1670, Bryan was well known as one who might "speedily Conveigh" a missive toward its final destination. He was well enough known, in fact, to earn complaints from those dissatisfied with his services. "[P]ray direct your Letrs to Capt. toping and he will dispach it to me," Daniel Lane insisted in July 1669, recommending a competitor of sorts, "for at Mr. Bryans thay are very Necklejent in sending them."[37]

Nor did the word "post" always carry a royal inflection. To send "post" on the King's account, one needed to be faced with a sufficiently pressing problem. Generally, this meant war, invasion, or the prospect thereof: When John Pynchon learned that French men of war had been found lurking off the Massachusetts coast in 1666, for instance, he sent word "Hast Post hast For his Maties. service" toward Colonel Nicolls in New York.[38] That language had been borrowed into colonial writing because of the King's directives. But all "posts" were not official. By the early 1670s the word had so infiltrated colonial speech that it often referred simply to any dispatch that went quickly and directly. Posts were generally reserved for emergencies, even if private. When Mrs. Winthrop's health flagged in August 1671, while her husband was away in Boston., her attendants "prepared apost . . . to have gonn post for your [Honor]" and "had Gott a Horss and all ready." But as the horse was being shoed, Mrs. Winthrop's condition unexpectedly improved. The danger passing, they ultimately sent word to her husband by "opportunety," rather than an express post.[39] To "go post" was to go fast, without detour.

This was the sort of news that had, for decades, been carried by Indians. But that, too, was changing. In the years that witnessed the English conquest of New Netherland, reliance on Indian couriers began to drop. By the 1660s, their numbers were waning. Into the 1650s, based on the Winthrops' correspondence, Indians had carried over a third of all letters. But in the next few decades that percentage fell considerably.[40] The decline owes, in part, to New England's changing demographics. As years wore on, the Indian population was falling and the English one growing. In 1670 (about the time John Ogilby was taking up his grand charge), perhaps 68,000 people lived in New England. One quarter were Indians. There were simply fewer Natives to hire.[41] As more English men and more English towns appeared, writers—some of whom may never have been comfortable using Indian messengers—were probably glad to pass off letters to their better-known neighbors. Algonquian couriers were generally the choice of last resort, and colonists' discomfort with them only grew. (It grew apace, in fact, with English-Indian tensions. Writing in the violent 1670s, one man confessed that he had been tempted to hire "an Indian on purpose" to carry an urgent letter, but feared "these troublesome times would have caused a dislike of it."[42]) But these factors, alone, do not explain the move from Native couriers to "posts."[43]

One clue lies with a final characteristic of *posts:* In general, they rode horses. The very word "post," to early modern English speakers, was inextricably associated with horse travel. In the sense of describing a messenger system for forwarding "letters and dispatches," it apparently entered the English language in the early sixteenth century, just about the time when Henry VIII began a relay system of mounted posts throughout England. *Posts* were, in fact, *horse-posts.* In the sixteenth and seventeenth centuries (and much beyond, in fact), the word "post" conjured a very particular image: that of postal riders, the hooves of their "fresh horses" beating a rhythm into the ground.[44] Hatfield rode on horseback, and perhaps even took along a second horse. (The governor had implored him to "provide yor selfe of a Spare Horse," lest his letters be delayed by a tiring animal.[45]) Without horses, swift exchange between Boston and New York—a distance topping 200 miles—would have been all but inconceivable. The phrase *post haste,* sneaking steadily into English letters and popping up on sealed papers in this period, thus betrays something quite specific. It points indirectly to a new company of characters, mute and snorting and endlessly important: horses.

It takes a bit of a leap, at first, to imagine that the arc of New England's history turned on these skittish beasts. In the world beyond the northeast's pastures and pathways, these were momentous years indeed. The 1660s was an active decade for news, as the wider Atlantic lurched and swelled with political tumult and war. As sleepy colonists dipped encrusted quills into inkpots in New England, plague and fire ripped through London, devouring thousands of buildings and lives. Charles II returned from exile, New Netherland was conquered, war with the Dutch Republic, dreadfully, was revived. Much about the empire had changed by the mid-1660s. But the ground was shifting beneath colonial feet, as well.

II.

Seventeenth-century travel accounts are frustratingly few. While early travelers left behind a rich trail of evidence, most of it comes in flashes. We see John Winthrop, Jr., stoking a "blazing fire," as he prepares to spend a frosty

night in Nipmuck; we glimpse William Wood, drinking tobacco and
feasting on bear; we hear of a servant who has lost her way.[46] Any portrait
of English travel must be cobbled together from these precious shards, as
virtually no sustained, lifelong records of travel have survived. There is,
however, one important exception: the diary of Thomas Minor.

Thomas Minor was one of the earliest settlers of coastal Connecticut. We
have already spied him several times—hiring Indian messengers, purchasing
canoes, chatting with Agedouset, traveling through Narragansett "afoot."
But don't be fooled by his frequent appearances. Thomas Minor was, inas-
much as any of his cohort could be called such a thing, ordinary. Were it
not for his diary, we would know very little about him. We could say, perhaps, this much: He was a farmer, a father, a sergeant, and, later in life, a
sometime deputy to the General Court. He had also been an early migrant
to the New World. In 1629, he left behind his native Somersetshire, England,
and sailed aboard the *Lyon's Whelp* to Massachusetts. After several removes,
a marriage, and the births of his five eldest children in Massachusetts Bay,
he drifted southward in the 1640s to help settle John Winthrop, Jr.'s new
plantation at Pequot.[47] Minor's life, and the world around him, come into
much sharper focus in 1653. That year, he began his diary.

Minor kept his diary from 1653 to 1684. As a thirty-year record of his journeys, the diary is an unmatched measure of everyday mobility. It is not a
travel diary but, rather, a farmer's almanac of events and activities: lambs
"ewed," butter exchanged, neighbors visited. Its language can be unforgiv-
ingly sparse, since Minor seldom paused for personal reflection. Nor did
he do much to describe the landscape as it passed underfoot. But as much as
he recorded what he did, Minor made note of where he went. Paging through
the diary, it is almost possible to follow in his footsteps. Effectively, the diary
is a map: it tells us, quite concretely, where, and when, Minor traveled.
Although the diarist seldom noted his reasons for traveling, a sampling of
some of his most favored destinations yields a sense of what compelled his
movements. When it came to traveling beyond his more immediate environs,
a few key motives drove Thomas Minor's journeys. What lured the diarist
away from his farm? Three things, principally: court, trade, and family.[48]

Among long-distance destinations, Hartford (or "Conecticut," as Minor
usually called the river towns) was his most frequently visited. In thirty
years, he made twenty-two trips to Connecticut. Judging from the dates of
travel, almost all were related to colonial government or justice. Fully half

of the trips came in either May or October, the two months in which the Connecticut General Court regularly sat. Although he was not always a deputy (only later in life did he achieve that post), Minor visited Hartford principally to attend court—whether to report to the General Court, to participate in a court of "Electtion," or to defend himself in the Particular Court. Moreover, some of his other long-distance trips were also on court business. In October 1681, when the assembly ordered him to "goe visitt Mrs Harris, and see how it fares with her," Minor duly traveled to Narragansett to do so. "I went to the widow Haris," he wrote in early December, and "came whome ffrom Naraganset" three days later.[49] Trade seems to have most often drawn Minor to Boston, where he was a relatively frequent visitor. He recorded seventeen trips to Massachusetts Bay. At least one of these was for the rather extraordinary purpose of witnessing Mary Dyer's 1660 execution on Boston Common.[50] But many of his other sojourns to the bay were aimed at bringing livestock to market. In 1668, for instance, he arrived in Boston "with the oxen"; the next year, "sould my horses." A 1667 entry hints at the larger pattern: "I went to Bostowne . . . with Catell," he wrote. Since the majority of Minor's trips to the bay happened in the fall, particularly in October, these travels were likely livestock drives. Autumn found many New England farmers transporting animals to market.[51]

Excluding Boston, the furthest Minor ventured was to Stratford, a small satellite of New Haven. Almost seventy-five miles distant from Minor's own homestead, and so far west that it nearly bordered on New Netherland, it seems a curious destination. But, with a quick look into Minor's family history, the diarist's six trips to Stratford begin to make more sense. In 1658, his eldest son, John, had married and moved to Stratford. John Minor's residing there was probably the prime motivation behind his father's visits. These were difficult journeys that grew more trying as the elder Minor aged. In late May 1672, Minor and three of his younger sons voyaged west to visit John. Minor's note about the journey back hints at his struggle. "[C]oming from stratford," he wrote, "I fayled in takeing a Cup of Sider . . . much to the greaving of my sons."[52]

In the thirty years covered by the diary, Minor averaged two or three long journeys per year.[53] These were seasonal, patterned movements, and it is fair to assume that other New Englanders were making similar journeys. Did these patterns change? Not dramatically. But because Minor was aging as the diary progressed (he was well into his seventies as he penned the final entries), it is difficult to gauge his mobility over time. The diary does not suggest that he was becoming significantly more, or less, mobile as years passed.[54] It does, however, point to some important shifts. The biggest change in travel witnessed by the diary can't be found among Minor's destinations. What changed was how he got there.

"[T]he mare have a white face," Thomas Minor scrawled, "a slit in the righte yeare," and ".3 white feet." Each of the animal's ears, he continued, was marked with a white ring and a "halpenie" cut. Here she was, in the flesh— one thousand pounds of notched, mottled flesh. This mare was one of many. At the time of this description, she was among a swiftly growing horde of equine inhabitants, roving southern New England. Yet, for Minor, she was the first to merit such careful portraiture. A stray horse or two had wandered into Thomas Minor's diary earlier than this, but only now did he begin to write about them in numbers—and in detail. It was October 1660.[55]

Horses had long been in short supply. While hogs and cattle had arrived in tremendous numbers with the earliest migrants to New England, horses had not. In 1630, the Winthrop fleet departed England carrying 700 migrants, but only sixty horses.[56] As more ships docked, horses continued to dribble in, in comparatively small numbers. In 1632, for instance, the *Charles* delivered a paltry six mares, though it carried eighty cattle.[57] The following year, likewise, a Yarmouth ship came bearing ninety-five passengers, thirty-four sheep, and just "2: mares."[58] Because English farmers did not use horses as draught animals, they simply did not bring many of them to the New World. While other livestock quickly outnumbered colonists, the number of horses lagged. As of 1632, Governor William Bradford was apparently the only man in Plymouth to own a horse. By 1640, according to one historian's count, New England was home to a scant two hundred horses, even as its English population climbed into the tens of thousands. Because they were relatively rare, horses also fetched staggering prices. A canoe was easily purchased for twenty-odd shillings; mares, by contrast, could sell for as much as thirty to forty pounds.[59] With so much money to be made, New Englanders were all too tempted to sell what few horses they possessed. Boston men had begun testing the export market by 1648. That year, a ship carrying eighty horses nearly toppled in the harbor. Perhaps fearing the consequences of sending so many horses away (or, worse, of seeing their investments swallowed by the bay), Massachusetts men soon after banned all exports of mares.[60]

Before midcentury, this scarcity was a profound bar on English mobility. With few horses to go around, borrowing was common. Even such prominent men as John Endecott made use of others' horses. When in 1645 the United Colonies combed the Massachusetts countryside for horses to be used by militia in Narragansett, Endecott protested against the pressing of a horse owned by his neighbor, the widow Goodwife Ingersoll. "[T]he trueth is," he confessed to the United Colonies commissioners, "it is a horse which I alwaies upon occasion ride on."[61] Complaints about the dearth of horses peaked in the 1640s. When John Winthrop, Jr., removed to the Pequot country in the mid-1640s, several of his correspondents lamented that, without horses, they were unable to visit the new plantation. "I should have bene very willing to have spent some parte of this winter with you," Adam Winthrop wrote to his brother in 1648, "if I could have had any hope of tollerable passage." But lacking "horsses," he was stuck in Boston. Should John have an animal that was "Fitte to travell," Adam promised, he would "bye it, or borrow for my Jurny, for I feare I shall hardly gett one heer."[62] For the same reason, the younger John Winthrop was no more successful in wooing a minister to the new settlement. John Jones of Fairfield, the man Winthrop wanted, also lacked transport. Jones would have been on his way, he assured Winthrop by letter in May 1647, "If love or money would have procured a horse in these parts." They wouldn't; and thus the minister was bound to wait until "Some pinnace," bound eastward, was willing to carry him.[63]

It was a common plight. For years New Englanders made do with few horses. Even the elite were sometimes caught without one. But this was beginning to change. Minor's notes suggest a significant shift, beginning in the 1660s. About that time, horses began to creep into his records and, gradually, to crowd the diary as they must have crowded the countryside. By 1661, he had begun a kind of petty trade in horses. "I received .3. mares by george Robinson," he wrote on 7 October 1661, and the next day, in a quick turnover, he "solde the wilde horse."[64] By March, Minor and his sons were "looking mares" as they had once searched for drifting canoes. Between 1661 and 1664, Minor mentioned either "looking" for horses or finding them no less than ten times. This was something new. Even as Minor fastidiously described his white-faced mare, horses were multiplying at a terrific speed. Recalling that "In the yeare 1626 or thereabouts there was not a Neat Beast Horse or sheepe in the Countrey," Samuel Maverick marveled in 1660 at what was now a "great number of Horses."[65]

Some of this "great number," alas, was destined to go elsewhere. Many ended up in the balmy sugar islands of the West Indies, where they provided power for crushing cane and hauling heavy loads. The West Indies trade, in fact, greatly stoked New England's stocks of cattle. Colonists had been sending "our Cattle" to the islands at least since the year 1647, when John Winthrop thanked the Lord for opening such a "gainfull" exchange. That year was droughty in the Caribbean, but the islands nevertheless had to eat. (Even in wetter years, they had little space, let alone the right environment, for raising their own cattle.) "[H]ere wants the English mans grasse," Beauchamp Plantagenet wrote, about Barbados, in 1648, "and so the English mans Beef, Mutton, Milk, Butter and Cheese." What the islands also wanted was power "to turn their Sugar mils," which was why "*New England* sendeth Horses, and *Virginia* Oxen."[66] Horses were not the only commodity that went sea-ward to the West Indies. New England also sent corn, peas, fish, pitch, tar, masts, and other livestock. But the profitability of horses soon got a great boost. In 1654, Parliament began taxing England's horse exports. As the flow from England slowed, colonists discovered what money could be made by raising their own horses.[67] It was their haste to send horses away, in part, that triggered a shift in New English ways of travel at home.

This, in fact, was the genesis of a swift and highly profitable horse trade. Tradition holds that the first man to comprehend the market for horses was Massachusetts "mint-master" John Hull, who in 1657 purchased a neck of land in Narragansett with the express intent of penning, and raising, horses. But others quickly followed suit. Within a few years, Rhode Island was "overtaken" with the English grasses preferred by its equine inhabitants.[68] By the late 1660s some parts of New England seemed overtaken with horses, too. John Winthrop, Jr., had his own "Great store," numerous enough to cause headaches for Winthrop's caretaker in Pequot.[69] Word of this supply traveled far. Several men wrote to Winthrop looking to buy horses from him, from places as far away as Maryland. "Sr. I having bin infformed that you have a Great store of horses and mares . . . ," wrote Robert Morris, "seend mee tow of your Largest well spred yong mares For Breeders."[70]

So rapidly did New England's "Breeders" multiply, in fact, that some English worried about the quality of such stock. Colonial governments began to pass regulations aimed at preventing small, inferior animals from reproducing. Fearing, in 1668, that "the breed of horses in the Country is utterly spoyled . . . through the smalenes & badnes" of its growing herds, Massachusetts explicitly decreed what sort of horses would be allowed to graze freely in its "Commons & woods."[71] New York passed a similar law in 1669. "[Y]ou have a mutch better Race of horses then wee have," Governor Francis Lovelace wrote enviously to Connecticut, that year. (The success of these efforts to control New England's breeding stock is dubious, since horses continued to range freely. "Horses there are numerous," John Josselyn observed of New England, in the early 1670s, and then added wryly, "and here and there a good one.")[72] Meanwhile, prices fell precipitously. By 1668 the official value of a "sounde horse" in Massachusetts had plummeted to a mere five pounds. Long Islanders complained, in the early 1670s, that horses no longer brought "halfe so much" profit as the colony figured when taxing its subjects, while in Connecticut prices endured a "catastrophic fall" over the years between midcentury and 1680.[73]

The coming of horses to New England's towns probably unfolded unevenly.[74] But there was a defining moment. In the Minor diary, horses arrive precipitously in the 1660s—a veritable herd. That timing corresponds with what was happening in Massachusetts Bay. Probate records, which sometimes include inventories of the things people owned at death, tell the tale: In these crude lists, one can watch pockets of horse ownership bloom across the colony.[75] In the 1640s, a mere 14 percent of households in Essex County, Massachusetts, listed any horses at all among their possessions. Climbing, that number reached 27 percent in the 1650s. But in the next decade, it doubled. By the 1660s, fully half of probated householders owned at least one horse. (Many owned several.) Very similar rates prevailed in Middlesex County, the sprawling reach of settlement to the west, where by the 1670s a majority of households owned a horse. Alongside the beasts themselves, assorted riding accessories began to crop up. About a third of probated households in both counties, by the 1670s, also kept saddles, bridles, pillions, stirrups, or, in one case, even a pair of "bootes & spurs."[76]

More horses, the Minor diary attests, changed travel quickly. Where Minor had once rowed, he now "rode." Canoes did not, by any means, disappear. But Minor's notes make clear that horse riding was ascendant. By the late 1660s, Minor's wife Grace was also regularly riding from town to town, though her mounted mishaps suggest that she was still adjusting to horse travel. In two years, she weathered three serious falls. In May 1667, Minor noted that, "my wife was hurt with the horse by the pond"; six months later, she "fell of[f] her mare and hurt her selfe verie much." In 1668 Grace Minor once again "ffell of the mare," this time at the cart bridge.[77] As those foibles suggest, greater numbers of horses did not translate into immediate ease of mobility. Horses threw riders, fell into Indian traps, and ran off inexplicably. They had a penchant for disappearing. John Hull himself was once "forced to lie in the woods" when his horse wandered off and refused to be caught. (Months later, the horse was returned; "He had been taken in an Indian trap, near Taunton," Hull noted.[78]) Long after horses had ceased to be rarities, those that went missing were still well worth seeking. When his brown gelding galloped off in 1668, Francis Lovelace wrote letters to Connecticut in hopes of reclaiming him. "[H]ee is Stragled from this Iland and was seene on the roade towards Hartford," Lovelace explained.[79]

Nor could horses go everywhere. Even those able to ride found some pathways yet impenetrable. Looking for a way through Podunk in the 1650s, an English scout found one possible route "worse for horse" than he had hoped. It was pitted with swamps and steep ravines. "[F]or foot men," he wrote, there were "bridges made by indeanes." But, he concluded ruefully, "I can not advise any man to come that way with an horse."[80] But such obstacles did not stop Englishmen from riding. Some now mused, casually, over whether to tackle long distances "by Sea" or "by land." "I most encline, by Land," thought John Richards, planning a trip to New Netherland. (He later reconsidered: Given "the season of the yeare, and bad traveleing specially for horses," Richards decided, on second thought, to make a "sea voyage thither.")[81] By the end of the 1660s, prodigious numbers of horses had reached even the remotest parts of New England. Riding had become so common, at least among elites, that some even "took horse" between places that were separated by no more than a simple boat trip—from Stamford to New York, for example.[82]

In the meantime, Thomas Minor devoted ever more time to buying, selling, seeking, finding, shoeing, and marking horses.[83] His diary now became a paper pen, overrun with notations about the animals. It is filled with elaborate descriptions of those horses born and branded under his care. Portraits of each animal are given in great detail. One was "somewhat whitish under the bely all white from the Eies downward to the very mouth"; another had "a black mussel & black lips"; others, still, were marked by a "star in the forehead" or a "litell spot of white."[84] Brown, bay, black, pibald, sorrel, roane—he carefully marked and recorded all.

III.

Historians, like colonial observers, have noted the increase in New England's horses in the latter part of the century.[85] But few, curiously, have pondered the effect this must have had on travel. It was momentous. In relatively short order, horses made English men and women much more mobile. In English letters, the shift is almost palpable. First a few stray drops, then a trickle, then more. If we could hover overhead, look down from above, we would see them: couriers, travelers, carts, and horsemen, traveling in new numbers. Tales of travelers gone astray, lost in the woods, go strangely silent. Indian guides fall away. Talk arises of making roads—great roads, to ease intercolonial travel. This is a marked change. Although some few English had been traveling through New England's great interior spaces for years, a perceptible tipping point came sometime during the 1660s. With new abandon, colonists took to the road.

Or, more properly, took to the path. To this point, New England's only roads—that is, ways cut and cleared by Englishmen—were local.[86] They ran from houselots to woodlots, to the mill, to outlying fields, or to the meetinghouse. As in England, where parishes bore the brunt of highway upkeep, New England's roads rested in the hands of local men. Because these responsibilities ended at town bounds, "town ways" remained virtually the sole English *roads* in New England for most of the century. Routes reaching between towns—let alone colonies—were far fewer.[87] So thoroughly local, most early roads had the effect of turning English travel inward, on itself. They were "centripetal"—that is, circling, like wagons. Well into the century, finds one historian, Little Compton, Rhode Island, for instance, was still "encircled by the forest," its roads either "turning along the civilized perimeter or ending at the forest edge."[88]

But with the rise of horse travel, more were tempted to strike beyond that "forest edge." Pushed by the impetus to bring goods to market, western colonists began to find their way over land. Whereas John Eliot's 1650 description of New England made no mention of roads or horses, Samuel Maverick's—just ten years later—nodded toward a fledgling carrying trade. Covering the forty miles between Boston and Rehoboth, Maverick found "a Comone trade, carrying & recarrying goods by land in Cart and on Horseback" (though he noted a "fayre conveyance of goods by water," as well). From Taunton, too, traders could find "good conveyance to Boston by Cart."[89] Eighty miles west in Hartford, Goodman Richard Fellows, well "fited for horses," was also gaining a reputation for hauling goods in his cart.[90] As the West Indies trade accelerated, ever-greater numbers of livestock—more, even, than there were horses—pounded the paths of New England, on their way to market. On market days, the ways between villages thronged with hogs, cattle and horses, on their way to be slaughtered or shipped.[91] These pilgrimages, more than the post, forged connections between colonies.

All travelers, of course, were not market-bound. Others went simply to visit relatives. At about the same time that Maverick found carts hurtling between Boston and Rehoboth in 1660, Antipas and Elizabeth Newman traveled that same route to visit family.[92] By 1667 Newman felt comfortable enough to make a hundred-mile trip on horseback, his young son "rideing very couragiously behinde mee." On the whole the two found it a "very comfortable Journey." Rather than hire a Native guide, Newman piloted himself—though not perfectly. When he missed a turn in the path, he simply blamed the folly on his horse's "being unaquainted with the way."[93] Perhaps Newman was too hasty in trying his trip alone. Mastery of northeastern travel routes did not happen instantly. Plenty still went missing.[94] Some corridors remained barely known. ("We have no English that are acquainted with the way towards Albany," admitted John Winthrop, Jr., in 1666, "but we thinke it were good some should know it." Decades later, John Pynchon was still relying on Native couriers in his communications with the place.[95]) Despite lingering uncertainties, though, colonists were nonetheless galloping off to their destinations with greater ease—and in greater numbers.[96]

Measuring travel is difficult. That English riders were traveling by land is plain to see. Letters and other records capture them, resting "at Nipnap" or turning back at Chickuppy. To discover the volume of such riders, however, is far trickier than simply detecting their presence. But suppose we consider one particular corridor—one main route. Would it then be easier to grasp the increase in English traffic along these paths? One of the northeast's central Indian arteries ran between Hartford and Boston. Later called the "Great Trail," this was the route that some had followed to settle the Connecticut towns in the mid-1630s. In 1645, John Winthrop, Jr., had tried it and gotten lost (he ran into trouble where it split with the "Bay Path" to Springfield). The path left Boston and hooked steadily southwest, finally depositing its travelers at the Windsor rapids on the Connecticut River.[97] The entire journey reached over one hundred miles, through a kind of "hollow" in middle New England, virtually all of which remained Indian territory.

English traffic along this route probably climbed slowly and steadily, from the time of Connecticut's founding. But until the late 1650s, few records point to much regular travel along its route. After midcentury, evidence suggests, more ordinary travelers took to the trail. In one of the first such scenes, in 1658, John Winthrop, Jr. himself voyaged over land from Boston to Hartford. From Sudbury, and then from "Neep-nett," he sent letters back toward Massachusetts Bay. (Recipient John Richards "rejoyced" at hearing, in the letters, about Winthrop's "soe farre, prosperous journey."[98]) Between New Haven, Hartford, and Boston, English correspondents began to consign their letters to passersby—a sure sign that travel along the Great Trail was becoming more commonplace. Writing to Massachusetts in the winter of 1659-1660, for instance, Lucy Winthrop sent a letter "by one David a Welshman who is gone directly through the woods." In 1660, New Haven's John Davenport quickly scribbled a letter to Hartford, after meeting a traveler bound that way. "[H]earing that one at the ordinary purposeth a journey towards the Baye, . . . who I suppose, will goe by Hartford," he sent a quick greeting. It was becoming easier to send news with ordinary passengers.[99]

English lodgings along this route, meanwhile, did not quite keep pace. With horses at the ready, sojourners were likely able to cover the route at a much quicker speed (about two or three days, it seems).[100] Yet they were still pressed to seek Indian hospitality. Traveling in 1657, Mrs. Winthrop planned to "ly in a Wiggwam both the nights."[101] Antipas Newman caught cold, when he "lay at Nipnap." By the late 1660s, demand for a place to stay had so outpaced English settlement that in 1668, Massachusetts Bay men recommended settling a town at Quansigamond Ponds (Worcester) precisely because it "willbe advantageous for travellers, it falling neere midway betweene Boston & Springfeild, and about a dayes journey from either."[102] To Englishmen much of this way remained "the woods," a still-wild place marked by swollen rivers and unfamiliar terrain. In winter, travel, here, ceased. It moved to the coast, as John Winthrop, Jr., wrote in 1668, "the upper way through the woods being almost impassable." But the stoppages were temporary. "Be pleasd with the first opening of the passage to Boston through the woods," Richard Nicolls requested, in 1667, "to put these few letters into one friends hand whose occasions shall draw him to breake the Ice first."[103] "Friends" would soon be going that way, Nicolls felt sure, and, moreover, they would be carrying his letters.

We will never be able to count precisely the number of travelers traversing this "Great Trail"—or any other—at a given moment. But the circumstantial case is a powerful one. In just the first five years of the 1670s, John Winthrop, Jr., sent nearly twice the amount of letters between Boston and Hartford that he had in the entire previous decade. All of these did not go over land; some surely went by sea. Yet, many others went with cattle drivers, ministers, traders, and other travelers who simply happened by. For anyone hoping to send letters, chance opportunities had taken a great leap forward.[104]

IV.

Hatfield's postal route struck directly through the heart of New England. From New York, he bent northward toward Hartford, his first stage. Here, he probably changed horses. (Lovelace expected Hatfield to "have a fresh one lie ledger" in Connecticut.) Then he would turn east, through Nipmuck country. This route, Lovelace imagined, would eventually become a "Post-Road." Along the way, Hatfield was to seek advice on "how to forme the best Post-Road" and, where necessary, to "marke some Trees that shall direct Passengers the best way." In the meantime, Lovelace implored John Winthrop, Jr., to enlist "some of the most able woodmen" to aid in the making of this road, "which in process of time would be the King's best highway."[105] There were, of course, well-trod routes already reaching through this very territory. One of them was the Great Trail.

There were still few English towns strung along this path. (What Hatfield would have seen, instead, were Pocumtuck or Nipmuck villages, a few of them "Praying Towns" of Christian Indians—thought it's not clear that these would have looked recognizably, or at all, different from other Native settlements.) But English towns were not the sole measure of command over this interior space. Roads could be that, too. Though it may seem a heavy burden to heap on Hatfield's hunched shoulders, Francis Lovelace understood completely what was at stake in sending the man off to find "the best and most facile way for a post."[106] It was no accident that Lovelace had begun to imagine roads—great, broad "Post-Roads," well-marked, and ridden by post riders who would happily assist "travailers." New Englanders began to show similar impulses. They thought consciously about facilitating travel between colonies, "the better to unite & strengthen the inland plantations."[107] It was not so much the settling of towns that first secured territory for the English, they understood; it was the opening of roads, inviting travel among colonial settlements. The horse ridden by the post, the growing numbers of travelers with whom he shared the route, Hatfield's very body—these things told of how the scene was changing. In each lived a message, broadcasting colonial power.

If Hatfield did "marke some Trees" along the route, he left no record. No account tells what he saw and did on that first journey, in winter 1673. But Hatfield can be glimpsed flitting through the letters he carried. From New York, he rode to Hartford—what Lovelace imagined would be the post's "first stage"—and, days later, arrived in Springfield. (Only because of Springfield's John Pynchon do we know Hatfield's name. "Recd yours per the Post Mr. Hatfeild," Pynchon wrote, after the postal courier brought John Winthrop, Jr.'s letters to town.[108]) Then, from Springfield onward to Boston. For at least the second half of his trek, Hatfield took guides. From Windsor to Springfield, he "had the Company hither of one of our Towne that was at Windsor," and then, departing Springfield for Boston, Pynchon reported, "he met with 2 men that were goeing to Boston." Weather may have necessitated the extra guidance. Heavy snows had blanketed pathways, leaving "noe track." "[B]eing 3 of them I hope they will doe well," he fretted.[109]

Hatfield did reach Boston. There, however, he seems to have met with a rather lukewarm reception. At least one recipient of letters, merchant John Richards, was unenthused. Although Hatfield had conveniently delivered letters directly to Richards' home, he had come at dusk, when "it was too darke to read," and then departed too quickly for Richards to address the contents of his mail. (Hatfield had made the error of failing to alert Richards to some pressing issue therein; "he said nothing of the matter," Richards sniffed, "so we parted.") A day later, Richards searched for Hatfield ("I went to his lodging & up & downe"), but never saw him again. The experience apparently soured him to the entire scheme. "As to the matter of encouraging the designe of Governr Lovelace for a constant Post from those p[ar]ts," Richards declared, he was skeptical. On prodding, he had discussed the post with Massachusetts Bay's deputy governor, who was also fairly uninterested. "[H]e thinks it will hardly be worth while," Richards reported dryly.[110]

At Boston, then, postal service met its first great obstacle: thudding indifference. This proved crippling, at least, if not fatal. After February, Hatfield slips out of view. If his postal deliveries continued—and they probably did, for a time—he nonetheless becomes impossible to track. In succeeding

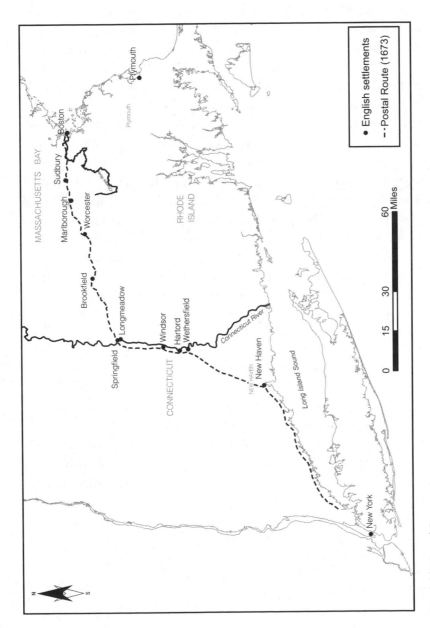

Hatfield's Postal Route, 1673

Legend:
- English settlements
- --Postal Route (1673)

Miles: 0 15 30 60

MASSACHUSETTS BAY

Plymouth

Boston
Sudbury
Marlborough
Worcester

Brookfield

Longmeadow
Springfield

Windsor
Hartford
Wethersfield

CONNECTICUT

RHODE ISLAND

Connecticut River

New Haven

New York

Long Island Sound

months, postal service connecting New York and its neighbors was likely not as regular as Lovelace would have liked. Still, some remained hopeful. In late February, John Winthrop, Jr., wrote cheerily to his son that "there wilbe now often oportunityes" to send, an apparent reference to the new post. But by June, the plan was in jeopardy, if still quite alive. That month, New York's Matthias Nicolls thanked Fitz-John Winthrop for his "kind Correspondence by our *intended* monthly Post"—the word 'intended,' here, perhaps betraying the post's recent irregularity.[111]

But if Bostonians saw little need for a New York post, Lovelace's scramble to establish one soon seemed terribly justified. In steamy July 1673, Lovelace was away visiting Hartford (perhaps, ironically, in hopes of bolstering the post), when disaster struck. Squinting through the summer haze, New Yorkers beheld an awful spectacle: a fleet of Dutch warships, lumbering toward Manhattan. After prowling up the Hudson, the vessels anchored in a "halfe moone" next to Fort James and promptly disgorged hundreds of Dutch soldiers into Manhattan. A "hot dispute" followed. Bursts of cannon fire unleashed thunderous reports that were "plentifully & amazeingly heard by all the Country," wrote one witness, miles away. (On his way back to New York from Hartford, Francis Lovelace must have stopped in his tracks, as the concussion of the "loud roaring Cannons voice" vibrated underfoot.)[112] Before long, Lovelace's worst fears were realized. New York fell, quickly. The island ground that had so recently opened up to swallow the withered, elderly body of Petrus Stuyvesant once again became Dutch soil. "[T]he .30. day of July being wensday," Thomas Minor scratched into his diary, with typical pith, "york was surrendered to the duch."[113]

Despite all the noise and furor, few died. Surrender came quickly. "[A]ll is done & over in one howrs time," went one estimate.[114] (Actually, it had been four hours.) Still traveling back from Hartford, Lovelace missed all of it. Only on reaching New Haven did he learn for certain what had happened. Under the circumstances, he could do little but complain. Particularly infuriating, he thought, were the Dutch invaders' depredations of his own personal chattel. On reaching New York, they had "breake-fasted on all my Sheepe and Cattell on Staten Island," he wrote bitterly.[115]

V.

So, it would seem, the post had failed. With the fall of New York, Lovelace's scheme was dead, obsolete. But that is not quite the end of the story. In the wake of the Dutch attack, hunger for news was rampant. Particularly in Connecticut, suddenly the uncomfortable neighbor of "New Orange" (what the Dutch now dubbed the former New York), many nervously sought "intelligence." Robert Treat, for one, could barely contain his curiosity. Treat had been escorting Lovelace in his "painfull and toilesome journey" homeward, when the sound of cannons shook the ground beneath their feet. After parting with the deflated governor, Treat rode furiously toward New York to "satisfie my longing appetite to heare further news." Eventually he bumped into a soldier who had been present at the siege. Having eagerly gobbled up the details—some of them fanciful, like the estimate that "3000" Dutchmen had stormed Manhattan—Treat then hastily penned a letter narrating the event to Governor Winthrop. On the overleaf, he scrawled a quick directive for the courier: "haste post haste," it read.[116]

Others also saw the wisdom in sending "post haste." New York's capture inspired several attempts to arrange postal service, particularly along the north shore of Long Island Sound. On learning of the city's plight, Rhode Island "Seteled a post" that would ride toward New London.[117] In Connecticut, meanwhile, some scrambled to establish more regular posts, aimed expressly at gathering news of Dutch actions. Fairfield's Nathan Gold, thinking it "exeding nessesary to settle a post from this Towne westward for Intelligence," mustered nearby constables for that very purpose. Gold's "Post messengers" rode daily between Eastchester and Fairfield. It was they who fetched Lovelace's crestfallen letter to John Winthrop, Jr., in which he groused that Dutch soldiers had feasted on his livestock. In that same letter, Lovelace endorsed Gold's postal service: "[Y]our Gent: have formed a post from Mr Richbels to you," he wrote. "[P]ray let it be continued for intelligence."[118]

These plans achieved mixed results. With the Dutch entrenched at New York, news soon slowed to a trickle. "[W]e have Continued the post ever Since [the attack]," Gold reported, days later, "but hath gayned Little Intellegence." Sending men westward, he was discovering, did little good. Twice, his posts had returned with "noe Letters" and "Little new Intellegence." (Even worse, the Dutch, who were in hot pursuit of Lovelace, had apparently realized precisely who might best be bullied into spilling such information. They had cleverly interrogated Mrs. Richbel, the wife of one of Gold's postmen, about "ware the Govr of yorke was.") Perhaps tiring of making futile journeys toward Manhattan, Gold's postal messenger informed him, rather bluntly, on August third, "that the passages of

Intellegence are Stopt." Still, if these frantic posts were temporary and largely unsuccessful, they nonetheless demonstrate that, by the time that New York fell, New Englanders had fully absorbed both the notion and the language of "posting." Like Robert Treat, Nathan Gold labeled his letters *"hast hast post hast for his maiesties Speciall Seruice."*[119] Accounts of the siege arrived at John Winthrop, Jr.'s doorstep carried by "a post sent expresse"; Winthrop, in turn, "sent post" to the governors of Massachusetts, Plymouth and Rhode Island. At Springfield, John Pynchon received an official letter from the Massachusetts Council "p[er] Post."[120] This was hardly the well-organized, orderly postal service imagined by Francis Lovelace. But it was, nevertheless, evidence that elite New Englanders had begun to warm to such a prospect.

In the meantime, New York did eventually revert to English control—though not through the efforts of New England's colonists. Despite their frenzied efforts to share information, the English colonies ultimately mounted virtually no challenge to the Dutch invasion. Instead, they spent much of the next year squabbling about what to do. This infighting kept the colonies from mustering any sort of organized military effort to expel the Dutch (though they engaged in plenty of posturing on paper). Only when the Third Anglo-Dutch War sputtered to an end, in February 1674, was New York restored to English rule. Without bloodshed, and merely as one of the terms of the Peace of Westminster, the States General simply agreed to give it back. Word of the agreement arrived in the colonies that spring, and in November 1674, Dutch leaders officially surrendered "New Orange" to its new governor, Sir Edmund Andros.[121]

What became of Francis Lovelace? On August 12, 1673, he limped back into the newly-Dutch Manhattan and was swiftly arrested. Later shipped back to England, disgraced, he eventually ended up in the Tower of London and was dead by 1675.[122] His dream of intercolonial postal service, needless to say, had been hobbled. Yet, in the long run, Francis Lovelace may have been more successful than he knew. Even Massachusetts well understood the worth of having posts at the ready, if not a "constant" post to New York. Acknowledging, in 1673 (almost at the precise moment in which Lovelace drew up his own postal plans, in fact), that the colony's "publick occasions . . . do frequently require that messengers be sent post," Massachusetts passed a law standardizing payment for men "travayling vpon the publicke service."[123] Connecticut followed suit in October 1674, with a law that painstakingly decreed how many shillings post riders were permitted to spend at ordinaries and "other places in the road."[124]

It is difficult to tell how well these laws stuck. But, in some ways, it does not matter. Lovelace's post failed, that is true. But there was already a steady march of hoofbeats through the wood. There were other travelers, driving cattle and carrying letters along the very trails through which Hatfield had ridden. That anonymous parade spoke just as loudly of English intentions. It did as much to broadcast English hegemony as any abstract law or deed. Surely this message was not lost on New England's Indians. For Indians, paths and byways had once connected people; they had now begun to contain them. But colonial travelers were about to meet a great and terrible obstacle, as paths through New England once again turned treacherous.

5

An Adder in the Path

Enter ye in at the strait gate:
for wide is the gate, and broad is the way,
that leadeth to destruction,
and many there be which go in thereat.
—Matthew 7:13

WILLIAM NAHAWTON HAD a very good reputation. He was known to
the English as "an ingenious person and pious man," as loyal to Massachusetts
Bay as his father, Nahawton, who had once carried the letter bearing news
of John Winthrop's death. He was a Christian and a preacher, the newly
appointed teacher at his father's Praying Town, Punkapoag. The English
used him as a messenger to unconverted Indians. Embracing Christianity
had not been easy, but he had done it, apparently, wholeheartedly. He had
sacrificed his own marriage to Christian ideals, when, in 1668, he accused
his wife Sarah of adultery. (She was sentenced to stand upon the Boston
gallows with a rope around her neck, and, according to local legend, later
took her own life.) "He is a promising young man, of a single and upright
heart," John Eliot gushed, in 1670. "He is studious and industrious, and
well accounted of among the English."[1]

When William Nahawton offered information, then, the English authorities listened. In the winter of 1674–1675, the bloated body of a Christian Indian named John Sassamon was discovered beneath the ice of
Assawompset Pond. Sassamon had just come from warning Plymouth's

leaders about impending attacks, being planned by the Wampanoags. When his corpse was discovered, the English concluded—partly because William Nahawton told them so—that Wampanoags had killed Sassamon to keep him quiet. (Nahawton claimed that he had heard about the murder from an eyewitness. Wampanoags protested that he had manufactured the story, because it "wold pleas the English so to think him a beter Christian.") Whether or not Sassamon was actually murdered is not clear. He might, as easily, have fallen through the fragile ice accidentally. But some of the Wampanoags were, in fact, planning a war. In June, Plymouth hanged three of them for Sassamon's murder. War came soon after.[2]

It began at Swansea. As dawn broke on the morning of June 21, 1675, a breathless post reached Governor Josiah Winslow's house. The news was grim: "phillip the Sachem and his men are now in action," the messenger informed him. With "drums beating," Wampanoags had begun harassing the English near Swansea, a marshy village in western Plymouth colony. This news probably came as no great surprise, since many a rumor had preceded it. On hearing it, Winslow promptly ordered seventy men to march toward the troubled town. He also penned a hasty letter to Massachusetts. It pled for help in keeping the Nipmucks and Narragansetts uninvolved and begged "a word of answer by the post." Winslow's message reached Boston by four o'clock that day.[3]

Meanwhile, the violence grew. Men were killed, houses robbed and burned. With Swansea aflame, news of the attack rippled outward. Letters, filled with fractured prose, document its spread: "Divers Inglish Cutt off at Swansy"; "A Considerable part of sea conk burned, and some killed"; a garrison house ablaze, "sivera men killed." Warnings went westward, perhaps tardily. A frantic letter dated 29 June traveled fifty miles southwest, to Thomas Stanton's trading post on the Pawcatuck River. "12 housis of Swanse are borened," announced its panicked script. Stanton forwarded the letter further west, and north, to Hartford. Only in early July did a certain account of the news finally reach Springfield: Indian war had begun.[4]

King Philip's War was the first and last war to engulf virtually the entire Indian and English northeast. For both sides, the war was tremendously destructive, though, in the long run, Algonquians suffered far worse than did the English.[5] When the violence began in June 1675, the stakes were not immediately clear. At first it seemed Plymouth's problem, a flaring of local tensions. It appeared to be a plot by Pokanokets, a group of Wampanoags seated just west of Swansea at Mount Hope. But in the cinders at Swansea lay the origins of a much larger conflict. With alarming speed, the war spread. By July Nipmucks were assailing Massachusetts towns. "There is cause to feare this Ind Plot is more Generall then we formerly expected," Edward Rawson gauged, in mid-July.[6] Over the next fourteen months, King Philip's War—so called for its supposed mastermind, Philip, sachem of the Pokanokets—would visit unthinkable suffering on the peoples of southern New England. Before the war turned in favor of the English, Indian attacks would all but push colonists back to the coasts.

Many things sent New England over the edge in 1675. King Philip's War has traditionally been related as a story about land, or, more pointedly, about the Native population's shrinking holdings thereof. Classic tellings find angry Indians rebelling against the crush of deeds wrung from various sachems in the years just prior to the war's outbreak (though, of course, nearly as soon as the war began, it proved a great many of those documents all but meaningless).[7] Many Native people were also angered by English missionaries' insistent spreading of the gospel. Philip, for one, was clearly dismayed by the diminishment of his own authority, as those who had once followed him increasingly embraced Christianity. By 1675 there were many Christian Indians in New England, canny characters like William Nahawton, who were all too eager to trade in information with Englishmen and seemed to be rewriting the rules of Native authority. Christian Indians, Philip himself complained, "wer in everi thing more mischivous, only disemblers." They wronged Native leaders "by ther lying." They became English, not Indian, subjects. That, in great part, was what the war was about. Colonists' increasingly voracious appetites for Indian land, the damages inflicted by wandering livestock, the campaign for Indian souls, the erosion of sachems' authority—all of these factors contributed.[8]

But one other important development directly preceded the war. In the years just before it, English travel shifted considerably. Where colonists had once been rigidly restricted to the region's waterways, they now moved confidently about the land. Interior trails had before served primarily Native voyagers. They now accommodated a new swell of English riders, drovers, oxen and carts. Horses were everywhere. Even as English traffic pounded through old trails, new roads were staked out. The early 1670s had even witnessed the faltering beginnings of a postal service, whose rider followed the route of one of the central Indian arteries between New York and

Boston. Englishmen, plainly, had begun to claim New England's travel routes as their own. That paths could be thought "English" is illustrated vividly in a passage from one of the war's most famous memorials. Captured and traveling with a party of Nipmuck Indians, Mary Rowlandson—goodwife of Lancaster, Massachusetts, and later, author of the widely read captivity narrative *The Soveraignty and Goodness of God*—nearly fainted at the mere sight of a byway that seemed, somehow, familiar. "[W]e came to an *English* path," she later wrote, "which so took with me, that I though I could have freely lyen down and died."[9]

But, of course, paths were only perceived as "*English.*" Proving that, for those who fought against the English, may have been part of the point. War presented a tremendous roadblock, as it were, in the swiftly advancing march of English towns, inns, couriers, and travelers. Before the war, colonists had been breeding horses, staking out roads, heedlessly riding about. This would stop. Communications crumpled, as inland routes became impassable. If roadlayers had been driving oxen through the woods between Boston and New York, they briskly abandoned their teams. Colonists who had been riding freely through these pathways suddenly encountered, as Cotton Mather later phrased it, an "adder in the path." (The phrase is lifted from Genesis 49:17, which declares that "Dan shall be a serpent by the way, an adder in the path, that biteth the horse heels, so that his rider shall fall backward.")[10]

To the historian's eye, the war is a confusion of motion: marches, pursuits, ambushes, and flights. Toward the end of it, Captain Daniel Henchman wrote that "all the Indians were in continual motion."[11] In fact he might have been describing any moment in the war. The entire episode witnessed "continual motion," among Indians and English alike. It plunged English soldiers into unfamiliar "boggy Woods," their "Eyes . . . muffled with the Leaves, and their Arms pinioned with the thick Boughs of the Trees," and sent others fleeing toward the safety of garrison houses and islands.[12] It likewise found Native people moving, pausing to camp and eat, fleeing English troopers, and tracking stray colonists. King Philip's War was not a war of battlefields. It was a war fought largely in New England's pathways. During the war those pathways became sites of terror, places where strong messages were delivered, or left, in blood. This was no accident. It was a measure of the recent English push to control New England's pathways and, consequently, the contested nature of traveled space.

I.

For Indians, the great shift of English travel onto land was not without consequences. Ballooning numbers of livestock did little good for New England's Native people.[13] Free ranging horses were heedless invaders of Indian cornfields. One need only note how much time Thomas Minor spent tracking down his own horses, which roamed freely in the woods north and east of town, to know how problematic this must have been. Those woods bordered Narragansett, and, early in his career as a horse owner, Thomas Minor knew the wrath of his Indian neighbors. In the spring of 1662, Minor took a bad journey into Narragansett, where he found Shumatucke's men both "deteyning" and "Ryding" his horses. When Minor demanded that Shumatucke surrender the stolen horses, the Indians volleyed "threatening speeches" at him. They even pledged to kill him. Minor devoted a good chunk of the diary, following this incident, to building a record of his efforts to recover the captive mares.[14]

Native animosity toward roaming livestock was not new. But there was something beyond the destruction of crops that may have angered Minor's Narragansett neighbors. Wandering horses not only ravaged Indian corn-fields. They also signaled English command of travel routes. Although horses' depredations of planting fields deeply angered Native people, it is possible, too, that Indians resented the traffic now rushing through Indian country.[15] Here and there are clues that Indians were losing patience. What Massachusetts considered "insolent dealing" by Shumatucke's men, for one thing, was more than just salty speech. The colony also pressed the Indians to stop "abusing any of our people in their travaile," whether by "throwing stones at them, robbing them, or seazing upon their horses & catle, & hiding them out of sight when demaunded."[16] A few years later, Englishmen complained again about the Narragansetts, after some of them killed "sundry horses." The Indians had also kept several men from going into the fields to mow and "assaulted others in the high way as they rode about."[17]

Indians admired horses greatly. As early as 1643, Roger Williams had noticed the Narragansetts' longing to own such animals. "Having no Horses," he wrote, "they covet them above all other Cattell." Riding, it seems, was more enticing than the milk and beef that other animals had to offer.[18] Decades later, some Native people did indeed own horses. Some even raised them. But there is little doubt that they also saw them as potent symbols of English colonialism. As if to drive home the point, the English jealously guarded their access to horses. New Haven decreed that "no horss" be sold to an Indian. Bay men could expect to pay a hefty fifty pounds for such an offense. And only by special license from Connecticut was Pequot sachem Robin Cassacinamon able, in 1673, to buy a horse.[19] So anxious was the New York government to keep horses out of Native hands that, in 1670, it ordered anyone who had previously sold horses to Indians to hastily "take them back againe."[20]

That was unlikely. But it is true, nonetheless, that even as Shumatucke's men got their jollies by "Ryding" Thomas Minor's horses, they surely sensed the ground quaking beneath them. For most of the century, Native people had controlled both knowledge and use of New England's travel routes. That was now changing. To a growing degree, Indian and English travelers began to share pathways. Mounted Englishmen rode the same trails used by Indian footmen. With horses came roads, and English roads often shadowed Indian paths. A 1669 plan for the "Highway" through Thomas Minor's own town is typical: Its course was to adhere "so near as may be" to the "old foot path." As it happened, the "old foot path" was the Pequot path. Passing various Indian landmarks, it ran "through the Indian field at Quaquataug," over Tetequack hill, and, finally, "to the wading place at Pawcatuck river above the Indian weare."[21] How Narragansetts, Pequots and other Native people felt about the growing numbers of Englishmen riding by their villages is hard to know. But by the late 1660s, it would have been an increasingly common sight.

This may seem an odd preface to war. But if we accept that King Philip's War emerged, most broadly, from Native frustration over colonial expansion, then we must consider carefully how "expansion" truly unfolded on the ground. For some of the region's Indians, the surest and most visible evidence of a soaring colonial presence did not manifest in the traditional trappings of colonization, such as towns, farms, and missions. It manifested, instead, in the pounding of horses' hooves through villages. The ruts cut by English carts along Indian trails; the building of bridges; the removal of stumps and stones necessary for road building. Historians of the American West are perhaps more accustomed to thinking in these terms: In the nineteenth century, Plains tribes quite clearly experienced American expansion as a thunderous parade of overland travelers, wagon trains and haphazard roads, and finally a transcontinental railroad that crudely sliced through the West's bison herds. The Sioux fought wars to stem the tide of hopefuls cutting through their territory along the Bozeman Trail. A similar pattern,

albeit on a smaller scale, unfolded in early New England. As they endeavored increasingly to hopscotch between colonies, colonial wayfarers pressed
habitually through Native space.[22]

What lay in the space through which much of this traffic churned was
Nipmuck country. "Deare Bro: We gott the last night in good time to
Concord," reported Wait Winthrop, mid-journey in 1663, "and now we are
going to take hors for Nipmong."[23] Nipmong. This was what lay in between.
This was the place through which the great paths struck. "There is a great
Countrey lying betweene *Conectacott* and the *Massachusets,* called Nipnet,"
John Eliot described, in 1651, "where there be many *Indians* dispersed."
These many Indians—these were the people with whom English travelers
lodged. These were the people whom they met, along the "*Connecticot*
Road."[24] Could they have failed to notice how many more were coming?

   "Nipmuck country" appears on early maps as a great, sprawling space in
middle New England. To those who knew it, it was a place of rolling green
hills and great pine stands, hundreds of square miles etched and creased by
plunging river valleys. The Native people who lived there were defined by
those waterways: "Nipmuck" meant "people of fresh waters." They were not
as cohesive as some other Native groups in New England. They are better
understood as a collection of loosely confederated bands, bound by geography and kinship. Their towns were widely "dispersed," as Eliot described,
clustered mostly at the edges of great lakes and old paths and tucked into
the hooks of riverbeds. In the early 1670s the Nipmucks probably did not
seem particularly threatening to English colonists. They were not seen as a
great Indian power. At least some of their bands had long been tributary
to the Narragansetts. In 1668, partly, perhaps, in hopes of casting off that
yoke, several Nipmuck sachems had submitted to the authority of Massachusetts Bay.[25]

   But when war began, Nipmucks joined almost immediately. Nipmuck
warriors were among the first, as William Hubbard so memorably phrased
it, to "*Philippize.*" Their motivations, however, have always been somewhat
mysterious. Classic explanations for Native war making—"economic, political, and cultural pressures," as historian Neal Salisbury puts it—do not
apply quite as well to the Nipmuck case. By all accounts, Nipmuck country
had not felt the brunt of colonial pressure in the same fashion as had the

Pokanokets and Narragansetts. English towns in Nipmuck territory (Sudbury, Lancaster, Marlborough, Brookfield, Mendon, and finally, Worcester)— were few and small, comprised mainly of "large numbers of nonresident shareholders." Even John Eliot's missionary work was comparatively paltry, amongst Nipmucks. In other words, as one scholar has concluded, "there was no rising tide of English expansion in the Nipmuck Country."[26] That is true, if you conceive of English "expansion" as towns, fences, and farms. But there were other developments that amounted to unmistakable new signals of colonial power.

Several major paths ran through Nipmuck country. Probably most important was what English colonists called the "Connecticut Path," the great trail that tethered Massachusetts Bay to the Connecticut River. Even in 1675 there was relatively little English settlement along this route. After it left Cambridge and ran along the Charles River for a while, its outermost colonial plots lay at the extreme southerly reaches of Sudbury (in what is now Framingham, Massachusetts), about twenty miles away. (It meanders through early Framingham town records: In 1655, Edmund Rice requested land "near the path leading to Connecticut" and soon after settled just south of "Conecticott path." About the same time, Richard Russell was granted land "in the wilderness, upon both sides of the path that leadeth from Sudbury toward Nipnop.") Beyond Sudbury the path moved into Nipmuck territory and arced toward various important Native settlements—Magunkaquog (also identified in English records as lying "neere unto the roade which leadeth from Sudbury unto Conecticot"), Hassanamesit, Chabanakongkomun. Only upon approaching Hartford, ninety miles beyond Sudbury, did an English townscape once again come into view.[27]

But by 1675, nevertheless, the English had a clear presence on this path. In recent years the Reverend John Eliot, following the Connecticut path, had been pressing Nipmucks to choose Christianity. (In a 1674 tour of Nipmuck villages, Eliot intimated that those who chose Christianity were more likely to see their land holdings protected by Massachusetts, thus implying that those who rejected Christianity might, by contrast, lose land). Many of the villages he had recently convinced to try Christianity—the so-called "new" Praying Towns—lay right along its route. But Eliot was by no means the only Englishman using the Connecticut path. It had come into heavy use by colonists. In the first five years of the 1670s, John Winthrop, Jr., alone, sent nearly two hundred letters from Hartford to Massachusetts Bay.

If that is suggestive of how many people were traveling this route regularly, then the Nipmucks must have played hosts to incalculable new numbers of Englishmen. By the time Francis Lovelace's post-master passed through Nipmuck in 1673, English traffic along this route was climbing steadily.[28]

But the English were not simply traveling more often along established Native routes. They were also building new roads. What Francis Lovelace may not have known, as he pushed Hatfield to discover the "best" way through New England, was that the routes through Nipmuck were shifting even as he wrote. In fact, by the 1670s, a new roadway had opened, arching directly through the space traveled by Hatfield. The new route ran from Massachusetts Bay through Marlborough and the newly-planted Brookfield toward, finally, Springfield. Piecing together its adoption is difficult, but English records reflect its usage by the early years of the 1670s. Writing in 1671, John Eliot described the Nipmucks as a people "well known to the *English* so long as the *Connecticot* Road lay that way," hinting that patterns of travel had recently shifted.[29] Three years later, in 1674, Daniel Gookin mentioned that Hassanamesitt, a Praying Town, lay "near unto *the old road way* to Connecticut." Packachoog, on the other hand, was not far off "the *new* road way that leadeth from Boston to Connecticut."[30] The United Colonies had discussed making an intercolonial road through Nipmuck country as early as the 1640s and 1650s, but it was only in winter 1674—just a few months before King Philip's War erupted—that a road was actually cut and cleared.[31]

To make an English road was no small thing. Colonists used the term "road" to refer to any route from place to place, as modern English speakers do, but it also carried some connotations of *making:* a way that had been constructed, shaped, even staked out purposefully. The word "road" seems to have evolved in English out of terms related to *riding,* and probably always "applied to the track ridden on." But it could also have emerged "from the verb 'to rid,' the track having been cleared of obstacles."[32] Clearing of obstacles was the major work involved in colonial road making. That meant felling trees and uprooting stumps. Then, the roadbed would be smoothed over and some fill or brush put down "in marshy places." (In England, the road's surface might be rounded, flanked with drainage ditches, even shored up with broken stones. Some parishes also kept special plows for turning over the road's surface each year, after it had become "rutted and distorted.") In the colonies, it is safe to say, most roads were

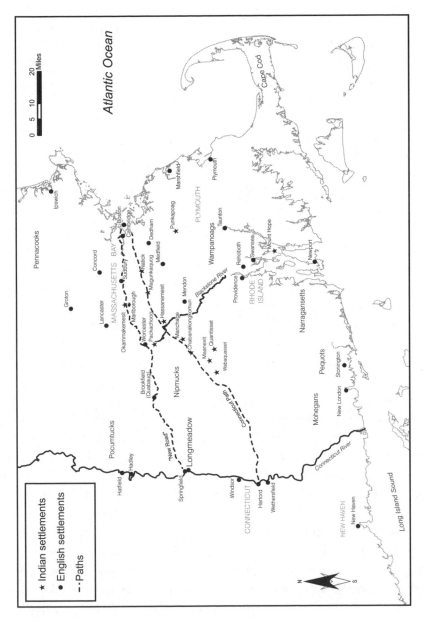

Southern New England, ca. 1675

simply made of "beaten earth."[33] Oxen did the hard work of pulling up stumps and boulders, then hauling them away in carts.[34]

This was arduous work, and it altered the landscape significantly. Because they were generally quite wide, English roads chewed through thousands of acres of forest. Most roads, like the road running from Watertown to Concord, or that from Concord to Lancaster, were four to six rods wide. But some were as wide as ten. (A rod being equivalent to sixteen and a half feet, colonial roads thus ranged regularly from 99 to 165 feet wide.) This great width was chiefly to provide room for animals to be driven to market. Roadways, ideally, were light and open, wide enough for grazing and even for stopping overnight. Mercifully, though, at least in the case of the highways crossing Watertown, Massachusetts, a few roadside trees were blazed with a "W" to remind townsmen not to fell them: For travelers, they provided much-needed shade.[35]

Roads were not all. To carry roads over water, bridges were constructed. In 1666, John Pynchon was sufficiently desperate for a bridge ("so useful and necessary a thing for travellers") to be built over Quabaug River that he was willing to contribute money personally. To name just a few others: In 1668, Mendon built a bridge in the way to Medfield "for the public good and care of traivelers," and in spring 1674, Samuel How built a bridge across the Sudbury River, on the new road through Nipmuck. He was even allowed to "take toll of all travellers."[36] Bridges do not seem terribly offensive. In fact they probably eased travel for many an Indian, as well as Englishmen. But they were also great monuments to the English takeover of the landscape, and they reached cumbersomely across the very rivers that defined Nipmuck country. (Mills, too, may have been provocative for this reason. In the first Nipmuck attack on an English town, Mendon's mill—squatting bulkily on a stream flowing into the Blackstone River—was burned.)

Consider, then, the scene in Nipmuck country on the eve of King Philip's War. For Nipmucks, changes in the landscape were unfolding terribly rapidly: roads, bridges, horses, carts, and markings on trees. Though it is difficult to tell how Native people read the changes converging on them, it is worth reconstructing something of what they saw. They glimpsed countless riders, heard hoofbeats come and go. They saw carts lurching toward Boston, even an official postman. They saw new roads plotted and cut, including a great road forged right through the heart of Nipmuck. Although few English towns had yet been planted in Nipmuck country, the growing colonial

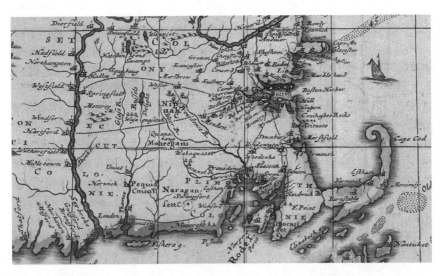

By the 1670s, roads were well enough established through interior New England that English maps began to include them. This one, by Richard Daniel, shows two routes reaching west from Boston, through Nipmuck country. Others swing southward from Massachusetts Bay. Richard Daniel, "A Map of ye English Empire in the Continent of America" (detail), ca. 1679. *(Courtesy of the John Carter Brown Library at Brown University)*

presence was unmistakable. Even where English towns had not sprouted, English traffic had appeared. As much as fenced pasture and plowed ground, this surely signaled the English push to control the landscape.

Although shaped humbly by animal feet and anonymous townsmen, these roads were, in some senses, imperial. Even to Englishmen, they were important symbols. The first maps of New England to portray roads appeared about the time of King Philip's War; in fact, they are nearly coincident with it. The earliest map of the region to include roadways, Richard Daniel's *A Map of ye English Empire in the continent of America,* dates to 1679. (In it, two roads reach westward from Boston, while a coastal route through New England hugs Narragansett Bay and another dips south, through Plymouth.) New England's roads appeared even more plainly, a few years later, in Philip Lea's *A new map of New England. New York. New Jarsey. Pensilvania. Maryland. and Virginia* (1685), their dotted lines disobediently stretching across all the rivers of Nipmuck country. The men who created these maps were not in New England. They were in London. But the timing is not accidental.

Roads, as well as the prominently labeled "Nipnak Country," also appear in this map: Philip Lea, "A New Map of New England. New York. New Jarsey. Pensilvania. Maryland. and Virginia" (detail), 1685. *(Courtesy of the John Carter Brown Library at Brown University)*

All of the maps show "Nipnak country," labeled plainly, at the center of the region. But they are pale reflections of Nipmuck people's intimate ties to this landscape. Nipmucks, of course, knew it to be theirs. Each brook and stream, each trail and crook of a river were familiar, even sacred. "The *Natives* are very exact and punctuall in the bounds of their Lands," Roger Williams once declared, "belonging to this or that Prince or People, (even to a River, Brooke) &c." By the 1670s Nipmuck people had sold some plots of their land to English colonists, and they probably had few illusions about what that meant.[37] But English roads and traffic were arguably more noticeable, even disruptive, because they reached brazenly beyond the small clusters of English settlement in Nipmuck country. Like the five-rod road between Concord and Lancaster, they ran boundlessly "beyond all the lots into the woods."[38] The very face of Nipmuck country, in other words, was changing. Some may have felt that it was being disfigured, even profaned.

Clues to how the Nipmucks were experiencing these signals reside in the tale of a murder that happened somewhere in Nipmuck country, four years before war began. In April 1671, the body of Zachary Smith turned up in the road outside of Dedham. Smith, a Watertown man, had been making his way southward to evade a fornication charge. He met a far worse fate. "[T]ravailing neer Dedham," he was suddenly and inexplicably gunned down—"shott through the body," went an early report. "It is vehemently suspected," the writer added, "to be by Indeans." Although the early proof that Smith's murderers were Native was tenuous (three Indians had been "seen to pass that way about an hour after him, one haveing a gun"), a suspect quickly emerged.[39]

Suspicion fell on Ascooke, a Native man who had been working at Roxbury and had "gone from his Master two days before the murder was committed." The reasons to suspect Ascooke were many. Firstly, he had been spotted fitting "a slug for his gun" shortly before the murder. Too, an Indian man fitting his description (wearing a "shirt & blew wastcote [waist-coat] & red Indian coat") had been "seen to Pass either before or after the man that was murthered within a few miles of him." But the smoking gun, so to speak, was a comment that Ascooke himself had made. At Roxbury, he had been overheard saying "how easy it was to shoote an Englishman alone in the road, if they had no one with them."[40] That remark betrays an important dimension of the coming war. Ascooke was a Nipmuck man, and in 1671 a slow and steady parade of colonists was invading his country, their clunky carts and cattle in tow. In some small way, he stood as an "adder" in their path. (One wonders whether Cotton Mather had this murder in mind, in fact, when he chose that metaphor: "Ascooke," or *Askùg*, to Algonquians, meant "snake.")[41] John Pynchon, on hearing what Ascooke had said, pushed to quash such impulses among Indians. Swift punishment was necessary, he wrote, to "prvent secret murthers of the English in their Travells."[42]

Punishment came indeed, when Ascooke was eventually executed. So that none would forget, his head was "fastened to a Pole, at one End of the Gallows," in Boston. But if English authorities had hoped to "prvent secret murthers" by punishing Ascooke, they instead reaped many, many more. There was one person, far removed from town, who never forgot about this incident. The very first attack on a Massachusetts town during King Philip's War happened four years later, in July 1675. It fell on Mendon, a remote little town roosting comfortably in the bright sunny hills of the Blackstone River valley. Mendon was the outermost English town on a relatively new road, the same road, in fact, upon which Zachary Smith's corpse had been found. The Nipmuck man who led the attack, a man who William Hubbard later called an "old malicious Villian," did not live nearby. His name was Matoonas. He also happened to be Ascooke's father.[43]

Matoonas is no longer famous. No history of King Philip's War begins by sketching his character. But if there were a face of the Nipmuck war, it might be his. It was he who, with the killings at Mendon, widened the war. He invited it into Nipmuck country, into Massachusetts, and then spread it to other English towns, too. (James Quanapohit, a Christian Indian spy, saw Matoonas "take the lead in the war dances" among Nipmucks.) His English contemporaries hated him bitterly for it. It was a measure of his renown as "the principal Ringleader" among Nipmucks that, at the end of the war, one of his compatriots sought to make amends with the English by offering up the person of Matoonas, captured and bound.[44]

Matoonas had watched closely the recent intrusions into Nipmuck country. He had a good vantage: He lived, at Packachoog, very nearby the "new road." He knew plenty of Englishmen. He had flirted with Christianity (though he later revealed himself, William Hubbard wrote acridly, to have "no Part nor Portion" in it). He knew Ephraim Curtis, whose trading house at Quansigamond, the tiny bunch of English shacks near Packachoog, lay on the same road. He robbed it. Then, in mid-July 1675, he left Packachoog, followed the jagged southeasterly course of the Blackstone River, picked up the English road that headed toward Dedham, and found Mendon. He burned it. Weeks later, he hugged the course of the new road leading west from Packachoog and did the same to Brookfield. Nipmuck attacks did not fall randomly. They moved through English settlements like flames burning down on candles, along the wicks of colonial roads.[45]

It isn't that English roads caused King Philip's War. It isn't that horses did. But the flow of people moving through Nipmuck country, and other Native places, was but one more signifier of English intent. Were these changes somehow leading, contributing, to what would happen next? Did the turning of Indian landscapes and footpaths into English "thorough-fares" help to precipitate war? Answers to those questions must remain, to some degree, elusive. But what is perfectly clear, nonetheless, is that King Philip's War was fought in such terms. It was a war of roads, posts, horses, woods, footprints, and ambushes. It unfolded, largely, along the very travel routes that the English had begun to think of as their own. It offered a bloody lesson, too, in how ephemeral that ownership had been.

II.

King Philip's War thoroughly interrupted English travel. In colonial accounts of the war, stopped passages and precarious journeys are ever-present themes. Imposed immobility became a kind of favorite leitmotif to which English writers continually returned. The pattern began early. When rumors of the Indian war reached Springfield, John Pynchon's first thought—before the violence had even spread beyond Plymouth—was that it "possibly may obstruct traveling to the Bay by land." Meanwhile, a Narragansett sachem warned nearby "English to take heed of remaining in Lone-out places & of travelling in the Common roade."[46] Early histories cast the war's origins with imperiled travelers. One reported that on June 20th, Philip's men had seized "a *Swansey* man, travelling from *Road Island,* through the land, and kept him prisoner," though they eventually released him unharmed. Days later, with Swansea's residents hunkered in garrisons, the "Indians shot at several men travelling through *Rehoboth*" and "killed six men, going with a Cart." Slain next were two others "that were travelling for a Chyrurgeon. Thus war began."[47]

Early in the war, nonetheless, plenty traveled safely. When John Pynchon griped that Massachusetts had been too slow in sending him news of Plymouth's plight, Edward Rawson simply replied that haste had not been necessary; after all, travelers had passed comfortably toward Springfield. "[W]e herd by Intelligence of Travelers that the danger was not much in yor p[ar]ts," he wrote defensively.[48] In fact, reported John Winthrop, Jr., "they have had no trouble there, [and] several have passed that way to & againe & are dayly passing." Not content to leave it at that, Winthrop decided for good measure to name these untroubled pilgrims. "Capt: Lewis Ens: Steele & Mr Wadsworth of Farmton & others came last weeke and severall of wethersfeild & goodma Catlin & his wife & divers others came this weeke, & Ed: Messinger is gone this weeke alone wth cattle & yesterday Jonatha Bull went hence towards Boston," he wrote exhaustively, barely stopping to lift his pen.[49] One wonders: Could any who read such a litany of proof have taken comfort in it? Did Winthrop himself?

People traveled. Things changed profoundly for the worse, however, when the Nipmucks stirred toward war. In August, Brookfield was attacked. Ten "English travelers coming from the Bay" found the town under siege and wisely "returned back forthwith to Boston." Marooned miles beyond

Brookfield, in Springfield, John Pynchon could only hope that they would summon "relief."[50] (They did. A soldier stranded at Brookfield during the attacks later confirmed that "some who were going to Connecticut" had quickly turned heel and, later, "sent a post" alerting nearby Major Willard.[51])

As these stories circulated, meanwhile, traffic thinned along inland routes. Many colonists retreated to the waterways, as they were inclined to do during dangerous times. Despite his earlier outpouring of optimism ("Ed: Messinger is gone this weeke alone wth cattle . . ."), even John Winthrop, Jr., soon fled, "by water," to safer ground. (Richard Smith learned that the Connecticut governor had "goone by water to Boston" when a party of men, driving Winthrop's horses toward Massachusetts, passed his trading house in Narragansett.) Rhode Island saw a mass exodus to Aquidneck. "[T]he pepel heare are gon and going of[f] towods [the] Island," Henry Stephens wrote, in late June. When Stonington passed that news along to Connecticut authorities, townsmen noted that a boat was "Come in to pawcatuck River to fetch Away people and there pvitions to Road Island." In the meantime, the colony arranged for patrols to sweep the inlets about Mount Hope.[52]

Winthrop's hasty departure from Hartford may have been prompted by an incident in which Indians shot at a man "travelling between Hartford and Simsbury."[53] As such incidents made plain the hazards of traveling, some English took measures to keep passengers safe. Connecticut colony, for instance, moved to protect any "English who may be traveling up and down upon their necessary occasions" from the sorts of "enemies that have done hurt by suddain shooting at such travilours unawares." Any armed Indians seen travelling without English company, and failing to identify themselves, Connecticut decreed, might be lawfully shot and killed. "Guards are kept Every day between Town & Towne for the safety of passengers," John Allyn averred to a correspondent, in late September. With these steps, colonial leaders hoped to check the "danger to travelours upon the road betweene towne and towne." Tellingly, however, they also canceled September court at New London, because "it is dangerous to pass upon the roads."[54]

The danger, of course, lay in the very fact that New England's roads were so terribly "Common," after all. So many of them were Indian pathways, lately adopted by English passengers who had gleefully clogged them with carts and beasts of burden. That the English used these as "common roads" was what made them so vulnerable to Native attackers, perched by the wayside and primed to "set on travellors."[55] When English men and women met with violence on the road, it was seldom random. More often, they fell victim to well-orchestrated attacks—ambushes. Natives proved frightfully adept at planning these.[56] Time and again, colonists found themselves surprised and helpless, "the common Road being waylaid with Indians on every Side."[57] English soldiers eventually learned to take evasive measures, such as "avoiding any thick woods" and "riding in open places," in order to avoid being surprised. One captain was happily saved, Daniel Gookin later described, when "his guides conducted him a private way." He was lucky: The enemy had, indeed, been waiting "in ambushment for him on the common road."[58]

But ambushes proved difficult to avoid. Indians learned that colonists tended to travel in clumps, making themselves easy targets. Large groups were the most vulnerable. Although accompanied by English troopers, a party bound for church at Longmeadow in March 1676 drew gunfire. A "Party of *Indians* lying in the Bushes as they rode along" fired upon those riding in the rear, killing two and seizing several others. When those riding ahead realized what was happening, they did not turn back to help the stragglers. They were too petrified to ride back through the "winding Road," which twisted for several miles through "a woody Place."[59] There was reason to be nervous about "woody places." Native informants suggested that Philip's men had waited to make war until "the woods were grown thick with green trees." With war finally underway, Native combatants even adorned themselves with branches and leaves, for concealment. Some dressed, wrote Daniel Gookin, "from the waist upwards with green boughs, that our Englishmen could not readily discern them, or distinguish them from the natural bushes; this manner of fighting our men had little experience of, and hence were under great disadvantages."[60] With these great disadvantages painfully apparent through the summer of 1675, Englishmen impatiently awaited winter. "[T]he Leaves that ar now greene I hope will bee drye Ear Long," wrote one, "& the Snow will discover the footing of Indians tho thaye travell."[61]

In writing about the war, some may have overstated the dangers. Daniel Gookin, for one, was interested in celebrating the role of "friendly" Indians during the war, and thus Native enemies became, in his rendering, almost supernaturally gifted warriors—warriors whose affinity with nature could only be combated by other Indians, acting as scouts and guides. Like John Winthrop subjecting Connecticut migrants to horrendous travails, Gookin sometimes meted out literary justice against his adversaries by "killing" them in their travels. A Watertown man foolish enough to make comments of which Gookin disapproved, for instance, met a watery death soon after: "Within a quarter of an hour after these words were spoken," Gookin wrote, with faint satisfaction, "this man was drowned passing the ferry between Charlestown and Boston; the ferry-boat being loaded with horses, and the wind high, the boat sunk; and though there were several other men in the boat and several horses, yet all escaped with life, but this man only."[62]

But if English accounts dwelled disproportionately on the terror of Indian "ambuscadoes," they had good reason. To be sure, many journeys unfolded uneventfully. Yet even those who avoided meeting a violent death, while on the road, risked encountering the gruesome remains of those who had. To modern readers, the word "road" suggests a conduit—a route followed, a way from one place to another. *Roads* are neither here nor there; instead, they simply connect. They merely cross the space between one's starting place and one's destination. English men and women themselves often thought this way (which may be why, in English tradition, suicides were sometimes buried, unceremoniously, at cross roads). But during King Philip's War in 1675–1676, New England's passageways became some of the central sites of warfare. Although it is difficult to tell precisely where some of the most famous attacks occurred, one thing is often very clear: they happened "upon the road."[63] Roads and paths embodied the danger of ambush. And in the wake of an attack, roads also provided Algonquians with opportune places to leave messages of horror. If left deep in a wood, or back from the path, such displays might never be seen. So, instead, disembodied heads and hands ghoulishly greeted English passengers "by the wayside," where they were sure to be encountered.

Englishmen first encountered such a sight just outside of Swansea, at the outset of the war. Riding into town, Massachusetts men came upon "some Heads, Scalps, and Hands cut off from the Bodies of some of the English, and stuck upon Poles near the Highway." Though clearly meant to stoke English fears, the mutilated corpses also presented a mocking invitation: *make war with us.*[64] The English were well able to read such grisly declarations, not least because they themselves had often used similar tactics. (Once war had subsided, the English victory was evinced in a gruesome display on Plymouth common: The disembodied head of Philip himself was planted on a post for all to see.[65]) Outside of Swansea, meantime, soldiers gingerly pulled the gnarled body parts off of their poles and somberly buried them.

The English worked ardently to bury such things. But, throughout the war, a crop of blackened heads and hands continued to sprout by the roadside like so many ghastly weeds. After ambushing a company of English soldiers near Squakheag, Indians again broadcast their might by "cutting off the Heads of some of the Slain, and fixing them upon Poles near the Highway." Here, as elsewhere, the scene achieved its desired effect: English soldiers, coming upon the display, "were much daunted to see the heads of Captain *Beers's* Souldiers upon Poles by the way side."[66] Other bodies also surfaced "by the way side," mute messengers forced to declare Algonquian intent posthumously and against their will. At Groton, in March 1676, two carts were ambushed as their owners frantically attempted to gather hay. One of the men was "slain, strip'd naked, his Body mangled," and finally "laid on his Back in a most shameful Manner." Shame, of course, is nothing if not public—thus the man's body was pointedly "dragged into the Highway," for all to see.[67]

Not all of the messages that Algonquians left, "by the way," came in bodily form. Some were fashioned from paper and ink. By 1675, some Indians, especially those who had undergone Christian tutelage, could write. Some few scraps of what they wrote, in fact, have survived. Almost all of them were written amidst Massachusetts Bay's attempts to redeem Mary Rowlandson, the wife of a Lancaster minister, from her Nipmuck and Narragansett captors. In April 1676, the colony sent Tom Nepanet, a Christian Native, into Nipmuck country with a letter opening negotiations for English captives. It also sent pen, paper, and ink, for a return. The answer, penned by "Peter Jethro Scribe" and signed by several men, made no effort to negotiate. "[Y]ou know, and we know," it read, in part, "you have great sorroful with crying; for you lost many, many hundred men, and all your house, all your land, and woman, child, and cattle." But a second ransom letter, written by James Printer, a literate Nipmuck who had spent years apprenticed to Samuel Green at the Cambridge press, was less cocky. "I am sorrow that I have don much wrong to you," it read, "and yet I say the falte is lay upon you."[68]

One piece of writing said, explicitly, what was meant by those other wordless wayside messages. In late February 1676, Nipmucks attacked Medfield. The town burning, one among them left a note, in English:

Thou English man hath provoked us to anger & wrath & we care not though we have war with you this 21 years for there are many of us 300 of which hath fought with you at this town[.] we hauve nothing but our lives to loose but thou hast many fair houses cattell & much good things.

As much as those English corpses left pointedly behind, this aimed to terrify. It was the proclamation of an endless will to assault colonists' "fair houses" and "cattell" and other "good things," as well as their bodies. Like many bodies, it appeared where it would be found quickly and easily: The note was left "stuck up in a cleft of one of the bridge posts," just outside of town. It was soon discovered by an English trooper.[69]

III.

The Reverend John Russell was restless. At Hadley, Englishmen were penned, like animals. "They hinder us from goeing fforth for wood," he moaned, and "ffrom goeing to mill two or three miles out of Towne," and even "ffrom seeking our Chattle . . . in the woods." By confining colonists to their various safe houses and hampering their movements, Russell wrote, Algonquians effectively kept the English "from interCours one with another." In other words, they could not communicate. There was no news, no letters, and no way to send for help.[70] At first blush, Russell's complaint seems utterly obvious. With travel so disrupted, opportunities to send messages with passersby all but collapsed. Gone were the days when the aptly named Edward Messenger—John Winthrop's carefree exemplar—had felt fine traveling through Nipmuck "alone with cattle." The war, in short, crippled communications.

Evidence of the war's heavy toll on English exchange is not difficult to find. "Sending is Soe enterupted by the war," wrote William Harris in August 1676, "that there is noe safe Sending nor pasing to & fro (without danger of life)." (Harris knew this personally: He had lost his own "deer son" in the war, when "Indians lay in waite . . . by the way and kild him.")[71] Blocked messengers and miscarried news frustrated colonists everywhere. John Leverett apologized for the tardiness of a post that failed when "the Messengers were obs[truc?]ted in theire passage by the Ind[ians] about Quabaugh."[72] Urgent posts from Brookfield were forced to fire upon enemies, to turn back twice, even to "creep on . . . hands and knees" to escape detection.[73] Even the most pressing letters returned to their senders. Some learned to avoid sending along particularly violent routes, or simply gave up trying to send at all. Rather than send through Nipmuck territory, for instance, John Pynchon sent letters from Springfield to Boston by way of Hartford. But he was also forever discouraged. "[W]ays here being obstructed," he wrote gloomily, "we cannot send to the Bay."[74]

Algonquians may have aimed actively to cut off English communications. At the beginning of the war, for instance, Philip's men seemed to target those who were positioned to give warnings or aid. On the outskirts of Swansea, an "English Sentinel was shot in the face." The Pawtucket ferryman was wounded. When Massachusetts sent soldiers toward the beleaguered town, Indians shot the guide who had been leading them "in their way to *Philips* Country." This last measure was particularly well calculated. Without a pilot, after all, the militia would be hopelessly slowed in its march toward Mount Hope. Not coincidentally, by the time the English arrived, Philip was no longer there. He and others had indeed bent for "the InLands," as Roger Williams had predicted.[75]

Trapped in a garrison house at Brookfield, Thomas Wheeler was convinced that the Nipmucks "waited to prevent our sending if they could have hindered it." The Indians were also bent on blocking incoming aid or information. They arranged "sentinels, (some nearer and some further off)," described Wheeler, "the furtherest about two miles from us, who if they saw any coming from the Bay they might give notice by an alarm." (This, too, was a measure enacted elsewhere: At Springfield, that October, raiding Indians fled before John Pynchon's English forces arrived when sentinels "signifyed their sence of his approch by their hoops or watchwords.") At Brookfield, Nipmuck sentinels identified the passages through which English aid would need to arrive and guarded them. Some encamped at an abandoned house, "by which if any help came from the said Bay, they must pass, and so they intended (as we conceive) . . . to cut them off."[76]

This strategy extended to destroying English means and modes of travel. Lest any Englishman should attempt a mounted escape from Brookfield, Wheeler noted, the Natives also "either killed or drove away almost all the horses of our company." Elsewhere, bridges burned or were pulled apart. Over the winter of 1675–1676, an Indian informant warned English authorities of planned attacks at Lancaster, Marlborough, and Groton, where "they intend first to cut of Lancaster bridge & then say they there can no releef come to them from Boston nor the people cannot escape." When the attacks came in February, this tactic was apparently tried, as anticipated: Those going to relieve Lancaster came to "a Bridg, [which] they gat over safe, though the Planks were pulled off by the Enemy." Retreating Nipmucks also burned a bridge at Medfield, so as not to be pursued.[77]

Indians also beset those carrying supplies to wandering English armies. The most famous such incident occurred in September 1675, when Captain Thomas Lathrop left Hadley to replenish English forces near Deerfield. Lathrop took with him "about eighty men to gaurd several Carts laden with Corn, and other Goods." They marched directly into an ambush. Almost all died, prompting William Hubbard to proclaim September 18, the day of the march, "that most fatal Day, the Saddest that ever befel *New-England*."[78] Whenever possible, reinforcements were sent by sea, but this was slow. Stranded soldiers were sometimes pressed to find reserves of patience, as supply boats and land-borne goods were equally delayed. "Our wounded men are greatly distressed for want of medicines," John Russell wrote in agitation to Massachusetts Bay, in October 1675. "Those by sea not yet come at us: those Expected by Capt: Waite last at Roxbury."[79]

Couriers may have attracted special, and strategic, punishment. At best, they might simply be stopped. "Yesterday sending post to Brookfield they were obstructed by 15 or 16 Indians . . . who endeavored to get the way of our messengers," John Pynchon once recounted. "I am in straits on every side what to do."[80] But posts sometimes met worse fates. "[W]ee Can here of none of our people that went to the bay from hence," Stonington townsmen wrote, early in the war, "but are informed that [the Indians] way Lay all Roade paths and Kill all posts or any that may Cary intelligence." Indeed, two posts sent "for Ayd" by Plymouth had disappeared ("there horses are found, but noe men"). By one account, the men were dead, "and Letters found with them."[81]

IV.

Not a few pens were stilled by this war. Still, many persisted in begging and praying for whatever tidings could be had. In letter upon letter, colonists clamored for news. They complained when there was none. They grumbled, too, about the quality of information, often little more than rumors and "flying reports." They lamented the "many Lame reports & blinde relations" concerning wartime events.[82] Not all wished for war-related news. Some longed painfully for word of their own families. Near the war's beginning,

Joseph Eliot had left his wife "ill in the Bay," and by August 1675 had still "not gained a word of intelligence from her, or about her, since." Now he hoped that some late-coming "travailers" might have gleaned "the least intimation" of her condition, though he was well aware that news was hard to come by. "[H]ard it is to gain any," he added, "in the sad interruption of passage."[83]

Such pleas were not always met with ominous silence. Much as writers bemoaned "the sad interruption of passage," that interruption was not, after all, total. Despite the war's clearly profound disruption of English communications, colonists indeed found ways to send the most important of news. Some accounts evoke a veritable barrage of news bearers. In their separate tellings, William Harris and Nathaniel Saltonstall both described "Fresh Messengers . . . howrly arriving to bring the Doleful Tidings of New Massacres, Slaughters and Devastations committed by the Brutish Heathens."[84] Edmund Browne felt compelled to apologize for troubling the Massachusetts Bay governor with relatively minor problems, when "soe much tidings of sad Executio pr Natives . . . come posting unto your and the Councills hands."[85] The news was bad, in these renderings, but it was also frequent. Roger Williams wrote so prolifically, during the war, that he ran out of paper: "Sir since I am oft occasioned to write upon the Publike busines," he nudged Governor Leverett, in January 1676, "I shall be thanckfull for a litle paper upon the Publike account being now neere destitute."[86]

To gather "intelligence," English authorities marshaled a host of forces. On some occasions they sent intelligencers, of sorts, charged with the chore of information getting. At the war's outset, for instance, boatman Caleb Carr was "sent on purpose to Swansie for tidings." It was from Carr that much of the initial news of Philip's actions derived.[87] Others culled precious bits from the mouths of nearby Indians, hopefully friendly. Before those around Springfield ultimately turned against him, John Pynchon learned a good deal from Native friends. Word of the attack on Brookfield, in August 1675, came thusly. "Our Indians have now brought me news of a fight between English and Indians two days ago," he wrote to Connecticut, ". . . about 11 English killed, some houses burnt." Days later, Pynchon confirmed what he had heard by sending an Indian to survey the scene in person.[88]

Even as New England burned, letters continued to flow. Few letters, though, were carried by Indians.[89] Well before the war had begun, English use of Algonquian couriers had been dropping. The war did nothing to reverse the trend. Of the surviving wartime Winthrop letters, a mere five passed through Indian hands. Nearly all of these were carried by Pequots, allies to the English during the war. But as distrust of Algonquians soared, even "friendly" Indians became suspect. Most English writers probably hesitated, as Giles Sylvester did, to hire an Indian. "I had sent an Indian on purpose," he wrote, "but that these troublesome times would have caused a dislike of it."[90] An alternative was to send by boat, since English shipmasters were relatively safe from Indian assault. Instead of sending overland through Nipmuck or Narragansett, for instance, several of the Winthrops' letters between Boston and Connecticut were carried by "Mr Belcher" or "Mr Belcher's vessell" (probably merchant Andrew Belcher, sailing the coast).

But far more prevalent than any one name, or any particular person, are the war's anonymous "posts." The outbreak of King Philip's War launched a thousand posts. In moments of emergency English writers festooned their letters with that newly popular label: "hast hast post hast." "[D]elliver upon the kings service," ordered one, "post hast post."[91] Posts reported fresh news—"[T]he post sayth they had a Hott engagement, & slew many of the Indians, neere a Hundred," went one breathless account—and also trucked important items. In October 1675, John Pynchon beseeched Hadley men to "send down by the post" his doublet coat, linen, and a supply of paper, while Samuel Stow begged for rubila, a medicine, to be sent "by som of the posts that may possibly com up."[92] Up, down, back and forth, posts carried the freshest news of the war. In ways unimaginable, the war tested and convulsed New England. It halted travel and cut off many from any news at all. Yet in it, too, small glimpses of a new order are detectable. It may be that the lamentations over stopped news, during the war, in some way reflect how communications had been quickening beforehand.

Undergirding these posts were hundreds of horses. On hearing of Plymouth's plight, the Massachusetts council did two things: First, they scrambled soldiers to march toward Mount Hope. But following that, they also ordered Boston's constable to "Impress forthwith five Able and Special horses for the service of the country." These horses, which would need to be especially fleet and healthy, were to serve as vehicles for posts.[93] Mounted men could cover ground in half the time (or less) required by those "afoot." Horse-posts were tremendously important in keeping English leaders apprised of what was happening in "the woods." So heavily did soldiers lean on letters, for sending updates or seeking advice, that Captain Daniel Henchman actually kept a letter-case with him as he marched. Trudging forward from Packachoog to Hassanamesit, Henchman realized that he had left behind this letter-case, "wherein his writings and orders were." At once, he sent men back—"on horseback"—to "find his papers."[94]

Bearing posts was, of course, not the only role played by horses during King Philip's War. They also carried soldiers. (Horses' importance in both capacities is captured well in a scene from the war's opening, when Captain James Oliver "rode post to Boston for some hundreths of Horse." One rider, in other words, begat a legion of others.[95]) Mounted Englishmen also used horses to scout for and harass wandering Indians, and to ravage Native food supplies. The "Horse was sent out upon all Occasions to scout about the Country," related William Hubbard, and "brought in daily much of the Enemies Corn and Beans, which they had hid in Barns and under the Ground." Because horses could tolerate "the Depth of the Snow" and "Sharpness of the Cold" far better than the "Foot," they did much to feed New England's frozen soldiers over the winter of 1675–1676.[96]

Horses also *became* food. Early on, Indians had sometimes slain English cattle and horses and simply left them to rot. But as victuals dwindled, little was wasted. The war took its toll in "Horse-flesh," as Indians literally began to consume the animals.[97] In at least one instance, later dubbed the "Hungry March," English soldiers were also forced to eat horses—an act they did not relish. Pursuing Philip into Nipmuck country in early 1676, the English began to run out of food. The "Scarcity of Victuals daily encreasing," went one account, "we were forced to kill several of our Horses for our Sustenance."[98] Lest anyone think that the ordinary soldiers alone had deigned to humble themselves so, the same author was careful to note, later, that of the "several Horses . . . killed and eaten," even General Josiah Winslow had eaten "his Part."[99]

How much military might was lent to New England's forces by horses, however, is not entirely clear.[100] King Philip's War witnessed no conventional "battles," and, as weapons, of sorts, horses offered little defense against the burning of English towns. They also invited ambushes. In sticky situations horses could provide a means of quick escape, as when Joseph Freeman met an Indian in the path near Sudbury, spied the man's gun, and quickly "mounted and rod for it." (One of Freeman's neighbors, by contrast, "saved himself by his leggs."[101]) But horses also exposed their riders to attack, by raising them high above the roadside brush. Later accounts made much of horses' usefulness in scouting, but even this tactic was curbed by Native knowledge of New England's best hiding places. Swamps, Indians' favored havens during war, made good refuges, in part, because they foiled horses.

A swamp, said William Harris, was "not pasable for horses." Swamps were so miry, echoed Nathaniel Saltonstall, that, "Horse cannot at all, nor English foot (without great Difficulty) passe."[102]

It would be wrong to say that any newfound English agility of communication contributed to the war's winning. What led to that outcome is complicated. English forces had an advantage in men and resources; Natives had a lack of both. Food was most problematic: After half a year of fighting, Algonquians were hobbled by a dearth of food. They never recovered from it. But Indian disadvantages did not make the English victory inevitable. What happened, it seems, was that Native people lost heart. They watched other Indians, like William Nahawton, fight against them. (Once, when an English soldier thought a Native man out of range of his musket, Nahawton encouraged him to shoot: "[T]ry said *Nahawton,* and God shall direct the bullet." When he did, and they saw the Indian "tumble down," Nahawton thanked God for the "successe.") They saw Indian guides, scouts, informants, and fighters aiding the English (aid which did, in fact, exert a hefty influence on the war's outcome). They were wearied by it. Colonists' victory in King Philip's War, one historian has argued, is attributable to the fact that the English remained "ideologically coherent," even as their Indian opponents gradually lost the will to fight.[103]

There was no decisive moment, in 1675–1676, when horses rode to the rescue, or posts prevented what might have been a finally disastrous assault. But if "ideological coherence" won the war for the English, we might ponder the mechanics that made such a thing possible. In perhaps just the last decade before the war, the English had begun to travel and to trade, to ride and to write, as never before. The war interrupted this progression, almost irreversibly. Nor did the war's end result in a perfect harmony among the English colonies. Instead, it unleashed a tide of bickering, as English interests competed to grab fastest at tracts of Indian land. But in New England's pressed posts and careening carts, in the hulls of sloops and on the backs of horses, a quieter conquest of territory was underway. In coming years, it would only hasten.

Philip was killed on August 12, 1676. He had been found just outside Mount Hope. One of his former followers had led English troops, very nearly, to the precise spot. News of his death radiated immediately outward. "This 12th of August 1676 in the morneing Phillip was Slayne," William Harris scribbled giddily into a letter. "Just now about three of the Clock newes therof is come to Newporte."[104] As the war waned, in the meantime, New England's woods grew eerily quiet. English travel began to rebound. "I hear some go this day from Hadley toward the Bay," John Pynchon noted, only days after Philip's death. The Indians now seemed to scatter. "We find only some skulking Indians in these parts," Pynchon reported. Some writers marveled at the woods' hush. "Some of Late have travelled through the Woods to *Connecticut*," William Hubbard wrote, toward the end of his narrative, "but met with no *Indians*, nor did they hear of any in their passing."[105]

V.

Near dusk on an evening in early June 1678, three Indian travelers were strolling southward along the road to New London. It had been a good afternoon. Nuckquittaty and his wife had spent it at Thomas Williams' ordinary, where they had met up with Keweebhunt.[106] At the Williams house, Keweebhunt had sold a bit of venison in exchange for a jug of rum, "a nutt shell of wch . . . he then tasted," Nuckquittaty later remembered. Shortly thereafter, the three left together and began making their way to town. En route, Keweebhunt decided to stop in at the Bowles house, a humble home perched by the wayside. He may have hoped to sell some more of his venison there. But when the travelers arrived, something seemed awry. The door was unlatched and ajar, and they could make out the figure of a child, sprawled on the floor and "making a noyse like snoring." When Keweebhunt poked at the dwindling fire, its light revealed the full scene: one child lay "wounded & gasping," while Mrs. Bowles and another child lay dead on the floor nearby. Surveying this slaughter from the doorway, Nuckquittaty began to tremble. What should they do? he asked Keweebhunt. "[F]or my part," Keweebhunt replied, "I will goe to Towne & informe: what I find."

The three then headed back into the road, toward town. But as they were "coming along in the way," they heard the sound of gunshots being fired "at the Towne" (probably an alarm, raised on earlier news of the murder). On hearing this, the Native woman traveling with Nuckquittaty and Keweebhunt grew afraid. She turned to the men and made a nervous plea: "[G]oe not in the path," she begged, "least you be killed." Nuckquittaty thought this good advice. Together, the two hastily "left the path."[107]

Those Indians traveling the pathways of southern New England in the years after King Philip's War were well advised to tread lightly. The war wrought great changes. It had been a horrific event for all involved, but Native people, there can be no doubt, took the worst of its blows. Of the thousands of souls who died during King Philip's War, perhaps two thirds were Indians. Several thousand more fled to the north and west (out of the path, so to speak, of English colonists), or were shipped into the most brutish of bondage in the West Indies. Some Christian Indians (many of whom had been interned on the bleak and barren Deer Island in Boston Harbor) filtered back into the old Praying Towns at Nonantum, Natick, or Punkapoag. But converted or not, most Native people in the years after the war found themselves pushed, increasingly, onto smaller and smaller tracts of marginal land. Some pockets of Native power persisted. But even the independence of Uncas's Mohegans dwindled as the decades passed. War's end, by some estimates, effectively marked the "end of Indian sovereignty" in this part of New England.[108] It is tempting to conclude from the nervousness of Nuckquittaty's companion that Indians also perceived a marked reversal in control of the region's pathways. The woman's plea—*Go not in the path least you be killed*—betrays an atmosphere very different indeed from what had once prevailed in southern New England. Earlier in the century, Narragansetts had warned the English to "be carefull on the high wayes," and, as late as 1675, to beware of "of travelling in the Common roade."[109] But now, when any flicker of danger arose, Indians would be the ones, instead, to shy from traveling "in the path."

It was not an unmitigated victory for New England's colonists. The war's end involved some loss of autonomy for the English as well. Its very disastrousness convinced the Crown that the colonies needed to be more closely watched. After decades of benign neglect in which the colonies "had mostly governed themselves," King Philip's War (along with other crises, including the uprising known as Bacon's Rebellion in Virginia) spurred England's Restoration government to seize control of its freewheeling American colonies. Royal agents were thus dispatched, new leaders implanted, and a tighter grip of authority exercised over the American colonies, which, in turn, lost their "political independence" for the next hundred years.[110] But in the meantime, they threw off much of their remaining dependence on Indians.

In the years after King Philip's War, lower New England underwent a veritable communications revolution. Northeastern pathways now began to metamorphose rapidly into English roads. By the 1680s teams across the region were laying out new "country highways" that stretched between plantations. (Diarist Thomas Minor and his fellow townsmen "Layd out the Contrie high ways" through Stonington in March 1680.[111]) Printed aids began to appear to help English travelers along these new, and sometimes unfamiliar, ways. Even regular postal service—that far-fetched dream of Francis Lovelace, in 1673—slowly fell into place along the eastern seaboard. The last years of the seventeenth century made way for a vastly different scene, at the dawn of the eighteenth.

Stories about King Philip's War, meanwhile, stiffened into place, as printers on both sides of the Atlantic fixed them to paper. The war generated quite a lot of writing. Well before it had ended, a frenzy of printing presented English readers with tales of the war that they were not soon likely to forget. It would be misleading to credit the war, alone, with creating a new market for print in the colonies, but it certainly fired quite a few English imaginations. Twenty-one printed accounts of the war, several of them published in multiple editions, found their way into booksellers' stalls during the years 1675–1682.[112] Booksellers also began to multiply quickly, most of them crowded into the noisy town house in Boston. (In the 1660s the city had had only two booksellers, but in the 1670s the number leapt up to nine, and by the 1680s there were seventeen, a number well above what one might expect given Boston's population.[113]) Printing itself expanded tremendously. Up to the mid-1670s, the sole colonial press had been that at Cambridge, Massachusetts. But in 1675, the very year of King Philip's War's outbreak, printing spread to Boston. By the final decades of the century the communications frontier was closing. It was, in effect, almost closed.

Almost, but not quite. Even after the war, English nervousness about Indians persisted. The Bowles murders, in fact, are suggestive of the seething tensions that remained. After Mrs. Bowles and her children were found slain, suspicion settled on a Native man named Kesuckquunch (or "Suckquuns"). Part of what landed Kesuckquunch in jail was that he seemed to know about the murders before the news had spread. (When English authorities seized him, he had reportedly blurted out, "[W]hat is the matter you lay hold of me[?] [I]s Thomas Bowles his wife & children dead[?]")[114] But what sunk him more deeply into trouble, in all likelihood, was that he belonged to a cohort of Indian (probably Nipmuck) "surrenderers" who had capitulated after the war, but remained within the bounds of English towns. These survivors, who were required to list their names with English authorities, had a somewhat hazy status. Shortly before the murders, Kesuckquunch had heard a rumor that the surrenderers would soon be "carried out of the

Country" (perhaps into West Indian slavery). But "before I will be Carried away," he had said, according to several Mohegan and Nipmuck testimonies, "I will doe some mischiefe."[115]

An angry, embittered Indian survivor of King Philip's War slaying an English mother and her children: Kesuckquunch, by all measures, seemed a very likely suspect. But this particular story ended with an unexpected twist. In July 1678, a disturbed young Englishman named John Stodder admitted to killing Mrs. Bowles and her children. His motivation may have been sexual. Having arrived at the Bowles house that evening, "he desired to ly there," he explained, but the woman "bid him begon & Thrust him out of dores." Spitefully, Stodder had entered the house again and "tooke the ax & Stroke mrs Bowles on the hinder part of the head." He had killed the children, he said, "for fear [they] should goe down to the Towne & tell of it," though he left the littlest one alive "Because there was no danger of its telling." In the fall, Stodder, Kesuckquunch and Keweebhunt were all charged with the murders. The Indians, though, were found "not Gillty."[116]

Stodder's shocking confession proved that danger sometimes prowled where it was least expected. The real lesson, though, is how willing some were to believe that the killings had been done by Indians. Stodder was revealed as the murderer, in fact, only because, two months after the Bowles slayings, his younger brother was found dead. Stodder tried to blame the boy's death (also caused by an ax wound) on Indians. That didn't work, but it might have, because even if King Philip's War was over, it continued to haunt people. The "deplorable and desolating effects of the late Indian Warre," wrote the men of Mendon, in a 1681 petition to Massachusetts, "have made, we doubt not, impressions on yr minds soe deep and abiding that they can not easily be forgotten, or erased."[117] That was not the half of it. Neither, as it turned out, was the violence over. John Stodder knew he could blame Indians for his brother's death because that was a believable story: Englishmen were still afraid of them. Probably that sense of anxiety had never been higher than in the immediate wake of the war, but it would deepen immeasurably in the decades to come. It would spread, first rushing down from the north, but then carried, to all parts, by folios and pieces of foolscap.

6

Terror Ubique Tremor

Mine enemies chased me sore, like a bird, without cause.
—Lamentations 3:52

For the present then, the *Indians* have *Done* Murdering;
They'l *Do so no more till next Time.*
Let us then have *done* Writing.
—Cotton Mather, *Decennium Luctuosum* (1699)

FAME WAS SOMETHING that few colonial English women experienced. But Hannah Dustan was a grand exception. Nothing, in her first several decades, marked her as extraordinary. But in March 1697 her life took a wild turn, when Indians raided the town of Haverhill, Massachusetts, where the Dustans lived. When the raiders reached her house, her husband, Thomas, and most of her children fled safely to a garrison. But Hannah, who had given birth only days earlier, was still abed. She and her nurse were taken captive. Her newborn, a girl named Martha, was killed. When Hannah Dustan began thinking of revenge is not clear. But, several weeks later, after being marched northward for dozens of miles along the Merrimack River, she pushed her fellow captives to action against their captors. One night, as the Abenaki family slept, Dustan and two others took up the Indians' own *"Hatchets"* and "struck such Home Blowes, upon the Heads of their *Sleeping Oppressors*," that all but two died. They also scalped the Indians. After "cutting off the Scalps of the *Ten Wretches,* who had Enslav'd 'em," they filched a canoe and rowed away.[1]

It was a remarkable story. The Reverend Cotton Mather, minister of Boston's North Church, recognized it as full of providential meaning, a splendid illustration of God's work. When Dustan and her comrades came to Boston soon after escaping, probably to claim bounties for the scalps they had collected, Mather preached about them. (He pointed them out in the pews: "I think I see, among you, at this Hour," the sermon reads, "*Three Persons,* namely, Two Women, and one Youth, who have just now, Received a Deliverance from a Captivity in the Hands of horrid Indians, with some very Singular Circumstances.") The sermon was pure jeremiad: "After all that is come upon us, for our Evil Deeds," Mather warned, quoting Ezra 9:13–14, "seeing thou, our God, hast given us such Deliverance as this, should we again break thy Commandments . . . ?" It also ratcheted up the terror of Dustan's experience to dizzying heights: You can almost hear the Abenaki raiders, "Raging Dragons" to Mather, breaking into the house. Once he had delivered it, Mather sent the text to Bartholomew Green's print shop, where it was transformed into a little book called *Humiliations Follow'd with Deliverances.* Copies sold briskly.[2]

Although captivity was a fate known to English men and women throughout the empire, this sort of tale was relatively new to New England. In coming years, however, there would be many more stories like it. The greater context of Hannah Dustan's captivity was grim and global. In the final years of the seventeenth century, European wars, especially between England and France, made northern New England a dangerous place to live. Crouched in the cold country north of the English colonies, and a rising threat in times of war, was New France. "New France" was actually little more than a diffuse collection of trading posts, villages, and mission towns. The French settlements were weaker, and far less numerous, than the English ones to their south. And they were separated from New England by what had always seemed a nearly impenetrable expanse of mountainous, unknown terrain. (To traverse it, as one early captive described, meant struggling over vast highlands through "dark and hideous wayes.")[3] But as the century wound down, English colonists discovered that their distance from New France had been something of an illusion.

The French had formidable Native allies. Northern Indians, some of them refugees who had fled in the wake of King Philip's War, found that the French shared their animosity toward the English. They began to see

New France as both an ally and a safe harbor. This was true of Hannah Dustan's captors, as well: The Abenaki family that claimed Dustan had ties to the French. In fact they were devout Catholics. Having been won over to the French faith, they held *"Prayers* in their Family, no less than Thrice every Day." Dustan's new "Master, whom she kill'd," was not new to Christianity. (Incredibly, he had once lived with the Rowlandsons, whose Lancaster home had been raided by Nipmucks during King Philip's War in 1676. Mary Rowlandson's resulting narrative of her own captivity—the immensely popular *The Soveraignty and Goodness of God,* published in 1682—is, arguably, the first early American captivity narrative.) "[W]hen he pray'd the English way, he thought that was good," the Indian man told Dustan, "but now he found the French way was better."[4]

That was about the last thing an English colonist would have wanted to hear. It is hard to overstate how deeply the rivalry with France bore down on English colonists in these years. The great fact of life in northern New England, during the late seventeenth and early eighteenth centuries, was imperial war with France. (Or, more precisely, the intermittent raiding that came with it.) The first English captives known to have been carried into French Canada were taken from Deerfield and Hatfield, Massachusetts, in 1677. But it was the 1688 outbreak of the War of the League of Augsburg— "King William's War," to English colonists—that truly began generations of violence. After that, raiding became endemic. With a remarkable economy of violence, northern enemies visited fear upon New England. English colonists learned quickly to dread the prospect of French and Indian warriors surprising their towns, carrying off captives, and leaving bloody spectacles behind.

It was a concerted campaign of terror. It was also very effective. Herein lies an irony: Widespread raiding emerged at a time when easier communications were beginning to fall into place among English colonists. As the colonies hurtled toward the new century, roads were being cut, printing presses hummed with activity, and a newspaper became available. Haltingly, and imperfectly, posts went flitting from town to town, and taverns opened for travelers. Southern New England was a changed place, a place of highways and byways that determinedly stitched together its once scattered settlements. But all of this was not, on the whole, a blessing. As gruesome news from the borderlands percolated throughout the colonies, those shared stories made all of New England more vulnerable to terror. As Samuel Penhallow wrote in his 1726 *History of the Wars of New-England with the Eastern Indians,* "Terror ubique tremor." Or, terror, it seemed, was everywhere.[5]

Hannah Dustan was unique. She was unusual in many ways, not the least of which was her gender, which was, after all, what made her escape so remarkable. "From women, ordinarily," one historian wrote dryly, several generations later, "attempts of this sort are not to be expected." (Mather, too, gave due attention to Dustan's womanhood. He even winked at readers in the opening line of a subsequent version he penned, which found Indians descending upon the "Skirts of *Haverhil.*")[6] But the curiosity of her gender was not the only thing that drew readers to her story. What made her tale appealing, in its own time, was how little it resembled most other captivity stories circulating in New England. It did not look, or end, like the kind of tale that colonists were accustomed to encountering. Instead, Hannah Dustan's escape momentarily reversed what was, in these years, an inescapable tide of bad news.

Mather published her story twice more, in his 1699 history of King William's War, *Decennium Luctuosum,* and in 1702's enormous chronicle of New England's history, *Magnalia Christi Americana.* In the meantime others, too, were writing and publishing about the terrors of war. "The Cruelties committed . . . ," someone remarked, about a raid in 1690, "no Penn can Write nor Tongue expresse."[7] But that was wrong. Many pens would write, and many tongues express, the "Cruelties" visited on English villages by raiders.

I.

It took years, following the ordeal of Francis Lovelace, for anything resembling regular postal service to take root in the English colonies. But in the 1680s, as colonists began to reclaim some of the weedy, abandoned towns that had emptied during King Philip's War, talk turned again to postal service. In 1684, Thomas Dongan, the new governor of New York, imagined building a string of post houses along the seaboard, from "Carolina to Nova Scotia."[8] He took some steps to see this vision realized. But little came of it. In the late 1680s there was chatter about a post riding regularly between Boston and Connecticut.[9] This plan, too, foundered. Postal plans were bedeviled by political upheavals. In 1685, Charles II revoked the Massachusetts charter and consolidated the government of the entire English northeast into an entity called the "Dominion of New England." Colonists were generally displeased with this new assertion of royal power. When, in 1689, they heard of the Glorious Revolution that had deposed the Stuarts in England, they toppled the unpopular governor of the Dominion, Edmund Andros. The rebel who momentarily seized New York, during this chaos, Jacob Leisler, arrested Andros's poor postman.[10]

But the next decade changed everything. In 1691 the new monarchs, William and Mary, granted Thomas Neale a monopoly to begin a postal service in the colonies. Although Neale himself never set foot in America, he put in charge of this venture the governor of New Jersey, Andrew Hamilton, a man who, at long last, was able to set the post in motion. Hamilton circulated among the colonies a draft law that he hoped they would enact, setting the rates and schedules of colonial postal service. It worked: While not all followed his stipulations, all of the northern colonies passed some sort of postal legislation. (Virginia and Maryland demurred.)[11] In May 1693, Massachusetts set rates along the hoped-for postal route: To send to Rhode Island from Boston—six pence; to send anywhere along the post road in Connecticut—nine pence; to New York—twelve pence; and the Jerseys and Pennsylvania—fifteen pence. Further south, letters to Maryland or Virginia cost two shillings. The postal route would also extend north and east of Boston, as far as Piscataqua (six pence). Massachusetts also moved to protect Neale's monopoly. Only the postmaster was permitted to carry letters for hire.[12]

It was one thing to draft such a law, and quite another to make it reality. All did not go smoothly. Postal rates were too expensive, and opportunities to send with other travelers too tempting, for postal service to become immediately the preferred means of sending. By the end of the decade, Neale's project was still struggling toward profitability. Instead of making him rich, the post drove Thomas Neale into debt. He begged for better enforcement of his monopoly, which colonists gleefully ignored.[13] (The habit of sending letters outside of the post would not die soon. Well into the eighteenth century, postmaster John Campbell crabbed about Bostonians who clambered aboard newly-arrived ships and grabbed up their letters before the missives could make it into his post office.) Colonial correspondence did not depend wholly on Thomas Neale's postal service. But, very clearly, English men and women had a new way to send news.

Letters and diaries make plain that postal service was running by the mid-1690s. By the early 1700s it was fairly regular.[14] In 1704, Sarah Kemble Knight, a woman traveling alone from Boston to New York, relied on the postman as a guide through several stages of her trip. (She liked nothing more than hearing "the Post's sounding his horn," which she found "musickall and agreeable" mostly because it meant they had arrived at some place "where we were to Lodg.")[15] Posted letters did not always break fresh news. But readers often gave more credence to what arrived by post. In March 1701, for instance, Boston's Samuel Sewall heard, unofficially, of the New York governor's death. "The Town is fill'd with the News of my Ld Bellomont's death, last Wednesday," he wrote. The news had left New York in a Saybrook-bound sloop, arrived with a magistrate in New London, and entered Boston "by Land" with Mr. Southmayd. Not until seven days later did the tale arrive by post. But Sewall seems not to have trusted the news until he saw it in posted letters. "The awfull News of the Lord Bellomont's death . . . confirmed by Letters received by the Posts!" he wrote. "The Town is sad."[16]

Meanwhile, New England's roads took shape. Post riders galloped through an increasingly settled set of highways. For years townsmen had been whacking through the brush to create, or widen, roads, but after King Philip's War, this work hastened. In 1683, Massachusetts Bay wanted a "better & nearer way" to Connecticut, less "hazardous to travelers." Indians were hired to help find one.[17] In 1684, Connecticut commanded its towns to clear the king's highways—the country roads that reached from plantation to plantation—of "dirty [sloughs], bushes, trees and stones."[18] (The colony had a difficult time of it. Years later, travelers still griped about the "great difficultie in journeying" through Connecticut. Once more, the General Court admonished that the highways be "sufficiently cleared" and punctuated "with marks erected for direction of travailers."[19]) In the 1690s a post road froze into place. Boston to New York, "278 *Miles, thus accounted*": Boston to Dedham to Billings' tavern to Woodcock's (or, alternatively, from Dedham to Medfield and Wrentham, "which is the smoother Road"), then to Providence, New London, Saybrook, New Haven and onward, with many a smaller village along the stony way.[20]

One can plot this route by reading what scores of colonists read: almanacs. Printed annually, almanacs charted tides, described the phases of the

A Defcription of the High Ways, & Roads.
From Bofton *to* New-York 278 *Miles, thus accounted.*
FRom *Bofton* to *Dedham* 10 miles, thence to *Whites* 6, to *Billings* 7, to *Woodcocks* 10. Or, from *Dedham* to *Medfield* 9, to *Wrentham* 10, to *Woodcocks* 4 (which is the fmoother Road) to *Providence* 15, to the *French* Town 20, to *Darby* 24, to *Pembertons* 3, to *Stonington* 12, to *New-London* 15, to *Say-Brook* 18, to *Killingfworth* 12, to *Guildford* 10, to *Branford* 12, to *New-Haven* 10, to *Milford* 10, to *Stratford* 4, to *Fairfield* 8, to *Norwalk* 12, to *Standford* 10, to *Horfeneck* 7, to *Rye* 7, to *Marineck* 4, to *New Rochel* 4, to *Eaft-Chefter* 4, to *Kings-bridge* 6, to the *Half-way-houfe* 9, and from thence to *New-York* 9 mile.
From New-York *to* Philadelphia 96 *mile, thus accounted.*
FRom *N-York* to *Elizabeth Town* (by water) 20 m. to *Woodbridge* 8 m. to *Pifcattawa* 8 m. to *J. inians* 2 m. thence (the new Road) to *Mill-ftone-brook* 14 m. to *Affimpinks* 4 m. to *Crofwicks-Bridge*, over *Doctors-brook* 8 m. then to *Burlington* by the *Mill* 12 m. thence to *Philadelphia* 20 mile.

F I N I S.

In the 1690s, almanacs began providing detailed itineraries for ordinary travelers. This one, printed in 1698, offered a "Description of the High Ways, & Roads" between Boston, New York, and Philadelphia. From John Tulley, *An almanack for the year of our Lord, MDCXCVIII* . . . (Boston, 1698). *(Courtesy of the American Antiquarian Society)*

moon, predicted weather, and proffered whatever other miscellany the average reader might find useful.[21] They were also the first colonial road maps. Almanac makers began printing descriptions of "High-wayes" in the 1690s. The first to do so was Daniel Leeds, who included a "short Description of High-wayes" in his almanac for 1695. It included itineraries radiating outward from New York and Philadelphia, including the "Old Road" between those towns. By following Leeds's lead, as it were, one could find the way from New York all the way to Maryland. "Probably another year I may give account of the Roads from *Boston,* along the Coast over these parts, to *Virginia,*" Leeds promised.[22] In 1697 three different almanacs offered such itineraries. John Tulley's described the entire route from Boston

to Philadelphia. In the early eighteenth century lists of the *"several Stages &*
Post-Roads" became regular features of almanacs.[23] Readers plainly wanted
advice on how to get from place to place. *"If you'r a stranger to the Way,"*
wrote Samuel Clough, in 1701, "Clough's *Almanack procure you may; / For*
that will guide you in the Road, / Besides the pastime t'will afford."[24]

Some almanacs guided travelers toward the warmth and hospitality of
inns. These were fast becoming fixtures of the colonial landscape. Puritans
had once been skittish about public houses, as they encouraged unseemly
drinking and gaming. But, by the 1690s, such places were acknowledged
necessities.[25] Expecting to find ordinaries aplenty, Sarah Kemble Knight
thought the road from Narragansett to Kingston a veritable desert, very
"poorly furnished wth accommodations for Travellers."[26] The clever John
Clapp charmingly combined his work writing almanacs with the business
of offering strangers a resting place. Only a couple of miles from the post
office in New York, Clapp ran a public house "which generally is the bating
place, where Gentlemen take leave of their Friends going so long a Journey."
After describing the route from Boston to New York, Clapp shrewdly advertised his own ordinary. There, Clapp beckoned, men could get "good
Entertainment," even hire a saddle horse or a hackney coach.[27]

Coaches began to populate the landscape in the 1680s.[28] They were rare
at first, but for those with means, all sorts of new contraptions—coaches,
calashes, chariots—soon became available. The term "hackney" indicated
that the coach could be hired.[29] One of the earliest mentions of a coach in
Samuel Sewall's diary had him hiring "Emms's Coach," wherein he and
friends rode to Roxbury, one afternoon, and then "sup[ped] together at the
Grayhound-Tavern." (By 1699 Sewall owned his own coach. His daughter
Betty hid in it for hours, one day, to avoid a suitor's visit.)[30] Some of the
best-off Bostonians kept their own coaches, and some even had coachmen
to drive them. In 1703 the governor's coachman, Thomas, misbehaved thoroughly enough to be exiled into military service in Maine (an assignment
that was, in these years, not appealing). By the 1710s coach driving was
associated with those on the lowest rungs of Boston's social ladder. Sewall
mentioned several Indian drivers in his diary, as well as a "Negro Charioteer."
He also wrote to Cape Cod on behalf of friends, looking for an Indian boy.
"They keep a Calash, and want a Lad to drive it," he explained.[31]

Coach travel could be awkward. In 1699, Rhode Island's governor was
beset when the horses tugging him along were "frighted with a Pistol" and

snapped his calash's pole.[32] During a trip to Rhode Island, the axel-tree of Samuel Sewall's coach "broke quite off."[33] And when several governors were to meet at New London in 1711, much handwringing accompanied the decision of whether or not the roads were good enough for Governor Dudley to ride from Boston to Connecticut "in the calash." Perhaps it was possible to "find a coach-way," wrote Wait Winthrop, but "if any thing should break, espetially a wheele or axeltre, remote from any habitation, how would thay be got hither?" Worriedly, he outlined proper preparations: "[S]ee that the wheels and axeltre be well greased, least it heat and burn off. You must be sure that every thing be sound, and that the coachman be not in drink."[34]

Pockets of very bad travel persisted. This passage through Narragansett country was one of them. "Here We found great difficulty in Travailing," Sarah Kemble Knight groused in 1704, "the way being very narrow, and on each side the Trees and bushes gave us very unpleasent welcomes wth their Branches and bow's." Many of the main roads remained so crude that Knight found them barely tolerable. The post road along the Connecticut shore, in particular, was dreadful. "The Rodes all along this way are very bad," she complained, "Incumbred with Rocks and mountainos passages, wch were very disagreeable to my tired carcass."[35] This coastal route was so notorious that travelers to New York often chose instead to cross Long Island Sound in a boat, and then to ride west over Long Island, whose flat plains offered "much better travelling."[36] (Notwithstanding such complaints, some found New England's roads perfectly welcoming. "They have very good roads all through the country," one English visitor wrote in 1709, "where I have been more agreeably entertained in travelling, than in either *France* or Italy."[37])

France or Italy it was not. But New England was plainly passing into a different age. Travel was becoming more common, sending news easier. Happily, Cotton Mather's freshly penned manuscript did not have to travel far, when it went to the printer in 1697. Only a few blocks away, on Newbury Street, stood the print shop of Bartholomew Green, the man who turned Mather's sermon into a slim little volume entitled *Humiliations Follow'd with Deliverances*. (This Green was on his way to becoming the "most distinguished American printer" of his time, according to one appraisal.)[38] But his medium, print, could carry Hannah Dustan's story much further. Opportunities to publish were quietly multiplying in Boston in the 1690s, and much could be made, Mather well knew, of print. He had learned that lesson from his father.

II.

Books mattered dearly to Increase Mather. So much so, in fact, that he almost died for their sakes. In November 1676, a fire tore through Boston and destroyed nearly all that Mather owned. "It is true that my house is burnt," he wrote to his stepbrother, John Cotton. The furniture had gone up in flames, along with his clothes, his father's letters, his mother's "trunk of writings," and the "winter provision . . . all consumed." But, as the fire had begun licking at the clapboards that morning, Mather related, "God (and I believe his angells)" had awakened him in time to save some of his most prized possessions. "I smelt the fire before the cry was made in the streets," he remembered. After rushing most of the children out of the house, he ran to his study. He pressed his most important manuscripts into the arms of his thirteen year-old son, Cotton, who fled the house with them. The elder Mather then began heaving books out of the study. People on the street helpfully "carried them away." (One of these was William Bradford's history *Of Plimoth Plantation,* one of the only surviving accounts of the early Plymouth Colony, flung out during the fire and later miraculously recovered.)

It was, for Mather, a close call. "I had . . . time to throw almost all my Bookes," he wrote, "but before I could quite clear my study some called to me I was a dead man if I stayed any longer[.] So I departed." Some of his library burned. But, Mather related with relief, "My Bookes and M.SS. are most of them safe."[39] Mather's love of books ran to those beyond his own collection. It was that love, perhaps, more than vanity, that motivated his patronage of the press in these last years of the seventeenth century. No matter what moved him to write, or to publish, one pattern was borne out very clearly in the career of Increase Mather: the rise of the colonial press. Writing had always been elemental to New England culture. But print—embodied by the various "Bookes" that Mather had so frantically worked to save—now emerged in the colonies, too.

New England had never really been without printing. The first printing press had arrived in the summer of 1638. Accompanied by boxes of type and bundles of paper, it crossed the Atlantic with the other migrants aboard the *John of London.* Its owner, the Reverend Jose Glover, did not live to see

American shores; he died at sea. But the orphaned press went with Glover's widow to Cambridge, where it anchored the first printing house in the English colonies. An official press, essentially, the Cambridge press in its early decades produced mostly official publications, almanacs, and little else. But its work grew measurably in the 1650s, when it became the cornerstone of John Eliot's mission to bring Christianity to neighboring Indians. It was put in service of creating a body of material for Eliot's Native converts, in the Massachusett language—what Cotton Mather later dubbed Eliot's "Indian Library." Almost from the first, the fate of the press was bound, messily, to the fate of New England's Indians.

The very location of the press suggested how thoroughly it was tied up in Eliot's project. The press had come to rest on the property of Harvard College in 1641, when Jose Glover's widow, Elizabeth, married the college's president, Henry Dunster. Eliot kept the Cambridge press so busy that, by 1655, it had "shaken the timbers of the President's house," where it was kept, so thoroughly as to threaten the building's ruin. Continuing to subject the house's joists to the vigorous pull of the press, the president worried, would be "dangerous & hurtful to the edifice." So it was moved, appropriately enough, to the newly-built "Indian College" at Harvard, a brick building that had been constructed, rather too hopefully, to accommodate Native students.[40] In the end not many Indians passed through the Indian College. But the Cambridge press remained seated there into the 1680s, when visitors peered into the broken window of the crumbling building and saw it, squatting quietly, inside.[41]

The Indian College, abandoned, was toppled in spring 1698. The "old Brick Colledge, commonly called the *Indian* Colledge," Samuel Sewall recorded wistfully, that May, "is pull'd down to the ground." But the press did not share this doleful end. Well before this, printing escaped Cambridge, where it had been confined for decades, and leapt across the Charles River into Boston.[42] For this New Englanders had to thank the irrepressible Marmaduke Johnson, erstwhile partner of Cambridge printer Samuel Green. Johnson, a trained printer, had been sent to New England to aid in the massive task of printing the Indian Bible. The task was indeed monumental, and it presented some difficulties. For one thing, printing in Algonquian quickly exhausted the type needed to produce O's and K's, both of which sounds were common in Indian speech. "Some defects there be in the work," Eliot apologized, toward the end of the first printing of Genesis, "which could not be helped for want of letters or tipes . . . Which hath put us upon the using of some unsuitable Characters." The New England Company answered this complaint by sending type, paper, and, eventually, Marmaduke Johnson.[43] But Eliot had not yet rid himself of "unsuitable Characters." Soon after arriving, and despite already being married to a woman who, although in England, was still very much alive, Johnson pursued the affections of Samuel Green's young daughter. Unsurprisingly, Johnson's partnership with Green broke up in 1671. In 1674, he petitioned for, and was granted, permission to print in Boston, where he thought he might get more business. Johnson died barely six months later; but, liberated from the ban that had once constrained it to Cambridge, printing burst out of its shackles.[44]

What Johnson had wrought was momentous. In 1675, John Foster set up the first Boston press, into the maw of which went numberless reams of stiff, new paper. Many of those sheets, including the first two imprints that Foster produced (*The Wicked mans portion*, an execution sermon, and *The Times of men are in the hand of God*, about an exploding ship), emerged bearing the compositions of the Reverend Increase Mather. Mather's record embodies the explosion of printing in the last quarter of the century. Before 1675, Mather had published but a few times in New England. But by the end of the decade, he had published several volumes of sermons, two histories of Indian war, two books on baptism, and a biography. He dispensed copies to readers in both England and America. "Mather's example encouraged others," writes one biographer. "His patronage of John Foster and the first press in Boston started an expansion of printing that accelerated to the end of the century, long after Foster himself was gone."[45] Foster himself was gone by 1681. But printing soldiered on without him.

Colonists had hardly been living in a world without print. On the contrary: Early New England had always had a booming book trade. But the market had long been fueled, mostly, by imported European imprints. (That remained true even after Boston printing took off in the 1680s. About 3500–4000 imported books reached Boston annually during that decade, and they generally sold out. By contrast, the 2000 or so colonial imprints printed in each of these same years sold more slowly.) Most early booksellers were clustered together at the Exchange in Boston, very near the waterfront, where imported books had only a few yards to travel before they could hit the stalls for sale.[46] The florescence of colonial printing in the last quarter of the century, therefore, did not revolutionize reading practices. What it did do, however, was make colonial news more available. Much more than the Cambridge press had ever done, and perhaps just as much as London printers did for the colonial market, Boston began printing news.[47]

In September 1690, Bostonians could even hold in their hands the colonies' first attempt at a regularly published newspaper, *Publick Occurrences, Both Forreign and Domestick*. Its publisher, Benjamin Harris, wanted simply to provide readers with accurate news, in a time when many of them were verily clamoring for it. When *Publick Occurrences* appeared, Massachusetts was in something of a political maelstrom: The royal governor had been toppled, and colonial emissaries were in London seeking a new charter. Pamphlet wars flared, repeatedly. While the provisional government tried to get its bearings, meanwhile, French and Indians had begun punishing towns to the north and east of Boston. The colony had scraped together an expedition to resist the raiders pounding the northern frontier, but it was not going well.[48]

The butchery would go on for decades more, but *Publick Occurrences* met an abrupt end. Harris had intended it to be published once a month, or sooner, charmingly, if "any Glut of Occurrences happen." Glut of occurrences or no, the governing council of Massachusetts quashed the paper after just one issue. This, apparently, because the newssheet was "not Licensed"; and because Harris had impugned the honor of both the French king and the Mohawk allies of the English. One senses that there was more to the story.[49] The governing council can perhaps be forgiven for its nervousness. Newspapers were relatively new to the English. Even England did not have a periodical press until the 1620s. (Early corantos, or printed half-sheets of news, appeared in Amsterdam in 1618; by December 1620, as the Pilgrims were warily poking about 'First Encounter' beach, English translations had surfaced in London.[50] At about the same time, epistolary newsletters emerged, as men with country estates hired letter writers to gather London news, compose it, and forward it by post. One of these reporters was Thomas Archer, who, in 1622, began printing his newsletter. The resulting work, *The Weekly Newes*, was, by all rights, the first English newspaper.[51])

Publishing news, it turned out, was politically perilous. Archer was arrested in 1621 for penning some snippet to which the Spanish ambassador objected.[52] Benjamin Harris fared better: After *Publick Occurrences* was silenced in 1690, he became a successful publisher and was named the colony's official printer in 1692 (though, when he returned to England in 1695, he once again ran afoul of the authorities).[53]

III.

In 1690, there was, indeed, plenty of news, almost more than Benjamin Harris could cram into his ill-fated newspaper, and much of it woeful. A February snowstorm drove some hapless boaters against the sandbar at Barnstable, "Bodies not found."[54] Smallpox bore down on Boston, killing hundreds. Babies were reportedly born bearing the marks of the disease, as it "infected even *Children in the bellies of Mothers.*" The city also suffered two great fires, one that devoured "*twenty Houses,*" and then, only weeks later, another. (This one Harris seemed to count as more disastrous, not least because it consumed "the best furnished PRINTING-PRESS, of those few that we know of in *America* . . . a loss not presently to be repaired.") In Watertown an old man, "*Sober* and . . . *Pious,*" hung himself in a barn. Others likely contemplated choosing a similar fate, this terrible year. " 'Tis not easy to relate the Trouble and Sorrow that poor *Boston* has felt," Harris wrote.[55]

And there was war. In the 1690s, French and Indian raiders began preying, with some regularity, on the northern fringes of English settlement. One of the first attacks came just as the decade opened. It must have seemed very far indeed from Harris's Boston. On the icy morning of February 9, 1690, the inhabitants of Albany, New York, awoke to an alarm: The nearby village of Schenectady had been attacked. First to reach Albany with the news was Symon Schermerhorn, "shott threw his Thigh" and bleeding. Then others, too, "came Running here," wrote one Albany witness. Schenectady was afire, they said, its streets "full of french and Indians." The town had foolishly assigned no watch. (Legend has it that their only sentinels were snowmen, stationed stiffly at the village entrances.) At least sixty died when raiders fell upon the town, and nearly thirty more were taken captive. Some twenty-five others stumbled frantically through the snow to Albany, "there limbs frozen in the flight."[56]

They told chilling stories. "The Cruelties committed at said Place," went one report, "no Penn can Write nor Tongue expresse: the women big with Childe rip'd up and the Children alive throwne into the flames, and there heads dash'd in pieces against the Doors and windows." That night, after much shuffling, were later released. But when French and Indian forces crushed Salmon Falls in 1690, Hope-Hood led them there.[66] The drive to visit revenge and terror on New England was powerful.

Abenakis shared this objective with the French. Especially during war, the French posts clustered against the cold in the St. Lawrence River valley needed to keep New England in a posture of defense. New France also relied heavily on Native allies, as buffers against both the English and other threats. (It was only after Abenakis had asked "for my help," wrote one French governor, that he had sent 250 men to raid an English settlement.[67]) A careful diplomatic calculus, therefore, lay behind decisions to attack English settlements. The raid on Schenectady in 1690, for instance, was designed to boost French morale and to bolster support from allies during a time when New France itself had been punished relentlessly by Iroquois raiders. To reaffirm French puissance, the governor of New France, Count Frontenac, planned several spectacular attacks on English towns. The first (initially planned for Albany, which had close ties to the Iroquois) fell on snowbound Schenectady, in February 1690. The second fell at Salmon Falls, the third at Falmouth. Nearly three hundred English colonists died, and almost two hundred more were taken captive, in these three attacks alone.[68]

"There are frownes on America, & on N.E.," thought Increase Mather, in March 1693. Mather was not especially cheerful, even in the best of times. As he grew older, and his bones more achy, he seemed at times to long for death. (He greeted the year 1704, for instance, by asking, "Is this the first day of that year in which I am to dye, & to go into the eternal world?") But the Indian wars seemed to cause him special distress. In the 1690s, he filled the pages of his diaries with evidence of God's reproofs, most of it news of the latest attacks by French and Indians. Twelve killed at Pascataway. Thirty captured at Haverhill. Eighteen killed at Lancaster. Every pen stroke suggests this news vexed him deeply. Mather customarily listed grounds for humiliation—signs that God was displeased—at the beginning of each month's diary entries. In 1695 almost every one of these monthly lists mentioned Indian attacks.[69]

Mather was not alone in his distraction. Other New Englanders also kept careful records, painfully rehearsing news from the ravaged north. "This day & yesterday [were] fatal for the desolating of Casco by the Enemy," wrote Lawrence Hammond in his diary, in May 1690. Although the details were "not known," little was left of the town: "all killed & taken." Hammond,

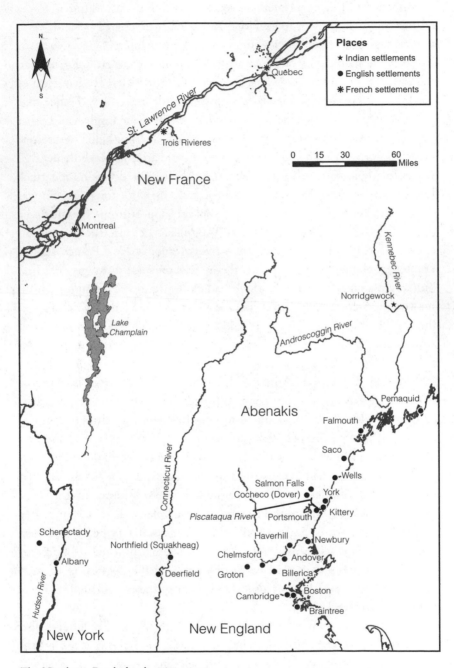

The Northern Borderlands, 1690s–1710s

1692; and Durham and Groton, July 1694. In August: killings at Spruce Creek, York, Kittery. In summer and fall 1695, Kittery, Billerica, Saco, and Pemaquid all suffered. Haverhill, March 1697. Lancaster again, September 1697: twenty killed, five taken. Andover, February 1698. The havoc came to an uneasy close in the late 1690s, with the end of King William's War. "The Indian War, which hath lasted a full ten years," wrote Samuel Sewall in November 1698, "is we hope, now at an End."[64] But it ratcheted up again painfully soon thereafter, with the outbreak of Queen Anne's War in 1702.

Much as it seemed so to English colonists, the violence was not random. It was not purposeless. Behind the raids lay complex Native and French motivations, both political and personal. Some Indians took captives because they intended to adopt them, as new kin replacing lost family members. Many raiders were of Iroquois heritage and had thus been steeped in a long tradition of "mourning wars." Mourning wars, marked by raids on enemy groups meant to collect new adoptees to cover the dead, probably predated contact with Europeans. But the practice seems to have escalated with colonization, not least because the arrival of colonists caused incalculable mortality among Native people. Captives taken for this reason underwent elaborate adoption rituals, which were, by most accounts, remarkably effective. Quite a few English captives chose to remain with their captors and live out the rest of their lives as Indians. But Native raiders' objectives were also, increasingly, economic. Raiding was lucrative: English captives could be sold as servants in New France or ransomed back to anxious relatives in New England.[65]

One of the basest motivations for raiding, however, was simply to terrify. Some of those involved in these attacks were Algonquians who had been pushed out of their homelands by the English. Others were struggling to stay autonomous. Abenakis, who lived in the vast territory between Iroquoia, New France, and New England (some in the very teeth of English settlement), fell under great pressures in these years. They lost land. They lost crops and fish, disrupted by English settlements. They lost patience. Meanwhile, the French pushed them to become Catholic, and, during war, to attack the English. Not all agreed, but English colonists gave them ample reason to grow resentful. King William's War began, in part, because anxious Englishmen, afraid the Indians were conferring with Frenchmen, arrested twenty Abenakis. Among them (though most were women and children) was an Androscoggin leader named Hope-Hood. The captives,

Schenectady in ashes, "a Snow fell above knee deep and dreadfull cold."[57] It blanketed the bodies, left resting mutely within the palisades. But when Albany sent Captain Jonathan Bull to "bury the dead," the next day, he was still able to identify some of them. Albany kept a "List of The People Kild and Destroyed," probably from Bull's own tally. One can almost imagine him walking the ruined village: "Barent Jansse Killd and Burned his Sonne Kild." "Ands Arentse Bratt shott and Burnt & also his childn." "David Christoffelse & his wife with 4 Children all burnt in there house." "Joh: Potman kild his wife kild & her scalp taken off."[58]

Samuel Sewall was hosting a dinner party on the twenty-fourth of February, the night that Boston received word that Schenectady had been "destroy'd by the French." One of Sewall's dinner guests that night, the governor, apparently thinking not of the appetites of the other attendees, "brought the Papers [describing the attack] and read them before and after dinner." As ghastly aperitifs, the story's details must have turned the stomachs of Sewall's poor dinner guests: "60 Men, Women and Children murder'd. Women with Child rip'd up, Children had their Brains dash'd out," Sewall scribbled into his diary.[59] The following month, as Mrs. Sewall was on her way to Dorchester in a hackney coach to dine with the Stoughtons, word came of another "Surprisal," at Salmon Falls, in New Hampshire. Here was more "dolefull news": A party that was "about half French, half Indians" had struck at dawn, "destroying the best part of the Town, with Fire and Sword."[60] Almost thirty died, Cotton Mather counted, "and more than *Fifty*," he wrote gloomily, "were led into what the Reader will by 'nd by call, *The worst Captivity in the World*."[61]

Thus began decades of violence in New England's northern borderlands.[62] The northern frontier had not been entirely quiet since King Philip's War, which sputtered on into the late 1670s, there, as Native refugees from southern New England brought the bitterness, and fury, northward. But sudden "surprisals" of violence became regular in northern New England with the 1688 outbreak of the War of the League of Augsburg, pitting England and the Dutch against France. (In the colonies it was called "King William's War," wryly, after the country's new king.) From the 1680s on, raiders repeatedly pummeled English towns: Cocheco, June 1689; Pemaquid, August 1689; Schenectady, February 1690; Salmon Falls, March 1690; Falmouth, May 1690; Wells, May 1691; York, January 1692 (Mather: "a *Storm* of Blood!"[63]); Lancaster, July 1692; Brookfield, July 1692; Billerica, August colony's official printer in 1692 (though, when he returned to England in 1695, he once again ran afoul of the authorities).[53]

III.

In 1690, there was, indeed, plenty of news, almost more than Benjamin Harris could cram into his ill-fated newspaper, and much of it woeful. A February snowstorm drove some hapless boaters against the sandbar at Barnstable, "Bodies not found."[54] Smallpox bore down on Boston, killing hundreds. Babies were reportedly born bearing the marks of the disease, as it "infected even *Children in the bellies of Mothers.*" The city also suffered two great fires, one that devoured "*twenty Houses,*" and then, only weeks later, another. (This one Harris seemed to count as more disastrous, not least because it consumed "the best furnished PRINTING-PRESS, of those few that we know of in *America* . . . a loss not presently to be repaired.") In Watertown an old man, "*Sober* and . . . *Pious,*" hung himself in a barn. Others likely contemplated choosing a similar fate, this terrible year. "'Tis not easy to relate the Trouble and Sorrow that poor *Boston* has felt," Harris wrote.[55]

And there was war. In the 1690s, French and Indian raiders began preying, with some regularity, on the northern fringes of English settlement. One of the first attacks came just as the decade opened. It must have seemed very far indeed from Harris's Boston. On the icy morning of February 9, 1690, the inhabitants of Albany, New York, awoke to an alarm: The nearby village of Schenectady had been attacked. First to reach Albany with the news was Symon Schermerhorn, "shott threw his Thigh" and bleeding. Then others, too, "came Running here," wrote one Albany witness. Schenectady was afire, they said, its streets "full of french and Indians." The town had foolishly assigned no watch. (Legend has it that their only sentinels were snowmen, stationed stiffly at the village entrances.) At least sixty died when raiders fell upon the town, and nearly thirty more were taken captive. Some twenty-five others stumbled frantically through the snow to Albany, "there limbs frozen in the flight."[56]

They told chilling stories. "The Cruelties committed at said Place," went one report, "no Penn can Write nor Tongue expresse: the women big with Childe rip'd up and the Children alive throwne into the flames, and there heads dash'd in pieces against the Doors and windows." That night, available. Much more than the Cambridge press had ever done, and perhaps just as much as London printers did for the colonial market, Boston began printing news.[47]

In September 1690, Bostonians could even hold in their hands the colonies' first attempt at a regularly published newspaper, *Publick Occurrences, Both Forreign and Domestick*. Its publisher, Benjamin Harris, wanted simply to provide readers with accurate news, in a time when many of them were verily clamoring for it. When *Publick Occurrences* appeared, Massachusetts was in something of a political maelstrom: The royal governor had been toppled, and colonial emissaries were in London seeking a new charter. Pamphlet wars flared, repeatedly. While the provisional government tried to get its bearings, meanwhile, French and Indians had begun punishing towns to the north and east of Boston. The colony had scraped together an expedition to resist the raiders pounding the northern frontier, but it was not going well.[48]

The butchery would go on for decades more, but *Publick Occurrences* met an abrupt end. Harris had intended it to be published once a month, or sooner, charmingly, if "any Glut of Occurrences happen." Glut of occurrences or no, the governing council of Massachusetts quashed the paper after just one issue. This, apparently, because the newssheet was "not Licensed"; and because Harris had impugned the honor of both the French king and the Mohawk allies of the English. One senses that there was more to the story.[49] The governing council can perhaps be forgiven for its nervousness. Newspapers were relatively new to the English. Even England did not have a periodical press until the 1620s. (Early corantos, or printed half-sheets of news, appeared in Amsterdam in 1618; by December 1620, as the Pilgrims were warily poking about 'First Encounter' beach, English translations had surfaced in London.[50] At about the same time, epistolary newsletters emerged, as men with country estates hired letter writers to gather London news, compose it, and forward it by post. One of these reporters was Thomas Archer, who, in 1622, began printing his newsletter. The resulting work, *The Weekly Newes*, was, by all rights, the first English newspaper.[51])

Publishing news, it turned out, was politically perilous. Archer was arrested in 1621 for penning some snippet to which the Spanish ambassador objected.[52] Benjamin Harris fared better: After *Publick Occurrences* was silenced in 1690, he became a successful publisher and was named the

But some must have wondered whether they truly *"Deserved"* the torrent of bloodshed that Mather insistently narrated. Readers were treated to unblinkingly violent descriptions of English bodies, broken and suffering. Mather lingered on images like that of the damage done by the *"Head-breakers"* (a "frightful Name," he thought) carried by Indian raiders. Of nine captives taken at Newbury in 1696, Mather wrote, "the *Indians,* in their going off, Strook them all so Violently on the Head with the *Clubs"* that nearly all died. If "the Doctors closed up the *wounds* of their *Heads,* they would grow *Light-headed,* and Faint, and Sick, and could not bear it; So at last, they Died, with their very *Brains* working out at their *Wounds.*"[95] Mather's purpose was to make sense of these episodes. He sought to find, as the title of a 1706 publication phrased it, the "Good Fetch'd Out of Evil." He tried to explain, somehow, these visitations of violence. But, in so doing, he also rehearsed them. He underlined them, replicated them, multiplied them. He enumerated them, as if driven compulsively to index New England's torments. "We have been sorely Lashed, with one Blow after another, for our Delinquencies," he wrote in 1697. "Who is there to *Number* the Blowes?"[96]

With Mather chronicling them, the "Blowes" seemed endless, and the gore spilled liberally. Even the stories of captives who had been "Recovered," and were now "Living Monument[s] of the Power and Goodness of God," were drenched in bloody description. At Deerfield, during King William's War, Mather wrote, raiders had "struck an Hatchet some Inches into the *Skull* of a Boy there," so deeply that his attackers were forced to "Wrench" it out. The boy had been found after spending "a long while Weltring in his *Blood,*" and survived; but for a space of time thereafter, "considerable Quantities of his *Brain* came out from time to time."[97] While many of Mather's colonists were brained, or left "Weltring" in blood, others were burned alive. Mather dwelled, for instance, on the example of Robert Rogers, a captive taken during the Salmon Falls raid: After being "Stript," "beat," and "prickt," when he could not keep pace with his Indian captors, he was roasted like a pig.[98]

But it was the suffering of northern New England's "Scattered Families" that especially offended Mather's sensibilities. The Puritan founders of New England thought "well-ordered families" the fundamental units of a healthy commonwealth, and thus raiders' indiscriminate slaughter of families, children even, must have read to English colonists as particularly horrific.[99] In writing about the wars, Mather resorted repeatedly to stories in which raiders and in Mather's own *Ecclesiastes* (1697), Mather's little book was read with "a greedy Attention," by people in "all Corners of the Countrey."[87]

He was not the first to understand readers' interest in captivity. Tales of captivity had circulated earlier, as Europeans began fanning out across the globe and coming into contact with exotic, new peoples.[88] Often these stories were woven into longer narratives, not focused wholly on the experience of capture. But only in the late seventeenth century did the captivity narrative, one of the most iconic genres of early American literature, truly emerge. The pattern began in 1682, with Mary Rowlandson's account of her capture during King Philip's War (a publication so popular that three more editions were issued within a year). But it took full shape under the pen of Cotton Mather. Forged largely in the convergence of Boston printing and imperial warfare, the captivity narrative assumed its now-famous form—a tale of capture by Indians, forced marches through the wilderness, and trials endured as tests of faith.[89] Such stories also circulated orally (and in manuscript), but in print they proved immensely popular. Mary Rowlandson's narrative was second only to the Bible in popularity; John Williams's *Redeemed Captive Returning to Zion* (1707) purportedly sold 1,000 copies in its first week of release.[90]

Captivity narratives were framed as spiritual instruction. They were written to spur feelings of humility at God's providence. Mather intended his to "promote . . . *general Repentance*."[91] Often they glorified God by gesturing toward captives that had been rescued, improbably, from the jaws of fate. One of the first accounts of captivity to be published in New England, Quentin Stockwell's, had appeared as part of a collection of providence tales, Increase Mather's *An Essay for the Recording of Illustrious Providences* (1684). It was nestled into a chapter profiling those who had survived experiences that, by all rights, should have killed them. Cotton Mather's writings also proffered "Numberless" examples of captives saved from certain death.[92] Yet captivity narratives were also embedded with stories of misery and death, of captives who had not been spared. In reading about such "Disasters," Mather hoped, New Englanders would be moved to reckon with their own transgressions.[93] "Have Bloody, Popish, and Pagan *Enemies*, made very dreadful Impressions upon us, and Captived and Butchered multitudes of our Beloved Neighbors?" he asked, in a 1697 sermon. "Let us Humbly Confess, our Sins have *Deserved*."[94]

who lived in Charlestown, Massachusetts, was not close to danger. Yet, like Mather, he recorded copious stories of this mayhem, whether the raids were major or not. Thus, his diary captured the astounding moment when York was "Attaqued by French & Indians," whereby most of the town was "burnt," 140 people had gone "missing" and "40 found killed." But Hammond also took note of smaller episodes, as when "one man, his wife & son & patrick Mark's Daughter" were killed at Dunstable in 1691.[70] In New Hampshire, the Reverend John Pike turned his diary into a litany of the dead and captured. Pike's tally included the distant and anonymous dead. But more often, he listed the names of people he knew, killed amidst familiar orchards and byways. "Mrs Ursula Cutt (with 3 others) was slain [by] Indians, . . . upon her plantation near boiling-Rock," he wrote in July 1694.[71]

Many seemed not to know what to do with such news, except to write it down. Most did not offer much in the way of interpretation, in relating these events. They only set them down in stark, stiff, numerical terms. A macabre formula took hold, a sort of grim mode of reportage, which almost all writers tended to follow, with slight variation depending on what was known: the town beset; how many killed; how many carried captive; how many houses burned; how many of the enemy; and, finally, the identities of those lost, if any names were known. "The Enemy at Nuchawannick have burned about 30 Houses & killd & carry'd away about 80 persons," Hammond tallied, after the Salmon Falls raid in March 1690, ". . . the Enemy said to be not above 60."[72] If these attacks could not be controlled, they could, nonetheless, be enumerated. The disordered could be given order, if only on paper. It could be named and numbered, and described, which observers—even those in comparatively little danger—seemed to do compulsively. Letters and diaries were turned into dour lists of the dead, of the taken, their inert language and numbers belying the chaos that drove writers, continually, to take up their pens.

"We hear of nothing but Rumors of War and Slaughter against us," Samuel Sewall wrote in July 1696. "I hope the Shepherd of Israel will rescue this his little flock out of the mouths of the Lion and cruel Bear, which gape upon it to devour it." Those who were not in the belly of the beasts, as it were, nonetheless understood the fright involved. News of northern terrors, it is clear, swept well south and west. One could hardly avoid it. Every so often, it seemed, a man would "hear of some slain here and there."[73] "The enemy Indians to the eastward did much hurt in this month," wrote John Marshall, in Braintree, Massachusetts, in July 1697. "Every week brought us the sad notices of it."[74] Sad notices were sometimes painfully intimate. Among those struck in a 1704 raid, Increase Mather counted, were "my Cousin Williams, & his wife & children. His wife was my brother Eleazars daughter. His children my brothers grandchildren. 3 of them killed."[75] After the "amazing stroke" at York, in 1692 ("about fifte persons kill'd and near ninty captivated"), Samuel Sewall lamented the loss of the Reverend Shubael Dummer, "which is the more sorrowfull to me, because [he was] my Mothers Cousin german and my very good friend."[76]

It is not easy to say, precisely, how all of this news traveled. But the Mathers' correspondence betrays some clues. Increase Mather was well known, by the 1690s, and lived in buzzing Boston. He had a healthy stable of correspondents. Some of them, like the Reverend John Pike (to whom Cotton Mather later acknowledged he was "much beholden" for news about the war), and Samuel Penhallow of Portsmouth, resided north and east of Boston, nearer to the borderlands. Penhallow sent intermittent letters and gifts to the elder Mather, who reciprocated gratefully. (Portsmouth being on the northern postal route, at least some of these missives likely traveled by post. A 1706 letter from Mather to Penhallow, for one, is marked "post payed. 12d.") In 1704, Mather thanked him for his generous "token" of "Furr gloves," which were impossible to get in Boston but "very beneficial" because of the gout in Mather's hands, which flared up painfully in the cold.[77]

Penhallow also sent extraordinary stories. One concerned a French army, nearly all of its men sickened after drinking "plentifully" from a well. Eight hundred died. Years later, wrote Penhallow, a French soldier who had robbed a church and "was sentenced to be burnt" admitted, incredibly, that he had killed "near eight hundred souls." Chastened by an officer, the soldier had gotten hold of a poison and "threw it all into a well, of which the thirsty army drank freely."[78] Mather, who found the story "Remarkable," sent several "small bookes" to Penhallow as a gesture of gratitude. "If you have any other Remarkable providences to acquaint me wth, you will oblige me," he wrote.[79] Further tales followed. When Cotton Mather published 1699's *Decennium Luctuosum*, a lurid relation of King William's War, he reprinted letters from both John Pike and Samuel Penhallow. Writing about the Indian wars elsewhere, he thanked his "Good Friend, *Samuel Penhallow* Esqr. (to whome I have been Endebted for many such Communications)."[80]

Cotton Mather, it turned out, had a lot to say about New England's Indian troubles. In him the emerging New England press soon met its greatest patron—greater, even, than his father. Increasingly, because of that patronage, one needed not to have watched a house burn, or to have lost a relative, in order to gain intimate knowledge of the violence vexing New England's outer reaches. There would soon be new ways to learn about such things, and to read about them. News, for years, had found its way—in various ways—to New England's fearful colonists. Letters had carried it, their writers attempting to give it order, and, always, chatter passed the word along less formally, less certainly. But increasingly, now, they would begin to see it captured in type.

IV.

Cotton Mather did not travel much. As late as 1705, the famed Boston minister thought twenty miles a long way to go, especially in winter. He thanked God for preserving him during a trip to Watertown Farms (now Weston), that December. "My Calash once oversett on the Road, and I was thrown out, but I received no manner of Harm," he noted, almost disbelievingly.[81] The following spring, the roads mired in mud, Providence intervened again: As Mather braved the journey to Andover ("a Town almost thirty Miles off"!), the Almighty prevented "my Calash from over-setting, when the bad Way brought me into extreme Danger of it."[82] But muddy ways and the occasional overset chariot may not have been all that deterred Mather. He balked, especially, at traveling north and west of Boston, and not without reason. Just before his journey to Andover, he noted, "a Descent of Indians from *Canada,* on this very Part of the Countrey, rendred the Road so unsafe, that I durst by no means have travelled it." Just a "few Dayes" later, a family he met along the way was "visited" by Indians and "murdered."[83]

Mather probably did not remember a time without Indian war. He had been only twelve years old at the outbreak of King Philip's War in 1675. Already, by that time, he was living a rather extraordinary life, a life full of providential twists of fate. At just eleven years old, he had entered Harvard, where he was hazed viciously. Despite stuttering as a child, he had become a renowned minister and orator, and by the mid-1690s, he was one of the best-known preachers in New England. He was married in May 1686 to Abigail Phillips, but the union was darkened by a string of sorrows: Mather lost thirteen children in his life, as well as Abigail herself in 1702. Through all of this, he wrote furiously, always. He published a staggering fifteen to twenty items per year. In just four years, he wrote nearly all of his famous ecclesiastical history *Magnalia Christi Americana* (1702). It is 800 pages long.[84]

Mather grasped the power of the press in ways that few others did. In the early 1690s he began noting in his diary whenever he had "composed and published" a book, and by 1692, he imagined that he had all but "filled my Countrey, with little BOOKS." In moments when his humility slipped, Mather allowed himself to think his "little BOOKS" so powerful as to be the special targets of the devil. (It was not lost on him, for instance, that when a rash of "horrid *Witchcraft*" broke out at Salem, the devil's method had been "to tender BOOKS unto the afflicted People." Was this hellish circulation of books, he wondered, "intended by *Hell,* as a particular Defiance, unto *my* poor Endeavours"?)[85] One senses, in his publication record, a kind of punishing ambition. He published at a volume far beyond any other colonial writer. For that, he sometimes allowed himself faintly smug moments of self-congratulation. In summer 1697 he thanked God for "publishing more of my Composures than any Man's, that ever was in *America,* while I am yett a young Man: and making my Studies, to bee readd, and priz'd, and serviceable, not only all over these *American* Colonies, but in *Europe* also."[86]

Indeed Mather's "Composures" kept the presses wildly busy. He wrote tirelessly, his pen stubbornly willing events into shape. One subject about which he was compelled to write, in the 1690s, was the violence of King William's War. Mather may have avoided the terrors of the frontier, but he did write about such things—prolifically. He preached sermons, penned histories, and published numbingly bloody accounts of French and Indian raids. He wanted to give meaning to these things, to put them into the service of his ministry. In 1696, he planned to publish *Great Examples of Judgment and Mercy,* a sermon including a "*Collection* of terrible and barbarous Things undergone by some of our *English Captives* in the Hands of the *Eastern Indians.*" This was the little book that became *Humiliations Follow'd with Deliverances,* after Hannah Dustan's escape. To Mather's apparent delight, it found a great readership. Partly because it was advertised in advance in Tulley's almanac for 1697 (though published afterward with a different title) "assassinated the Children."[100] Infants, and pregnant mothers, seemed to suffer worst. Their bodies bore all of the symbolic promise and the cruel vulnerability of the English colonies, and thus were badly battered in print. When Mehetabel Goodwin's infant cried because it was hungry, Mather related, her Indian captor "Snatcht the Babe out of its Mothers Arms, and before her Face knockt out its *Brains*." She was not allowed to bury it.[101] Some of these images eventually became standard tropes in American captivity narratives, the ultimate examples of Indian barbarity. But as colonists encountered them for the first time, perhaps in Cotton Mather's blistering reports, they must have summoned almost inexplicable horror.

Mather's graphic descriptions were meant to shock readers out of religious complacency.[102] But one wonders whether his writings had the desired effect. In 1707, he penned *Frontiers Well-Defended*, a "little Book" that offered spiritual direction and consolation to residents of "our exposed Plantations," those poor frontier families living in a "Land of unwalled Villages."[103] But it must have been cold comfort. Frontier residents hardly needed reminding of the dangers they faced: namely, the "*Killing* of some," as Mather spelled out needlessly, "and siezing and snatching away others, for a *Captivity*, full of miseries." In writing, he reenacted the terrors of frontier surprisals. "Ever now and then," he wrote, "we hear of some, who in Planting their *Corn*, alas, have their *Fields water'd with their Blood;* . . . Some, who stepping forth to look their *Cattel*, have themselves become *Sheep for the Slaughter*." Indeed, the north country was a "*Countrey of Death*." Then came a lesson, about family prayer: "O Hearts harder than Rocks," he rebuked, "You know not, but your Houses may be rifled and burned, and your Children weltring in their *Blood*, before to morrow; And will you not *Pray?*"[104]

Whether *Frontiers Well-Defended* even reached readers along the edges of English settlement is not clear. But it was soon available for sale in Benjamin Eliot's bookshop in Boston.[105] This may be where Mather's publications found their greatest audience and wrought the greatest effects: away from scenes of war. Mather was a master at promoting his own writing. A description in his diary suggests how this likely worked: In 1705 he penned a "Discourse" to spur men to family prayer. Promptly, he printed 1000 copies. "These I bound up in Bundles," he explained, "and printed a short Letter to be added unto each of the Bundles; entreating the Person, whose Name I inserted with my Pen, to find out what *prayerless Families* there may be in the Town where he lives, and to lodge these Essayes of Piety in them." To "every Town in all these Colonies" went a bundle.[106] In 1706, Mather esti-mated that he had given away "at least *six hundred Books* in a Year."[107]

By the early eighteenth century, itinerant peddlers were also selling books. Mather himself grumbled, in 1713, that, "the Minds and Manners of many People about the Countrey are much corrupted, by foolish Songs and Ballads, which the Hawkers and Peddlars carry into all parts of the Countrey." He hoped to counter these "foolish" materials by distributing "Composures full of Piety" in "all Corners of the Land."[108] But if Mather's pious "Composures" found an audience in "all Corners of the Land," then so too did the terror they described. Mather forced war into homes throughout New England. His writing brought the imperial wars home to roost. It ensured that those in other parts of the region felt fright, too, because, by all accounts, Mather sold a lot of "little BOOKS." *Good Fetch'd Out of Evil,* for instance, flew off the bookseller's racks. "In a weeks time," Mather tallied, "he sold off a thou-sand of the Impression."[109] But Mather was not the only one spreading the news. There were other ways to read about the carnage, as well. More car-nage was coming, and more print, as well.

V.

In the winter of 1704 the English village of Deerfield, Massachusetts, was perched, nervously, in the hills overlooking the Connecticut River valley. It was nested into rolling folds of snow, white drifts bunched up against its palisade. Townsmen had turned the town into a garrison. But the wooden pales set staunchly around the town ultimately proved of little aid. When French and Indian raiders arrived in the hushed darkness of early morning on February 29, they simply clambered up the piles of snow alongside the village walls and fell upon the houses inside. Deerfield's slumbering resi-dents awoke to the sound of hatchets whacking through their doors. "The enemy came in like a flood upon us," wrote the Reverend John Williams. Only a few English escaped. Some desperately pursued the raiders, as they retreated. But they fell back for fear of the captives' lives, after finding "many dead bodies" and "prints on the snow," where others had been dragged toward the river. Fifty were dead, by the end of the raid; 112 more were taken captive. Twenty died during the march toward Canada.[110]

A pall of fear had long darkened Deerfield. The town rested on the outer-most edge of English settlement. John Pynchon worried that the colonial government was too little concerned about such a lonely outpost. A "laish-like indiscretion," he warned, "may procure some smart blow (as it did at Scenectoke)."[111] ("Laishlike" referred to a biblical city, Laish, attacked and burned to the ground by the Tribe of Dan. The story appears in the Book of Judges.) Attacks did come, several times in the 1690s. "These towns are dayly Infested by the enymy," Pynchon wrote, beleaguered, in September 1695. Town residents were exhausted, awash "wth feares." Many cursed the decision to plant themselves in a place so pestered by threats. As Pynchon described, Deerfield's harried settlers were "in a sence in the enemy's Mouth almost," and thus "are often & so continualy Pecked at."[112] By the summer of 1703, a persistent drumbeat of warnings suggested that a major blow was coming.[113] When it finally came, in February, the town was left a "mangled Remnant."[114]

News of the Deerfield raid did not spread as fast as the fires eating through the town's ruins. Smoke was spotted, soon enough, by colonists a few miles downriver at Hatfield. Perhaps they even smelled smoke rising against the inert winter air. Colonel Samuel Partridge, commander of the militia in western Massachusetts, arrived soon enough after the raid to make a grim tally of the havoc and death left behind. This he sent to Hartford, to summon help. Towns dotting the riverbanks south of Deerfield, then, probably heard about the raid fairly quickly—in some cases, within hours. But the news took days to reach Boston. Samuel Sewall wrote in his diary that the "dismal News of the Slaughter made at Deerfield" was made "certainly and generally known" on March 5, five days later.[115] That same day, in his sermon at Windsor, Connecticut, the Reverend Timothy Edwards lamented the "dreadful dispensation of God's hand at Deerfield."[116] By late spring the tale had traveled as far as Maryland, where leaders balked at sending aid to New England, being "very apprehensive of their own danger from the Indians and French . . . since the cutting off of Dearfield."[117]

As an act of terror, the Deerfield raid succeeded spectacularly. It visited crippling panic on the Connecticut River towns, where colonists remained tremulous for months. "O[u]r people are so tranceported with the late stroak at Derefd that I can hardly pacifie them," Samuel Partridge wrote, in mid-March. Partridge sent a cascade of desperate letters to Connecticut, pleading for aid. "The awfull appearences of warr, blood, fire & dessolations by the comon enemy," he described plaintively, "moves & shakes o[u]r people with such consternation & amazement that its hard for us here to sitt quiet under o[u]r present circumstances."[118] But the fears awoken by the raid were not limited to those who witnessed the raid or its aftermath. Deerfield's woes became widely known. However distant some colonists may have been from this terror, they followed it carefully. They wrote about it in diaries, preached about it in sermons, and put it into letters. The Deerfield raid did better what other raids had also done, and would do: It took English networks of communication and turned them against themselves. It woke up the English frontier of correspondence and sent bursts of terror throughout.

For months afterward, there were frequent panics that another catastrophic raid was coming. In May 1704 came word from New York that the *"French* of *Canada* are sending out 300 men to attack some parts of *N. England."* A month later: "We hear 500 French and Indians are Marched from *Canada,* to attaque some parts of *New-England."* In his diary, Increase Mather wrote that there were "reports" of "800 French & Indians" descending on the colonies. Sometimes the uncertainty of these rumors made them the more frightening. The year after Deerfield, another French army was said to be coming "over the Ice, but on what place was kept secret." None of these rumors was borne out. But the panics took their toll. "It is a dismal time in N.E.," Increase Mather moaned. "We are advised of 500 Indians & French designing to fall on the western plantations in the province, as many on the eastern. Never was there the like distress." The distress was difficult to escape. Letters communicated it, like plague.[119]

But colonists could soon follow the drama in print, as well. Barely two months after the Deerfield raid, Boston postmaster John Campbell set about publishing English America's first recurrent newspaper, the *Boston News-letter.* Campbell left behind no writing to explain why, in 1704, he thought it a good time to revive Benjamin Harris's failed experiment. But he was in a good position to do it. As postmaster he was privy to incoming shipping news, as well as the American posts. (Early issues of the *News-letter* make clear that Campbell timed the printing of the paper to coincide with the Saturday arrival of postmen from parts beyond Boston; the "eastern post" arrived weekly from Maine and New Hampshire, while the "western post" from New York—and further south—came every other Saturday.[120]) He was also used to sharing news. For several years he had been penning handwritten newsletters and dispatching them via post to various eminent New Englanders, in some cases weekly and apparently for free. (Campbell's surviving manuscript newsletters are marked "ffranke," to signal that no money should be collected upon delivery.)[121] These were widely circulated.[122] So, Campbell moved to a medium in which he could reproduce a greater number of copies: print. The *Boston News-letter* appeared for the first time on April 24, 1704. It was to be America's first successful newspaper.[123]

It hardly looked the part. And that was for good reason: Campbell did not make the mistake of failing to get his publication licensed, as Benjamin Harris had done. Unlike *Publick Occurrences,* the *News-letter* was "published by authority," sanctioned by the colonial government. It was also, therefore, something of a bore—utterly uncontroversial, and, worse, composed in a manner that was "graceless and dull."[124] Cotton Mather sneeringly called it "our paltry news-letter" and "a thin sort of diet of news."[125] It was also unabashedly imitative: It looked exactly like the *London Gazette,* and Campbell more or less copied most of its news out of European newsprints. In its early years the *News-letter* had a rather modest circulation of only 250 copies or so. Most of those reading the newspaper were likely merchants and colonial officials, located around Boston.[126] Beset by the production costs, John Campbell printed repeated, pained pleas for help in keeping it afloat.[127] In 1709 he even suspended printing for a short time. ("Campbell prints no more newes," one reader wrote, whether or not with disappointment is unclear.)[128] We should thus be careful not to overstate the paper's influence.

Nonetheless, it did find an audience. During Campbell's 1709 hiatus from printing, at least one reader found writing letters to be more burdensome, since he was forced to relate news which the *News-letter* ordinarily would have included. "Mr. Campbell's not printing his news now makes me thus perticuler & tedious," the young John Winthrop apologized to a Connecticut correspondent.[129] The comment suggests that at least some Connecticut readers did get news, even fresh news, from the paper. Campbell himself insisted that he had printed a goodly amount of "Intelligence" that a few "Gentlemen and Merchants" might already know, "yet for the most part the people in general, in this and the Neighbouring Provinces, have it not."[130] (Campbell saw his production of the *News-Letter* as a public duty, and he was wounded by those who were "so apt & ready to carp at his weakness."[131]) Samuel Sewall read the *News-letter* carefully, making notes in the margins and retaining his copies, which he later bound together. Sewall's notes prove how the paper's readership was bolstered when

N. E.　Numb. 1.

The Boston News-Letter.

Published by Authority.

From **Monday** April 17. to **Monday** April 24. 1704.

London Flying-Post from *Decemb.* 2d. to 4th. 1703.

Letters from *Scotland* bring us the Copy of a Sheet lately Printed there, Intituled, *A Seasonable Alarm for* Scotland. *In a Letter from a Gentleman in the City, to his Friend in the Country, concerning the present Danger of the Kingdom and of the Protestant Religion.*

This Letter takes Notice, That Papists swarm in that Nation, that they traffick more avowedly than formerly, & that of late many Scores of Priests and Jesuites are come thither from *France*, and gone to the North, to the Highlands & other places of the Country. That the Ministers of the Highlands and North gave in large Lists of them to the Committee of the General Assembly, to be laid before the Privy-Council.

It likewise observes, that a great Number of other ill-affected persons are come over from *France*, under pretence of accepting her Majesty's Gracious Indemnity; but, in reality, to increase Divisions in the Nation, and to entertain a Correspondence with *France*. That their ill Intentions are evident from their talking big, their owning the Interest of the pretended King *James* VIII. their secret Cabals, and their buying up of Arms and Ammunition, wherever they can find them.

To this he adds the late Writings and Actings of some disaffected persons, many of whom are for the Pretender, that several of them have declar'd they had rather embrace Popery than conform to the present Government; that they refuse to pray for the Queen, but use the ambiguous word Sovereign, and some of them pray in express Words for the King and Royal Family; and the charitable and generous Prince who has shew'd them so much Kindness. He likewise takes notice of Letters not long ago found in Cypher, and directed to a Person lately come thither from *St. Germains*.

He says that the greatest Jacobites, who will not qualifie themselves by taking the Oaths to Her Majesty, do now with the Papists and their Companions from St. *Germains* set up for the Liberty of the Subject, contrary to their own Principles, but meerly to keep up a Division in the Nation. He adds, that they aggravate those things which the People complain of, as to *England's* refusing to allow them a freedom of Trade, &c. and do all they can to foment Divisions betwixt the Nations, and to obstruct a Redress of those things complain'd of.

The Jacobites, he says, do all they can to perswade the Nation that their pretended King is a Protestant in his Heart, tho' he dares not declare it while under the Power of *France*; that he is acquainted with the Mistakes of his Father's Government, will govern us more according to Law, and endear himself to his Subjects.

They magnifie the Strength of their own Party, and the Weakness and Divisions of the other, in order to facilitate and hasten their Undertaking; they argue themselves out of their Fears, and into the highest assurance of accomplishing their purpose.

From all this he infers, That they have hopes of Assistance from *France*, otherwise they would never be so impudent; and he gives Reasons for his Apprehensions that the *French* King may send Troops thither this Winter, 1. Because the *English* & *Dutch* will not then be at Sea to oppose them. 2. He can then best spare them, the Season of Action beyond Sea being over. 3. The Expectation given him of a considerable number to joyn them, may incourage him to the undertaking with fewer Men if he can but send over a sufficient number of Officers with Arms and Ammunition.

He endeavours in the rest of his Letters, to answer the foolish Pretences of the Pretender's being a Protestant, and that he will govern us according to Law. He says, that being bred up in the Religion and Politicks of *France*; he is by Education a stated Enemy to our Liberty and Religion. That the Obligations which he and his Family owe to the *French* King, must necessarily make him to be wholly at his Devotion, and to follow his Example; that if he sit upon the Throne, the three Nations, must be oblig'd to pay the Debt which he owes the *French* King for the Education of himself, and for Entertaining his supposed Father and his Family. And since the King must restore him by his Troops, if ever he be restored, he will see to secure his own Debt before those Troops leave *Britain*. The Pretender being a good Proficient in the *French* and *Romish* Schools, he will never think himself sufficiently aveng'd, but by the utter Ruine of his Protestant Subjects, both as Hereticks and Traitors. The late Queen, his pretended Mother, who in cold Blood when she was *Queen of Britain*, advised to turn the West of *Scotland* into a hunting Field will be then for doing so by the greatest part of the Nation; and, no doubt, is at Pains to have her pretended Son educated to her own Mind. Therefore, he says, it were a great Madness in the Nation to take a Prince bred up in the horrid School of Ingratitude, Persecution and Cruelty, and filled with Rage and Envy. The *Jacobites*, he says, both in *Scotland* and at *St. Germains*, are impatient under their present Straits, and knowing their Circumstances cannot be much worse than they are, at present, are the more inclinable to the Undertaking. He adds, That the *French* King knows there cannot be a more effectual way for himself to arrive at the Universal Monarchy, and to ruine the Protestant Interest, than by setting up the Pretender upon the Throne of *Great Britain*, he will in all probability attempt it; and tho' he should be perswaded that the Design would miscarry in the close, yet he cannot but reap some Advantage by imbroiling the three Nations.

From all this the Author concludes it to be the Interest of the Nation, to provide for Self defence; and says, that as many have already taken the Alarm, and are furnishing themselves with Arms and Ammunition, he hopes the Government will not only allow it, but encourage it, since this Nation ought all to appear as one Man in the Defence
of

The front page of the first edition of the *Boston News-letter* (17–24 April 1704). Boston: B. Green, 1704. *(Courtesy of the Massachusetts Historical Society)* well-heeled Bostonians passed copies on to acquaintances. In 1704, he carried the first issue across the Charles River into Cambridge; he also sometimes forwarded the *News-letter* to other parts of the northeast, including New York, New Jersey, Connecticut, and western Massachusetts.[132] Later, he gave copies to the women he courted.[133]

Historians have not pictured Campbell as having been terribly interested in the raids. Perhaps it was merely accidental that he began publishing his paper so soon after Deerfield was lain waste. Perhaps it was coincidence. Admittedly, Campbell allotted less space to local events than to European ones.[134] But what better illustration of the intrusion of European affairs into New England than the Deerfield raid? The new publication followed the trials of the Deerfield captives, reported other deadly episodes from the New England hinterlands, and, on one occasion, prayed ardently that "GOD would not destroy *Dearfield* any more."[135] The inaugural issue spared its readers of any blood spilled. But hints of trouble appeared in the very second edition: A man, near Dover, had been "found Dead and Scalpt." About the same time, in a different part of Oyster River, the paper reported, another man was waylaid by Indians, who "shot him through the thigh & leggs, then took, Scalpt, kill'd, and stript him Naked." In the third issue Campbell reported that some Indians had told a young servant that her master shouldn't bother planting his orchard. He would have no chance to "eat the Apples, nor drink the Cyder," they said, because Indians would "have him . . . and roast him, and she should see it." One of them then bashed the girl over the head and "left her for Dead." Exasperated, in light of the "Calamitous Wars" in Europe and the "*Hostilities acted against us by the treacherous Murderous Salvages within our own Limits,*" the governor of Massachusetts proclaimed a fast day on May 18, 1704. Campbell announced it in the paper.[136]

In the newspaper's first decade, as Queen Anne's War clawed at the edges of the northeast, the *Boston News-letter* printed innumerable items like those described above—items that rehearsed the gruesome punishments beating at the very doors of northern New England. A weekly post now tethered Boston to these northern reaches ("The *Eastern* and *Piscataqua* Post sets out from *Boston* every *Monday* night at seven of the Clock, and all Persons are desired to bring their Letters to the Post-Office before six," went a November 1704 announcement), and by that means countless frightful stories flowed into Campbell's post house.[137] It all amounted, in print, to a persistent chronicle of those stripped, scalped, vanished, found dead, found, even, headless. ". . . Found Mr. *Shaplies* Body, and his head cut off, but cannot tell what is become of the Son," read a dispatch from June 1706. In 1712: Stephen Gillman, "stript, scalpt and battered" by hatchets and left "in the Thickets weltering in his blood." John Waldron's children, near Dover, killed and beheaded.[138] More than any singular incident, it is the relentlessness of these stories that is striking. Some readers must have become numb to them. Some may even have read for entertainment, or with relief that they had been spared such experiences. But others, of course, absorbed this grisly imagery in ways impossible to quantify or to describe.

The wars did have an other side. Englishmen committed violence, as well as suffering it. Many of the major English expeditions against New France were disastrous, even embarrassing.[139] But, even as they fell victim to raids, the English routed Abenaki and French villages, too, with equal ruthlessness. (A brutal English "reprisal against Acadia," in fact, followed the Deerfield raid. It prompted one French official to question New France's strategy entirely.)[140] Massachusetts offered militiamen twenty-pound bounties for Indian scalps. English scouting parties, sometimes accompanied by Indian allies, ransacked Native camps and effectively ended the threat of large raids.[141] Occasionally, a glimpse of English violence snuck into the *News-letter*. In rare moments the newspaper even pictured English soldiers visiting the same sort of terror on Indians and Frenchmen. When Englishmen found the fort at Norridgewock ("the Head Quarters of the Eastern Indians") deserted in 1705, wrote Campbell, they speculated that the enemy had fled the place because they were afraid. The *News-letter* had briefly touched on Colonel Benjamin Church's assaults on French and Native coastal settlements in summer 1704; now, it attributed their fleeing to "consternation that seized them at the Ransacking of the Eastern *French & Indian* Settlements the last Summer."[142]

But what often lingered, despite Campbell's groping for a triumphal tone, was a sense of persistent danger. An undertone of unease poisoned even the reports of raids that had been stopped. The "Enemy was beaten off with loss," the *News-letter* observed, of Lancaster in 1704, "but are yet hovering on the head of those Towns, to make some further Impression, if not prevented."[143] Another lamented: "The Indians are Sculking every where on our Frontiers."[144] The *Boston News-letter* contributed to the sense, among English readers, that colonists could do little to defend themselves against these attacks. It amplified the sense that violence might arrive, out of nowhere, without warning. As Isaac Addington wrote in August 1704: Raiders "continue still hovering in those woods and keep the parts alarm'd; its uncertain where they may fall next, or whether they may not divide and come upon several places at once, so that we are necessitated to strengthen all our frontiers."[145]

By the summer of 1707 the war on English colonists had devolved into a relentless series of smaller incidents: skirmishes, ambushes, and attacks on unsuspecting plowmen or churchgoers. There would be no more great raids like the one on Deerfield. "The Indians are everywhere upon me in small party's," Joseph Dudley moaned, in a letter to the governor of Connecticut.[146] The *News-letter* did not keep up with these episodes systematically, although it did chronicle some. But, years later, when Judge Samuel Penhallow sat down to write his *History of the Wars of New-England with the Eastern Indians,* he *did* seek to create an exhaustive account. Penhallow was a life-long resident of New Hampshire, and his *History* is evocative of how constant the danger must have seemed in these years. In May 1707, "they took two at *Oyster River,*" and in June, "killed one at *Groton*"; soon after, William Carpenter was slain at Kittery, "with his whole Family." July 8, two men "shot dead" on the road from Dover to Oyster River. August 10, a party of travelers struck between York and Wells. Several slain near Marlborough. At Exeter, one killed, two days later, another at Kingston. And on and on it went.[147]

Because Penhallow lived in northern New England, he did not need to resort to secondary accounts of this violence in compiling his book. He had ample access to living memory, his own and others'. He had also kept some sort of written record, which, "in as much as the Divine Providence has placed me near the Seat of Action," he thought his "Duty." In his introduction, Penhallow wrote that his own recollections had been "assisted" by "abstracts of original letters," as well as by consulting with "persons of the best credit and reputation."[148] But his prose suggests that he also consulted the *Boston News-letter,* or that he and Campbell shared sources. In a July 1707 report, for instance, the *News-letter* related the story of brothers Stephen and Jacob Gilman, "ambusht" by Indians. The Indians "shot their Horses under them," the *News-letter* described, and "the first having his Horse dead, was in great danger of being slain . . . [but] got clear; the other Brother was shot at with 7 bullets which grazed his belly." Penhallow echoed:

One brother had "his Horse shot under him, and was in danger of being scalpt before he could get clear. The other brother had several Shot thro' his cloaths and one that graz'd his Belly . . ." In both accounts the brothers escaped harm.[149]

Later readers may have taken little notice of such episodes. After a time, they dissolve into a kind of faceless string of incidents. Penhallow's narrative tests the reader's ability to follow these events, even to absorb them. It deadens understanding. Sentences, dates, names begin to run together, robbed of context. But in his rehearsal of northern New England's torment resides a lesson. If the spectacular blow at Deerfield had sent quakes of fear through the colonies, this parade of smaller attacks—one horseman here, a small child there—was in some way just as terrifying. Penhallow put his finger on it, only a few pages into the narrative. The "Enemy dispersing into small parties," he wrote, "did much more mischief than in larger." It "put the Country into a far greater Confusion," for all who lived in the shadow of the imperial wars knew that "there was no safety to him that went out, nor unto him that came in, but dreadful Calamity on every side." He then described this state of being, in a tight but powerful phrase, set apart from the rest of the text and bordered by long, dark dashes: "____Terror ubique tremor____." Terror everywhere.[150]

Penhallow may not have known how right he was. Frontier fears spread far and wide. Even those in Connecticut harbored "great feers." Settlers living in the many "out-places" along New England's fringes began to have thoughts of abandoning their towns. In the winter of 1707 William Whiting found colonists at the western towns of Woodbury and Waterbury "much possess'd with fear" and "under great apprehentions of approaching danger . . . If some speedy reliefe be not afforded," he warned, "they will break up and desert the place."[151] The "Frontier Towns" in Connecticut, the Boston News-letter confirmed, "have been lately alarmed, with apprehensions of danger from some of the Indians that are on the back of these Towns."[152] Of course, not everyone was afraid. The governor of Connecticut grew bitter when flights of terror in Massachusetts drew his men to the north, for no good reason. "The late alarme made by your scout (frighted with Jack in the Lanthorne)," he wrote acerbically to Joseph Dudley in March 1707, "put us to a great deale of trouble."[153] But even those who did not succumb to such fear left evidence of its prevalence. "I am so amused with multitudinous stories and reports of the Indeans malicious suddaine attempts to do mischief from both East & West," Robert Treat scoffed in 1700. To him, it was "little more than a great pannick fear . . . upon slender grounds." But, slender grounds or not, Treat had seen people truly terrified. The "great pannick fear" was real.[154]

VI.

Many of the captives taken during Queen Anne's War eventually came home. In the meantime, Cotton Mather kept them in his prayers (though he admitted, in his diary, that he would sometimes "forgett to mention them"). He also preached about them. In May 1706 he lectured, among other things, about "Our own Dangers. Our Captives."[155] In November 1706, nearly sixty of the Deerfield captives were redeemed, among them the "pious and worthy Minister, Mr. *Williams*," who had been gone almost three years. If his congregants were in any way inclined to forget about the Deerfield raid (as some of them surely must have wanted to do), Mather made sure they did not. He implored Williams to preach to his congregation at Boston, "a great Auditory," and "to show how great Things God had done unto him."[156] He also pressed Williams to publish his story, which he did, in what became one of the best selling captivity narratives in American history, *The Redeemed Captive Returning to Zion* (1707). In the first ten years of the eighteenth century, according to one estimate, only three books sold fully three thousand copies. One of them was Williams's *Redeemed Captive*.[157]

Queen Anne's War ended, on paper at least, in 1713. But memories of the wars were entrenched early, and they took root deeply. In a lecture that was later published as *Duodecennium Luctuosum* (1714), Mather once more reminded hearers of the seven hundred English that had known captivity— many of them taken "one, or two" at a time, but, in other towns, "a greater Effusion of Blood." "*Haverhil* at once Loses above Thirty of it's Inhabitants," he cried, "and, Poor *Deerfield!*—Never to be forgotten *Deerfield!*"[158] Deerfield wasn't likely to be forgotten. Others followed in Mather's footsteps, long after he was dead. The Reverend Timothy Harrington's *Century Sermon,* celebrating Lancaster's centennial in 1753, for one, stubbornly remembered all of the raids and slayings that had befallen the town, all of the families "barbarously butcher'd by their Hatchets, and weltring in their Gore.—"[159]

Other wars followed, as well. In his 1720 *History of New-England*, Daniel Neal claimed that most of the noteworthy towns in Maine had erected garrisons, which were necessary "to prevent the Incursions of the Eastern *Indians* who might otherwise over-run the Country in 24 Hours."[160] This was exaggeration. But the sense of peril that it reflected was sincere, and this would last a very long time. "I much fear Eastern Indians," a weary Increase Mather wrote in September 1721, nearing death, as colonists faced yet another war.[161] Only a year after Harrington's Lancaster sermon was printed, in 1754, a young Virginia militiaman named George Washington stumbled into a diplomatic hornet's nest in the Ohio country and ignited yet another war with French and Indians. The pattern would repeat.

The post soldiered on, though not without some hiccups. One legacy of Queen Anne's War was truly public postal service. In 1707, several years before Thomas Neale's patent was to expire, the Queen took over his monopoly and embarked on a grand project to unite postal service throughout the empire. In 1710, in part because revenue was needed to fund the continuing war, Parliament passed the Post Office Act. It standardized rates and incorporated colonial postal service into a greater network of transatlantic letter bearing. Giddier about this, no doubt, than his readers, John Campbell published the text of the Act—albeit in slightly abbreviated form—in the *Boston News-letter*. Never again would the post's fate rest in private hands.

In the colonies, though, some grumbled about the cost of posting. "Camell had 18d. for your letter," Wait Winthrop wrote bitterly to his son John, in July 1713. Up to this point, the Winthrops had been using the post liberally; but now, they hired another courier to carry all of their "little bundles" (for "bigg bundles" they paid extra) and made efforts not to let their packets "come to Camells hand."[162] Cotton Mather, too, grew resentful of Campbell and his post office, where ordinary letters were "render[ed] . . . very chargeable." "My dear," he wrote to a Connecticut friend in 1718, "Don't send packets for me to *Campbel*. The last cost me 2s & 10d." He, too, seems to have settled on a "cheaper way" to send letters. ("That costly way may do now & then: But not to make a Trade on't," he advised.) Still, a year or so later, chilled by "dreadful cold" and struggling to find a way to send, Mather betrayed his continued reliance on the post. "My Ink-glass in my Standish is froze & splitt," he wrote gloomily. "My Ink in my very pen suffers a congelation; but . . . by the next post, you may (if we live) hear further from me."[163]

In the meantime, the ever-beleaguered John Campbell's station grew no easier. Shortly after news of the Queen's Post Office Act reached the colonies in the fall of 1711, a "Great Conflagration" tore through Boston. The post office burned to the ground.[164]

Milestones

IN SOME PARTS of New England, still, there are milestones. They are knee-high and red, hidden in hillocks and stuck in tufts of roadside grass. They are not always easy to find. Some have been moved, to stay snug with the drifting path of the post road, and others have long since disappeared. They are carved with numbers, but not uniformly. Most tell the distance to Boston, but a few also measure the miles from Springfield. Number sixty-eight, in West Brookfield, Massachusetts (sixty eight miles to Boston), was years ago polished, lovingly, and cast into a small memorial. It now gazes proudly over the town green. Number sixty-seven rests more humbly, a mile down the road, not far from where Ephraim Curtis crawled through the weeds, on his stomach, to escape a Nipmuck siege in 1675.

These stones were placed along the post road in the mid-eighteenth century. Although they helped ordinary souls with wayfinding, to be sure, they were intended for post riders. Tradition credits Benjamin Franklin, appointed deputy postmaster general in 1753, with ordering these monuments into the loam. He toured the post road himself, the story goes, and personally measured the miles. "Franklin set out on the Boston Post Road," a 2004 Associated Press article imparts, "in a carriage with a homemade odometer attached to the wheel. Every mile a stake was driven into the ground. A crew followed behind, setting stone markers."[1] Some of that may be apocryphal. But Franklin did drag the lumbering American postal service into a new age, and his milestones are like a dwarfish army, marking the rent in time and space.

Most histories of American postal service begin with Franklin. But Franklin is also a conclusion. The middle years of the eighteenth century, those covering his lifetime, are very hard to measure. There were many violent turns. War. Religious revival. Depression, and inflation. A great breach with Britain. One searches for footholds, or landmarks, to cling to, amidst the upheaval. But it is difficult to escape the feeling that somewhere in the middle of the century, right about the time Franklin's men were placing those stones in the road, something ended. The plows and the oxen and the rhythms of life remained the same, for many. But in the lives of some men, whether Mohegan, or Nipmuck, or English, you can almost watch the old New England slipping away. The more you look, the more those stones along the post road start to look like epitaphs.

Franklin was born in Boston in 1706, into a squat and humble little house on Milk Street. "Benjamen Son of Josiah Frankling & Abiah his Wife born 6 Janry 1706," reads the record of his birth in Boston's city registry.[2] Little Ben had many siblings. He was born ninth, but his household eventually included seventeen children ("of which I remember 13 sitting at one time at [the] Table," Franklin later recalled). The Franklins were poor. Josiah Franklin had tried his hand as a dyer, but found he could not make a living that way. So he became a "Tallow chandler and Sope-boiler," a lowly business in which his young son Benjamin sometimes assisted, by "cutting Wick for the Candles, filling the Dripping Mold," and "going of Errands" (though he made no secret of the fact that he "dislik'd" it). By his own account, Franklin's was a childhood of "Poverty and Obscurity."[3]

He was a bookish child. Young Ben Franklin dreamed of going to sea, but his father, recognizing his son's wits, wanted him to become a minister. "My early Readiness in learning to read (which must have been very early, as I do not remember when I could not read) and the opinion of all his Friends that I should certainly make a good Scholar," Franklin wrote, "encourag'd him in this Purpose of his."[4] It was not to be. But in about 1718, when he was twelve or so, Franklin landed in another place that suited his talents with letters: the print shop of his older brother, James. Within a few years he was no longer merely setting type, but also writing essays (albeit anonymously) for his brother's newspaper, *The New-England Courant*. (His pen name, 'Silence Dogood,' mocked the titles of two of Cotton Mather's more tiresome sermons.)

The New-England Courant was not the first newspaper to challenge John Campbell's *Boston News-letter*. Franklin had been born into a world with only one colonial newspaper, but soon after he took up his printing apprenticeship, there were others. Campbell's monopoly on news lasted until 1719. By then he was scandalously far behind in printing European news (over a year behind, to be exact). His postmastership ended in 1718 (possibly because he was pressured to leave it), and, to his chagrin, the new postmaster, William Brooker, commenced publishing a new journal, *The Boston Gazette*. (By some remarkable coincidence, Philadelphia's Andrew Bradford also debuted his new paper, *The American Weekly Mercury*, at almost the very same moment.) While Campbell continued to produce issues of the *Boston News-letter*, he now had competition. But no other newspaper anticipated the "Short and Merry Life" of the *New-England Courant*, whose first edition appeared in 1721.[5]

The *Courant* was a very different sort of newspaper. One historian has called it an "impertinent and precocious brat that never survived its own adolescence."[6] Whereas Boston's official newspapers—the *News-letter* and the *Gazette*—were staid, respectful, and aimed at elite readers, James Franklin's paper was irreverent and partisan. (Its origins lay partly with the controversy over smallpox inoculation, a new and disputed technique. William Douglass, the chief opponent of inoculation, was one of the 'couranteers' who provided James Franklin with letters, essays, and other content.) The *Courant* did not usher in a new age of journalism. It landed James Franklin in jail, twice, and its run ended abruptly in 1726. But the paper anticipated later trends, and, if nothing else, it schooled Benjamin Franklin in the idea of a free press. "The Opinions of Men are almost as various as their Faces," he wrote, in a 1731 'Apology for Printers.' "[I]f all Printers were determin'd not to print any thing till they were sure it would offend no body, there would be very little printed."[7]

The eighteenth century looks different, and then it doesn't. Certainly there were milestones. Newspapers multiplied, as new printers opened shops across the colonies. In 1729 Herman Moll drafted the very first map of the post road in America, its route curving cheerfully through brightly water-colored towns. Postal service, meanwhile, now a public enterprise, remained a bit of a mess. It ran, but it was expensive, inefficient and disorganized. It made no money. No neat, linear progression, and not even the steady march of time, brought news and letters predictably into eighteenth-century households. Nor did Benjamin Franklin's life continue predictably. Franklin, in Boston, was restless, and tired of the beatings that his brother's anger "too often urg'd him to bestow on me." In 1723 he ran away, and landed in Philadelphia, where bread could be bought much more cheaply than in Boston. By 1731, when he wrote his Apology for Printers, he was already publishing his own newspaper, the *Pennsylvania Gazette.* John Campbell, by then, was dead.[8]

In 1723, the year that Ben Franklin ran from his brother, a baby boy was born at Mohegan to Sarah Samson and Joshua Occom. They called him Samson. "I Was Born a Heathen in Mmoyanheeunnuck alias Mohegan in N. London North America," he wrote, later, in the first draft of his autobiography. That sentence betrays a uniquely global perspective. In this later writing, he emphasized his own Indian-ness, his Native roots. "[M]y Parents were altogether Heathens, and I Was Educated by them in their Heathenish Notions," Occom wrote, almost insistently. "[T]hey led a wandring Life up and down in the Wilderness." But Samson Occom's life took him far from Mohegan and those supposedly "Heathenish" origins. He became perhaps the most visible Christian Indian of the eighteenth century, a missionary, a councilor, a traveler, and a leader among many tribes. He preached and taught before Native groups across the northeast. He visited Philadelphia, New York, London, and Iroquoia. He sat for portraits.[9]

Occom, unlike Franklin, remembered a time when he could not read. He remembered a time, in fact, when most Mohegans "were unacquainted with the English Toung." As a child, he had first become familiar with English letters through an Englishman who "went about among the Indian Wigwams," chasing down children and "mak[ing] them read." (The man "Us'd to Catch me Some times and make my Say over my Letters, and I believe I learnt Some of them," Occom recalled.)[10] As for so many others, true literacy came, for him, with Christianity. In 1743, amidst the fervor of the Great Awakening, the young Occom approached the Reverend Eleazar Wheelock, who was then instructing young Englishmen at Lebanon Crank, near Mohegan, to be his teacher. He learned English, Hebrew, Latin, and

Greek. In later life, Occom wrote prodigiously. His surviving letters, journals, sermons, and petitions are all suggestive of a man awakening to the exigencies of using letters, in the broadest sense, to do well for his Indian brethren.[11]

Samson Occom no more speaks for all of New England's Indians than Benjamin Franklin speaks for every Englishman. He was also not the first, of course, to appropriate English writing nor to bend it toward Native concerns. Literate Indians had been doing that almost as long as they had had any experience with the English language, whether by penning wartime ransom notes or by composing expressions of self and belief in the margins of Bibles. ("I Josiah Attaunitt made this on March 18, 1716. I am going to the ocean.")[12] During his own lifetime, even, some questioned whether Occom could stand for other Indians. He wrote his autobiographical narrative, or, as he called it, "a Short Plain and Honest Account of myself," as a defense of his own character, and of his Indian-ness, after both had been called into question. All of the "wigwams" and the "Heathenish" allusions in that piece, therefore, were meant to prove that a true, lowly Indian could, in fact, become an exemplary Christian.[13] But if Occom is not entirely representative, he, like Franklin, does provide a sort of augur.

The mid-eighteenth century was a bleak time for many Indians. Even after the catastrophe of King Philip's War in the 1670s, many Native communities had been able to maintain a hard-fought autonomy, in large part because French and Indian raids kept English colonists very nervous. But the end of Queen Anne's War in 1713 stopped the terror, at least for a good while. It was after 1713 that English men and women truly flooded into Nipmuck country, into the wide interior of New England, and began hungrily grabbing up land. Within a few years, a new social geography defined Native New England. Indians increasingly lived in larger, and fewer, enclaves. Some few plots of land were reserved for them, mostly marginal lands, and Native people from various villages throughout the region drifted toward these. Often, they settled in ways that overlooked old rivalries and divisions. But, by the 1720s, the human map of New England looked very different: Native people, now, comprised the "islands," and the English the surrounding sea.[14]

For some, Christianity formed a kind of bulwark against the century's oncoming miseries. In Massachusetts and the former Plymouth, Indian faith often dated well back into the seventeenth century. Native people in lower New England generally came into the fold later. Some, like Occom, were swept up in the frenzy of the Great Awakening. Practicing Christianity, across groups, contributed to a new "common, separate identity" among Indians, as Native converts tended not to stay with English churches but to form their own. Some others, not caught up in the religious enthusiasm, quietly moved into English towns or went to work in English households. Some lost their way. By the 1750s, as Occom moved toward ordination and began touring Native communities, New England was haunted by unsettling numbers of "wandering Indians." These anonymous travelers, dislodged from their histories, moving from place to place, turned up in documents only when English towns or families were forced to take care of them or, even, to "bury them." But they were there, at sea, in a sense, in a landscape that was no longer theirs.[15]

In 1723, the year Samson Occom was born, the *New-England Courant* printed a satirical letter describing the funeral of Ninigret II (son of the sachem who had gone, in 1653, to Manhattan). It "being usual to favour the Publick with some Account of the Lives and Death of great Personages," the account opened snidely, how could the newspaper fail to honor this sachem? Notwithstanding he had died, reportedly, from "drinking too largely of that Princely Liquor vulgarly called Rhum" ("two Gallons at a Sitting"!), his queen had stood over his grave and "pour'd in a Bottle." (The writer added, a bit more soberly, that tobacco, bread, and "a Pot of Nokaeg" had also gone into Ninigret's coffin, possibly to ease his travels in the beyond.) The *Courant* also mocked the idea that Ninigret's son, the future "king," might be well educated. "'Tis said the Young King is to be sent to the Grammar-School, in order to be educated at Harvard College," pronounced the letter. "[T]is not doubted but that in a few Years time he will be able to write a Latin Epitaph on his Father."[16]

That was the world into which Samson Occom was born. That was what he was up against.

Those stout red milestones went into the New England soil a bit later, after Franklin was already a well-known public figure. In 1753, when he was forty-seven years old, Franklin was appointed deputy postmaster general of North America. (He shared the appointment with a Virginian, William Hunter.) The postal service that Franklin inherited was still somewhat

Milestone, at West Brookfield, Massachusetts. *(Author photo)*

unpredictable. It was unprofitable. Roads had been laid out from Penobscot, in Maine, to St. John's River in Florida, dipping and swelling over an astonishing fifteen hundred miles. But they were rough. In the north service was regular, but, south of Philadelphia, riders left only when sufficient mail had piled up. Post riders themselves, meanwhile, stole brazenly. They simply collected the fees for delivered letters, without ever depositing them at post offices. The rider at the Portsmouth stage, for instance, was wont to "Bring and Carry almost all the Letters in a privet way[,] deliver them at his Lodgings[,] and take the money for them." A "Tablefull of Letters" was eventually discovered at his house.[17]

Franklin cleaned up this mess. He sketched postal guidelines that kept letters moving speedily across colonies. Riders now traveled during night, as well as day, and they faced penalties for delaying. To prevent fraud, letters were tallied and listed. Unclaimed (or "dead") letters were to be kept for a month at the local post office, and then sent to Philadelphia. Franklin understood that these measures were necessary because he twice toured the post roads, personally. (It was on the second tour, in the early 1760s, that he reportedly hitched a homemade odometer to the wheel of his carriage and set down milestones to aid post riders.) The success of these measures is not in dispute. By 1761, for the first time in history, the colonial postal service turned a profit.[18]

But in the meantime, there was war. In Franklin's lifetime, there was almost always war. In July 1710, on hearing that his young nephew (and namesake) had shown some interest in "Martial affaires," the elder Benjamin Franklin had sent a poem to little Ben. "Beleeve me Ben. It is a Dangerous Trade— / The Sword has Many Marr'd as well as Made," he wrote. "By it doe many fall, Not Many Rise; / Makes Many poor, few Rich and fewer Wise; / Fills Towns with Ruin, fields with blood beside." The poem's final couplet is a fitting summation of the century: "Ruin'd Estates, The Nurse of Vice, broke limbs and scarts / Are the Effects of Desolating Warrs."[19] Franklin was only four years old when he received the poem. But he lived to see his uncle's words borne out.

The Seven Years War, or, as it was called in the colonies, the "French and Indian War," was sparked, partly, in spring 1754, when a young Virginian militiaman named George Washington went into the Ohio country to order the French to abandon their forts there. Years of bloodshed followed. The coming of this war likely spurred Franklin's carriage along a bit more speedily, as he rushed to reform the post. The colonies were not quite ready to unite politically, yet, which they proved by rejecting the Plan of Union that Franklin proposed, in summer 1754. (He imagined, for better governance and defense, a "President-General" and an elected legislature of colonial delegates.) The hills and hollows of the backcountry, meanwhile, were so scarified by the war that, at its end, although victorious, the British government all but conceded that colonists could not live peaceably with Indians. It drew a line down the spine of the Appalachians in 1763 and declared everything west of it "Indian country." (That decision spelled trouble very quickly, when Parliament tried to fund the policing of this frontier by imposing unwanted new taxes on the colonies.)[20]

Samson Occom, in the meantime, fought his own wars. In 1765 he went to London to raise money for educating young Native men to be ministers. He was embittered, though, when his mentor Eleazar Wheelock, a man he had known since very young, used the money to open a school for Englishmen, instead. Occom fell into heavy drinking in the late 1760s, and by 1773, when his people, the Mohegans, lost a long-fought case to preserve their lands in Connecticut, he seems to have relinquished some hope that Indians could live well in southern New England. In the 1770s Occom and various other Mohegans, Pequots, Narragansetts, Montauketts, and Niantics began to discuss the idea of beginning anew, somewhere distant, and building a new community of Christian Indian brethren. In 1774, the Oneidas granted them a tract of several hundred square miles on which to do it. It was called "Brothertown."[21]

Franklin died in 1790, famous, in the wake of the colonies' war of independence against Britain. Occom died in 1792, more despondent. "[I]t seems that Heaven and Earth, are in Combination against us," he wrote, close to the end of his life. "I am, Some Times, upon the Borders of Desperation."[22]

There are, in the lives of Franklin and Occom, some striking parallels. Both toured the northeast. Both went to London. Both wrote autobiographies. Both tried valiantly to unite those whom they imagined to be their own people, just as those people were awakening to new ways of union. There are also some markedly perpendicular aspects to their lives, mirroring but not matching. Franklin could not remember when he hadn't been able to read; Occom remembered vividly his tutoring. Occom was born into a traditional Mohegan family, and yet became a minister; Franklin's father hoped for him to become a minister, and yet he became one of the more secular figures of the eighteenth century. One expects these lives to intersect, somehow, like two carriages meeting on the post road. But ultimately, there are not so much parallels as slippages. It's as if their histories brush up against one another, but begin to move in very different directions.

"The whole race of *mankind* is generally infected," Roger Williams wrote in 1643, "with an *itching desire* of hearing *Newes*." New England's early history bore this out. Men would go to great lengths to get news, and in the confusion of planting colonies, they had to. News was essential. It rooted people, told them who they were. It gave the impression of warding off dangers, whose powers crumbled with discovery. But its pursuit had a way of leading men astray, into fools' errands and labyrinths of fear and confusion. It was hard to satisfy that "*itching desire*" for news, Williams acknowledged. "Mans *restlesse soule hath restlesse eyes and eares, / Wanders in change of sorrows, cares*

and feares," he wrote. *"Faine would it* (Bee-like) *suck by the ears, by the eye /
Something that might his hunger satisfie."* Eyes and ears were not always
faithful guides.[23]

That struggle for news, that restless wandering, went into the making of
New England. Communication, in the end, was an arm of colonization. It
made real the imagined community that John Winthrop had rather ambi-
tiously described aboard the *Arbella* in 1630. It drove, as did deeds and crude
promises of transferred land, the taking of the northeast. As much as English
colonists claimed the landscape by carving out farms and towns, they
claimed it by traveling through it. They claimed it by sending and collecting
news. New England was not won, or lost, on the back of a horse. It did not
rest, entirely, on the beaten earth of a post road. But colonial communications were part of the appropriations that accompanied English settlement.
Just as their livestock, those famous bovine invaders, overran Native fields
and villages, the English themselves—the human wanderers of the northeast—also pulsed through Native space.[24] Franklin's milestones, after all,
and among their many other duties, are markers of possession.

Along the way, though, there were blunders and horrors, like the
"Backward Turnings" in John Ogilby's *Britannia.* The wandering wood
that was early New England was a thicket of errors, a contingent place, in
which English bewilderment sometimes led to violence. There was a price to
pay for getting news, and things, and for the remaking of Native trails and
networks into English ones. It was not just the knee-jerk slaughter of the
Pequot War, nor the devastation of King Philip's War, nor any of the other
problems triggered somewhat, unexpectedly, by English communications.
There was also a kind of tenacious fear, peaking and receding, but never
retreating fully. So much of what coursed through the communications
frontier, in whispers and letters and rumors, was frightening. It's hard to
avoid the conclusion that, even as travel and exchange went into the settling
of English New England, a parallel process, a sort of *unsettling,* also
unfolded. Colonists unsettled Native New England; in some ways, they
also unsettled themselves.

Meanwhile, in time, memory faded. The earliest years of New England's
history, the uncertain years, went into the deeper reaches of the past.
Penowayanquis, the Nipmuck trader who had once fatally stopped to drink
tobacco with Arthur Peach, had been dead for a hundred years by the time
Franklin began his career as a postmaster. In the years after the death of

Franklin, and of Samson Occom, New England's history was smoothed over, romanticized. Writers penned dozens of histories of New England towns, many of which painstakingly rehearsed local geography but also, simultaneously, erased Indians from it. The descendants of Occom (and Ninigret, and Uncas, and Matoonas, and Nahawton) remained in New England; but, in books, they disappeared.[25] The land changed, too. New England's woods all but vanished, cut down for fuel and lumber and farmland, so that by the time of the American Revolution, the rebels could watch British soldiers approaching, in their lurid red coats, across mile-wide treeless pastures. Roads, however, don't change much. Their courses are stubbornly consistent. Somewhere, along some road in Wampanoag country, Route 44, or maybe Route 118, if you look closely enough, you might still see Penowayanquis, crouched at the water's edge, resting, mid-journey.

Abbreviations

LETTER WRITERS

CM   Cotton Mather
FJW   Fitz-John Winthrop
IM   Increase Mather
JW   John Winthrop
JWJ   John Winthrop, Jr.
RW   Roger Williams
SS   Samuel Sewall
WW   Wait Winthrop

ARCHIVES AND SERIALS

BNL   *Boston News-letter*

CCR   James Hammond Trumbull, ed., *The Public Records of the Colony of Connecticut 1636–1776.* 15 vols. Hartford, 1850–1890.

DHNY   E. B. O'Callaghan, ed., *The Documentary History of the State of New York.* 4 vols. Albany, 1850–51.

IMP   Increase Mather Papers (microfilm). 4 reels. Massachusetts Historical Society, Boston, Massachusetts.

MBR   Nathaniel B. Shurtleff, ed., *Records of the Governor and Company of the Massachusetts Bay in New England.* 5 vols. Boston, 1853–54.

MHSC   Massachusetts Historical Society, *Collections*

MHSP   Massachusetts Historical Society, *Proceedings*

NYCD   John Romeyn Brodhead, ed, *Documents Relative to the Colonial History of the State of New York.* 15 vols. Albany, 1853–87.

Winthrop Papers Microfilm   Marjorie F. Gutheim, ed., *Winthrop Family Papers* (microfilm). 53 reels. Boston, 1976.

WMQ   *William and Mary Quarterly*

circumstances were uncertain, others have been placed in the "Unknown" category. I have also excluded a handful of letters (small enough in number to have a negligible effect on my results), where I could not determine whether they originated in Europe or in the Americas.

I have counted only those couriers attached to surviving letters (as the extant letters represent solid proof of carriage). But I also kept notes on all of the couriers *mentioned* in the Winthrop letters, both bearers linked to existing correspondence and those merely mentioned, in passing. Their stories, although not included in my quantitative analysis, are woven into the narrative wherever possible.

A Note on Method

Much of this study is based on letters. Each letter had to be delivered, and, thus, each is the physical artifact of a journey—tangible documentation of one of the most ephemeral and difficult things to measure. Thousands of seventeenth-century letters survive. By surveying these letters together, we can begin to see the dimensions of correspondence in early America: who was writing, how often, and from where. We can begin to see "corridors" of correspondence, hooking through Nipmuck territory or across Long Island Sound. We can even tell, on occasion, whether letters sailed aboard ships or rode on horseback.

To pull patterns from this early correspondence, I built a database of nearly 3,000 letters. All of the letters in the database come from the Winthrop Family Papers, housed primarily at Massachusetts Historical Society. To help tell the story, I supplement these letters with many other sources, but my quantitative evidence is confined to this group. The collection is not without biases. The Winthrops were elite. They kept mostly to a few particular places (Massachusetts Bay and Connecticut, primarily), so the collection has some geographic bents. But the Winthrops drew correspondence from all over the colonial world, from all sorts of people. The Winthrop Papers are also the wellspring for innumerable other collections.[1] In short, these letters are the best available portrait of scribal New England in the seventeenth century.

My inquiry reaches from 1635 to 1675.[2] Within that period, I have been as exhaustive as possible, with one exception. My analysis is limited to those letters that circulated *within* colonial America; it excludes letters exchanged between Europe and America. Because Atlantic scholars such as David Cressy and Ian K. Steele have thoroughly explored trans-Atlantic communications, that story is less pressing. (Too, in part because the English Civil War disrupted trans-Atlantic correspondence for many of New England's early years, letters sent to and from Europe make up a relatively small portion of the Winthrop collection.) Geographically, then, my database—like the letters themselves—extends to all parts of colonial America, English or not: New England, New Netherland, the Chesapeake, Bermuda, the Caribbean, and elsewhere. With few exceptions, I have tried to count *every* letter contained in the Winthrop Papers that falls within my date range.[3] The final tally is 2,856.

For each letter, I collected specific pieces of information: date; author; addressee; direction (how the letter was addressed); place of origin; destination; carrier's identity (if known); speed of delivery (if noted); and, of course, the subject of the letter (what news it contained). To reflect colonial geography, I have broken the colonial world into "regions," rather than colonies. These are: Bermuda / the Caribbean; Connecticut (what we would think of as Hartford and surrounding towns); Long Island; Maine / New Hampshire; Massachusetts Bay; Narragansett; New Haven; New Netherland / New York; Pequot; Plymouth; Providence; Rhode Island (the island itself); Springfield; the Chesapeake; and other, unknown, destinations. In classifying letters within these zones, I have tried to stay true to colonists' view of geography and to the way New England developed.

In collecting this evidence, some choices were necessary. One choice concerns dating. Many of the letters are dated, clearly (2490, or about 87 percent of them, in fact). But some are not. Here, I have relied on the Winthrop Papers' editors, who have often made thoroughly reasoned decisions about a letter's dating, given its content. Some letters, however, simply cannot be reliably placed in a given time period. Similar caveats apply to places of origin and destination. Although many letters are clearly labeled as departing from "Hartford" or "Newport" or "Providence," some are not marked. For correspondents about whose locations I could be reasonably certain (John Pynchon in Springfield, or John Davenport in New Haven, for example), I used discretion in identifying letters' origins. But, where

Notes

FOOTPRINTS

1. William Bradford, *Of Plimoth Plantation 1620–1647* (Boston: Wright & Potter Printing Co., 1899), 433. I prefer this edition of Bradford's history for its preservation of the author's original, and variable, spelling. In using the Commonwealth Edition of Bradford, I follow the practice of one of the most recent students of Bradford's writings, literary scholar Douglas Anderson. See Anderson, *William Bradford's Books: Of Plimmoth Plantation and the Printed Word* (Baltimore: Johns Hopkins University Press, 2003), 253, n.2. I have, however, silently modernized some transcriptions, substituting "th" for "y," "u" for "v" (and vice versa), and "j" for "i," in Bradford and in other transcribed sources.

2. Roger Williams to John Winthrop, ca. 1 August 1638, in *Winthrop Papers, 1498–1654,* 6 vols. Allyn B. Forbes et al., eds., (Boston: Massachusetts Historical Society, 1929–1992), 4: 48–49.

3. John Winthrop, *The Journal of John Winthrop*, Richard S. Dunn, et. al., eds. (Cambridge, Mass: The Belknap Press of Harvard University Press, 1996), 260.

4. Roger Williams to John Winthrop, Jr., 7 November 1648, *Winthrop Papers,* 5: 279.

5. Winthrop, *Journal*, 163–164. On Williams's life, see Samuel Hugh Brockunier, *The Irrepressible Democrat, Roger Williams* (New York: Ronald Press, 1940); Edwin S. Gaustad, *Roger Williams* (Oxford: Oxford University Press, 2005); and Ola E. Winslow, *Master Roger Williams* (New York: Macmillan, 1957).

6. William Wood, *New England's Prospect: A True, Lively, and Experimentall Description of that Part of America, Commonly Called New England,* ed. Alden T. Vaughan (1634; Amherst: University of Massachusetts Press, 1977), 90.

7. Wood, *New England's Prospect*, 89–90.

8. Glenn Warren LaFantasie, "Murder of an Indian, 1638," *Rhode Island History* 38:3 (August 1979), 67. My description of the trail's geography is also informed by this article.

9. RW to JW, ca. 1 August 1638, *Winthrop Papers*, 4: 50. William Bradford tells the story of their capture slightly differently. In his rendering, Miantonomi knew the men's identities *before* they tried to gain passage to Aquidneck. When they approached some Narragansetts for "a canow to sett them over a water, (not thinking their facte had been known,)," Miantonomi was alerted to their presence. If they then showed him Williams's letters, he may not have fallen for the ruse; according to Bradford, he soon helped arrange their capture. See Bradford, *Of Plimoth Plantation*, 434.

10. On how the "ignorance of western American geography influenced in unfamiliar and surprising ways the contest for America and empire," in a later period (and different place, the eighteenth-century West), see Paul W. Mapp, *The Elusive West and the Contest for Empire, 1713–1763* (Chapel Hill: University of North Carolina Press, 2011). (Quote from p. 3.)

11. This is not, of course, the first study to portray an early American frontier as fragile or fluid. Studies exploring the permeability, the vulnerability, and the many exchanges in frontier settings are legion; for some that inform the chapters that follow, see, for example, Evan Haefeli and Kevin Sweeney, *Captors and Captives: The 1704 Raid on Deerfield* (Amherst: University of Massachusetts Press, 2003); Ann M. Little, *Abraham in Arms: War and Gender in Colonial New England* (Philadelphia: University of Pennsylvania Press, 2007); Peter Silver, *Our Savage Neighbors: How Indian War Transformed Early America* (New York: W.W. Norton & Company, 2008); and Richard White, *The Middle Ground: Indians, Empires and Republics in the Great Lakes Region, 1650–1815* (Cambridge: Cambridge University Press, 1991). But virtually none gives sustained, systematic attention to communications. Exceptions include Alejandra Dubcovsky, "Connected Worlds: Communication Networks in the Colonial Southeast, 1513–1740" (Ph.D. diss., University of California, Berkeley, 2011), and James H. Merrell, *Into the American Woods: Negotiators on the Pennsylvania Frontier* (New York: W.W. Norton & Company, 1999).

Historians of the Atlantic have more extensively studied the circulation of people, goods, and news. In recent years, scholars have broken free from traditional national and regional boundaries by using oceanic connections to define a new realm of study—the early modern "Atlantic world." And, too, some histories of early America now march broadly across the North American continent, "ranging across cultural and national boundaries" to follow elaborate "processes of exchange" and "human interaction." In exploring exchange and communication in the northeast during the earliest years of English colonization, this book takes some inspiration from those trends. Introductions to Atlantic history include David Armitage and Michael J. Braddick, eds., *The British Atlantic World, 1500–1800* (New York:

Palgrave Macmillan, 2002); Bernard Bailyn, *Atlantic History: Concept and Contours* (Cambridge: Harvard University Press, 2005); and Elizabeth Mancke and Carole Shammas, eds., *The Creation of the British Atlantic World* (Baltimore: Johns Hopkins University Press, 2005). For a recent historiographical review, see Alison Games, "Atlantic History: Definitions, Challenges, and Opportunities," *American Historical Review* 111 (June 2006): 741–757. Illustrative of the move toward continental history is Alan Taylor, *American Colonies: The Settling of North America* (New York: Penguin Books, 2001), a synthesis of early American history. Also see Taylor, "Continental Crossings," *Journal of the Early Republic* 2004 24 (2): 182–188, from which the previous quotes are taken (from p. 184). Most lately, global histories of the early modern period have asked whether even Atlantic or continental perspectives may be too confining. See, for example, Alison Games, "Beyond the Atlantic: English Globetrotters and Transoceanic Connections," *William and Mary Quarterly* 3rd ser., 63 (October 2006): 675–692.

12. For critical approaches to reading maps, see, for example, James R. Akerman and Robert W. Karrow Jr., eds., *Maps: Finding Our Place in the World* (Chicago: The University of Chicago Press, 2007); Emerson W. Baker et al., eds., *American Beginnings: Exploration, Culture, and Cartography in the Land of Norumbega* (Lincoln: University of Nebraska Press, 1994); J. B. Harley, *The New Nature of Maps: Essays in the History of Cartography* (Baltimore: Johns Hopkins University Press, 2001); and Gregory H. Nobles, "Straight Lines and Stability: Mapping the Political Order of the Anglo-American Frontier," *Journal of American History* 80:1 (1993): 9–35.

13. For studies focusing mostly on the eighteenth century and beyond, see Richard D. Brown, *Knowledge Is Power: The Diffusion of Information in Early America, 1700–1865* (New York: Oxford University Press, 1989); Konstantin Dierks, *In My Power: Letter Writing and Communications in Early America* (Philadelphia: University of Pennsylvania Press, 2009); Wayne Fuller, *The American Mail* (Chicago: Chicago University Press, 1972); Eric Jaffe, *The King's Best Highway: The Lost History of the Boston Post Road, the Route that Made America* (New York: Scribner, 2010); Richard R. John, *Spreading the News: The American Postal System from Franklin to Morse* (Cambridge: Harvard University Press, 1995); and Richard B. Kielbowicz, *News in the Mail: The Press, Post Office, and Public Information, 1700–1860s* (New York: Greenwood Press, 1989). Print culture in the seventeenth century, unlike other modes of communication, has received significant attention; see, for example, David D. Hall, *Worlds of Wonder, Days of Judgment: Popular Religious Belief in Early New England* (New York: Alfred A. Knopf, 1989), and Jill Lepore, *The Name of War: King Philip's War and the Origins of American Identity* (New York: Alfred A. Knopf, 1998).

Greater strides have been made toward charting trans-Atlantic communications in the seventeenth century. See, for example, David Cressy, *Coming Over: Migration and Communication between England and New England in the Seventeenth Century*

(New York: Cambridge University Press, 1987), and Ian K. Steele, *The English Atlantic, 1675–1740: An Exploration of Communication and Community* (New York: Oxford University Press, 1986). April Lee Hatfield, *Atlantic Virginia: Intercolonial Relations in the Seventeenth Century* (Philadelphia: University of Pennsylvania Press, 2004), and Carla Gardina Pestana, *The English Atlantic in an Age of Revolution, 1640–1661* (Cambridge: Harvard University Press, 2004), are among the few to consider both intercolonial and trans-Atlantic communications in this period.

14. Historical memory of colonial New England is still shaped, to a surprising extent, by imagery that emerged in the nineteenth century, especially during the Colonial Revival. A cultural movement beginning in about the 1870s, the Colonial Revival looked back nostalgically to a "stable, communal, small-town Yankee world," untainted by industrialization or the social upheavals associated with labor and immigration. The image of old New England conjured by the Colonial Revival was simplified and romanticized; from it, we have inherited tenacious ideas about colonial women huddled about the hearth and well-ordered towns centered on village greens and white-steepled churches. A spate of preservation efforts during the Revival, which ranged from the historical to the material and architectural, helped secure this idealized memory of early New England. See Joseph A. Conforti, *Imagining New England: Explorations of Regional Identity from the Pilgrims to the Mid-Twentieth Century* (Chapel Hill: University of North Carolina Press, 2001), Laurel Thatcher Ulrich, *The Age of Homespun: Objects and Stories in the Creation of an American Myth* (New York: Knopf, 2001), and Joseph S. Wood, *The New England Village* (Baltimore: The Johns Hopkins University Press, 1997). (Quote is from Conforti, p. 203.)

Generations of scholarship have, by now, presented a more complex portrait of early New England, though the influence of the Colonial Revival retains a powerful hold on popular memory. For some of the most recent studies that depict a more complex and diverse cultural scene in early New England, see, for example, Richard Bailey, *Race and Redemption in Puritan New England* (New York: Oxford University Press, 2011); Allegra di Bonaventura, *For Adam's Sake: A Family Saga in Colonial New England* (New York: Liveright, 2013); Linford D. Fisher, *The Indian Great Awakening: Religion and the Shaping of Native Cultures in Early America* (New York: Oxford University Press, 2012); R. Todd Romero, *Making War and Minting Christians: Masculinity, Religion, and Colonialism in Early New England* (Amherst: University of Massachusetts Press, 2011); and Wendy Anne Warren, " 'The Cause of Her Grief': The Rape of a Slave in Early New England," *Journal of American History* 93:4 (2007): 1031–1049.

15. The familiar tale of Indian land dispossession is, of course, far better understood. See, for instance, Stuart Banner, *How the Indians Lost their Land: Law and Power on the Frontier* (Cambridge: The Belknap Press of Harvard University Press, 2005); Jean M. O'Brien, *Dispossession by Degrees: Indian Land and Identity in Natick, Massachusetts, 1650–1790* (Cambridge: Cambridge University Press, 1997);

and Alan Taylor, *The Divided Ground: Indians, Settlers, and the Northern Borderland of the American Revolution* (New York: Alfred A. Knopf, 2006).

16. For studies that look at communication, colonization and empire in other periods and places, see, for example, Kenneth J. Banks, *Chasing Empire Across the Sea: Communications and the State in the French Atlantic, 1713–1763* (Montreal: McGill-Queen's University Press, 2002); C. A. Bayly, *Empire and Information: Intelligence Gathering and Social Communication in India, 1780–1870* (Cambridge: Cambridge University Press, 1996); Barry Crosbie, *Irish Imperial Networks: Migration, Social Communication and Exchange in Nineteenth-Century India* (New York: Cambridge University Press, 2012); and Dubcovsky, "Connected Worlds."

17. Nina Baym et al., eds., *The Norton Anthology of American Literature*, 6th ed., 5 vols. (New York: W.W. Norton & Company, 2003), A: 105.

18. Bradford, *Of Plimoth Plantation*, 95.

19. Estimate is from Joseph Conforti, *Saints and Strangers: New England in British North America* (Baltimore: Johns Hopkins University Press, 2006), 6. Synthesizing recent estimates, Kathleen Bragdon offers a range of between 71,900–156,200 Native inhabitants of the region that later became New England and eastern New York, prior to European exploration and colonization. See Bragdon, *The Columbia Guide to American Indians of the Northeast* (New York: Columbia University Press, 2001), 7. Also see S. F. Cook, *The Indian Population of New England in the Seventeenth Century* (Berkeley: University of California Press, 1970) and Dean R. Snow and Kim M. Lamphear, "European Contact and Indian Depopulation in the Northeast: The Timing of the First Epidemics," *Ethnohistory* 35(1988): 15–33. The effect of European disease on Native population is more broadly explored in Albert W. Crosby, *Ecological Imperialism: The Biological Expansion of Europe, 900–1900* (New York: Cambridge University Press, 1986); Henry F. Dobyns, *Their Number Become Thinned: Native American Population Dynamics in Eastern North America* (Knoxville: University of Tennessee Press, 1983); and William A. Starna, "The Biological Encounter: Disease and the Ideological Domain," *American Indian Quarterly* 16 (1992): 511–519.

20. On the Native peoples who lived in what became New England, see especially Kathleen Bragdon, *Native People of Southern New England, 1500–1650* (Norman: University of Oklahoma Press, 1996); Neal Salisbury, *Manitou and Providence: Indians, Europeans, and the Making of New England, 1500–1643* (New York: Oxford University Press, 1982); Howard S. Russell, *Indian New England Before the Mayflower* (Hanover, N.H.: University Press of New England, 1980); and William S. Simmons, *Spirit of the New England Tribes: Indian History and Folklore, 1620–1984* (Hanover, N.H.: University Press of New England, 1986). For a synthesis of recent work on Native America in the contact period, more generally, see Daniel K. Richter, *Facing East from Indian Country: A Native History of Early America* (Cambridge: Harvard University Press, 2001).

21. Giovanni da Verrazano, "Narragansett Bay," in *Sailors Narratives of Voyages Along the New England Coast 1524–1624,* ed. George Parker Winship (Boston: Houghton, Mifflin & Co., 1905), 16.

22. For introductions to New Netherland, see Michael Kammen, *Colonial New York: A History* (New York: Oxford University Press, 1996); Jaap Jacobs, *New Netherland: A Dutch Colony in Seventeenth-Century America* (Leiden: Brill, 2005); and Henri A. and Barbara van der Zee, *A Sweet and Alien Land: The Story of Dutch New York* (New York: Viking Press, 1978).

23. Any discussion of the word "frontier" must begin with Frederick Jackson Turner's "The Significance of the Frontier in American History" (1893), in which Turner famously declared the American frontier "closed." The essay can be found in Frederick Jackson Turner, *History, Frontier, and Section: Three Essays* (Albuquerque: University of New Mexico Press, 1993), 59–91. Following from Turner's thesis, the word "frontier" in the American imagination has traditionally conjured a line in space, usually the foremost edge of Anglo-European settlement. In the latter part of the twentieth century, however, scholars began to critique Turner's work as both ethnocentric and too simplistic to describe what was, in truth, a quite complex set of human exchanges, relationships, and conflicts. I follow such works as Richard White, *The Middle Ground: Indians, Empires and Republics in the Great Lakes Region, 1650–1815* (Cambridge: Cambridge University Press, 1991), which attend to the frontier as both *process* and *place.* For a recent synthesis of work on American frontiers, see Gregory H. Nobles, *American Frontiers: Cultural Encounters and Continental Conquest* (New York: Hill and Wang, 1997).

24. See "A Note on Method," at end. My qualitative evidence is, of course, drawn from a much wider range of sources.

25. Jill Lepore was the first to push me to think of my research in these terms, and this question, although originally phrased a bit differently, was hers.

26. Bradford, *Of Plimoth Plantation,* 433 ("cloth & beads," "meett him"); RW to JW, ca. 1 August 1638, *Winthrop Papers,* 4: 50 ("little way").

27. RW to JW, ca. 1 August 1638, *Winthrop Papers,* 4: 50; Roger Williams, *A Key into the Language of America, Or, An Help to the Language of the Natives in that Part of America, Called New England* (1643; Bedford, Mass.: Applewood Books, 1997), 124–125.

1. "THE OCEAN OF TROUBLES AND TRIALS WHEREIN WE SAILE"

1. John Winthrop, *The Journal of John Winthrop,* Richard S. Dunn, et al., eds. (Cambridge, Mass: The Belknap Press of Harvard University Press, 1996), 179–180 ("old seyne," "starke naked"); John Underhill, *Newes from America; or, A New and Experimentall Discoverie of New England* (London: J.D. for Peter Cole, 1638), in Charles Orr, ed., *History of the Pequot War: The Contemporary Accounts of Mason, Underhill, Vincent and Gardiner* (Cleveland: The Helman-Taylor Company, 1897),

50–51; and Thomas Cobbet, "A Narrative of New England's Deliverances," *New England Historical and Genealogical Register* 7: 3 (July 1853), 209–219 ("perceived," "bloody head," 211), which includes a purportedly first-hand telling of the event by an eyewitness, Gallop's son. On hands and feet as trophies among Algonquians, see Andrew Lipman, "'A meanes to knitt them togeather': The Exchange of Body Parts in the Pequot War," *William and Mary Quarterly* 65:1 (January 2008): 3–28.

2. Alison Games, *Migration and the Origins of the English Atlantic World* (Cambridge: Harvard University Press, 1999).

3. Virginia DeJohn Anderson, *New England's Generation: The Great Migration and the Formation of Society and Culture in the Seventeenth Century* (New York: Cambridge University Press, 1991); Joseph A. Conforti, *Saints and Strangers: New England in British North America* (Baltimore: Johns Hopkins University Press, 2006); Jack P. Greene, *Pursuits of Happiness: The Social Development of Early Modern British Colonies and the Formation of American Culture* (Chapel Hill: University of North Carolina Press, 1988); and Gloria L. Main, *Peoples of a Spacious Land: Families and Cultures in Colonial New England* (Cambridge: Harvard University Press, 2001).

4. Discussions of the hypothetical circumstances behind Oldham's death can be found in Alfred Cave, *The Pequot War* (Amherst: University of Massachusetts Press, 1996), 108; Francis Jennings, *The Invasion of America: Indians, Colonialism, and the Cant of Conquest* (Chapel Hill: University of North Carolina Press, 1975), 207–208 ("Perhaps a drunken Englishman blurted out a brag or threat?" Jennings speculates); and, especially, Andrew Lipman, "Murder on the Saltwater Frontier: The Death of John Oldham," *Early American Studies* 9:2 (Spring 2011), 268–294.

5. On the war itself, see Cave, *The Pequot War;* Alden T. Vaughan, "Pequots and Puritans: The Causes of the War of 1637," *WMQ* 21:2 (April 1964): 256–269; Vaughan, *New England Frontier: Puritans and Indians, 1620–1675* (Boston: Little, Brown and Company, 1965), 93–154; Jennings, *The Invasion of America,* 177–227; and Neal Salisbury, *Manitou and Providence: Indians, Europeans, and the Making of New England, 1500–1643* (New York: Oxford University Press, 1982), 203–224.

6. William Bradford, *Of Plimoth Plantation 1620–1647* (Boston: Wright & Potter Printing Co., 1899), 232.

7. See especially Edmund Morgan, *American Slavery, American Freedom: The Ordeal of Colonial Virginia* (New York: W.W. Norton & Company, 1975), esp. 72–90.

8. Karen Ordahl Kupperman, *The Jamestown Project* (Cambridge: The Belknap Press of Harvard University Press, 2007), 175. Leftover scraps of copper used for trade have recently been unearthed by the Jamestown Rediscovery archaeological excavation. For examples from the dig, see the Association for the Preservation of Virginia Antiquities' website, search under "copper" and "trade," http://www.apva.org/. For Powhatan's protestations, as well as discussion of the

environmental context of Chesapeake settlement, see Kupperman, *Jamestown Project,* 166–176, 223–225.

9. Dorothy Bradford's death remains something of a mystery. No contemporary accounts explain her death, and Bradford barely mentioned the incident in his own history *Of Plimoth Plantation.* Cotton Mather first suggested she had fallen overboard accidentally; see Mather, *Magnalia Christi Americana,* 2 vols. (1702; Hartford : Silus Andrus & Son, 1853), 1: 111. But speculation that she committed suicide persists.

10. John Smith, *The Generall Historie of Virginia, New England, and the Summer Isles* (London, 1624), 106.

11. Phinehas Pratt, "A Declaration of the Affairs of the English People that First Inhabited New England" (1662), in Massachusetts Historical Society *Collections* 4th ser., 4 (1858), 479 ("begun to insult"), 483 ("kill all the Einglish," "ffoot steps"). A more detailed relation of this incident can be found in Salisbury, *Manitou and Providence,* 125–140.

12. Bradford, *Of Plimoth Plantation,* 197. Plymouth's food supplies fell short that year, as well. See Edward Winslow, *Good Newes from New England: or A True Relation of Things Very Remarkable at the Plantation of Plimouth in New-England* (1624), in *Chronicles of the Pilgrim Fathers of The Colony of New Plymouth, From 1602 to 1625,* ed. Alexander Young (Boston: Charles C. Little and James Brown, 1841), 292, 296–297, and Bradford, *Of Plimoth Plantation,* 152.

13. Bradford, *Of Plimoth Plantation,* 401–402; Nathaniel Morton, *New-Englands Memoriall . . .* (Cambridge, Mass., 1669), 95. For other contemporary descriptions of the great hurricane of 1635, see Samuel Danforth, *An Almanack for the Year of Our Lord 1649 . . .* (Cambridge, Mass., 1649), n.p.; William Hubbard, *A General History of New England: From the Discovery to MDCLXXX* (Boston, 1848), 199–201; John Hull, "The Diaries of John Hull, Mint-Master and Treasurer of the Colony of Massachusetts Bay," in *Transactions and Collections of the American Antiquarian Society* 7 (1857): 109–316, esp. 169; and Winthrop, *Journal,* 151–153. A strikingly detailed account survives of Anthony Thacher's pinnace being caught in the storm and subsequently shipwrecked off the coast of Massachusetts. See A. Thacher to Peter Thacher, September 1635, in Everett Emerson, ed., *Letters from New England: The Massachusetts Bay Colony, 1629–1638* (Amherst, Mass., 1976), 167–174. Climatologists at the National Hurricane Center analyzed some of these historical descriptions and now theorize that the storm was a major hurricane—a category three—with maximum winds of 130 miles per hour and a vicious storm surge. See Associated Press, "Great New England Hurricane of 1635 Even Worse Than Thought," Nov. 21, 2006.

14. Karen Ordahl Kupperman, "Climate and Mastery of the Wilderness in Seventeenth-Century New England," in David D. Hall and David Grayson Allen, eds., *Seventeenth-Century New England* (Boston: Colonial Society of Massachusetts, 1984), 6–7.

15. Winthrop, *Journal*, 162 ("70: men & woemen"), 174 ("greatest parte").

16. Winthrop, *Journal*, 171–172, 174.

17. Lion Gard[i]ner, "Leift Lion Gard[i]ner His Relation of the Pequot Warres," in Orr, *History of the Pequot War*, 123–124.

18. "The very successes of colonies could cause scarcity," notes Alison Games, contrasting New England's early years with the struggles of Bermuda, Virginia, and other colonial projects. See Games, *Migration and the Origins*, 86.

19. Roger Thompson, *Mobility and Migration: East Anglian Founders of New England, 1629–1640* (Amherst: University of Massachusetts Press, 1994), 14. In fact the phenomenon reached far beyond New England; other regions of the British New World received far greater numbers of immigrants. In 1630, estimates Alison Games, the colonial population hovered somewhere near 9500; ten years later, it had ballooned to 53,700. Games has called the 1630s an "originative moment," in which westward migration essentially "secured England's Atlantic World." See Games, *Migration and the Origins*, 4.

20. Robert Charles Anderson et al., eds., *The Great Migration: Immigrants to New England 1634–1635*, 7 vols. (Boston: New England Historic Genealogical Society, 1999–2011), 1: xvii (quotation); Robert Charles Anderson, "A Note on the Pace of the Great Migration," *New England Quarterly* 59:3 (Sept. 1986): 406–407.

21. William Wood, *New England's Prospect*, ed. Alden T. Vaughan (1634; Amherst: University of Massachusetts Press, 1977), 67–68.

22. On the timing of Atlantic migration to New England, see Anderson, *New England's Generation*, 65–66. Virginians also complained of new arrivals from England disembarking with too few provisions, and at the wrong time of year, no less. In 1620, Governor George Yeardley wrote to the Virginia Company that if such immigrants continued to arrive "to late to sett Corne," then he would not be able to "feed them owt of others labors." He asked that they be sent before Christmas, instead. See Morgan, *American Slavery, American Freedom*, 105.

23. Edward Trelawny to Robert Trelawny, 10 January 1635/1636, in Emerson, *Letters from New England*, 186.

24. Winthrop, *Journal*, 132.

25. Kupperman, "Climate and Mastery of the Wilderness," 6.

26. Winthrop, *Journal*, 108–109. Here, and in the rest of the book, I have modernized "old style" dates; that is, dates between January 1 and March 25, which in seventeenth century writing would have been rendered as "January 1633/1634," are here given as "January 1634."

27. Bradford, *Of Plimoth Plantation*, 402 ("mortalitie"). On the several Pequot sachems who "renounced their allegiance to the grand sachem," see Cave, *The Pequot War*, 66.

28. Linda Murray Berzok, *American Indian Food* (Westport, Conn.: Greenwood Press, 2005), 123.

29. On the Algonquian diet, see Howard S. Russell, *Indian New England Before the Mayflower* (Hanover, New Hampshire: University Press of New England, 1980), 72–95, and Kathleen J. Bragdon, *Native People of Southern New England, 1500–1650* (Norman: University of Oklahoma Press, 1996), 102–118.

30. Sarah F. McMahon, "A Comfortable Subsistence: The Changing Composition of Diet in Rural New England, 1620–1840," *William and Mary Quarterly* 42:1 (Jan. 1985), 28, 31, 35–39, 44, and passim (quotation, 28).

31. John Mason, *A Brief History of the Pequot War: Especially of the Memorable Taking of Their Fort at Mistick in Connecticut in 1637* (Boston, 1736), in Orr, *History of the Pequot War*, 17. Also see Bradford, *Of Plimoth Plantation*, 386–387, and Winthrop, *Journal*, 108. The details and significance of John Stone's death are analyzed closely in Alfred A. Cave, "Who Killed John Stone? A Note on the Origins of the Pequot War," *WMQ* 49 (1992): 509–521.

32. John Winthrop to Sir Simonds D'Ewes, June [24] 1636, in Allyn B. Forbes et al., eds., *Winthrop Papers, 1498–1654*, 6 vols. (Boston: Massachusetts Historical Society, 1929–1992), 3: 276. Hammond's death has barely registered in recent readings of the war, but Massachusetts named it as a grievance against the Pequots shortly thereafter; see "Commission and Instructions from the Colony of Massachusetts Bay to John Winthrop, Jr., for Treating with the Pequots," 4 July 1636, in ibid., 285.

33. Mason, *Brief History*, and Underhill, *Newes from America*, both in Orr, *History of the Pequot War*, 17, 50; Bradford, *Of Plimoth Plantation*, 232.

34. Lion Gardiner, "Relation of the Pequot War," 123.

35. Jennings, *Invasion of America*, 189–190.

36. Bradford, *Of Plimoth Plantation*, 207, 209, 219, 230. On Oldham's life, see Robert Charles Anderson, *The Pilgrim Migration: Immigrants to Plymouth Colony, 1620–1633* (Boston: New England Historic Genealogical Society, 2004), 345–348, and Henry Bond, *Genealogies of the Families and Descendants of the Early Settlers of Watertown, Massachusetts* (Boston: Little, Brown & Co., 1855), 861–864.

37. Bradford, *Of Plimoth Plantation*, 231–232.

38. Lynn Ceci, "Native Wampum as a Peripheral Resource in the Seventeenth-Century World System," in Laurence M. Hauptman and James D. Wherry, eds., *The Pequots in Southern New England: The Fall and Rise of an American Indian Nation* (Norman: University of Oklahoma Press, 1990), 60.

39. Mark Meuwese, "The Dutch Connection: New Netherland, the Pequots, and the Puritans in Southern New England, 1620–1638," *Early American Studies* 9:2 (Spring 2011), 295–323; Michael Leroy Oberg, *Uncas: First of the Mohegans* (Ithaca: Cornell University Press, 2003), 40–44; Salisbury, *Manitou and Providence*, 203–213.

40. Winthrop, *Journal*, 181.

41. Ceci, "Native Wampum," 48. Noting that the amount of wampum collected in the war's aftermath amounted to "the partial underwriting of New

England colonization costs by the conquered natives," Ceci gives wampum causal import in the escalation to violence in the 1630s. In her reading, Oldham's death and other incidents provided an "excuse to punish the mintmasters and extract wampum payments" (60, 61).

42. Roger Williams to John Winthrop, 3 July 1637, in Glenn W. LaFantasie, ed., *The Correspondence of Roger Williams,* 2 vols. (Providence, R.I.: Published for The Rhode Island Historical Society by Brown University Press, 1988), 1: 91–92.

43. Edward Johnson, *Johnson's Wonder-Working Providence of Sions Saviour in New England,* ed. J. Franklin Jameson (1654; New York: Charles Scribner's Sons, 1910), 151.

44. "Water-bailies," or water bailiffs, were shore patrolmen who collected customs. For Providence's 1647 choice of "Water Bailies for the Colonie," see John Russell Bartlett, ed., *Records of the Colony of Rhode Island and Providence Plantations, in New England,* 10 vols. (Providence: A. Crawford Greene and Brothers, 1856–65), 1: 151. Also see "The Oath of the Water Bayley" in Nathaniel B. Shurtleff, ed., *Records of the Colony of New Plymouth in New England,* 12 vols. (Boston, 1855–1861), 5: 62.

45. Seymour Dunbar, *A History of Travel in America* (Indianapolis: The Bobbs-Merrill Company, 1915), 28–29 (quote); William Avery Baker, "Vessel Types of Colonial Massachusetts," in *Seafaring in Colonial Massachusetts* (Boston: The Colonial Society of Massachusetts, 1980), 3–29.

46. John Endecott to John Winthrop, 12 April 1631, *Winthrop Papers,* 3: 24.

47. Wood, *New England's Prospect,* 64.

48. Charles J. Hoadly, editor and transcriber, *Records of the Colony and Plantation of New Haven, From 1638 to 1649* (Hartford, 1857), 212–213.

49. New London Town Records, 1648–1666, Book 1A, New London City Clerk's Office, New London, Connecticut.

50. Thomas Minor, *The Diary of Thomas Minor, Stonington, Connecticut. 1653 to 1684,* ed. Sidney H. Miner and George D. Stanton, Jr. (New London, 1899; reprint edition, 2001), 8–9, 14, 26–28, and passim. On canoe varieties and construction, see especially Wood, *New England's Prospect,* 108–109; John Josselyn, *An Account of Two Voyages to New-England,* ed. Paul J. Lindholdt (1674; Hanover: University Press of New England, 1988), 23, 102; and Williams, *Key,* 106–108.

51. A "shallop" was a small, open boat, used in relatively shallow waters; a "pinnace" could be "a flat-sterned small schooner-rigged vessel" or "a man-o-war's boat, with six or eight oars." See Grant Uden and Richard Cooper, eds., *A Dictionary of British Ships and Seamen* (New York: St. Martin's Press, 1980), 376, 467.

52. Lipman, "Murder on the Saltwater Frontier"; Horace P. Beck, *The American Indian as a Sea-Fighter in Colonial Times* (Mystic, CT.: The Marine Historical Association, Inc., 1959).

53. John R. Stilgoe, "A New England Coastal Wilderness," in *New England Prospect: Maps, Place Names, and the Historical Landscape,* ed. Peter Benes (Boston: Boston University, 1982), 89–105 (quotations, 89).

54. Winthrop, *Journal,* 43–44.

55. For letters carried by boat between Connecticut and Massachusetts Bay in the years 1635–1640, see, for example, JW to JWJ, 4 April 1636, *Winthrop Papers,* 3: 244 ("the Rebecka," "mr. Oldhams Pinace"); JWJ to JW, 7 April 1636, *Winthrop Papers,* 3: 247 ("mr. Gibbon"); JW to JWJ, 26 April 1636, *Winthrop Papers,* 3: 255–56 ("the Blessing," "mr. Hodges," "mr. Oldham," "mr. Tilly," unnamed "Shipp"); JWJ to JW, 16 May 1636, *Winthrop Papers,* 3: 260 ("the Bacheler"); Israel Stoughton to JWJ, ca. June 1636, *Winthrop Papers,* 3: 264 ("Mr. Tilley"); JW to JWJ, 10 June 1636, *Winthrop Papers,* 3: 268 ("the Rebecka"); JW to JWJ, 23 June 1636, *Winthrop Papers,* 3: 275 ("the Wrenne," "Jo: Gallop," "The Batchelor"); Adam Winthrop to JWJ, 3 July 1636, *Winthrop Papers,* 3: 283 ("the bacheldor"); Thomas Hooker to JW, ca. May 1637, *Winthrop Papers,* 3: 408 ("these pynaces"); and Israel Stoughton to JW, ca. 28 June 1637, *Winthrop Papers,* 3: 435–436 ("Giggles" pinnace).

56. Winthrop, *Journal,* 156 ("goeinge"), 161 ("cast awaye"), 238 ("small pinnace"). For similar stories of boat wrecks, including the story of "2. shallops going to Coonigtecutt with goods from the Massachusetts," cast away in an "easterly storme," see Bradford, *Of Plimoth Plantation,* 415.

57. Evidence of landborne exchange is harder to find, though some did occur. Some of the Connecticut migrants braved the hundred-mile trek westward and took letters with them. But the land route was little known and mostly untested. See William Pynchon to JWJ, Roxbury to Saybrook, 4 July 1636, *Winthrop Papers,* 3: 285; and JW to JWJ, 10 June 1636, *Winthrop Papers,* 3: 268.

58. Winthrop, *Journal,* 50 ("5:dayes"), 97 ("over land"), 108 ("miserye," 158 ("teadious"), 161 ("10:dayes"), 164 ("Conectectott"). Given his disapproval of their break with Massachusetts Bay, Winthrop may have been exaggerating their troubles. Emphases are his.

59. Jonathan Brewster to JWJ, 18 June 1636, *Winthrop Papers,* 3: 271.

60. Gardiner, "Relation of the Pequot War," 134–135 ("Tille's folly"); Underhill, *Newes from America,* 67; Winthrop, *Journal,* 193; and Lion Gardiner to JWJ, 6 November 1636, *Winthrop Papers,* 3: 321 ("no vessels").

61. Gardiner, "Relation of the Pequot War," 135 ("in our sight"); Underhill, *Newes from America,* 62 ("put poles"); Daniel Patrick to the Governor and Council of War in Massachusetts, 19 June 1637, *Winthrop Papers,* 3: 430 ("ruinated").

62. For a discussion of the importance of early coastal trading in New England, see esp. Daniel Vickers with Vince Walsh, *Young Men and the Sea: Yankee Seafarers in the Age of Sail* (New Haven: Yale University Press, 2005), 7–24.

63. Winthrop, *Journal,* 132.

64. James Hammond Trumbull, ed., *The Public Records of the Colony of Connecticut 1636–1776*, 15 vols. (Hartford: Lockwood & Brainard Company, 1850–1890), 1: 3. How the "Corne of Mr. Olda" was ultimately dispensed is not clear.

65. John Winthrop to Sir Simonds D'Ewes, June [24] 1636, *Winthrop Papers*, 3: 276; and "Commission and Instructions from the Colony of Massachusetts Bay to John Winthrop, Jr., for Treating with the Pequots," 4 July 1636, in ibid., 285.

66. "Grievances of the Servants at Saybrook," ca. July 1636, in *Winthrop Papers*, 3: 281.

67. John Winthrop, Jr., to John Winthrop, 16 May 1636, *Winthrop Papers*, 3: 260.

68. Winthrop, *Journal*, 179.

69. For discussion of this phenomenon, see, for instance, Colin G. Calloway, *New Worlds for All: Indians, Europeans, and the Remaking of Early America* (Baltimore: Johns Hopkins University Press, 1997), 109.

70. Sandra L. Oliver, *Food in Colonial and Federal America* (Westport, Conn.: Greenwood Press, 2005), 9–11, 40–41; Anderson, *New England's Generation*, 150–151; Joyce E. Chaplin, *Subject Matter: Technology, the Body and Science on the Anglo-American Frontier, 1500–1676* (Cambridge: Harvard University Press, 2001), 209–212.

71. William Wood, *New England's Prospect*, 86–87; Williams, *Key*, 11. On the importance of maize to Native cultures, see especially Berzok, *American Indian Food*, 50–55. On green corn ceremonies—according to Berzok, "almost universal among maize-growing Native Americans" as a ritual honoring the late-summer growth of immature corn—see pp. 154–156.

72. Underhill, *Newes from America*, 54–55.

73. Alfred Cave also notes this discrepancy; see Cave, *The Pequot War*, 117.

74. Gardiner, "Relation of the Pequot War," 123–124.

75. Gardiner, "Relation of the Pequot War," 124.

76. Gardiner, "Relation of the Pequot War," 126–127.

77. Underhill, *Newes from America*, 59 and passim.

78. In his narrative, Gardiner fingered Cutshamakin—a Massachusett man acting as interpreter and guide to the English, during the Block Island expedition—as the prime culprit precipitating the war. Gardiner asserted that the war's main point of ignition occurred when Cutshamakin killed and scalped a Pequot—a provocation that could not go unanswered. That Gardiner thought nothing had issued from his own orders to plunder wantonly, however, seems a bit convenient. At the very least, the tale neatly excuses Gardiner from responsibility for the bloodshed that followed.

79. Winthrop, *Journal*, 189–190.

80. Gardiner, "Relation of the Pequot War," 128.

81. Winthrop, *Journal*, 200.

82. Lion Gardiner to John Winthrop, Jr., 6 November 1636, *Winthrop Papers,* 3: 319–320.

83. Mason, *Brief History,* 44–46; emphasis added.

84. Mark Nicholls, "George Percy's 'Trewe Relacyon': A Primary Source for the Jamestown Settlement," *The Virginia Magazine of History and Biography,* 113: 3 (2005), 242.

85. Increase Mather, *A Relation of the Troubles which Have Hapned in New-England by Reason of the Indians there . . .* (Boston, 1677), 42. (Pages 24–43 of Mather's narrative contain an early version of Mason's *Brief History* of the Pequot War.)

86. Mason, *Brief History,* 28–29.

87. Underhill, *Newes from America,* 81.

88. Witness the debate over whether English actions amounted to intended genocide; on this, see Stephen T. Katz, "The Pequot War Reconsidered," *New England Quarterly* 64:2 (June 1991): 206–224; Michael Freeman, "Puritans and Pequots: The Question of Genocide," *New England Quarterly* 68:2 (June 1995): 278–293; and Stephen T. Katz, "Pequots and the Question of Genocide," *New England Quarterly* 68:4 (December 1995): 641–649. For two articles that closely examine the burning of Mystic Fort, see Adam J. Hirsch, "The Collision of Military Cultures in Seventeenth-Century New England," *Journal of American History* 74:4 (March 1988): 1187–1212, and Ronald Dale Karr, " 'Why Should You Be So Furious?': The Violence of the Pequot War," *Journal of American History* 85:3 (December 1998): 876–909.

89. [Philip Vincent], *A True Relation of the Late Battell Fought in New-England, between the English and the Pequet Salvages,* in Orr, *History of the Pequot War,* 109.

90. There is little evidence to suggest that Native groups in New England engaged in warfare for the purpose of raiding grain or other plunder, though they undertook campaigns to gain trade and tributaries. Still, the Narragansetts in particular had been hard hit by the 1635 hurricane and may have had special incentive to plunder Pequot corn. According to Roger Williams, "they desire[d] the Pequts Corne might be enjoyed by the English and themselves as Mr. Governour please." See RW to JW, [10 July 1637] #2, in *Winthrop Papers,* 3: 448.

91. Winthrop, *Journal,* 257 ("rotted in the ground," "corn beyond expectation"), 256 ("flakes").

92. Mason, *Brief History of the Pequot War,* 40 ("supplant them," my emphasis), 41 ("there was Plenty"), 43.

93. Vincent, *A True Relation;* John Underhill, *Newes from America* (quotation, title page). According to an Underhill biographer, Vincent's account was available as early as November 1637 and Underhill's in April 1638. See Henry C. Shelley, *John Underhill: Captain of New England and New Netherland* (New York: D. Appleton and Company, 1932), 240–243, 250–251.

94. Winthrop, *Journal*, 261. On the Pequot war narratives and their effect on English migration to New England, see David Cressy, *Coming Over: Migration and Communication between England and New England in the Seventeenth Century* (Cambridge: Cambridge University Press, 1987), 25–26.

95. Katherine A. Grandjean, "The Long Wake of the Pequot War," *Early American Studies* 9:2 (Spring 2011): 379–411.

96. RW to Sir Henry Vane and John Winthrop, [15 May 1637], *Winthrop Papers*, 3: 414 ("any more land travel," "confederates"); RW to JW, [10 July 1637] #2, *Winthrop Papers*, 3: 448 ("hope"); Pulsifer, *Acts of the Commissioners of the United Colonies*, 9: 55 ("have no guides"); RW to JW, 14 August 1638, *Winthrop Papers*, 4: 52 ("be carefull").

97. RW to JW, 28 February 1637/1638, *Winthrop Papers*, 4: 16; RW to JW, 10 January 1637/8, *Winthrop Papers*, 4: 7.

98. Quote is from Cave, *The Pequot War*, 161.

99. RW to JW, 10 January 1637/1638, *Winthrop Papers*, 4: 7.

100. Williams, *Key*, 75.

101. "The magistrates' reliance on a Separatist clergyman whom they had earlier expelled from the Bay Colony . . . ," notes one historian, "is indicative of their desperate need for contacts in the Indian villages west of Cape Cod." See Cave, *The Pequot War*, 123.

102. RW to JW, [10 July 1637], *Winthrop Papers*, 3: 446.

103. See, for example, RW to JW, [10 July 1637], *Winthrop Papers*, 3: 446–448; RW to the Governor of Massachusetts, 13 May 1637, *Winthrop Papers*, 3: 410–412; RW to JW, 24 October 1636?, *Winthrop Papers*, 3: 314–318; RW to JW, 2 June 1637, *Winthrop Papers*, 3: 426–428.

104. RW to JW, 27 May 1638, *Winthrop Papers*, 4: 34 ("Nahigonsick"); RW to JW, ca. 14 June 1638, *Winthrop Papers*, 4: 40 ("forced me").

105. Daniel Patrick to JW, 23 May 1637, *Winthrop Papers*, 3: 421; Daniel Patrick to JW, 19 June 1637, *Winthrop Papers*, 3: 431; Edward Winslow to JWJ, 5 June 1637, *Winthrop Papers*, 3: 428 (Winslow writes that Plymouth men learned "this evening," from "Capt. Standish his Indian who was sent this morning to Namasket" that the fort had been taken); and RW to JW, 20 August 1637, *Winthrop Papers*, 3: 488–489 ("letters to Pequt").

106. John Winthrop, "A Modell of Christian Charity" (1630), *Winthrop Papers*, 2: 292 ("sinewes"), 294 ("shipwracke," "rejoye together"), 295 ("Citty").

107. Winthrop, "A Modell," 289 ("ligamentes"), 292 ("farre distant").

2. A Messenger Comes

1. Adam Winthrop to John Winthrop, Jr., Boston to Pequot, 14 March 1648/1649, in Allyn B. Forbes et al., eds., *Winthrop Papers, 1498–1654*, 6 vols. (Boston: Massachusetts Historical Society, 1929–1992), 5: 319.

2. John Wilson and others to JWJ, 26 March 1649, Boston to Pequot, *Winthrop Papers,* 5: 325.

3. David D. Hall, *Ways of Writing: The Practice and Politics of Text-Making in Seventeenth-Century New England* (Philadelphia: University of Pennsylvania Press, 2008), 19.

4. E. Jennifer Monaghan, *Learning to Read and Write in Colonial America* (Amherst and Worcester: University of Massachusetts Press, in association with American Antiquarian Society, 2005), 15.

5. Though many have charted the print and postal explosions of later years, studies of early American communications have neglected the seventeenth century. Some scholars of the Atlantic, meanwhile, have recovered the networks of news that tethered the colonies to old England. But patterns of delivery *within* seventeenth-century America remain somewhat mysterious. For trans-Atlantic communications and the English post in the seventeenth century, see especially David Cressy, *Coming Over: Migration and Communication between England and New England in the Seventeenth Century* (Cambridge: Cambridge University Press, 1987); Howard Robinson, *Carrying British Mails Overseas* (New York: New York University Press, 1964); and Ian K. Steele, *The English Atlantic, 1675–1740: An Exploration of Communication and Community* (New York: Oxford University Press, 1986). For studies of early American communications, most of which focus on the eighteenth century and beyond, see especially Richard D. Brown, *Knowledge Is Power: The Diffusion of Information in Early America 1700–1865* (New York: Oxford University Press, 1989); Konstantin Dierks, *In My Power: Letter Writing and Communications in Early America* (Philadelphia: University of Pennsylvania Press, 2009); Wayne Fuller, *The American Mail: Enlarger of the Common Life* (Chicago: Chicago University Press, 1972); Richard R. John, *Spreading the News: The American Postal System from Franklin to Morse* (Cambridge: Harvard University Press, 1995); and Richard B. Kielbowicz, *News in the Mail: The Press, Post Office, and Public Information, 1700–1860s* (New York: Greenwood Press, 1989).

6. The elder John Winthrop led the charge to found the Massachusetts Bay colony in 1630. His son, John Winthrop, Jr., founded several other New England settlements, before becoming governor of Connecticut in the 1650s. On the Winthrops, see especially Robert C. Black, *The Younger John Winthrop* (New York: Columbia University Press, 1966); Francis J. Bremer, *John Winthrop: America's Forgotten Founding Father* (Oxford: Oxford University Press, 2003); Richard S. Dunn, *Puritans and Yankees: the Winthrop Dynasty of New England, 1630–1717* (Princeton: Princeton University Press, 1962); Edmund S. Morgan, *The Puritan Dilemma: The Story of John Winthrop* (New York: HarperCollins, 1958); and Walter W. Woodward, *Prospero's America: John Winthrop, Jr., Alchemy, and the Creation of New England Culture, 1606-1676* (Chapel Hill: University of North Carolina Press, 2010).

7. John Endecott to JW, ca. 5 April 1639, *Winthrop Papers,* 4: 109; William Pynchon to JW, 19 February 1643/1644, in ibid., 443 (Nippumsint); Roger Williams to JW, ca. 1 August 1638, in ibid., 51 (Will); John Haynes to JW, 29 March 1643, in ibid., 373 ("Indian messendger"); Richard Odell to JWJ, 16 November 1652, *Winthrop Papers,* 6: 230 ("send an Indian"); Samuel Stone to JWJ, 28 February 1652/1653, in ibid., 257 ("procure some Indian").

8. RW to JW, 16 April [1638], *Winthrop Papers,* 4: 26.

9. Some irony lurks in that fact, as much recent scholarship shows that writing and literacy were profoundly powerful tools against Native people. See, for example, James Axtell, "The Power of Print in the Eastern Woodlands," *WMQ* 44:2 (April 1987): 300–309; Jill Lepore, *The Name of War: King Philip's War and the Origins of American Identity* (New York: Knopf, 1998); and David Murray, *Forked Tongues: Speech, Writing, and Representation in North American Indian Texts* (London: Pinter Publishers, 1991). Though, for a contrary argument, see Peter Wogan, "Perceptions of European Literacy in Early Contact Situations," *Ethnohistory* 41:3 (Summer 1994): 407–429.

10. On Nahawton (or Ahauton) and his family, see Nathaniel B. Shurtleff, ed., *Records of the Governor and Company of the Massachusetts Bay in New England,* 5 vols. (Boston: Press of William White, 1853–1854), 2: 23 (serves as guide and interpreter on diplomatic mission); Thomas Shepard, *The Clear Sun-shine of the Gospel Breaking Forth upon the Indians in New-England* (London, 1648), reprinted in Michael P. Clark, ed., *The Eliot Tracts: With Letters from John Eliot to Thomas Thorowgood and Richard Baxter* (Wesport, Conn.: Praeger, 2003), 126 ("worldly matters," "sober good man"); John Eliot, *A Brief Narrative of the Progress of the Gospel amongst the Indians in New England* (London, 1671), in Clark, *The Eliot Tracts,* 403 ("Chief Ruler," "more loved than feared"); Daniel Gookin, *Historical Collections of the Indians in New England* (New York: Arno Press, 1972), 44; and Daniel T. V. Huntoon, *History of the Town of Canton, Norfolk County, Massachusetts* (Cambridge: John Wilson and Son, 1893), 22–24.

11. Shurtleff, ed., *MBR,* 4: 85 ("badly written," "slurred paper"); and Edward Howes to JWJ., 18 March 1632/1633, *Winthrop Papers,* 3: 110 ("sea water").

12. "The Receipt for Ink," in JW to JWJ, 14 May 1647, *Winthrop Papers,* 5: 162. Another ink recipe followed, a year later: "Take the quantyty of a good walnutt of this Gume Arabeck, and putt it into ¼ of a pint of Aquavitae, sett it on the fire in a brasse skillet, and keepe it stirring till it be dissolved . . . you must beware it take not fire nor burne to the posnet." See JW to JWJ, 3–26 July 1648, *Winthrop Papers,* 5: 236.

13. On ink-making in early America, see Jane E. Harrison, *Until Next Year: Letter Writing and the Mails in the Canadas, 1640–1830* (Quebec: Canadian Museum of Civilization, 1997), 14, and William E. Burns, "Reading and Seeing: The Technology of Words and Images," in *Science and Technology in Colonial America* (Westport, Conn.: Greenwood Press, 2005), 89–95.

14. Harrison, *Until Next Year*, 14.

15. William Pynchon to JWJ, 2 June 1636, *Winthrop Papers*, 3: 267; JWJ to Wait Winthrop, 16 August 1659, in Marjorie F. Gutheim, ed., *Winthrop Family Papers* Microfilm, 53 reels (Boston, Mass.: Massachusetts Historical Society, 1976), Reel 6. Paper would not be manufactured in the colonies until 1690, when a paper mill opened in Germantown, Pennsylvania. On the history of papermaking, see especially Dard Hunter, *Papermaking: The History and Technique of an Ancient Craft* (New York: Dover Publications, 1978); Dard Hunter, *Papermaking in Pioneer America* (Philadelphia: University of Pennsylvania Press, 1952); and Richard L. Hills, *Papermaking in Britain, 1488–1988: A Short History* (London: Athlone Press, 1988).

16. RW to JWJ, ca. 23 May 1650, *Winthrop Papers*, 6: 43.

17. James Daybell, *The Material Letter in Early Modern England: Manuscript Letters and the Culture and Practices of Letter-Writing, 1512–1635* (Basingstoke: Palgrave Macmillan, 2012), 98–99; Peter Stallybrass, "What is a Letter?" (Elizabeth Turner Jordan '59 lecture), Susan and Donald Newhouse Center for the Humanities, Wellesley College, December 3, 2012.

18. Harrison, *Until Next Year*, 37; RW to JWJ, 29 January 1648/1649, *Winthrop Papers*, 5: 309.

19. Jonathan Brewster to John Winthrop, Jr. 31 January 1656/1657, Massachusetts Historical Society *Collections*, 4th ser., 1 (Boston, 1865): 81.

20. New England writers were sharply conscious of letters' power to overcome distance. One thought corresponding with John Winthrop, Jr., a means "to visit you by proxe." Others called their letters "papr: Messengr" or "paper pilgrim," as if correspondence traveled of its own accord. See John Davenport, Jr., to JWJ, 12 December 1668, *Winthrop Papers* microfilm, Reel 9, and John Talcott to JWJ, 25 October 1670, in ibid. On the concept of "imagined communities," built upon modes of communication, see Benedict Anderson, *Imagined Communities: Reflections on the Origin and Spread of Nationalism* (London: Verso, 1983).

21. Shurtleff, *MBR*, 4: 85.

22. "news, *n.*": "The report or account of recent (esp. important or interesting) events or occurrences, brought or coming to one as new information; new occurrences as a subject of report or talk; tidings." *Oxford English Dictionary Online*, December 2006, Oxford University Press, accessed 19 January 2007, http://dictionary.oed.com.ezp2.harvard.edu/cgi/entry/00323998.

23. David Pulsifer, ed., *Acts of the Commissioners of the United Colonies of New England*, Vol. I, in *Records of the Colony of New Plymouth in New England*, 12 vols. (Boston: William White, 1859), 9: 3.

24. See Mary Winthrop Dudley to Margaret Winthrop, 15 January 1635/1636, *Winthrop Papers*, 3: 223 ("fine thred"); MWD to JWJ, 26 February 1635/1636, in ibid., 228–229; MWD to Margaret Winthrop, 28 March 1636, in ibid., 239

("cloutes," "sheets," "pillow-beeres"); MWD to Margaret Winthrop, ca. April 1636, in ibid., 242 ("childs chaire"); and MWD to Margaret Winthrop, ca. June 1636, in ibid., 263 (sugar, "sope," "dwelling so farre").

25. Recent years have witnessed a spate of new scholarship historicizing letter writing as a practice, as well as several studies seeking to identify the conventions of early modern correspondence. See especially Daybell, *The Material Letter;* Gary Schneider, *The Culture of Epistolarity: Vernacular Letters and Letter Writing in Early Modern England, 1500–1700* (Newark: University of Delaware Press, 2005); Eve Tavor Bannet, *Empire of Letters: Letter Manuals and Transatlantic Correspondence, 1688–1820* (Cambridge: Cambridge University Press, 2005); David Barton and Nigel Hall, eds., *Letter Writing as a Social Practice* (Amsterdam and Philadelphia: John Benjamins Publishing, 2000); and Harrison, *Until Next Year.* For ancient and medieval communications, see Mogens Trolle-Larsen, "What they wrote on clay," in *Literacy and Society,* ed. Karen Schousboe and Mogens Trolle-Larson (Copenhagen: Akademisk Forlag, 1989), 121–148; Alain Boreau, "The Letter-Writing Norm, a Mediaeval Invention," in *Correspondence: Models of Letter-Writing from the Middle Ages to the Nineteenth Century,* ed. Rogier Chartier, Alain Boreau and Cecile Dauphin (Princeton: Princeton University Press, 1997), 24–58; Rebecca Earle, "Introduction: letters, writers and the historian," in *Epistolary Selves: Letters and Letter-Writers, 1600–1945,* ed. Rebecca Earle (Aldershot: Ashgate, 1999), 1–12; and Anne Kolb, "Transport and Communication in the Roman State: The *cursus publicus,*" in *Travel and Geography in the Roman Empire,* ed. Colin Adams and Ray Laurence (New York: Routledge, 2001), 95–105. Among the first studies to ponder the role of communications in empire, broadly, was H.A. Innis, *Empire and Communications* (Oxford: Clarendon Press, 1950). Quote is from Schneider, *The Culture of Epistolarity,* 13.

26. On the conventions of early modern English letters, see especially "An Introduction to Early Modern Epistolarity," in Schneider, *The Culture of Epistolarity,* 22–74. Quote is from Thomas Cobbett to John Winthrop, 13 March 1643/1644, *Winthrop Papers,* 4: 451 ("howse in Boston").

27. English posts had only begun carrying letters under Henry VIII, and their service was generally reserved for court use. A more public and efficient postal service was beginning to take shape just as the Winthrops and others departed for the New World (about 1630), of which they were likely aware; William Brewster, for instance, had been postmaster of Scrooby before leaving with the other Separatist pilgrims for Holland. The English Civil War, however, profoundly disrupted these developments. On English postal service, see Howard Robinson, *The British Post Office: A History* (Princeton: Princeton University Press, 1948); Robinson, *Carrying British Mails Overseas;* and J. Crofts, *Packhorse, Waggon and Post: Land Carriage and Communications Under the Tudors and Stuarts* (London: Routledge, 1967).

28. Schneider, *The Culture of Epistolarity,* 82.

29. Daybell, *The Material Letter*, 142.

30. Samuel Symonds to JWJ, 10 September 1652, *Winthrop Papers*, 6: 219.

31. Roger Williams to John Winthrop, ca. October 1638 *Winthrop Papers*, 4: 65 ("came to hand"); Jonathan Brewster to JWJ, 2 December 1648, *Winthrop Papers*, 5: 286 (writes twice); Edward Palmes to JWJ, 20 November 1673, *Winthrop Papers* microfilm, Reel 10 ("gon Back").

32. That letters often identify their bearers may, in fact, be a clue into New England's problems of communication. According to historian Gary Schneider, the custom of naming letter bearers was aimed at preserving "epistolary continuity," or the successful flow and exchange of letters. Correspondents wanted to know how and when their letters found passage. Attaching a bearer to each letter—like dating—was a kind of shorthand. It provided a gauge of how quickly letters had arrived, if at all. See Schneider, *The Culture of Epistolarity*, 56–60. An important note: No apparent logic explains why some bearers are named and others are not. I do not detect any inherent slant toward naming English couriers, rather than Indians, or vice versa.

33. JW to Peter Stuyvesant, 30 September 1647, *Winthrop Papers*, 5: 185 ("neighbour"); JWJ to JW, 17 January 1648/1649, in ibid., 303 ("vessell").

34. William Bradford, *Of Plimoth Plantation 1620–1647* (Boston: Wright & Potter Printing Co., 1899), 262–263 ("speake English," "sente 2. men"); 269 ("offered").

35. RW to JW, 10 July 1637, *Winthrop Papers*, 3: 446 (Assotemuit); RW to JW, 16 April [1638], *Winthrop Papers*, 4: 26.

36. Thomas Minor, *The Diary of Thomas Minor, Stonington, Connecticut. 1653 to 1684,* ed. Sidney H. Miner and George D. Stanton, Jr. (New London, 1899; reprint edition, 2001), 46, 54, 58, 63, 64.

37. Connecticut Archives: Colonial Boundaries, Series I, Vol. I, Doc. 23a-b, Connecticut State Library, Hartford, Connecticut; Elisha Potter, *The Early History of Narragansett; With an Appendix of Original Documents, Many of Which are Now for the First Time Published* (Providence: Marshall, Brown and Company, 1835), 195; Pulsifer, *Acts of the Commissioners of the United Colonies*, 10: 146 ("carry letters").

38. Edward Winslow to JW, 22 May 1637, *Winthrop Papers*, 3: 420; JWJ to Fitz-John Winthrop, 8 February 1654/1655, *Winthrop Papers* microfilm, Reel 1; Edward Winslow to John Winthrop, 7 January 1643/1644, *Winthrop Papers*, 4: 428–429 ("messenger cals").

39. Richard Nicolls to JWJ, 11 August [1666], *Winthrop Papers* microfilm, Reel 8.

40. John Pynchon to JWJ, 30 July 1666, *Winthrop Papers* microfilm, Reel 8.

41. On John Winthrop, Jr.'s medical knowledge, see Woodward, *Prospero's America,* 160–209, and Dunn, *Puritans and Yankees,* 80–83. His letters find him forever sending herbs, rubila, and other unidentified powders to various 'patients.'

42. John Bishop to JWJ, 6 May 1672, *Winthrop Papers* microfilm, Reel 10.

43. John Davenport to JWJ, 20 August 1653, *Winthrop Papers,* 6: 322.

44. Richard Smith to JWJ, 26 May 1673, Wickford to Hartford, *Winthrop Papers* microfilm, Reel 10. This is only one of several instances when Smith sought medical advice from Winthrop via Indian messengers. See also, for example, Richard Smith to JWJ, 17 April 1666, *Winthrop Papers* microfilm, Reel 8.

45. See, for example, Nathaniel Sylvester to JWJ, 15 March 1654/1655, *Winthrop Papers* microfilm, Reel 5; Stephen Goodyear to John Winthrop, Jr., 24 January 1650/1651, *Winthrop Papers,* 6: 92–93 ("send an Indian purposly"); Jonathan Brewster to JWJ, 2 December 1648 (collecting debt), *Winthrop Papers,* 5: 286.

46. Benedict Arnold to JW, 19 January 1643/1644, *Winthrop Papers,* 4: 431 ("Mow-hoaugs"); Jireh Bull to Thomas Stanton et al., 8 August [1673], *Winthrop Papers* microfilm, Reel 10 ("duches prosedings"); Stephen Goodyear to John Winthrop, Jr., 29 November 1655, *Winthrop Papers* microfilm, Reel 5 ("hyred").

47. The Winthrop letters hint that English travelers who carried letters, though not formally "hired," could expect some nominal reward for their troubles. Sending letters via an English stranger in 1674/1675, for instance, John Winthrop, Jr., instructed his son Wait to "thanke" the man for his "curtesy." Similarly, when the first intercolonial postal carrier brought letters to John Richards, he "thanked him (as we use to do travellers for the like courtesy)." See JWJ to Wait Winthrop, 22 March 1674/1675, *Winthrop Papers* microfilm, Reel 11, and John Richards to JWJ, 17 February 1672/1673, *Winthrop Papers* microfilm, Reel 10.

48. Speed and payment were often linked. Sending an important letter in 1672/1673, Edward Palmes set aside extra money for a careful and quick courier: "Rather then It should lye longe," he wrote, "I have order to Disburse 20s for Its Speedy and Saife Delivery." Another writer promised his courier, Zachary Crispe, an extra five or ten shillings to deliver letters within a few days. "I do it to cause him to make the more haste," the man wrote. See Jireh Bull to Thomas Stanton, 8 August 1673, *Winthrop Papers* microfilm, Reel 10 ("pay him at his returne"); Samuel Maverick to JWJ, 9 August [1666], *Winthrop Papers* microfilm, Reel 8 ("add to what I have given him heare 5 or 10 ss."); and Edward Palmes to JWJ, 6 January 1672/1673, *Winthrop Papers* microfilm, Reel 10 ("20s for Its Speedy and Saife Delivery").

49. William Pynchon to Stephen Day, 8 October 1644, *Winthrop Papers,* 4: 495.

50. Jonathan Brewster to JWJ, 2 December 1648, *Winthrop Papers,* 5: 286; Richard Odell to JWJ, 16 November 1652, *Winthrop Papers,* 6: 229–230; Samuel Stone to JWJ, 28 February 1652/1653, *Winthrop Papers,* 6: 257 ("please him").

51. John Davenport to JWJ, [23 December 1660], *Winthrop Papers* microfilm, Reel 6.

52. See Daniel Patrick to Governor and Council of War in Massachusetts, 19 June 1637, *Winthrop Papers,* 3: 431 ("Coate and a pare of shoes"); RW to JW, 10 July

1637, *Winthrop Papers,* 3: 448 ("Coate"); RW to JWJ., 10 November 1649, *Winthrop Papers,* 5: 376 ("pair of breeches"); and RW to JWJ, ca. 15 December 1648, *Winthrop Papers,* 5: 289 ("awle blades").

53. On average, 27 percent (27/101) of letters dated during January, February, and March were carried by Indians.

54. JW to JWJ, 22 January 1637/1638, *Winthrop Papers,* 4: 10 ("shutt up with snowe"); William Wood, *New England's Prospect: A True, Lively, and Experimentall Description of that Part of America, Commonly Called New England,* ed. Alden T. Vaughan (1634; Amherst: University of Massachusetts Press, 1977), 27–28. Cold weather letters teem with complaints about the season's toll on communications. For other examples, see Lucy Downing to JW, ca. January 1648/1649, *Winthrop Papers,* 5: 297; Thomas Olcott to JWJ, 8 January 1648/1649, *Winthrop Papers,* 5: 301 ("vessell frozen in"); JWJ to Richard Nicolls, 6 March 1666/1667, *MHSC,* 5th ser., 8 (Boston, 1882): 115; John Pynchon to JWJ, 26 February 1674/1675, *Winthrop Papers* microfilm, Reel 11; and Edward Winslow to JW, 17 February 1639/1640, *Winthrop Papers,* 4: 193.

55. JWJ to Francis Lovelace, 19 November 1669, *Winthrop Papers* microfilm, Reel 9. Travel remained rigidly seasonal over the entire course of the century. Thomas Minor's diary, recording his travels between the 1650s and 1680s, confirms the tyranny of winter. A mere six (or less than 8 percent) of his extra-local trips came during December, January, or February. Virtually all of these were in December (one marked the singular experience of traveling into Narragansett to participate in 1675's Great Swamp Fight). Never once, in three decades, did Minor set out to travel beyond the local during the month of January. By contrast, fully 35 percent (27/78) of his longer journeys fell in May or June. Another peak came in October (15/78, or 19 percent). See Chapter Four for a fuller discussion of Minor's travels.

56. JWJ to Sir Robert Carr, Hartford to Narragansett, 9 March 1664/1665, *Winthrop Papers* microfilm, Reel 7.

57. Roger Williams, *A Key into the Language of America, Or, An Help to the Language of the Natives in that Part of America, Called New England* (1643; Bedford, Mass.: Applewood Books, 1997), 71.

58. On Native literacy, see Kathleen J. Bragdon, "'Another Tongue Brought In': An Ethnohistorical Study of Native Writings in Massachusett" (Ph.D. Dissertation, Brown University, 1981); Lisa Brooks, *The Common Pot: The Recovery of Native Space in the Northeast* (Minneapolis: University of Minnesota Press, 2008); Kristina Bross and Hilary E. Wyss, eds., *Early Native Literacies in New England: A Documentary and Critical Anthology* (Amherst: University of Massachusetts Press, 2008); Ives Goddard and Kathleen J. Bragdon, *Native Writings in Massachusett* (Philadelphia: American Philosophical Society, 1988); Jill Lepore, "Dead Men Tell No Tales: John Sassamon and the Fatal Consequences of Literacy," *American Quarterly* 46

(December 1994): 479–512; Birgit Brander Rasmussen, *Queequeg's Coffin: Indigenous Literacies & Early American Literature* (Durham: Duke University Press, 2012); and Hilary E. Wyss, *Writing Indians: Literacy, Christianity, and Native Community in Early America* (Amherst: University of Massachusetts Press, 2000). On early American literacy more generally, see Monaghan, *Learning to Read and Write in Colonial America,* and Kenneth Lockridge, *Literacy in Colonial New England: An Enquiry into the Social Context of Literacy in the Early Modern West* (New York: W.W. Norton, 1974).

59. Sir John Clotworthy to JWJ, ca. 6 March 1634/1635, *Winthrop Papers,* 3: 190–191 (casement); James Fitch to JWJ, 18 July 1654, *Winthrop Papers,* 6: 404. Translation is from ibid., 405, n. 4, Mason Hammond, translator. In a letter from the ailing neighbor himself, Joseph Gerrard, we get a better sense of his affliction: "My watter is verie burning to me and my watter is verie thike and att the last thare is some blood," he described. See Joseph Gerrard to JWJ, [18 July 1654], *Winthrop Papers,* 6: 405.

60. RW to JW, [August 1639], *Winthrop Papers,* 4: 137.

61. Quoted in Garrick Mallery, *Picture-Writing of the American Indians,* 2 vols. (New York: Dover, 1972), 2: 666. See pp. 666–674 for Mallery's discussion of these birch bark writings.

62. Quoted in Rasmussen, *Queequeg's Coffin,* 18.

63. Rasmussen, *Queequeg's Coffin,* 49–78; Michael K. Foster, "Another Look at the Function of Wampum in Iroquois-White Councils," in Francis Jennings et al., eds., *The History and Culture of Iroquois Diplomacy: An Interdisciplinary Guide to the Treaties of the Six Nations and Their League* (Syracuse: Syracuse University Press, 1985), 99–114.

64. Peter Nabokov, *Indian Running: Native American History and Tradition* (Santa Fe: Ancient City Press, 1987), 11–36. See also James H. Howard, "Notes on the Ceremonial Runners of the Fox Indians," *Contributions to Fox Ethnology* (Washington: Bureau of American Ethnology, Bulletin 85, 1927), 1–50; Paul H. Ezell, "The Cocomaricopa Mail" (San Diego: Corral of the Westerners, Brand Book No. 1, 1968); Hazel Hertzberg, *The Great Tree and the Longhouse* (New York: Macmillan, 1966); and Lewis Henry Morgan, *League of the Ho-De-No-Sau-Nee or Iroquois* (New York, 1901), on Iroquoian messengers; John H. Rowe, "Inca Culture at the Time of the Spanish Conquest" (Washington: Bureau of American Ethnology, Bull. 143, 1946). For Indian mobility and paths (and early European use of them), elsewhere, see April Lee Hatfield, *Atlantic Virginia: Intercolonial Relations in the Seventeenth Century* (Philadelphia: University of Pennsylvania Press, 2004), 8–38; Philip Levy, *Fellow Travelers: Indians and Europeans Contesting the American Trail* (Gainesville: University Press of Florida, 2007); Jon Parmenter, *The Edge of the Woods: Iroquoia, 1534–1701* (East Lansing: Michigan State University Press, 2010); Helen Rountree, "The Powhatans and Other Woodland Indians as Travelers," in

Rountree, ed., *Powhatan Foreign Relations, 1500–1722* (Charlottesville: University Press of Virginia, 1993), 21–52; and Helen Hornbeck Tanner, "The Land and Water Communications Systems of the Southeastern Indians," in Peter H. Wood, Gregory A. Waselkov, and M. Thomas Hatley, eds., *Powhatan's Mantle: Indians in the Colonial Southeast* (Lincoln: University of Nebraska Press, 1989), 6–20.

65. Kathleen J. Bragdon, *Native People of Southern New England, 1500–1650* (Norman: University of Oklahoma Press, 1996), 91–92; James Bradley, "Native Exchange and European Trade: Cross-Cultural Dynamics in the Sixteenth Century," *Man in the Northeast* 33 (1987): 31–46; Eric S. Johnson and James W. Bradley, "The Bark Wigwams Site: An Early Seventeenth-Century Component in Central Massachusetts," *Man in the Northeast* 33 (1987): 1–26; Kevin McBride and Robert Dewar, "Prehistoric Settlement in the Lower Connecticut River Valley," *Man in the Northeast* 22 (1981): 37–66.

66. Williams, *Key*, 60.

67. RW to JW, 10 July 1637, *Winthrop Papers*, 3: 446.

68. Williams, *Key*, 54 ("desire"), 55 ("their manner"), 60 ("mutuall hollowing"), 68 ("admirable").

69. Thomas Pownall, *A Topographical Description of Such Parts of North America* . . . (1776), quoted in Archer Butler Hulbert, *Historic Highways of America*, 16 vols. (Cleveland: The Arthur H. Clark Company, 1902–1905): 2: 33.

70. RW to Sir Henry Vane and John Winthrop, [15 May 1637], *Winthrop Papers*, 3: 414.

71. Historians have devoted little attention to these questions, but see Seymour Dunbar, *A History of Travel in America* (Indianapolis: The Bobbs-Merrill Company, 1915), and James E. McWilliams, *Building the Bay Colony: Local Economy and Culture in Early Massachusetts* (Charlottesville: University of Virginia Press, 2007), which offers some perspective into early travel, transportation and economic exchange.

72. Scholars view Puritans' bemoaning of the "howling wilderness" as mostly polemic and trope, at once stripping the land of its Indian inhabitants, setting the Native landscape as a "wild" foil to the more "civilized" English one, and glorifying the Puritan migrants as having overcome this chaos. For one skeptic's viewpoint, see Cressy, *Coming Over*, 13–14. No early literature cast New England as a menacing "wilderness," Cressy objects; only later, after the "successful settlement of New England" did such discourse appear—and only to "depict the first comers as heroes, made of sterner stuff" (14).

73. For my characterization of English beliefs and fears about the forest, I am indebted to Simon Schama, *Landscape and Memory* (New York: Vintage Books, 1995), esp. 81–100 and 142–174; and Keith Thomas, *Man and the Natural World: Changing Attitudes in England 1500–1800* (New York: Oxford University Press, 1996), esp. 192–197.

74. John R. Stilgoe, *Common Landscape of America, 1580 to 1845* (New Haven: Yale University Press, 1982), 21. Keith Thomas detects a more sympathetic view of the "woods" beginning in about the mid-seventeenth century. On the shift, see Thomas, *Man and the Natural World*, 192–197.

75. Thomas, *Man and the Natural World*, 193–194; Schama, *Landscape and Memory*, 142.

76. Williams, *Key*, 59–60.

77. See Francis Higginson, *New-Englands Plantation* (1630), *Massachusetts Historical Society Proceedings* 62 (1929), 314; Henry Martyn Dexter, ed., *Mourt's Relation, or Journal of the Plantation at Plymouth* (1622; Boston, 1865), 2.

78. Edward Johnson, *Johnson's Wonder-Working Providence of Sions Saviour in New England*, ed. J. Franklin Jameson (1654; New York: Charles Scribner's Sons, 1910), 111–112.

79. Johnson, *Wonder-Working Providence*, 113; John Winthrop, *The Journal of John Winthrop 1630–1649*, Richard S. Dunn, James Savage and Laetitia Yeandle, eds. (Cambridge: The Belknap Press of Harvard University Press, 1996), 87 ("mayd"), 130 ("torne").

80. A caveat, here: Much has been made of the "parklike" appearance of New England's forests, due to Indians' habitual burning of the underbrush. "One must not visualize the New England forest at the time of settlement as a dense tangle of huge trees and nearly impenetrable underbrush covering the entire landscape," insists William Cronon. "Along the southern coast, from the Saco River in Maine all the way to the Hudson, the woods were remarkably open, almost parklike at times." But this was not true in all cases; by the 1630s, the ravages of disease had caused some of the forest underbrush that Indians were accustomed to burning to rebound. "In some places," described William Wood, "where the Indians died of the plague some fourteen years ago, is much underwood . . . because it hath not been burned." He fingered the "midway" between Wessagusset and Plymouth as one of the region's thornier passages: "Certain rivers stopping the fire from coming to clear that place of the country," Wood explained, "hath made it unuseful and troublesome to travel through, insomuch that it is called ragged plain because it tears and rents the clothes of them that pass." See Wood, *New England's Prospect*, 38–39. On the northeast's "parklike" forests and Indian burning, see especially Cronon, *Changes in the Land: Indians, Colonists, and the Ecology of New England* (New York: Hill and Wang, 1983), 25–26, 49–51.

81. Bremer, *John Winthrop*, 249.

82. Winthrop, *Journal*, 129–30 ("wandered"); 137 ("homewardes"); 412–413 ("benighted").

83. *Mourt's Relation*, 18–19, 32; Wood, *New England's Prospect*, 89.

84. See, for example, Wood, *New England's Prospect*, 89–90, and John Josselyn, *An Account of Two Voyages to New-England*, ed. Paul J. Lindholdt (1674; Hanover:

defended his "life and goods" by killing a person "attempting to rob or murthr in thyee feild or high way . . . shalbe holden blameles." See Richard W. Cogley, *John Eliot's Mission to the Indians before King Philip's War* (Cambridge, Mass.: Harvard University Press, 1999), 113; Shurtleff, *MBR,* 2: 212.

107. On John Winthrop, Jr.'s settlement at Pequot, see Frances Manwaring Caulkins, *History of New London, Connecticut, from the First Survey of the Coast in 1612 to 1852* (New London, 1852), and Woodward, *Prospero's America,* esp. 75–137.

108. I owe the concept of "corridors" of communication to Michael McCormick, *Origins of the European Economy: Communications and Commerce, A.D. 300–900* (Cambridge: Cambridge University Press, 2001).

109. Destinations are trickier to pin down. Since most of the surviving Winthrop letters are incoming pieces of correspondence, the collection is weighted toward those places where the Winthrops spent the most time. It's worth noting, nonetheless, how often Indians delivered letters to these places. Incoming letters to Massachusetts Bay arrived via Native messenger about 19 percent of the time (23/119), and to Connecticut about 13 percent. About 20 percent of letters to New York (earlier New Netherland) traveled with Native couriers. Pequot, where John Winthrop, Jr., spent several years, saw 33 percent of mail delivered by Indians.

110. Gookin, *Historical Collections,* 44.

111. Jonathan Brewster to JWJ, 1 December 1648, *Winthrop Papers,* 5: 286. Emphasis added.

112. Were Indian couriers truly faster? The evidence is inconclusive. For many letters, it is possible to gauge the speed of delivery. Over five hundred (or about 18 percent of all those examined) include endorsements or other evidence of how quickly they arrived. Unfortunately, a mere sixteen of the letters carried by Indians include this same kind of information.

113. William Pynchon to Stephen Day, 8 October 1644, *Winthrop Papers,* 4: 495.

114. John Wilson and others to JWJ, 26 March 1649, Boston to Pequot, *Winthrop Papers,* 5: 325.

115. Pulsifer, *Acts of the Commissioners of the United Colonies,* 10: 224. On New Netherland's use of Indian messengers, see Wheaton Lane, *From Indian Trail to Iron Horse: Travel and Transportation in New Jersey 1620–1860* (Princeton: Princeton University Press, 1939), 23–25.

116. Pulsifer, *Acts of the Commissioners of the United Colonies,* 9: 116.

3. Native Tongues

1. On New Netherland, see, for example, Joyce D. Goodfriend, ed., *Revisiting New Netherland: Perspectives on Early Dutch America,* Vol. IV of *The Atlantic World: Europe, Africa and the Americas, 1500–1830,* ed. Wim Klooster and Benjamin Schmidt (Leiden: Brill, 2005); Michael Kammen, *Colonial New York: A History*

(New York: Oxford University Press, 1996); Jaap Jacobs, *New Netherland: A Dutch Colony in Seventeenth-Century America* (Leiden: Brill, 2005); and Henri A. and Barbara van der Zee, *A Sweet and Alien Land: The Story of Dutch New York* (New York: Viking Press, 1978). Donna Merwick examines New Netherland's evolution through the eyes of one man, a notary named Adriaen Janse van Ilpendam, in her *Death of a Notary: Conquest and Change in Colonial New York* (Ithaca: Cornell University Press, 1999).

2. Thomas Morton, *New English Canaan* (Amsterdam, 1637), contains the famous description of the Massachusetts woods as a "new found Golgotha."

3. For discussion of New Netherland's influence and import (despite its sometimes being dismissed by early Americanists), see Daniel K. Richter, "Dutch Dominos: The Fall of New Netherland and the Reshaping of Eastern North America," in his *Trade, Land, Power: The Struggle for Eastern North America* (Philadelphia: University of Pennsylvania Press, 2013), 97–112.

4. Amos Richardson to JWJ, 28 December 1652, in Allyn B. Forbes et al., eds., *Winthrop Papers, 1498–1654*, 6 vols. (Boston: Massachusetts Historical Society, 1929–1992), 6: 238.

5. See "Letter from the Directors at Amsterdam to Director Stuyvesant," 6 August 1652, in Charles T. Gehring, trans. and ed., *Correspondence 1647–1653*, New Netherland Documents Series, Volume XI (Syracuse: Syracuse University Press, 2000), 184, and for the letter's capture by the English, "Letter from the Directors at Amsterdam to Director Stuyvesant," 13 December 1652, in ibid., 188. Ironically, the West India Company had begun to take measures to secure transatlantic mail. In the very letter that was eventually seized, directors suggested that New Netherland's incoming mail be inspected and each ship captain questioned, "so that we do not carry a snake in our own bosom . . . by transporting, to our detriment, the letters of those who would do us harm." See Gehring, *Correspondence*, 184.

6. Frances Manwaring Caulkins, *History of New London, Connecticut, From the First Survey of the Coast in 1612, to 1852* (New London: Press of the Case, Tiffany and Company, 1852), 84–85.

7. David Pulsifer, ed., *Acts of the Commissioners of the United Colonies of New England*, Vol. II, in *Records of the Colony of New Plymouth in New England*, 12 vols. (Boston: William White, 1855–1861), 10: 237.

8. Only a handful of scholars have examined this particular episode. Narratives of the feared Dutch-Narragansett plot (with differing verdicts on whether such a plot existed) can be found in Julie A. Fisher and David J. Silverman, *Ninigret, Sachem of the Niantics and Narragansetts: Diplomacy, War, and the Balance of Power in Seventeenth-Century New England and Indian Country* (Ithaca: Cornell University Press, 2014), 73–79; Andrew Charles Lipman, "The Saltwater Frontier: Indians, Dutch, and English on Seventeenth-Century Long Island Sound" (Ph.D. diss., University of Pennsylvania, 2010), 240–249; Michael Leroy Oberg, *Uncas:*

First of the Mohegans (Ithaca: Cornell University Press, 2003), 132–137; Jenny Hale Pulsipher, *Subjects Unto the Same King: Indians, English, and the Contest for Authority in Colonial New England* (Philadelphia: University of Pennsylvania Press, 2005), 32–34; and van der Zee and van der Zee, *Sweet and Alien Land*, 235–245. But for studies that approach different rumors much as I approach the one in consideration here, see Gregory Evans Dowd, "The Panic of 1751: The Significance of Rumors on the South Carolina-Cherokee Frontier," *WMQ* 53:3 (Jul. 1996): 527–560; James Merrell, *Into the American Woods: Negotiators on the Pennsylvania Frontier* (New York: W.W. Norton & Company, 1999), 184–185; and Tom Arne Midtrød, "Strange and Disturbing News: Rumor and Diplomacy in the Colonial Hudson River Valley," *Ethnohistory* 58:1 (Winter 2011): 91–112.

9. For studies of the seventeenth century American colonies that give sustained attention to the Dutch, as well as the English, see, for example, Bernard Bailyn, *The Barbarous Years: The Peopling of British North America: The Conflict of Civilizations, 1600–1675* (New York: Knopf, 2012); Christian J. Koot, *Empire at the Periphery: British Colonists, Anglo-Dutch Trade, and the Development of the British Atlantic, 1621–1713* (New York: New York University Press, 2011); and Lipman, "The Saltwater Frontier."

10. On "entangled history" as a model for studying the early modern Atlantic's communities, see "*AHR* Forum: Entangled Empires in the Atlantic World," *American Historical Review* 112:3 (June 2007): 710–799. Within that forum, see especially Eliga H. Gould, "Entangled Histories, Entangled Worlds: The English-Speaking Atlantic as a Spanish Periphery," 764–787, which argues that "the history of the Spanish and English-speaking Atlantic worlds is often best approached not from a comparative standpoint, but as a form of interconnected or 'entangled' history" (766).

11. John Winthrop, *The Journal of John Winthrop,* ed. Richard S. Dunn, et. al. (Cambridge, Mass: The Belknap Press of Harvard University Press, 1996), 491.

12. William Bradford, *Of Plimoth Plantation 1620–1647* (Boston: Wright & Potter Printing Co., 1899), 267 ("letters"), 269 ("farr northward," "halfe a days"), 281 (sugar, linen).

13. Koot, *Empire at the Periphery*; and Kim Todt, "Trading Between New Netherland and New England, 1624–1664," *Early American Studies* 9:2 (Spring 2011), 348–378.

14. Winthrop, *Journal*, 124. "[W]e had from them about 40: sheepe, & beaver, & brasse pannes & sugar &c: for sacke, stronge waters linnen clothe & other Comodityes," Winthrop detailed.

15. Bernard Bailyn, *The New England Merchants in the Seventeenth Century* (Cambridge: Harvard University Press, 1955), 58.

16. In autumn 1648, for example, Roger Williams was visited by a "Dutchman for an old debt," even as he was busily preparing "peag for Mr Throgmorton," an English trader who had lived in both Rhode Island and New Netherland. RW to

JW, ca. mid-November 1648, in Glenn W. LaFantasie, ed., *The Correspondence of Roger Williams,* 2 vols. (Providence, R.I.: Published for The Rhode Island Historical Society by Brown University Press, 1988), 1: 259.

17. Winthrop, *Journal,* 388.

18. Bailyn, *New England Merchants,* 40–41.

19. Bradford, *Of Plimoth Plantation,* 310 ("swime . . . betweene both"), 326 ("plaid his owne game"). On Allerton's life, see Isaac J. Greenwood, *Allertons of New England and Virginia* (Boston, 1890) and Cynthia J. Van Zandt, *Brothers Among Nations: The Pursuit of Intercultural Alliances in Early America, 1580–1660* (New York: Oxford University Press, 2008), 86–115.

20. Fisher and Silverman, *Ninigret,* vii–xx. The preface contains a lengthy discussion of the portrait.

21. Fisher and Silverman, *Ninigret;* Oberg, *Uncas,* 74–75, 126–132. Walter W. Woodward, *Prospero's America: John Winthrop, Jr., Alchemy, and the Creation of New England Culture, 1606–1676* (Chapel Hill: University of North Carolina Press, 2010), 93–137, also contains a useful examination of the complex Native and English politics, and Indian rivalries, that arose after the Pequot War.

22. J. Seke, "Ninigret's Tactics of Accommodation: Indian Diplomacy in New England, 1637–1675," *Rhode Island History* 36 (1977): 44–53.

23. Pulsifer, *Acts of the Commissioners of the United Colonies,* 10: 96.

24. Adriaen van der Donck, "The Representation of New Netherland," in *Narratives of New Netherland, 1609–1664,* ed. J. Franklin Jameson (New York: C. Scribner's Sons, 1909), 305.

25. Pulsifer, *Acts of the Commissioners of the United Colonies,* 10: 12 ("Aide and assistance"), 44–45.

26. Pulsifer, *Acts of the Commissioners of the United Colonies,* 10: 9.

27. Jaap Jacobs, *Petrus Stuyvesant: Een Levensschets* (Amsterdam: Bert Bakker, 2009); Donna Merwick, *Stuyvesant Bound: An Essay on Loss Across Time* (Philadelphia: University of Pennsylvania Press, 2013); Henry Howard Kessler and Eugene Rachlis, *Peter Stuyvesant and his New York* (New York: Random House, 1959); and Hendrik Willem van Loon, *Life and Times of Pieter Stuyvesant* (New York: H. Holt & Company, 1928). My characterization of Stuyvesant also draws from Kammen, *Colonial New York,* 48–49 (from which is taken the description of the silver embroidery on Stuyvesant's wooden leg).

28. For an overview of the relations between New Netherland and New England, from the perspective of leaders and high political diplomacy, see Franklin Bowditch Dexter, "The Early Relations between New Netherlands and New England," *New Haven Colony Historical Society Papers* 3 (New Haven, 1882): 443–469. On how the Dutch used their superiority in cartography to balance English claims of territory, see Benjamin Schmidt, "Mapping an Empire: Cartographic and Colonial Rivalry in Seventeenth-Century Dutch and English

North America," *WMQ* 54:3 (July 1997): 549–578. Quote ("chronic bones of contention") is from John Demos, "Searching for Abbotsij Van Cumminghuysen, House Carpenter in Two Worlds," in *The Impact of New Netherlands upon the Colonial Long Island Basin: Report of a Yale-Smithsonian Seminar held at Yale University, New Haven, Connecticut, May 3–5, 1990,* ed. Joshua W. Lane (New Haven: Yale-Smithsonian Seminar on Material Culture, 1993), 15.

29. On Kieft's War, see especially Evan Haefeli, "Kieft's War and the Cultures of Violence in Colonial America," in Michael A. Bellesiles, ed., *Lethal Imagination: Violence and Brutality in American History* (New York: New York University Press, 1999), 17–40; Lipman, "The Saltwater Frontier"; Donna Merwick, *The Shame and the Sorrow: Dutch-Amerindian Encounters in New Netherland* (Philadelphia: University of Pennsylvania Press, 2006), 135–179; Paul Andrew Otto, *The Dutch-Munsee Encounter in America: The Struggle for Sovereignty in the Hudson Valley* (New York: Berghahn Books, 2006); and Allen W. Trelease, *Indian Affairs in Colonial New York: The Seventeenth Century* (Ithaca: Cornell University Press, 1960), 60–84.

30. Pulsifer, *Acts of the Commissioners of the United Colonies,* 10: 10.

31. Thomas Minor to JWJ, 2 April 1653, *Winthrop Papers,* 6: 275.

32. William Morton to JWJ, 28 February 1652/1653, *Winthrop Papers,* 6: 255. Morton's meaning isn't entirely clear, here. The Winthrop Papers' editors suspect that "Morton presumably [meant] he had learned at Fishers Island from the Dutchman who brought Ninigret from Manhattan of the Indian's return to the New London area." See p. 256, n. 6.

33. John Mason to JWJ, March? 1652/1653, *Winthrop Papers,* 6: 258; Richard Odell to JWJ, undated, *Winthrop Papers,* 6: 271.

34. See, for example, Oberg, *Uncas,* 132–138.

35. Pulsifer, *Acts of the Commissioners of the United Colonies,* 10: 11–12.

36. Richard Smith, Sr., to JWJ, 9 April 1653, *Winthrop Papers,* 6: 278.

37. Pulsifer, *Acts of the Commissioners of the United Colonies,* 10: 23–24.

38. Pulsifer, *Acts of the Commissioners of the United Colonies,* 10: 22 ("Duch sloop"), 23 ("halfe the prise"), 24 ("guns powder"), 49 ("as well as most").

39. Pulsifer, *Acts of the Commissioners of the United Colonies,* 10: 22 ("Round about"), 23 ("Discourse," "wholy"), 24 ("Indians," "Newes").

40. Petrus Stuyvesant to JWJ, 6 March 1653, *Winthrop Papers,* 6: 258.

41. Petrus Stuyvesant to JWJ, 6 March 1653, *Winthrop Papers,* 6: 258; Petrus Stuyvesant to John Endecott, 6 March 1653, in Pulsifer, *Acts of the Commissioners of the United Colonies,* 10: 425–426.

42. Stuyvesant's letter took a mere ten days—March 6 to March 16—to travel from Manhattan to Salem. (Endecott noted that he had received the "Dutch Governors packett" from Winthrop's "Indean" on the 16th.) For the entire exchange, see Stuyvesant to JWJ, 6 March 1652/1653, *Winthrop Papers,* 6: 258–259; John Endecott to JWJ, 18 March 1652/1653, in ibid., 264; Edward Rawson to JWJ,

18 March 1652/1653, in ibid., 265–266; and JWJ to Stuyvesant, 28 March 1653, in ibid., 273 ("all possible," "messinger").

43. Pulsifer, *Acts of the Commissioners of the United Colonies,* 10: 23.

44. Bradford, *Of Plimoth Plantation,* 373.

45. Pulsifer, *Acts of the Commissioners of the United Colonies,* 10: 4.

46. This fact likely explains why Stanton remains so little studied, despite his clearly critical role as "Interpreter-General" of New England. Unlike Roger Williams and "apostle" John Eliot, arguably New England's most famous interpreters of Algonquian languages, Thomas Stanton left behind a relatively sparse paper trail. He produced precious little correspondence and no "Key" into the mysteries of Algonquian grammar. To do so, in fact, would have been foolish. As a trader and a paid interpreter, it behooved him to protect the secrets of his trade. Given his elusiveness, unfortunately, no biographer has yet attempted to piece together his life's story. But see William A. Stanton, *A Record, Genealogical, Biographical, Statistical, of Thomas Stanton, of Connecticut, and His Descendants, 1635–1891* (Albany: Joel Munsell's Sons, Publishers, 1891), 9–29, which offers a valuable introduction to Stanton's appearances in the historical record.

47. This incident is related in Lion Gard[i]ner, "Leift Lion Gard[i]ner His Relation of the Pequot Warres," in Charles Orr, ed., *History of the Pequot War: The Contemporary Accounts of Mason, Underhill, Vincent and Gardener* (Cleveland: The Helman-Taylor Company, 1897), 131–133.

48. Richard Anson Wheeler, *History of the Town of Stonington, County of New London, Connecticut, From Its First Settlement in 1649 to 1900, With a Genealogical Register of Stonington Families* (Mystic, Connecticut: Lawrence Verry Incorporated, 1966), 576–577.

49. Pulsifer, *Acts of the Commissioners of the United Colonies,* 10: 5.

50. Smith's trading house seems the likeliest meeting place, since both the trader himself and his agent Valentine Whitman (mentioned in Stanton's transcription as "Voll") were also present. See ibid., 6.

51. Pulsifer, *Acts of the Commissioners of the United Colonies,* 10: 5–6.

52. Pulsifer, *Acts of the Commissioners of the United Colonies,* 10: 6–7.

53. Pulsifer, *Acts of the Commissioners of the United Colonies,* 10: 8–9.

54. Pulsifer, *Acts of the Commissioners of the United Colonies,* 10: 5 ("what hath passed"), 8–9.

55. Pulsifer, *Acts of the Commissioners of the United Colonies,* 10: 44, 45.

56. Pulsifer, *Acts of the Commissioners of the United Colonies,* 10: 10, 23.

57. Henry Ackerly testimony, in Pulsifer, *Acts of the Commissioners of the United Colonies,* 10: 48–49.

58. "privatt talkes": This quote is drawn from an earlier panic that occurred in 1642, when rumors arose that the Narragansett sachem Miantonomi was organizing a pan-Indian alliance against the English colonies. In late August 1642, an

unnamed Indian stepped out of the shadows growing "towards the eveinge" and approached Roger Ludlow, who was then raking hay. In a "privatt talke," the man told Ludlow of a broad Native conspiracy. See "Relation of the Plott—Indian," in *MHSC,* 3rd. series, 3 (Boston, 1833): 161; and, for a recent interpretation of Miantonomi's intentions, see Michael Leroy Oberg, " 'We Are All the Sachems from East to West': A New Look at Miantonomi's Campaign of Resistance," *New England Quarterly* 77:3 (Sep. 2004): 478–499.

59. But for a few lonely studies, the language encounter in early America remains largely uncharted territory. But see, especially, James Axtell, "Babel of Tongues: Communicating with the Indians," in his *Natives and Newcomers: The Cultural Origins of North America* (New York: Oxford University Press, 2001), 46–78; Ives Goddard, "The Use of Pidgins and Jargons on the East Coast of North America," in *The Language Encounter in the Americas, 1492–1800: A Collection of Essays,* ed. Edward G. Gray and Norman Fiering (New York: Berghahn Books, 2000), 61–75; James H. Merrell, " 'The Customes of Our Countrey': Indians and Colonists in Early America," in *Strangers Within the Realm: Cultural Margins of the First British Empire,* ed. Bernard Bailyn and Philip D. Morgan (Chapel Hill: University of North Carolina Press, 1991), 126–131; and Robert Michael Morrissey, " 'I Speake It Well': Language, Cultural Understanding, and the End of a Missionary Middle Ground in Illinois Country, 1673–1712," *Early American Studies* 9:3 (Fall 2011): 617–648. Broader studies on how attitudes about Native language and race shaped encounters in early America include Edward G. Gray, *New World Babel: Languages and Nations in Early America* (Princeton: Princeton University Press, 1999); Jill Lepore, *A is for American: Letters and Other Characters in the Newly United States* (New York: Vintage, 2002); and Sean P. Harvey, *Native Tongues: Colonialism and Race from Encounter to the Reservation* (Cambridge: Harvard University Press, 2015).

Study of language exchange has often centered on the cultural brokers who crossed linguistic borders, rather than ordinary people. On cultural brokers, see, for example, Nancy L. Hagedorn, " 'A Friend to Go Between Them': The Interpreter as Cultural Broker During Anglo-Iroquois Councils, 1740–1770," *Ethnohistory* 35:1 (Winter 1988): 60–80; Frances Karttunen, *Between Worlds: Interpreters, Guides, and Survivors* (New Brunswick, N.J.: Rutgers University Press, 1994); Jill Lepore, "Dead Men Tell No Tales: John Sassamon and the Fatal Consequences of Literacy," *American Quarterly* 46:4 (December 1994): 479–512; Merrell, *Into the American Woods;* Daniel K. Richter, "Cultural Brokers and Intercultural Politics: New York-Iroquois Relations, 1664–1701," *Journal of American History* 75:1 (June 1988): 40–67; and Margaret Connell Szasz, ed., *Between Indian and White Worlds: The Cultural Broker* (Norman, OK: University of Oklahoma Press, 1994).

60. "Second Letter from Governor Eaton of New Haven to Director General Stuyvesant," 8 October 1647, in Gehring, *Correspondence,* 13–14. Englishman

Edward Gibbons, on the other hand, adjudged Stuyvesant a man of "good Languige"; see Edward Gibbons to JW, 27 November 1648, *Winthrop Papers,* 5: 283–284.

61. Bradford, *Of Plimoth Plantation,* 22, 267, 271.

62. John Milton became the Secretary of Foreign Tongues in March 1648/1649. For Williams reading Dutch to him, see RW to JWJ., 12 July 1654, in *Correspondence of Roger Williams,* 2: 393 and 395, n. 19.

63. See, for instance, the example of mariner John Thickpeny, in Charles J. Hoadly, editor and transcriber, *Records of the Colony and Plantation of New Haven, from 1638 to 1649* (Hartford, 1857), 106.

64. Kammen, *Colonial New York,* 37.

65. Quoted in Kammen, *Colonial New York,* 61.

66. Adriaen an der Donck, "Description of the New Netherlands," in *Collections of the New-York Historical Society* 2nd ser., 1 (New York, 1841): 206. On Dutch-Native communication in New Netherland more generally, see Lois M. Feister, "Linguistic Communication between the Dutch and Indians in New Netherland 1609–1664," *Ethnohistory* 20:1 (Winter 1973): 25–38.

67. See fn.59, above.

68. Roger Williams, *A Key into the Language of America, Or, An help to the Language of the Natives in that Part of America, Called New England* (1643; Bedford, Mass.: Applewood Books, 1997), 54, 56.

69. For definitions of *jargon* and *pidgin,* see Axtell, "Babel of Tongues," 56 ("reducing . . . native speech") and Goddard, "The Use of Pidgins and Jargons," 62 ("absolute minimum of vocabulary").

70. Axtell, "Babel of Tongues," 60.

71. Bernard Bailyn and Philip D. Morgan, introduction to *Strangers Within the Realm,* 22–23 ("linguistic imperialism"); Merrell, " 'The Customes of Our Countrey'," in ibid., 127 ("help England rule"). William Wood noted that, among the Massachusetts, the ability to speak English was a cherished talent. The Indians "are . . . not a little proud that they can speak the English tongue, using it as much as their own when they meet with such as can understand it, puzzling stranger Indians, which sometimes visit them from more remote places," he wrote. See William Wood, *New England's Prospect: A True, Lively, and Experimentall Description of that Part of America, Commonly Called New England,* ed. Alden T. Vaughan (1634; Amherst: University of Massachusetts Press, 1977), 110.

72. Edward Winslow, *Good Newes from New England: or A True Relation of Things Very Remarkable at the Plantation of Plimouth in New-England* (1624), in *Chronicles of the Pilgrim Fathers of The Colony of New Plymouth, From 1602 to 1625,* ed. Alexander Young (Boston: Charles C. Little and James Brown, 1841), 366–367.

73. Wood, *New England's Prospect,* 109.

74. *Strength Out of Weaknesse; or A Glorious Manifestation of the Further Progresse of the Gospel among the Indians in New-England* (London, 1652), in Michael P.

Clark, ed., *The Eliot Tracts: With Letters from John Eliot to Thomas Thorowgood and Richard Baxter* (Westport, CT: Praeger, 2003), 243.

75. William Castell, *A Petition of W[illiam] C[astell] Exhibited to the High Court of Parliament Now Assembled, for the Propagating of the Gospel in America, and the West Indies* (London, 1641), 6 ("principall Ende"). On Eliot and early efforts at Christianizing New England's Indians, see Clark, *The Eliot Tracts,* 1–52, and Richard W. Cogley, *John Eliot's Mission to the Indians before King Philip's War* (Cambridge: Harvard University Press, 1999).

76. John Eliot, *The Indian Grammar Begun* (Cambridge: Marmaduke Johnson, 1666), 65 ("pregnant witted"); *The Glorious Progress of the Gospel amongst the Indians in New England* (London, 1649), in Clark, *The Eliot Tracts,* 160 ("first that I made use of").

77. *Strength Out of Weaknesse,* 225.

78. *Tears of Repentance: Or, A Further Narrative of the Progress of the Gospel Amongst the Indians in New England* (London, 1653), in Clark, *The Eliot Tracts,* 282.

79. John Eliot, *A Late and Further Manifestation of the Progress of the Gospel Amongst the Indians in New-England* (London, 1655), in Clark, *The Eliot Tracts,* 305. In retrospect Eliot deemed the panic "utterly groundlesse," though "a great damping and discouragement upon us."

80. Thomas Shepard, *The Clear Sun-shine of the Gospel Breaking Forth Upon the Indians in New-England* (London, 1648), in Clark, *The Eliot Tracts,* 118.

81. *The Day-Breaking if not the Sun-Rising of the Gospell with the Indians in New-England* (London, 1647), in Clark, *The Eliot Tracts,* 95.

82. See Kathleen J. Bragdon, "Native Languages as Spoken and Written: Views from Southern New England," in Gray and Fiering, eds., *The Language Encounter in the Americas,* 173–188, for the persistence of Native languages in the face of "linguistic colonialism."

83. Most scholars view English claims of fluency with suspicion. "Europeans who learned the various forms of pidginized Algonquian *believed* that they were using the real Indian language," Ives Goddard writes (emphasis mine). See Goddard, "Some Early Examples of American Indian Pidgin English from New England," *International Journal of American Linguistics* 43, no. 1 (1977): 41. But, for an argument that missionary John Eliot's work in translating Massachusett was "a relatively successful attempt to accurately describe the language," see Stephen Andrew Guice, "The Linguistic Work of John Eliot" (Ph.D. Dissertation, Michigan State University, 1990), introduction, np.

84. Hoadly, *Records of the Colony and Plantation of New Haven,* 24.

85. Goddard, "Some Early Examples," 40. The term appears both in William Wood's "nomenclator" of Indian terms and in Roger Williams' *Key,* with similar definitions.

86. The word *weregin*—alternately rendered as "wereagea," "wunegin," "wunnégin," "weneikinne," and "waureegun,"—appears elsewhere in New England

records. It seems to have been borrowed rather quickly into English. Tellingly, Roger Ludlow used the word (given as *wereagea*) in a 1638 letter to John Winthrop, also without translating. See Roger Ludlow to JW, 3 July 1638, *Winthrop Papers,* 4: 44. *Weregin* enjoyed a long life as a borrowed term. In the eighteenth century, it was etched into Samuel Uncas's gravestone (as "waureegan") and gave an eastern Connecticut town its name ("Wauregan"). As late as the 1870s, the term *wauregan* was apparently still used by those living around Norwich, Connecticut, to mean "fine" or "showy." For additional examples of its use in early New England, see Alexander F. Chamberlain, "Wauregan," in *Handbook of American Indians North of Mexico,* ed. F. W. Hodge (Washington, DC, 1907–1910), 923, and Goddard, "Some Early Examples," 40.

87. According to William Wood's (admittedly flawed) Algonquian dialogue, "*Titta*" meant "I cannot tell." See Wood, *New England's Prospect,* 121.

88. John Hammond Trumbull, ed., *The Public Records of the Colony of Connecticut, Prior to the Union With New Haven Colony, To May, 1665,* 15 vols. (Hartford: Brown & Parsons, 1850), 1: 218–219.

89. "Mattamoi": to die. Wood, *New England's Prospect,* 119.

90. Charles J. Hoadly, ed and transcriber, *Records of the Colony or Jurisdiction of New Haven, From May 1653, to the Union. Together with the New Haven Code of 1656* (Hartford: Case, Lockwood and Company, 1858), 80. Italics added.

91. Thomas Minor, *The Diary of Thomas Minor, Stonington, Connecticut. 1653 to 1684,* ed. Sidney H. Miner and George D. Stanton, Jr. (New London, 1899; reprint edition, 2001), 9, 77, 196. "Nunip" is an Algonquian word for 'beans.' Italics added.

92. See Thomas Stanton to JWJ, 15 May 1649, in *Winthrop Papers,* 5: 344, in which Stanton writes, "I Left sum goodes with an Indyan to trad for mee" and later identifies his agent as "An Andouhu" of Pawcatuck. For Agedouset's appearances in the Minor diary, see Minor, *Diary,* 60, 72, 77, 85, 91, 196.

93. As with Thomas Stanton, it is unclear how Minor gained knowledge of the language, but he may simply have absorbed it through conversation with local Pequots. In the latter part of his life, he worked, on occasion, as an interpreter. See, for example, his mediation in the case of Taphanse, an Indian accused in 1662 of murder. Pidgin Algonquian words ("netop," "machet") are also present, in that record: Hoadly, *Records of the Colony or Jurisdiction of New Haven,* 458–462. For Grace Minor, see Deposition of Thomas Minor, Robert Hempstead, and William Nicholls, 17 April 1650, in *Winthrop Papers,* 6: 34–35.

94. "Algonquian" is a family of distinct languages, not simply a collection of varying dialects. How much intelligibility existed, across these languages, is debatable. Kathleen Bradgon describes at least five different "languages" among southern New England Algonquians: Loup A and B, Narragansett and Niantic, Massachusetts, Mohegan-Pequot-Montauk, and Quiripi-Unquachog. Despite trade and kin connections, she finds "significant dialectal and language variation within the region." Edward G. Gray also writes that, "linguists now describe most of what

was spoken in southern New England not as dialects but as distinct—although not unrelated—languages," with "some mutual intelligibility." William Simmons, on the other hand, minimizes the differences among Algonquian speakers. "Speakers of one Eastern Algonquian dialect could generally converse in the one spoken by their neighbors," he writes, although "communication became more difficult the farther one traveled away from home." See Bragdon, "Native Languages as Spoken and Written," 174; Lyle Campbell, *American Indian Languages: The Historical Linguistics of Native America* (New York: Oxford University Press, 1997); Ives Goddard, "Eastern Algonquian Languages," in *Handbook of American Indians,* ed. William C. Sturtevant, Volume 15, *Northeast,* ed. Bruce G. Trigger (Washington: Smithsonian Institution, 1978), 70–77; Gray, *New World Babel,* 15; and William S. Simmons, *Spirit of the New England Tribes: Indian History and Folklore, 1620–1984* (Hanover: University Press of New England, 1986), 11.

95. Pulsifer, *Acts of the Commissioners of the United Colonies,* 9: 54–55.

96. By the 1670s, many English along the southern shores of New England may have known some Algonquian. In 1674, Daniel Gookin wrote that, "In Rhode Island and Providence plantations there are sundry English live, that are skilful in the Indian tongue." See Daniel Gookin, *Historical Collections of the Indians in New England* (1792; New York: Arno Press, 1972), 70.

97. Connecticut Archives, Indian Papers, Series I, Docs. 10 & 17, Connecticut State Library, Hartford, Connecticut.

98. Connecticut Archives, Indian Papers, I, Doc. 17.

99. Pulsifer, *Acts of the Commissioners of the United Colonies,* 10: 44.

100. I have encountered Newcome / Mattake in several other records, as well, including: "A Copy of a deed of purchase to Porter & partners" and "Copy Deed Petaquamset Jan 1657" in "Pettaquamscutt Papers (old copies), 1657–1734," Elisha Reynolds Potter, Jr. Papers, Mss 629, SG3, Box 4, Folder 23, Rhode Island Historical Society, Providence, Rhode Island; and "The Coppie of Allumpps and Haquontuses giveing Posession of Quenebauge" (28 April 1659), Robert C. Winthrop Papers, Vol. 1: 110, Connecticut State Library, Hartford, Connecticut. His name also surfaces on several of the Westerly deeds that appear in Elisha R. Potter, *The Early History of Narragansett* (Providence, 1835), 243–248.

101. Pulsifer, *Acts of the Commissioners of the United Colonies,* 10: 10–11 ("somtimes"). "My good Sonne, your severall Lettres by this Indian Newcome I received," wrote the elder John Winthrop, in February 1648/1649. See John Winthrop to John Winthrop, Jr., 3 February 1648/1649, *Winthrop Papers,* 5: 311; Adam Winthrop to JWJ, 14 March 1648/1649, *Winthrop Papers,* 5: 319.

102. Indian Newe-come to JWJ, 1 December 1652, *Winthrop Papers,* 6: 234–235.

103. Another possibility: "Newcome" may have been a phonetic bastardization of an Algonquian name. In the later 1650s, a man named "Wonacomtone" appears in Rhode Island records. Was this Newcome? Even if it was, is it possible that

"Wonacomtone" was an Algonquian interpretation of the English-origin "Newcome"? See Wood, *New England's Prospect,* title page; Rhode Island, *Records of the Court of Trials of the Colony of Providence Plantations 1647–1662* (Providence: Rhode Island Historical Society, 1920), 52.

104. Pulsifer, *Acts of the Commissioners of the United Colonies,* 10: 10. Emphasis mine.

105. Pulsifer, *Acts of the Commissioners of the United Colonies,* 10: 11, 116, 169.

106. Pulsifer, *Acts of the Commissioners of the United Colonies,* 10: 8.

107. For a description of internal New Netherland politics, including Van der Donck's opposition, see Bailyn, *The Barbarous Years,* 191–241.

108. Pulsifer, *Acts of the Commissioners of the United Colonies,* 10: 22.

109. Pulsifer, *Acts of the Commissioners of the United Colonies,* 10: 12.

110. Bradford, *Of Plimoth Plantation,* 496.

111. Bradford, *Of Plimoth Plantation,* 509–510.

112. Pulsifer, *Acts of the Commissioners of the United Colonies,* 10: 23.

113. Pulsifer, *Acts of the Commissioners of the United Colonies,* 10: 56.

114. Pulsifer, *Acts of the Commissioners of the United Colonies,* 10: 44–45.

115. Pulsifer, *Acts of the Commissioners of the United Colonies,* 10: 428–429.

116. Pulsifer, *Acts of the Commissioners of the United Colonies,* 10: 56; Samuel Stone to Richard Blinman, 12 June 1653, *Winthrop Papers,* 6: 298.

117. *The Second Part of the Tragedy of Amboyna; or, A True Relation of a Most Bloody, Treacherous, and Cruel Design of the Dutch in New-Netherlands in America* (London, 1653), 5–7.

118. "Letter From the Directors at Amsterdam to Petrus Stuyvesant and the Council of New Netherland," 4 November 1653, in Gehring, *Correspondence,* 230.

119. Samuel Maverick, "A Briefe Description of New England . . . ," *MHSP,* 2nd ser., 1 (1884–1885): 246. On the divisions between the "Western Colonies" (New Haven and Connecticut) and the Eastern (Plymouth and Massachusetts), see especially Dexter, "The Early Relations between New England and New Netherland," 461–464.

120. Neal Salisbury, *Manitou and Providence: Indians, Europeans, and the Making of New England, 1500–1643* (New York: Oxford University Press, 1982), 215.

121. For Thomas Stanton's bad journey into Niantic in September 1653, see Pulsifer, *Acts of the Commissioners of the United Colonies,* 10: 94–95.

122. Henry C. Shelley, *John Underhill: Captain of New England and New Netherland* (New York: D. Appleton and Company, 1932), 360–362.

123. Pulsifer, *Acts of the Commissioners of the United Colonies,* 10: 44. Emphasis mine.

4. POST HASTE

1. Thomas Minor, *The Diary of Thomas Minor, Stonington, Connecticut. 1653 to 1684,* ed. Sidney H. Miner and George D. Stanton, Jr. (New London, 1899; reprint edition, 2001), 115 ("the 24th was the great storme of rayne").

2. The English capture of New Netherland in 1664 came as a distant aftershock of the Restoration. Charles II gifted a large swath of territory along North America's eastern seaboard—including that between the Connecticut and Delaware Rivers—to his brother James, the Duke of York. Eager to seize his prize, James sent a fleet of warships commanded by Colonel Richard Nicolls to capture and claim the Dutch territory. The task done, Nicolls became the first governor of the new colony of "New York" (and a frequent correspondent of the Winthrops and other New Englanders). On the 1664 capture itself, I am fond of the narrative in Henri van der Zee and Barbara van der Zee, *A Sweet and Alien Land: The Story of Dutch New York* (New York: The Viking Press, 1978), 445–464.

3. Dominie Henricus Selyns, quoted in van der Zee and van der Zee, *Sweet and Alien Land,* 481.

4. This was how Colonel Richard Nicolls, commander of the invading fleet and New York's first English governor, signed the letter he sent to Massachusetts, announcing his victory; see Michael Kammen, *Colonial New York: A History* (New York: Oxford University Press, 1975), 72.

5. Lovelace has no biography, but see J. Hall Pleasants, "Francis Lovelace, Governor of New York, 1668–1673," *New York Genealogical and Biographical Record* 51 (1920), 175–188; and Kammen, *Colonial New York,* 79.

6. Kammen, *Colonial New York,* 79, 95.

7. "A Proclamacon for a Post . . . ," in Victor Hugo Paltsits, ed., *Minutes of the Executive Council of the Province of New York, Administration of Francis Lovelace 1668–1673,* 2 vols. (Albany: Published by the State of New York, 1910), 2: 794.

8. Lovelace to JWJ, 27 December 1672, *MHSC,* 5th ser., 9 (Boston, 1885): 83–86.

9. Francis Lovelace to Secretary of State Joseph Williamson, 3 October 1670, excerpted in W. Noel Sainsbury, ed., *Calendar of State Papers, Colonial Series: America and the West Indies, 1669–1674* (London, 1889), 7: 111.

10. Francis Lovelace to JWJ, 22 September 1669, Marjorie F. Gutheim, ed., *Winthrop Family Papers* Microfilm, 53 reels (Boston, Mass.: Massachusetts Historical Society, 1976), Reel 9.

11. "A Lettr to Major Genrll Leverett at Boston," 23 April 1672, in John Romeyn Brodhead, ed, *Documents Relative to the Colonial History of the State of New York,* 15 vols. (Albany: Weed, Parsons and Company, printers, 1853–1887), 14: 662 ("receiv'd Practice"); Francis Lovelace to JWJ, 27 December 1672, *MHSC,* 5th ser., 9 (Boston, 1885): 83.

12. Pleasants, "Francis Lovelace, Governor of New York."

13. Francis Lovelace to JWJ, 27 December 1672, *MHSC,* 5th ser., 9 (Boston, 1885): 83.

14. Francis Lovelace to JWJ, 22 January 1673, in Winthrop Family, Winthrop Family Papers [transcripts], 1630–1741, 10 boxes, Box 9, Massachusetts Historical Society, Boston, Massachusetts.

15. Francis Lovelace to JWJ, 27 December 1672, *MHSC,* 5th ser., 9 (Boston, 1885): 83–86; JWJ to Wait Winthrop, 6 February 1672/73, *Winthrop Papers* microfilm, Reel 10, refers to Lovelace's plan as a "constant Post."

16. JWJ to Wait Winthrop, 6 February 1672/1673, *Winthrop Papers* microfilm, Reel 10.

17. Virtually no study has delved deeply enough into the colonial origins of postal service to witness it taking shape in the hundred years before Benjamin Franklin stepped into his acclaimed role, in the 1750s, as Postmaster-General. On the history of early American postal service, the major works are Konstantin Dierks, *In My Power: Letter Writing and Communications in Early America* (Philadelphia: University of Pennsylvania Press, 2009); Wayne Fuller, *The American Mail: Enlarger of the Common Life* (Chicago: Chicago University Press, 1972); Richard R. John, *Spreading the News: The American Postal System from Franklin to Morse* (Cambridge: Harvard University Press, 1995); and Richard B. Kielbowicz, *News in the Mail: The Press, Post Office, and Public Information, 1700–1860s* (New York: Greenwood Press, 1989).

18. Francis Lovelace to JWJ, 27 December 1672, *MHSC,* 5th ser., 9 (Boston, 1885): 83.

19. William Pratt to JWJ, 29 July 1666, *MHSC,* 5th ser., 1 (Boston, 1871): 413–414 ("letter by Post"; "post haste . . . without delay"); William Jones and John Nash to JWJ, 7 August 1673, *Winthrop Papers* microfilm, Reel 10 ("post him away"); John Allyn to JWJ, 28 August 1671, in ibid. ("gonn post"); John Corwin to Fitz-John Winthrop, [August 1669], *Winthrop Papers* microfilm, Reel 9 ("post payd").

20. Richard Nicolls to JWJ, 15 March 1664/1665, *Winthrop Papers* microfilm, Reel 8.

21. Mark Kishlansky, *A Monarchy Transformed: Britain 1603–1714* (London: Penguin Books, 1997), 222. For an overview of the Restoration and reign of Charles II, see ibid., 213–262.

22. Howard Robinson, *The British Post Office: A History* (Princeton: Princeton University Press, 1948), 21–23, 47. In fits and starts, postal service had long been developing in England. Early in the sixteenth century, Henry VIII appointed a Master of the Posts, charged with breaking routes into postal stages of ten to fifteen miles. The Master also ensured that horses and post boys were available for service along each stage, in the event of a royal emergency. But the system remained somewhat ad hoc, with temporary posts laid where needed. Later in the century, the service began to take more shape. "Ordinary posts"—that is, those responsible for speeding messages along a given stage—were even ordered to own a particular number of horses, leather bags, and horns (three of each). Under Elizabeth I, the speed at which posts were to travel—seven miles per hour in summer and five miles per hour in winter—was fixed. Despite these edicts, postal service was not entirely organized, nor was it intended as a public privilege (in fact, Henry VIII and

Elizabeth I both went to great lengths to keep potentially treasonous letters *out* of postal carriers' hands). Not until the first decades of the seventeenth century did postal service for "public use" come to England. In these years, English service became quicker, began to take in private letters, and even witnessed the rise of by-posts who carried letters to towns removed from the main postal routes. Upheavals related to the looming Civil War interrupted this progress, and in 1637 the embattled Charles I once again limited postal service to royal business. Not until 1660, when the monarchy was restored to Charles II, did England enjoy the advent of a truly organized postal service. After years of "unsettlement and confusion," attests postal historian Howard Robinson, the Restoration brought to England a real, permanent post. See Robinson, *The British Post Office*, 7, 15, 21, 23, 29, 33–34, 47.

23. Edwin A. Pratt, *A History of Inland Transport and Communication in England* (New York: Dutton, 1912), 39.

24. Dierks, *In My Power,* 28–29.

25. Catherine Delano-Smith, *English Maps: A History* (Toronto: University of Toronto Press, 1999), 159, 166–167.

26. Warrant appointing Ogilby, quoted in Catherine Delano-Smith, "Milieus of Mobility: Itineraries, Route Maps and Road Maps," in James R. Akerman, ed., *Cartographies of Travel and Navigation* (Chicago: University of Chicago Press, 2006), 50.

27. Delano-Smith, "Milieus of Mobility," 50; Delano-Smith, *English Maps,* 167.

28. John Ogilby, *Britannia . . . Or, An Illustration of the Kingdom of England and Dominion of Wales: By a Geographical and Historical Description of the Principal Roads thereof.* (London: Printed by the Author, 1675), B1 ("Geographers"), 2 (London to Aberistwith), 4 ("Backward Turnings").

29. Delano-Smith, *English Maps,* 171–172. Catherine Delano-Smith is skeptical about whether Ogilby intended his massive tome as a travel guide, since at 300 pages it was not particularly practical—"destined not for use on horseback, or even in a carriage, and far too costly to risk mistreatment," she adjudges. "It sold well, though, and as a delightful library book one has to assume it was read and pored over in the drawing rooms as well as the libraries of those country houses Ogilby had taken pains to include on the maps." (Ibid.) Ogilby's work was more nationalistic than it was about everyday wayfinding, Delano-Smith posits: It promoted the sense that the realm was "economically wealthy, its people prosperous, and its national security under no threat from any direction" (Delano-Smith, "Milieus of Mobility," 54).

But Ogilby biographer Katherine S. Van Eerde is less certain that *Britannia* was purely ornamental: ". . . [F]or the traveler, an often unlucky but far from unfamiliar figure of the seventeenth century," she writes, "Ogilby's *Britannia* had much utility: it gave him precise distances, locations of towns, and the best prospect of comprehending what his journey involved." Indeed, "many owners did not hesitate to cut

out strips of maps in their local areas or of the places to which they were journeying, and presumably carried these strips with them." See Van Eerde, *John Ogilby
and the Taste of His Times* (Folkestone, England: Dawson, 1976), 137.

30. Ogilby, *Britannia,* A1–A2.

31. Ian K. Steele, *The English Atlantic, 1675–1740: An Exploration of
Communication and Community* (New York: Oxford University Press, 1986), 120.
"There was less likelihood that postal services would be launched or subsidized in
the colonies [than in England] to support the distribution of court newspapers or
the gathering of political intelligence . . . ," Steele writes. "If they are seen in the
context of legitimate expectations and the limited political and commercial need,
the surprise is that comparatively expensive horse posts, connecting small settlements that were far apart, developed as soon as they did in North America."

32. Fuller, *The American Mail,* 15.

33. Robinson, *The British Post Office,* 53.

34. Henry Oldenburg to JWJ, 1669 [March or earlier], Winthrop Family Papers
[transcripts], 1630–1741, Box 8.

35. On Bryan's life, see C. C. Baldwin, *Alexander Bryan, of Milford,
Connecticut, His Ancestors and His Descendants* (Cleveland: Leader Printing
Company, 1889).

36. Boats played an important role in Alexander Bryan's forwarding "service."
Several letters hint that the mail he handled was usually sent over water ("Mr.
Bryans vessell lyes Icebound, and Mr. Maltby must now goe by Land to Milford,"
moaned one, while another noted that the "skipper that brings this to Mr. Bryan is
now ready to sett saile for Boston"). But not all were waterborne. At least one that
"Came by watter" to Bryan was propelled onward with a horse messenger ("my
man," to Bryan). See Richard Nicolls to JWJ, [12] January [1667], *Winthrop Papers*
microfilm, Reel 8 ("Icebound"); Richard Nicolls to JWJ, 22 June [1667], *Winthrop
Papers* microfilm, Reel 9 ("ready to sett saile"); and Alexander Bryan to JWJ, 5 April
1669, in ibid. ("my man Returnes with the horse").

37. Nathaniel Brewster to JWJ, 23 August 1670, *Winthrop Papers* microfilm,
Reel 9 ("speedily Conveigh"); Daniel Lane to JWJ, 12 July 1669, *Winthrop Papers*
microfilm, Reel 8.

38. In the mid-1660s French and Dutch threats sent numerous posts careening
across New England. When two French ships seized John Plumb's vessel off the
coast of Martha's Vineyard in 1666, Plymouth sent "a letter by poste" toward
Connecticut; from Saybrook, in turn, William Pratt sent the news upriver to
Hartford "post haste." That French men of war were lurking off the Massachusetts
coast was similarly "posted" to John Pynchon in Springfield, who also—like
Pratt—sent word "Hast Post hast For his Maties. service" toward Colonel Nicolls in
New York. And when news of the threat reached Rhode Island, Governor William
Brenton acted in like fashion: "the first thing I did was to procure a poste . . . that

the western parts might have speedy notice," he later wrote. William Pratt to JWJ, 29 July 1666, *MHSC,* 5th ser., 1 (Boston, 1871): 413; John Pynchon to JWJ, 30 July 1666, *Winthrop Papers* microfilm, Reel 8; William Brenton to JWJ, 27 August 1666, in ibid.

39. JWJ to Fitz-John Winthrop, 10 March 1673/1674, *Winthrop Papers* microfilm, Reel 11 (sending "post" versus "operunity"); JWJ to Wait Winthrop, 8 December 1673, *Winthrop Papers* microfilm, Reel 10; John Allyn to JWJ, 28 August 1671, in ibid.

40. If the Winthrop correspondence provides any indication, Indians were far more likely to carry letters in the years before 1655. Between 1635 and 1655, they made up about 35 percent (57/164) of all letter bearers. Between 1656 and 1675, Indians carried only about 13 percent of letters (35/272). If the number of Indian couriers within New England was falling by the 1660s, much evidence nonetheless suggests that the pattern would repeat, elsewhere—westward, and along other frontiers. In the 1670s, John Pynchon was actively using couriers to correspond with traders in Albany. He dispatched them to collect debts owed to him. "Whatever beaver you shall send to clear the account," he wrote frostily, in 1674, "you may safely send it by the Indians, the bearer hereof Wallump or Cranbeane." Deep into the 1680s and 1690s, such messengers continued to connect Springfield and Albany. See John Pynchon to Andreas Dreyer and Gerrit Van Slichtenhorst, Springfield to Albany, 29 June 1674, in Carl Bridenbaugh, ed., *The Pynchon Papers Volume I: Letters of John Pynchon, 1654–1700* (Boston: The Colonial Society of Massachusetts, 1982), 127–129.

41. Joseph A. Conforti, *Saints and Strangers: New England in British North America* (Baltimore: Johns Hopkins University Press, 2006), 6.

42. Giles Sylvester to Fitz-John Winthrop, 14 July 1676, *Winthrop Papers* microfilm, Reel 11.

43. "Posts" and Indian messengers were not necessarily mutually exclusive; the two categories did occasionally collide, as when Rhode Island men sent an Indian "post" to Hartford in 1673, in hopes of hearing news about the threat of a Dutch invasion. See Jireh Bull to Thomas Stanton et. al., 8 August 1673, *Winthrop Papers* microfilm, Reel 10.

44. "post, *n.*3": "Any of a series of men stationed at suitable places along appointed post-roads, the duty of each being to ride with, or forward speedily to the next stage, the monarch's (and later also other) letters and dispatches, and to provide fresh horses for express messengers riding through. ***to lay posts***: to establish a chain of such riders and horses along a route for the speedy delivery of dispatches. *Obs.*" Also "post, *v.*3": "I. To travel in the manner of a post-rider, and related senses. 1. *intr.* To travel with relays of horses, originally as a courier or bearer of letters. Now *hist.*," *Oxford English Dictionary Online,* March 2007, Oxford University Press, accessed 22 May 2007, http://dictionary.oed.com.ezp2.harvard.edu/cgi/entry

/50184804 and http://dictionary.oed.com.ezp2.harvard.edu/cgi/entry/50184815. Examples of use cited in the OED refer frequently to horses.

45. See "Instructions for the Post-Mastr," in Paltsits, ed., *Minutes of the Executive Council of the Province of New York,* 2: 796.

46. John Winthrop, Jr., "A Diary of 1645," in Harral Ayres, *The Great Trail of New England* (Boston, 1940), 372.

47. On Minor's life, see Robert Charles Anderson, ed., *The Great Migration Begins: Immigrants to New England 1620–1633,* 3 vols. (Boston: New England Historic Genealogical Society, 1995), 2: 1262–1267.

48. In order to track Minor's travels, I created a database of every place that he mentioned visiting in the diary, including the date and Minor's reason for visiting (if given). With this method, I identified patterns in his recorded movements. Here, I have concentrated on discovering the motives behind Minor's longer journeys. For the purposes of this chapter, I define as "long-distance" any trip that took him further than fifteen miles from his Mystic property. (This was about the extent covered by early Stonington and neighboring settlements.)

49. James Hammond Trumbull, ed., *The Public Records of the Colony of Connecticut 1636–1776,* 15 vols. (Hartford: Lockwood & Brainard Company, 1850–1890), 3: 90; Minor, *Diary,* 169. That he often traveled on official business somewhat explains his diligence in recording both destinations and travel time. The task fulfilled, he could collect reimbursement for his expenses.

50. Minor, *Diary,* 39.

51. Minor, *Diary,* 81, 86, 90–91.

52. Minor, *Diary,* 110.

53. Locally, of course, Minor was much more mobile. To nearby New London alone, he recorded over one hundred visits. Town meetings, worship, surveying, county courts, planting, reaping and trading with neighbors all kept Thomas Minor moving, constantly, within about a ten mile radius from his farm.

54. Overall, his longer trips peaked in the 1660s and dropped off slightly afterward. It's hard to know why. Was it because Minor was getting older? Was it because New England was sprouting new towns and ports, thus requiring less long-distance travel? Both, probably. As Minor aged, he may have been less likely to drive livestock to the Bay, but in his stead, son "samuell went to the bay with horses" (169). And as nearby New London developed into a buzzing seaport, Minor could more frequently turn to local merchants for imported goods or special services.

55. Minor, *Diary,* 41–42.

56. By contrast, the migrants took with them 240 cattle, of which 170 survived. If a similar rate of attrition ravaged the ships' horses, only forty or so may have made it to New England. In fact, Winthrop's own mare died en route from England.

57. Howard S. Russell, *A Long Deep Furrow: Three Centuries of Farming in New England* (Hanover, NH.: University Press of New England, 1976), 31–32.

58. Winthrop, *Journal,* 91.

59. Robert West Howard, *The Horse in America* (Chicago: Follett Publishing Company, 1965), 31–32. In June 1635, Flanders mares arriving in New England aboard Dutch ships sold for an astronomical "34li: a mare," according to John Winthrop. See Winthrop, *Journal,* 147. On the use and presence of horses in early America, see also Virginia DeJohn Anderson, *Creatures of Empire: How Domestic Animals Transformed Early America* (New York: Oxford University Press, 2004), 99–103, 146, and passim; William Cronon, *Changes in the Land: Indians, Colonists, and the Ecology of New England* (New York: Hill and Wang, 1983); and Deane Phillips, *Horse Raising in Colonial New England* (Ithaca: Cornell University Agricultural Experiment Station, Memoir 54, 1922), 889–941.

60. Winthrop, *Journal,* 713; Howard, *The Horse in America,* 40.

61. John Endecott to JW, 20 August 1645, in *Winthrop Papers,* 5: 41.

62. Adam Winthrop to JWJ., 2 February 1648/49, *Winthrop Papers,* 5: 310.

63. See JWJ to John Jones, 5 December 1646, *Winthrop Papers,* 5: 122 ("Some pinnace"), and John Jones to JWJ, 13 May 1647, *Winthrop Papers,* 5: 159.

64. Minor, *Diary,* 47.

65. Minor, *Diary,* 49 ("looking mares"); Samuel Maverick, "A Briefe Description of New England . . . ," *Massachusetts Historical Society Proceedings,* 2nd ser., 1 (1884–1885): 247. Before his death in 1657, William Bradford of Plymouth also noted—in verse!—how horses had begun to increase in numbers. "Horses here likewise now do multiply," he rhymed, "They prosper well, and yet their price is high." See "A Descriptive and Historical Account of New England in Verse; From a MS. of William Bradford, Governour of Plymouth Colony," *MHSC* 1st ser., 3 (Boston, 1794): 78.

66. Winthrop, *Journal,* 692; Beauchamp Plantagenet, "A Description of the Province of New Albion . . ." (1648), in Peter Force, ed., *Tracts and Other Papers, Relating Principally to the Origin, Settlement, and Progress of the Colonies in North America* (Washington, 1838), 2: 5; Daniel Romani, Jr., "The Pettaquamscut Purchase of 1657/8 and the Establishment of a Commercial Livestock Industry in Rhode Island," in Peter Benes, ed., *New England's Creatures: 1400–1900,* The Dublin Seminar for New England Folklife Annual Proceedings 1993 (Boston: Boston University, 1995), 52.

67. Anderson, *Creatures of Empire,* 227.

68. On this, see Romani, Jr., "The Pettaquamscut Purchase of 1657/8," 45–60.

69. As early as 1660, John Tinker—Winthrop's steward in Pequot—was complaining of his patron's disorderly herds. Tinker griped that he knew "not what number of horses your worshipp hath, nor wheare." He resolved to gather and brand them all "IW," for he fretted that Winthrop was losing animals "for want

of a marke." See John Tinker to JWJ, 23 April 1660, *MHSC,* 4th ser., 7 (Boston, 1865): 244.

70. Robert Morris to JWJ, 8 February 1667/1668, *MHSC,* 3rd ser., 10 (Boston, 1849): 70.

71. Massachusetts Archives Collection, Vol. I, Doc. 22, Massachusetts State Archives, Boston, Massachusetts.

72. For New York's law, see Peter R. Christoph, ed., *New York Historical Manuscripts, English,* Vol. 22, *Administrative Papers of Governors Richard Nicolls and Francis Lovelace, 1664–1673* (Baltimore, 1980), 26; Francis Lovelace to JW, enclosure in Alexander Bryan to JWJ, 22 April 1669, *Winthrop Papers* microfilm, Reel 9; John Josselyn, *An Account of Two Voyages to New-England,* ed. Paul J. Lindholdt (1674; Hanover: University Press of New England, 1988), 132.

73. Robert West Howard, *The Horse in America* (Chicago: Follett Publishing Company, 1965), 32; Massachusetts Archives, Vol. I, 24; Christoph, *New York Historical Manuscripts,* 27; Jackson Turner Main, *Society and Economy in Colonial Connecticut* (Princeton: Princeton University Press, 1985), 57, 368.

74. Even in the 1680s, one-third of Connecticut property owners left behind horse-less probate inventories. Main, *Society and Economy,* 77–78.

75. Probate inventories are often the best available evidence of colonists' material lives, but they are not perfect representations of what people owned. They carry some biases. On the uses of probate records in early American history, see especially Gloria L. Main, "Probate Records as a Source for Early American History," *WMQ* 32 :1 (Jan. 1975), 89–99; and Holly V. Izard, "Random or Systematic? An Evaluation of the Probate Process," *Winterthur Portfolio* 32 (1997), 147–167.

76. These percentages are based on my own count of 773 Essex County probate inventories, covering the years 1636–1681, and 400 Middlesex County probate inventories, covering the years 1645–1677. The Essex County inventories are drawn from George Francis Dow, ed., *The Probate Records of Essex County, Massachusetts* (Salem, Mass.: Essex Institute, 1916–1920), 3 vols., and the Middlesex inventories from Robert H. Rodgers, *Middlesex County in the Colony of the Massachusetts Bay in New England: Records of Probate and Administration, October 1649–December 1660* (Boston: New England Historic Genealogical Society, 1999) and from two micro-filmed reels of Middlesex County probate records, Middlesex County Probate Records First Series, Vols. 1–3 (1654–1673), and Middlesex County Probate Records First Series, Vols. 4–6 (1672–1705), both housed at New England Historic Genealogical Society, Boston, Massachusetts.

Rates of horses listed in Essex County probate inventories climb as such: in the 1640s, 14.5 percent (8/55) listed at least one horse; in the 1650s, 27.5 percent (33/120); in the 1660s, 48 percent (93/194); in the 1670s, 48 percent (172/355); and in the 1680s (an incomplete decade), 42.5 percent (20/47). Rates of horses listed in Middlesex County inventories look somewhat similar: in the 1640s, 16 percent (1/6); in the

1650s, 28 percent (29/102); in the 1660s, 45 percent (76/169); and in the 1670s, 54 percent (67/123). Riding accessories appear in 28 percent (100/355) of Essex County inventories, in the 1670s, and in 35 percent (43/123) of Middlesex County inventories. For the "pr. bootes & spurs," see Thomas Flint's 1668 inventory in Dow, *Probate Records of Essex County,* 2: 139.

77. Minor, *Diary,* 79, 81, and 87.

78. John Hull, *The Diaries of John Hull, Mint-Master and Treasurer of the Colony of Massachusetts Bay* (Boston, 1857), 149, 152.

79. Francis Lovelace to JWJ, 9 December 1668, *Winthrop Papers* microfilm, Reel 9.

80. Thomas Lord, Jr., to JWJ, 12 November [1652?], *Winthrop Papers,* 6: 228.

81. John Davenport to JWJ, 4 January 1655/1656, *Winthrop Papers* microfilm, Reel 5 ("by Sea," "by land"); John Richards to JWJ, 29 December 1659, *Winthrop Papers* microfilm, Reel 6; John Richards to JWJ, 25 February 1659/1660, in ibid. Richards' return presented a similar choice: "I doe not yet know whether they purpose to returne to Boston, by land, or sea," John Davenport wrote, of Richards' party. Of course, such journeys were not confined strictly to water or to land; in his return, Richards sailed to Rhode Island, and then went home to Boston "by Land." See John Davenport to JWJ, 13 April 1660, in *Winthrop Papers* microfilm, Reel 6, and John Richards to JWJ, 13 April 1660, in ibid.

82. JWJ to Richard Nicolls, 18 September 1667, *Winthrop Papers* microfilm, Reel 9 (Richard Lord travels on horseback between Oyster Bay and Westchester); Mathias Nicolls to JWJ, 17 June 1674, *Winthrop Papers* microfilm, Reel 11; and John Lederer to JWJ, 17 November 1674, in ibid. (Stamford—New York).

83. In 1669, Stonington made him "brander of horses." That office, along with his involvement in the burgeoning horse market, demanded careful records.

84. Minor, *Diary,* 69, 202, and 207.

85. See especially Anderson, *Creatures of Empire.*

86. Few histories consider early American roads. But, for early road making in New England, see James E. McWilliams, *Building the Bay Colony: Local Economy and Culture in Early Massachusetts* (Charlottesville: University of Virginia Press, 2007), esp. 17, 28–29; Isabel S. Mitchell, *Roads and Road-Making in Colonial Connecticut* (New Haven: Yale University Press, 1933); and Robert N. Parks, "The Roads of New England, 1790–1840" (PhD. Dissertation, Michigan State University, 1966). Quote is from Mitchell, 7.

87. In some places, like the Connecticut River valley, more vigorous efforts were made to connect roads between towns. (I owe this caveat to personal communication with Walter Woodward, May 12, 2014.) County courts, in some cases, also appointed men to organize intertown roadmaking. But roadmaking, during the seventeenth century, nonetheless remained almost wholly local.

88. John R. Stilgoe, *Common Landscape of America, 1580 to 1845* (New Haven: Yale University Press, 1982), 51–53.

89. Maverick, "A Briefe Description," 243–244. By this time, a far more elaborate carrying trade—including stagecoaches—was in place, in England. On England's common carriers, see especially J. Crofts, *Packhorse, Waggon and Post: Land Carriage and Communications under the Tudors and Stuarts* (London: Routledge, 1967), and Dorian Gerhold, *Carriers and Coachmasters: Trade and Travel before the Turnpikes* (Chichester, West Sussex: Phillimore, 2005).

90. For Richard Fellows hauling lead and shoes from interior Connecticut to the coast, see William Paine & Thomas Clark to JWJ, 29 March 1658, *Winthrop Papers* microfilm, Reel 5, and Abigail Montague to Sister Barnard, about July 1663, *Winthrop Papers* microfilm, Reel 7.

91. Anderson, *Creatures of Empire,* 149.

92. See Antipas Newman to JWJ, 10 March 1658/1659, *Winthrop Papers* microfilm, Reel 5, and Antipas Newman to JWJ, 26 March 1659, in ibid.

93. Antipas Newman to JWJ, 12 June 1667, *Winthrop Papers* microfilm, Reel 8.

94. One man "lost his way" between New Haven and Hartford, after he "tooke a wrong path twice and was so bewildered that he . . . lay in the woods, in a very cold night." Another traveler wound up dead, after seeking a "pilatt" in Narragansett. John Davenport to JWJ, 11 August 1660, *MHSC,* 3rd ser., 10 (Boston, 1849): 37–39; William Thomason to JWJ, 15 January 1660/1661, *Winthrop Papers* microfilm, Reel 6.

95. JWJ to Richard Nicolls, 30 July 1666, *Winthrop Papers* microfilm, Reel 8; JWJ to Richard Nicolls, 17 July 1666, in ibid.

96. Hints of this change are not simply anecdotal. Patterns of correspondence also reflect a new fluidity of movement across territory. Sorting the Winthrops' letters over time, for instance, is revealing. Over the years 1635–1665, the number of letters collected every five years remained fairly constant (except for an anomalous drop in the years 1641–1645)—that is, until the late 1660s and early 1670s, when there was a marked leap in volume. Clumping the letters into twenty year periods renders the pattern even more striking: 36 percent of the letters (1019/2856) were sent in the first two decades, 1635–1655. But after 1655, the amount of letters nearly doubled—to 64 percent (1837/2856). Surely some of this growth was due to a fundamental increase in those writing, as New England's towns filled with greater numbers of people. But it also points to a greater number of couriers, whose travels across the northeast presented John Winthrop, Jr., with ever increasing opportunities to correspond.

97. The apparent trajectory of the "Great Trail" (also called the "Connecticut Path") is painstakingly recreated in Harral Ayres, *The Great Trail of New England* (Boston, 1940). The trail likely continued southwestward, possibly to New Haven and even into Dutch territory (later New York). Leaman F. Hallet has it turning into the Westchester Path, "the ancient Indian trail by which the Mahicans of New York kept in communication with their kinsmen of the Connecticut Valley," and Ayres notes that Indian trails did indeed run between Windsor and Milford / New Haven. See Hallet, "Indian Trails," 42, and Ayres, *Great Trail,* 85, n.2.

98. John Richards to JWJ, 29 October 1658, *Winthrop Papers* microfilm, Reel 6.

99. JWJ to Wait Winthrop, 2 January 1659/1660, *Winthrop Papers* microfilm, Reel 6 ("David a Welshman"); John Davenport to JWJ, 17 October 1660, in ibid.

100. In the 1630s, by contrast, the same trip might have taken five or more days, even for experienced footmen.

101. Richard and Sarah Lord to JWJ, 11 October 1657, *Winthrop Papers* microfilm, Reel 5. For those with horses, travel between Boston and the River apparently decreased from Wahginnicut's "five days" to two to three days. From the mine at Tantiusques (in what is now northeastern Connecticut), William Paine and Thomas Clarke estimated the travel time to Boston to be "but two dayes Jurney." William Paine and Thomas Clarke to JWJ, 29 March 1658, *Winthrop Papers* microfilm, Reel 5.

102. Shurtleff, *MBR,*. 4 (Part 2): 408.

103. JWJ to Francis Lovelace, 28 November 1668, *Winthrop Papers* microfilm, Reel 9; John Pynchon to JWJ, [1667 before 12 January], *Winthrop Papers* microfilm, Reel 8; and Richard Nicolls to JWJ, 14 February 1667, in ibid.

104. The increase in the volume of letters sent along this corridor, in the early 1670s, is noteworthy. Of all letters traveling between Massachusetts Bay and Connecticut over the period 1635–1675, 28 percent (117/413) were sent during the 1660s. But the amount sent in just the first five years of the 1670s far surpassed the entire previous decade, at 44 percent of the total (181/413). To put it another way, nearly half of *all* the letters in the Winthrop collection that traveled between Massachusetts and Connecticut were sent in the years 1671–1675.

105. Francis Lovelace to JWJ, 27 December 1672 *MHSC,* 5th ser., 9 (Boston, 1885): 83; "Instructions for the Post-Mastr," in Paltsits, ed., *Minutes of the Executive Council of the Province of New York,* 2: 795. For the evolution of what later became the Boston Post Road, see Eric Jaffe, *The King's Best Highway: The Lost History of the Boston Post Road, the Route that Made America* (New York: Scribner, 2010).

106. Francis Lovelace to JWJ, 27 December 1672, *MHSC,* 5th ser., 9 (Boston, 1885): 83.

107. Records of the Massachusetts Bay General Court, quoted in William Lincoln, *History of Worcester, Massachusetts, From Its Earliest Settlement to September 1836* (Worcester, 1837), 4–5.

108. John Pynchon to JWJ, 10 February 1672/1673, *Winthrop Papers* microfilm, Reel 10. John Winthrop, Jr., seems to have learned Hatfield's name from Pynchon. Soon after, he repeated it, writing to son Wait in Boston, "I wrote last weeke by Mr Hatfeild the N:Yorke Post." See JWJ to Wait Winthrop, 16 February 1672/1673, *Winthrop Papers* microfilm, Reel 10.

109. John Pynchon to JWJ, 10 February 1672/1673, *Winthrop Papers* microfilm, Reel 10.

110. John Richards to JWJ, 17 February 1672/1673, *Winthrop Papers* microfilm, Reel 10.

111. JWJ to Wait Winthrop, 26 February 1672/1673, *Winthrop Papers* microfilm, Reel 10 ("often oportunityes"); Matthias Nicolls to Fitz-John Winthrop, 27 June 1673, in ibid. ("intended monthly Post"), italics added.

112. The Dutch recapture of New York in July 1673 is an understudied event, but see Ronald D. Cohen, "The New England Colonies and the Dutch Recapture of New York, 1673–1674," *New-York Historical Society Quarterly* 56 (1972): 54–78, and, for a narrative incorporating Dutch sources and perspective (as well as English), see van der Zee and van der Zee, *Sweet and Alien Land,* 482–494. For contemporary English accounts of the siege and surrender, see especially Robert Treat to JWJ, 2 August 1673, in *Winthrop Papers* microfilm, Reel 10; William Leete et al. to JWJ, 2 August 1673, *MHSC,* 4th ser., 7 (Boston, 1865): 570–571; JWJ to Fitz-John Winthrop, 2 August 1673, *MHSC,* 5th ser., 8 (Boston, 1882): 150–151; and "Governor Lovelace to Governor Winthrop," 31 July 1673, "Edward Palmes to Governor Leverett," 3 August 1673, "Robert Hodge's Account of the Capture of New-York," 6 August 1673, "Nathaniel Gould's Account of the Capture of New-York," and "Nathaniel Gould to Governor Winthrop," 8 August 1673, all in Brodhead, *NYCD,* 3: 198–203. Quotes in this paragraph are drawn from Lovelace to JWJ, 31 July 1673, and Robert Treat to JWJ, 2 August 1673.

113. Minor, *Diary,* 108.

114. Robert Treat to JWJ, 2 August 1673, *Winthrop Papers* microfilm, Reel 10.

115. "Governor Lovelace to Governor Winthrop," 31 July 1673, in Brodhead, *NYCD,* 3:198.

116. Treat to JWJ, 2 August 1673, *Winthrop Papers* microfilm, Reel 10.

117. William Coddington to JWJ, 6 August 1673, *MHSC,* 4th ser., 7 (Boston, 1865): 292–293.

118. Nathan Gold to JWJ, 31 July 1673, *Winthrop Papers* microfilm, Reel 10; Francis Lovelace to JWJ, 31 July 1673, *MHSC,* 3rd. ser, 10 (Boston, 1849): 86. Robert Treat also discussed this postal plan with Gold, though he thought it advisable to keep the main stages "within our Collonie," lest "our letters be intercepted." See Robert Treat to JWJ, 2 August 1673, *Winthrop Papers* microfilm, Reel 10.

119. Nathan Gold to JWJ, 3 August 1673, *Winthrop Papers* microfilm, Reel 10.

120. John Pynchon to JWJ, 9 August 1673, *Winthrop Papers* microfilm, Reel 10.

121. Kammen, *Colonial New York,* 88–89; van der Zee and van der Zee, *Sweet and Alien Land,* 486–494; Dunn, *Puritans and Yankees,* 175–181. For the argument that "endemic particularism" prevented the New England colonies from repelling the Dutch in 1673–1674, see Cohen, "The New England Colonies and the Dutch Recapture of New York, 1673–1674," 54–78.

122. Kammen, *Colonial New York,* 88.

123. Shurtleff, *MBR,* Vol. 4 (Part 2): 574–575.

124. Trumbull, *CCR,* 2: 242–244.

5. An Adder in the Path

1. Daniel Gookin, *Historical Collections of the Indians in New England* (New York: Arno Press, 1972), 44 ("ingenious"); "Instructions from the Church at Natick," *MHSC*, 1st ser., 6 (Boston, 1799): 201–203; John Eliot, *A Brief Narrative of the Progress of the Gospel amongst the Indians in New England* (London, 1671), in Michael P. Clark, *The Eliot Tracts: With Letters from John Eliot to Thomas Thorowgood and Richard Baxter* (Westport, Conn.: Praeger, 2003), 403 ("promising"); Jill Lepore, *The Name of War: King Philip's War and the Origins of American Identity* (New York: Knopf, 1998), 22–24, 40–41, 144, 157; Daniel T. V. Huntoon, *History of the Town of Canton, Norfolk County, Massachusetts* (Cambridge: John Wilson and Son, 1893), 23–24 (Sarah Ahhaton's suicide); and Ann Marie Plane, *Colonial Intimacies: Indian Marriage in Early New England* (Ithaca: Cornell University Press, 2000), 1–13 (adultery case).

2. Increase Mather, *A Brief History of the War with the Indians in New-England* (London, 1676), reprinted in *The History of King Philip's War*, ed. Samuel G. Drake (Boston, 1862), 48; John Easton, "A Relacion of the Indyan Warre, by Mr. Easton, of Roade Isld. 1675," in *Narratives of the Indian Wars, 1675–1699*, ed. Charles H. Lincoln (New York: Charles Scribner's Sons, 1913), 7–8 ("beter Christian"). On the Sassamon case, see especially James D. Drake, "Symbol of a Failed Strategy: The Sassamon Trial, Political Culture, and the Outbreak of King Philip's War," *American Indian Culture and Research Journal* 19:2 (1995): 111–141; Yasuhide Kawashima, *Igniting King Philip's War: The John Sassamon Murder Trial* (Lawrence: University Press of Kansas, 2001); Lepore, *The Name of War*, 21–47; and James P. Ronda and Jeanne Ronda, "The Death of John Sassamon: An Exploration in Writing New England Indian History," *American Indian Quarterly* 1:2 (1974): 91–102.

3. Massachusetts Archives Collection, Vol. 67, Doc. 202, Massachusetts State Archives, Boston, Massachusetts.

4. Stonington to Governor & Council, 30 June 1675, in Marjorie F. Gutheim, ed., *Winthrop Family Papers* Microfilm, 53 reels (Boston, Mass.: Massachusetts Historical Society, 1976), Reel 11 ("Divers," "Considerable"); Henry Stephens to Mr. Stanton, 29 June 1675, *MHSC*, 3rd. ser., 10 (Boston, 1849): 117 ("sivera men," "12 housis"); and John Pynchon to John Winthrop, Jr., 2 July 1675, in Carl Bridenbaugh, ed., *The Pynchon Papers Volume I: Letters of John Pynchon, 1654–1700* (Boston: The Colonial Society of Massachusetts, 1982), 137. In this last, Pynchon notes that Winthrop's confirmation of the events at Plymouth was "the first and all the intelligence I have had except flying reports."

5. For broad accounts of the war, see especially James D. Drake, *King Philip's War: Civil War in New England, 1675–1676* (Amherst: University of Massachusetts Press, 1999); Douglas Edward Leach, *Flintlock and Tomahawk: New England in King Philip's War* (New York: Macmillan, 1958); Lepore, *The Name of War*; Daniel

R. Mandell, *King Philip's War: Colonial Expansion, Native Resistance, and the End of Indian Sovereignty* (Baltimore: Johns Hopkins University Press, 2010); and Jenny Hale Pulsipher, *Subjects Unto the Same King: Indians, English, and the Contest for Authority in Colonial New England* (Philadelphia: University of Pennsylvania Press, 2005). I have also profited from reading George Madison Bodge, *Soldiers in King Philip's War* (Leominster, MA, 1896).

6. Edward Rawson to John Pynchon, 10 July 1675, *Winthrop Papers* microfilm, Reel 11.

7. See, for example, Francis Jennings, *The Invasion of America: Indians, Colonialism, and the Cant of Conquest* (Chapel Hill: University of North Carolina Press, 1975), 179, 254–281, and the synopsis of "King Philip's War," in Kathleen J. Bragdon, *The Columbia Guide to American Indians of the Northeast* (New York: Columbia University Press, 2001), 130.

8. Drake, "Symbol of a Failed Strategy"; John Easton, "A Relacion of the Indyan Warre," 10 ("only dissemblers"); Virginia DeJohn Anderson, "King Philip's Herds: Indians, Colonists, and the Problem of Livestock in Early New England," *WMQ* 51:4(Oct. 1994): 601–624; Leach, *Flintlock and Tomahawk,* 14–49; Philip Ranlet, "Another Look at the Causes of King Philip's War," *New England Quarterly* 61:1 (March 1988): 79–100.

9. Mary Rowlandson, *The Soveraignty & Goodness of God, together, with the faithfulness of his promises displayed; being a narrative of the captivity and restoration of Mrs. Mary Rowlandson . . .* (Cambridge: Samuel Green, 1682), 21.

10. Cotton Mather, *Magnalia Christi Americana,* ed. Samuel G. Drake, 2 vols. (1702; Hartford: S. Andrus & Son, 1853), 2: 565.

11. Captain Daniel Henchman to Massachusetts Bay Council, 30 June 1676, quoted in Bodge, *Soldiers in King Philip's War,* 57.

12. William Hubbard, *The Present State of New-England, Being a Narrative of the Troubles with the Indians in New-England* (London, 1677), reprinted in *The History of the Indian Wars in New England,* ed. Samuel G. Drake, 2 vols. (Roxbury: Printed for W. Elliot Woodward, 1865), 1: 87. I prefer this edition of Hubbard's narrative for Drake's "Extensive Notes," which provide a wealth of detail on the war.

13. See especially Anderson, "King Philip's Herds."

14. Thomas Minor, *The Diary of Thomas Minor, Stonington, Connecticut. 1653 to 1684,* ed. Sidney H. Miner and George D. Stanton, Jr. (New London, 1899; reprint edition, 2001), 50, 190–191; Nathaniel B. Shurtleff, *Records of the Governor and Company of the Massachusetts Bay in New England,* 5 vols. (Boston: Press of William White, 1853–1854), 4 (Part 2): 54.

15. Virginia DeJohn Anderson, *Creatures of Empire: How Domestic Animals Transformed Early America* (New York: Oxford University Press, 2004), 227 and passim. Later, as their relations with the English crumbled, Narragansetts grew angry at Providence's status as a "Throughfare Town." In 1676, they complained

about Plymouth's "Entrtaining, Assisting, [and?] Guideing" their enemies. Roger Williams to [Robert Williams?], 1 April 1676, in Glenn W. LaFantasie, ed., *The Correspondence of Roger Williams,* 2 vols. (Providence, R.I.: Published for The Rhode Island Historical Society by Brown University Press, 1988), 2: 722.

16. Minor, *Diary,* 50, 190–91; Shurtleff, *MBR,* 4 (Part 2): 54.

17. Massachusetts's government to the Narragansett sachems, 5 September 1668, MHS photostats, quoted in Pulsipher, *Subjects Unto the Same King,* 81–82.

18. Roger Williams, *A Key into the Language of America, Or, An help to the Language of the Natives in that part of America, called New England* (1643; Bedford, Mass.: Applewood Books, 1997), 72.

19. Charles J. Hoadly, editor and transcriber, *Records of the Colony or Jurisdiction of New Haven, From May 1653, to the Union. Together with the New Haven Code of 1656* (Hartford: Case, Lockwood and Company, 1858), 217; Shurtleff, *RMB,* 4: 277; New London County, County Court, Trials, Vol. 3: 58, Connecticut State Library, Hartford, Connecticut.

20. Peter R. Christoph, ed., *New York Historical Manuscripts, English,* Vol. 22, *Administrative Papers of Governors Richard Nicolls and Francis Lovelace, 1664–1673* (Baltimore, 1980), 24.

21. Stonington Records, Vol. I, 1664–1723, Stonington Town Clerk's Office, Stonington, Connecticut.

22. For a recent study that looks at travel routes as markers of territoriality and sovereignty, though in a different time and place, see Angela Pulley Hudson, *Creek Paths and Federal Roads: Indians, Settlers, and Slaves and the Making of the American South* (Chapel Hill: University of North Carolina Press, 2010).

23. Wait Winthrop to Fitz-John Winthrop, [October 1663], Winthrop Family Papers [transcripts], 1630–1741, 10 boxes, Box 5, Massachusetts Historical Society, Boston, Massachusetts.

24. *Strength out of Weaknesse; Or a Glorious Manifestation of the Further Progresse of the Gospel among the Indians in New-England,* in Clark, *The Eliot Tracts,* 226.

25. Dennis A. Connole, *The Indians of the Nipmuck Country in Southern New England, 1630–1750: An Historical Geography* (Jefferson, N.C.: McFarland & Co., 2001). (Quote on p. 7.)

26. Neal Salisbury, "Indians and Colonists in Southern New England after the Pequot War: An Uneasy Balance," in Laurence M. Hauptman and James D. Wherry, eds., *The Pequots in Southern New England: The Fall and Rise of an American Indian Nation* (Norman: University of Oklahoma Press, 1990), 93 ("economic, political"); Richard W. Cogley, *John Eliot's Mission to the Indians before King Philip's War* (Cambridge: Harvard University Press, 1999), 162–165 ("large numbers," "no rising tide," 162). As Cogley writes, any attempt to diagnose Nipmuck motivations for waging war in 1675 must remain "highly speculative." But, Cogley

points out, Nipmucks appear not to have felt the same pressures as other Native groups. Over most of the Nipmuck territory, English settlement and heavy mission-izing—what most scholars cite as the chief catalysts of war—had yet to bear down. By contrast, says Cogley, "the pressures on Metacom and the Pokanokets were severe." (Quotes, pp. 162 and 165.)

27. Harral Ayres, *The Great Trail of New England* (Boston, 1940); J. H. Temple, *History of North Brookfield, Massachusetts* (Boston, 1887), 24; Framingham town records, quoted in J. H. Temple, *History of Framingham, Massachusetts* (1887), 87–89, 95.

28. Connole, *The Indians of the Nipmuck Country*, 116–120 (Eliot's visits). Not all letters went over land; some went by sea, and water communications were devel-oping, too. But judging from the Winthrop Papers, the inordinate leap in the amount of letters sent between Boston and Hartford in the early 1670s suggests a growing rush of travelers.

29. John Eliot, *A Brief Narration of the Progress of the Gospel Amongst the Indians in New-England* (London, 1671), in Clark, *The Eliot Tracts*, 403.

30. Daniel Gookin, *Historical Collections*, 45, 52, emphases mine. The "new road" seems to have been formally opened in 1674. In December 1673, men at a Middlesex County Court meeting called for the laying of a new roadway between Boston and Brookfield, via Marlborough. How it happened: John Stone of Sudbury, John Woods of Marlborough, and Thomas Eams of Framingham were charged with laying out "a highway for the use of the country leading from the house of John Livermore in Watertown, to a Horse Bridge (then being) near the house of Daniel Stone, Jun., and thence the nearest and best way to Marlborough, and thence to Quabaugh [Brookfield]."

Though this may have been the formal call for a roadway, the passage was prob-ably in use—at least sporadically—years earlier. In the 1660s, Mohawks attacked some Indians living near "Quabage about the way from Springfeild to Massachusett." John Pynchon lobbied for a bridge over Quabaug River in 1666, possibly indicating use of the new route by the English as early as the mid-1660s. In the fall of 1668, Massachusetts men planned to plant Quansigamond Ponds (later Worcester) twelve miles west of Marlborough "neare the road to Springfield," "the better to unite & strengthen the inland plantations." This route seems to have been the "Usual Way" by 1675, which is how John Pynchon referenced it in an August 1675 letter. By 1677, it was no longer the "new road": in his history of King Philip's War, William Hubbard identified Marlborough and Brookfield as towns lying, simply, in the "Road to *Connecticut*." Similarly, two 1677 mortgages secured by John Wampas, a Nipmuck man, used land near Quansigamond as collateral; both parcels were described as abutting "the Connecticut high way."

For the evolution of the route, see Harral Ayres, *The Great Trail of New England* (Boston, 1940), 335; Leaman F. Hallet, "Indian Trails and Their Importance to the Early Settlers," *Bulletin of the Massachusetts Archaeological Society* 17, no. 3 (April 1956), 42–43; J. H. Temple, *History of North Brookfield, Massachusetts* (Boston, 1887), 25; JWJ to Richard Nicolls, [ca. 15 July 1666], Winthrop Family Papers [transcripts], 1630–1741, Box 7 (Mohawks); John Pynchon to JWJ, 24 December 1666, *Winthrop Papers* microfilm, Reel 8 (Pynchon's bridge); Shurtleff, *MBR*, 4 (Part 2): 408 (settling of Quansigamond); and John Pynchon to JWJ, 19 August 1675, *Pynchon Papers*, 146 ("Usual Way"); Hubbard, *A Narrative of the Troubles*, 98, 155; Connole, *The Indians of the Nipmuck Country*, 128.

31. David Pulsifer, ed., *Acts of the Commissioners of the United Colonies of New England*, Vol. I, in *Records of the Colony of New Plymouth in New England*, 12 vols. (Boston: William White, 1855–61), 9: 25; 10: 108.

32. J. W. Gregory, *The Story of the Road* (London, 1931), 11–12.

33. Geoffrey Hindley, *A History of Roads* (London: P. Davies, 1971), 88 ("beaten earth"); M. G. Lay, *Ways of the World: A History of the World's Roads and of the Vehicles that Used Them* (New Brunswick: Rutgers University Press, 1992), 67–68 (plowman's roads in England); Gregory, *Story of the Road*, 167; Thomas Procter, *A Worthy Worke* (1610).

34. In 1668 Mendon, for instance, used four oxen per day to remove rocks and trees. Mendon town meeting records, quoted in John G. Metcalf, *Annals of the Town of Mendon, from 1659 to 1880* (Providence, 1880), 32.

35. Carl Bridenbaugh, "Yankee Use and Abuse of the Forest in the Building of New England, 1620–1660," Massachusetts Historical Society *Proceedings*, 3rd. ser., 89 (1977): 34–35.

36. John Pynchon to John Winthrop, Jr., 24 December 1666, Winthrop Family Papers [transcripts], Box 7, Massachusetts Historical Society, Boston, Massachusetts; Mendon town records, quoted in Metcalf, *Annals of the Town of Mendon*, 32; Temple, *History of Framingham*, 110.

37. Howard S. Russell, *Indian New England Before the Mayflower* (Hanover, New Hampshire: University Press of New England), 1980, 43–44; Willliams, *Key*, 95. On Indian concepts of property, see Cronon, *Changes in the Land*, 58–68.

38. Abijah P. Marvin, *History of the Town of Lancaster, Massachusetts* (Lancaster, Mass.: 1879), 67.

39. John Richards to John Winthrop, Jr., 18 April 1671, *Winthrop Papers* microfilm, Reel 10. Another hint that the shooter was an Indian: Smith was shot, according to John Pynchon, with a "slug or plug." George Bodge notes that Indians in this period tended to use "slugs, or heavy shot instead of bullets." See John Pynchon to JWJ, 10 May 1671, *Winthrop Papers* microfilm, Reel 10; Bodge, *Soldiers in King Philip's War*, 46.

40. John Pynchon to JWJ, 10 May 1671, *Winthrop Papers* microfilm, Reel 10. In the version of this letter published in the *Pynchon Papers*, the transcription of this line is rather different. Instead of bragging about shooting an Englishman in the

83. Joseph Eliot to JWJ, 16 August 1675, *MHSC*, 5th ser., 1 (Boston, 1871): 430–431.

84. N. S., *A New and Further Narrative of the State of New-England . . .* (London, 1676), reprinted in Lincoln, *Narratives of the Indian Wars*, 78. William Harris echoed: "Mesengers like Jobes came soone one after another" with news of "burneing houses, takeing cattell, killing men & women & Children: & carrying others captive." See Harris, *A Rhode Islander Reports*, 18.

85. Edmund Browne of Sudbury to Gov. Leverett, 26 September 1675, Massachusetts Archives, vol. 67: 268.

86. RW to Governor John Leverett, 14 January 1675/1676, in *Correspondence of Roger Williams*, 2: 714.

87. Roger Williams to John Winthrop, Jr., 27 June 1675, *Winthrop Papers* microfilm, Reel 11.

88. John Pynchon to Governor & Magistrates of Connecticut, 4 August 1675, *Pynchon Papers*, 139; John Pynchon to JWJ, 7 August 1675, *Pynchon Papers*, 142.

89. Few letters written during 1675–1676, unfortunately, offer up the identities of their couriers. Of the twenty surviving letters written by John Pynchon, for instance, none can be linked to any particular bearer. The case is much the same with Roger Williams's correspondence; only one of ten letters mentions its courier by name ("Mr. Scot"). Roughly thirty of the Winthrop letters (of 156 written between June 1675 and April 1676) identify their own couriers.

90. Giles Sylvester to Fitz-John Winthrop, 14 July 1676, *Winthrop Papers* microfilm, Reel 11.

91. Robert Chapman to Wait Winthrop, 5 July 1675, *Winthrop Papers* microfilm, Reel 11.

92. John Allyn & Connecticut Council to Fitz-John Winthrop & Lt. John Mason, 5 September 1675, *Winthrop Papers* microfilm, Reel 11 ("post sayth"); John Pynchon to Rev. John Russell of Hadley, 5 October 1675, *Pynchon Papers*, 157 ("send down"); Samuel Stow to JWJ, 29 October 1675, *Winthrop Papers* microfilm, Reel 11 (rubila).

93. Capt. Savage and Capt. Oliver were to "have charge" of these animals. Anonymous letter, reprinted in Bodge, *Soldiers in King Philip's War*, 46.

94. Gookin, *Doings and Sufferings*, 479.

95. Roger Williams to JWJ, 27 June 1675, *Winthrop Papers* microfilm, Reel 11.

96. Hubbard, *A Narrative of the Troubles*, 158.

97. Hubbard, *A Narrative of the Troubles*, 164, notes that on one occasion a party of Native travelers left "no less than sixty Horses Heads in one Place."

98. N. S., *A Continuation of the State of New-England; Being a Farther Account of the Indian Warr, And of the Engagement betwixt the Joynt Forces of the United English Collonies and the Indians . . .* (London, 1676), in Lincoln, *Narratives of the Indian Wars*, 67.

99. N. S., *New and Further Narrative*, 80.

road, Ascooke imagines firing at an Englishman "alone in the *wood*" (emphasis mine). The second part of the quote is also different, so that the entire line, in this printed version, is given as: ". . . speaking at Roxbury how easy it was to shoot an Englishman alone in the *wood* if they had *war* with them." Ultimately, the meaning of Ascooke's remarks probably is not changed drastically by these discrepancies; but, having carefully examined the original letter, I am confident that his comments refer to a lone Englishman traveling in the "road." For the alternate transcription, see John Pynchon to JWJ, 10 May 1671, in *Pynchon Papers,* 87.

41. Williams, *Key,* 105. My gratitude to Walter Woodward for bringing this to my attention.

42. John Pynchon to JWJ, 10 May 1671, *Winthrop Papers* microfilm, Reel 10.

43. *A True Account of the Most Considerable Occurrences . . .* (London, 1676), 8 ("fastened"); Hubbard, *A Narrative of the Troubles,* 260. On the "Mendon Way," which crossed Dedham, see Connole, *The Indians of Nipmuck Country,* 23.

44. Samuel G. Drake, *The Book of the Indians; Or, Biography and History of the Indians of North America, From Its First Discovery to the Year 1841* (Boston, 1841), 79–80; *A True Account of the Most Considerable Occurrences,* 8.

45. Hubbard, *A Narrative of the Troubles,* 261; Drake, *Book of the Indians,* 79–80.

46. John Pynchon to Joseph Pynchon, ca. 30 June 1675, *Pynchon Papers,* 136; Roger Williams to JWJ, 27 June 1675, *Winthrop Papers* microfilm, Reel 11.

47. Anonymous, *A Brief and True Narration of the Late Wars Risen in New-England: Occasioned by the Quarrelsom Disposition, and Perfidious Carriage of the Barbarous, Savage and Heathenish Natives There* (London, 1675), 4–5. See also Letter of Massachusetts Council to Governor Winthrop, James Hammond Trumbull, ed., *The Public Records of the Colony of Connecticut 1636–1776,* 15 vols. (Hartford: Lockwood & Brainard Company, 1850–1890), 2: 336.

48. Edward Rawson to John Pynchon, 10 July 1675, *Winthrop Papers* microfilm, Reel 11.

49. JWJ to Fitz-John Winthrop, 9 July 1675, *MHSC,* 5th ser., 8 (Boston, 1882): 170–171.

50. Edward Rawson to John Pynchon, 10 July 1675, *Winthrop Papers* microfilm, Reel 11 (Curtis's trading house robbed); John Pynchon to John Winthrop, Jr., or John Allyn, 6 August 1675, *Pynchon Papers,* 139–140.

51. Thomas Wheeler, *A Thankefull Remembrance of Gods Mercy To Several Persons at Quabaug or Brookfield; Partly in a Collection of Providences about Them, and Gracious Appearances for Them: And Partly in a Sermon Preached by Mr. Edward Bulkley, Pastor of the Church of Christ at Concord, upon a Day of Thanksgiving, Kept by Divers for their Wonderfull Deliverance There* (Cambridge, 1676), reprinted in Jeffrey H. Fiske, *Wheeler's Surprise: The Lost Battlefield of King Philip's War* (Towtaid, 1993), 58, 61.

52. Richard Smith to JWJ, 3 September 1675, *Winthrop Papers* microfilm, Reel 11; Henry Stephens to Mr. Stanton, 29 June 1675, *MHSC*, 3rd ser., 10 (Boston, 1849): 117; Stonington to Governor & Council, 30 June 1675, *Winthrop Papers* microfilm, Reel 11; RW to JWJ, 27 June 1675, in ibid.

53. Trumbull, *CCR*, 2: 358.

54. Trumbull, *CCR*, 2: 359, 361, 366; John Allyn to Richard James, 27 September 1675, *Winthrop Papers* microfilm, Reel 11.

55. *A Brief and True Narration*, 5 ("set on travellors").

56. "Ambushing," as a Native military tactic, has not received much in-depth attention from scholars. But see Patrick M. Malone, *The Skulking Way of War: Technology and Tactics Among the New England Indians* (Baltimore: Johns Hopkins University Press, 1993), 106–109 and 114–119. For other studies considering Native and European strategies, see also Guy Chet, *Conquering the American Wilderness: The Triumph of European Warfare in the Colonial Northeast* (Amherst: University of Massachusetts Press, 2003); John E. Ferling, *A Wilderness of Miseries: War and Warriors in Early America* (Westport, Conn.: Greenwood Press, 1980); and John Grenier, *The First Way of War: American War Making on the Frontier, 1607–1814* (Cambridge: Cambridge University Press, 2005).

57. Hubbard, *A Narrative of the Troubles*, 99.

58. Wheeler, *Thankefull Remembrance*, 56; Daniel Gookin, *An Historical Account of the Doings and Sufferings of the Christian Indians in New England, in the Years 1675, 1676, 1677* (1677), in American Antiquarian Society, *Archaeologia Americana: Transactions and Collections of the American Antiquarian Society*, 7 vols. (Cambridge, 1836), 2: 490.

59. Hubbard, *A Narrative of the Troubles*, 206.

60. Gookin, *Doings and Sufferings*, 441. Several sources mention how Native men used branches and brush to camouflage themselves. Cotton Mather's *Magnalia Christiana* described Indians "covering themselves with green boughs," so as to adopt the color of their surroundings like "cuttle fish," and to more easily slay the English from their cover behind "the thick under-woods" and "prodigious thicket." See Mather, *Magnalia*, 2: 564.

61. Thomas Stanton to Richard Smith, 13 September 1675, *Winthrop Papers* microfilm, Reel 11.

62. Gookin, *Doings and Sufferings*, 467.

63. John Allyn to Fitz-John Winthrop, 4 September 1675, *Winthrop Papers* microfilm, Reel 11.

64. Hubbard, *A Narrative of the Troubles*, 71 (Hubbard read the display as mocking, "bidding us Defiance."); Massachusetts Archives, vol. 67: 247.

65. On the display of "war trophies," including Philip's head and hand, see Lepore, *The Name of War*, 178–180. Importantly, notes Lepore, Algonquian and English customs of display differed in that "while the English displayed body parts in the commons of colonial towns, where they encouraged the public celebration

and commemoration of English victories, Indians placed their displays where English soldiers were likely to find them. Algonquians hoped to terrorize their enemies; the English hoped to cheer themselves" (180).

66. Hubbard, *A Narrative of the Troubles*, 111 ("cutting off"); Mather, *Brief History*, 80 ("much daunted").

67. Hubbard, *A Narrative of the Troubles*, 196.

68. Sam Quanohit and Kutquen with Peter Jethro as scribe to the Massachusetts Council, 12 April 1676, in Gookin, *Doings and Sufferings*, 508; James Printer to the Massachusetts Council, 27 April 1676, Massachusetts Archives, Hutchinson Papers, 2: 282. On literate Indians in King Philip's War, see Lepore, *The Name of War*; and Hilary E. Wyss, *Writing Indians: Literacy, Christianity, and Native Community in Early America* (Amherst: University of Massachusetts Press, 2000), 17–51.

69. Gookin, *Doings and Sufferings*, 494; Lepore, *The Name of War*, 94–96.

70. John Russell to [unknown], enclosure, John Allyn & Connecticut Council to Fitz-John Winthrop & Lt. John Mason, 5 September 1675, *Winthrop Papers* microfilm, Reel 11.

71. Willliam Harris, *A Rhode Islander Reports on King Philip's War; the second William Harris letter of August, 1676*, ed. Douglas Leach (Providence: Rhode Island Historical Society, 1963), 16, 18.

72. John Leverett to JWJ, 31 July 1675, *Winthrop Papers* microfilm, Reel 11.

73. Wheeler, *Thankefull Remembrance*, 57–58.

74. John Pynchon to JWJ, 7 August 1675, *Pynchon Papers*, 142; John Pynchon to John Winthrop, Jr., 12 August 1675, *Winthrop Papers* microfilm, Reel 11 ("ways").

75. RW to JWJ, 27 June 1675, *Winthrop Papers* microfilm, Reel 11 ("Sentinel," "InLands"); Mather, *Brief History*, 57–58 ("in their way"). Although the English frequently used sympathetic Natives as pilots during the war, Mather clarifies, on page 58, that this was an *"English Guide* slain" (emphasis his).

76. Wheeler, *Thankefull Remembrance*, 58, 62; John Russell to MBC, 8 October 1675, Massachusetts Archives, vol. 67: 288–289 ("hoops or watchwords").

77. Wheeler, *Thankefull Remembrance*, 64; James Quanapohit testimony, in Fiske, *Wheeler's Surprise*, 87; Hubbard, *A Narrative of the Troubles*, 167 ("Bridg"), 171 (burned bridge).

78. Hubbard, *A Narrative of the Troubles*, 112–113.

79. John Russell to MBC, 8 October 1675, Massachusetts Archives, vol. 67: 288–289.

80. John Pynchon to JWJ, 12 August 1675, *Pynchon Papers*, 143–144.

81. Stonington to Governor & Council of Connecticut, 30 June 1675, *Winthrop Papers* microfilm, Reel 11.

82. Nathaniel Brewster to JWJ, 12 July 1675, *Winthrop Papers* microfilm, Reel 11; Lepore, *The Name of War*, 60–63.

"full of french and Indians," "being no Watch"); P. Schuyler, Dirck Wessell, and K. V. Rensselaer to the Massachusetts Governor and Council, 15 February 1689/1690, in *The Andros Tracts*, 3: 114 ("limbs frozen").

57. P. Schuyler, Dirck Wessell, and K. V. Rensselaer to the Massachusetts Governor and Council, 15 February 1689/1690, in *The Andros Tracts*, 3: 114–115.

58. O'Callaghan, *DHNY*, 1: 303–305.

59. Sewall, *Diary*, 1: 251. The "amazing news" took two weeks to reach Boston.

60. Sewall, *Diary*, 1: 254; Cotton Mather, *Decennium Luctuosum*, 46 ("best part").

61. Mather, *Decennium Luctuosum*, 46.

62. As many as fourteen hundred colonists may have been captured during the imperial wars of 1675–1713. Daniel Richter and Alden Vaughan, "Crossing the Cultural Divide: Indians and New Englanders, 1605–1763," *American Antiquarian Society Proceedings* 90:1 (April 1980): 23–99, and Richard Slotkin, *Regeneration through Violence: The Mythology of the American Frontier, 1600–1860* (Middletown, CT: Wesleyan University Press, 1973). Vaughan and Richter estimate about 700 were taken in the period 1675 to 1713; Slotkin thinks twice that. For reference works on captives taken during this period, see Charlotte Alice Baker, *True Stories of New England Captives Carried to Canada during the Old French and Indian Wars* (Greenfield, MA: Press of E.A. Hall & Co., 1897), and Emma Lewis Coleman, *New England Captives Carried to Canada between 1677 and 1760, During the French and Indian Wars* (Portland, ME: Southworth Press, 1925).

63. Mather, *Decennium Luctuosum*, 83.

64. SS to ___ Storke, 14 November 1698, *MHSC* 6th ser., 1 (Boston, 1886): 208. On King William's War, see Samuel Adams Drake, *The Border Wars of New England, Commonly Called King William's War and Queen Anne's Wars* (New York: C. Scribner's Sons, 1897); Evan Haefeli and Kevin Sweeney, *Captors and Captives: The 1704 French and Indian Raid on Deerfield* (Amherst: University of Massachusetts Press, 2003), 78–85; Norton, *In the Devil's Snare*, 82–111; Jenny Hale Pulsipher, "'Dark Cloud Rising from the East': Indian Sovereignty and the Coming of King William's War in New England," *New England Quarterly* 80:4 (Dec. 2007): 588–613; and Owen Stanwood, *The Empire Reformed: English America in the Age of the Glorious Revolution* (Philadelphia: University of Pennsylvania Press, 2011), 54–81.

65. James Axtell, "The White Indians of Colonial America," *WMQ* 32:1 (Jan. 1975): 55–88; Haefeli and Sweeney, *Captors and Captives;* Daniel K. Richter, *The Ordeal of the Longhouse: The Peoples of the Iroquois League in the Era of European Colonization* (Chapel Hill: University of North Carolina Press, 1992); Brett Rushforth, *Bonds of Alliance: Indigenous and Atlantic Slaveries in New France* (Chapel Hill: University of North Carolina Press, 2012).

66. Haefeli and Sweeney, *Captors and Captives*, 78–92; Kenneth M. Morrison, *The Embattled Northeast: The Elusive Ideal of Alliance in Abenaki-Euroamerican*

Relations (Berkeley: University of California Press, 1984); Norton, *In the Devil's Snare,* 82–111.

67. "Letter from Philippe de Rigaud de Vaudreuil to the Minister of the Marine, 1704," in Evan Haefeli and Kevin Sweeney, *Captive Histories: English, French, and Native Narratives of the 1704 Deerfield Raid* (Amherst: University of Massachusetts Press, 2006), 81.

68. Francis Parkman, *Count Frontenac and New France under Louis XIV* (Boston: Little, Brown and Company, 1880), 208–220; Haefeli and Sweeney, *Captors and Captives,* 34–54; Jon Parmenter, *The Edge of the Woods: Iroquoia, 1534–1701* (East Lansing: Michigan State University Press, 2010), 207–211.

69. Increase Mather diary, March 1693, in *IMP,* Reel 16 ("frownes"); ibid., 1 January 1703/1704 ("Is this the first day"); ibid., 11 July 1696 (Pascataway); ibid., 29 March 1696/1697 (Haverhill); ibid., 2 October 1697 (Lancaster).

70. Lawrence Hammond diary, 17 May 1690 (Casco); 25 January 1691/1692 (York); ibid., 2 September 1691 (Dunstable), Pre-Revolutionary Diaries Collection, Reel 5, Massachusetts Historical Society, Boston, Massachusetts.

71. "Journal of the Rev. John Pike," in *MHSP* 14 (Boston, 1875–1876): 121, 126, 127, 128 (Ursula Cutt), 130, and passim.

72. Lawrence Hammond diary, 21 March 1689/1690, in Pre-Revolutionary Diaries Collection, Reel 5.

73. SS to John Storke, 31 July 1696, *MHSC* 6th ser., 1 (Boston, 1886): 165 ("Rumors of War"); SS to John Ive, nd, in ibid., 169 ("hear of some slain").

74. John Marshall diary, Pre-Revolutionary Diaries Collection, Reel 6.

75. Increase Mather diary, 11 March 1703/1704., in *IMP,* Reel 16.

76. SS to John Ive, 19 February 1691/1692, *MHSC,* 6th ser., 1 (Boston, 1886): 129.

77. Mather quoted in *Collections of the New Hampshire Historical Society,* 3 (1832): 40 ("much beholden"); IM to Samuel Penhallow, 14 October 1706, *IMP,* Reel 16 ("post payed"); IM to Samuel Penhallow, 4 December 1704, ibid. ("Furr gloves").

78. "Copy of a Letter from the Hon. Samuel Penhallow, to Dr. Cotton Mather," Portsmouth, 27 February 1698/1699, in *Collections of the New Hampshire Historical Society,* 1 (1824): 133–135. Although this letter is labeled as having gone to Cotton Mather, Increase Mather answered it.

79. IM to Samuel Penhallow, 3 March 1698/1699, *IMP,* Reel 16.

80. Mather, *Decennium Luctuosum,* 15–16 (John Pike's letter) and 42–45 (Penhallow's letter); Mather, *Duodecennium Luctuosum. The History of a Long War with Indian Salvages, and Their Directors and Abettors; from the Year, 1702. To the Year, 1714* (Boston: B. Green for Samuel Gerrish, 1714), 27 ("Endebted").

81. Cotton Mather diary, *MHSC* 7th ser., 7 (1911): 528.

82. Cotton Mather diary, *MHSC* 7th ser., 7 (1911): 565.

83. Cotton Mather diary, *MHSC* 7th ser., 7 (1911): 566.

road, Ascooke imagines firing at an Englishman "alone in the *wood*" (emphasis mine). The second part of the quote is also different, so that the entire line, in this printed version, is given as: ". . . speaking at Roxbury how easy it was to shoot an Englishman alone in the *wood* if they had *war* with them." Ultimately, the meaning of Ascooke's remarks probably is not changed drastically by these discrepancies; but, having carefully examined the original letter, I am confident that his comments refer to a lone Englishman traveling in the "road." For the alternate transcription, see John Pynchon to JWJ, 10 May 1671, in *Pynchon Papers,* 87.

41. Williams, *Key,* 105. My gratitude to Walter Woodward for bringing this to my attention.

42. John Pynchon to JWJ, 10 May 1671, *Winthrop Papers* microfilm, Reel 10.

43. *A True Account of the Most Considerable Occurrences . . .* (London, 1676), 8 ("fastened"); Hubbard, *A Narrative of the Troubles,* 260. On the "Mendon Way," which crossed Dedham, see Connole, *The Indians of Nipmuck Country,* 23.

44. Samuel G. Drake, *The Book of the Indians; Or, Biography and History of the Indians of North America, From Its First Discovery to the Year 1841* (Boston, 1841), 79–80; *A True Account of the Most Considerable Occurrences,* 8.

45. Hubbard, *A Narrative of the Troubles,* 261; Drake, *Book of the Indians,* 79–80.

46. John Pynchon to Joseph Pynchon, ca. 30 June 1675, *Pynchon Papers,* 136; Roger Williams to JWJ, 27 June 1675, *Winthrop Papers* microfilm, Reel 11.

47. Anonymous, *A Brief and True Narration of the Late Wars Risen in New-England: Occasioned by the Quarrelsom Disposition, and Perfidious Carriage of the Barbarous, Savage and Heathenish Natives There* (London, 1675), 4–5. See also Letter of Massachusetts Council to Governor Winthrop, James Hammond Trumbull, ed., *The Public Records of the Colony of Connecticut 1636–1776,* 15 vols. (Hartford: Lockwood & Brainard Company, 1850–1890), 2: 336.

48. Edward Rawson to John Pynchon, 10 July 1675, *Winthrop Papers* microfilm, Reel 11.

49. JWJ to Fitz-John Winthrop, 9 July 1675, *MHSC,* 5th ser., 8 (Boston, 1882): 170–171.

50. Edward Rawson to John Pynchon, 10 July 1675, *Winthrop Papers* microfilm, Reel 11 (Curtis's trading house robbed); John Pynchon to John Winthrop, Jr., or John Allyn, 6 August 1675, *Pynchon Papers,* 139–140.

51. Thomas Wheeler, *A Thankefull Remembrance of Gods Mercy To Several Persons at Quabaug or Brookfield; Partly in a Collection of Providences about Them, and Gracious Appearances for Them: And Partly in a Sermon Preached by Mr. Edward Bulkley, Pastor of the Church of Christ at Concord, upon a Day of Thanksgiving, Kept by Divers for their Wonderfull Deliverance There* (Cambridge, 1676), reprinted in Jeffrey H. Fiske, *Wheeler's Surprise: The Lost Battlefield of King Philip's War* (Towtaid, 1993), 58, 61.

52. Richard Smith to JWJ, 3 September 1675, *Winthrop Papers* microfilm, Reel 11; Henry Stephens to Mr. Stanton, 29 June 1675, *MHSC*, 3rd ser., 10 (Boston, 1849): 117; Stonington to Governor & Council, 30 June 1675, *Winthrop Papers* microfilm, Reel 11; RW to JWJ, 27 June 1675, in ibid.

53. Trumbull, *CCR*, 2: 358.

54. Trumbull, *CCR*, 2: 359, 361, 366; John Allyn to Richard James, 27 September 1675, *Winthrop Papers* microfilm, Reel 11.

55. *A Brief and True Narration*, 5 ("set on travellors").

56. "Ambushing," as a Native military tactic, has not received much in-depth attention from scholars. But see Patrick M. Malone, *The Skulking Way of War: Technology and Tactics Among the New England Indians* (Baltimore: Johns Hopkins University Press, 1993), 106–109 and 114–119. For other studies considering Native and European strategies, see also Guy Chet, *Conquering the American Wilderness: The Triumph of European Warfare in the Colonial Northeast* (Amherst: University of Massachusetts Press, 2003); John E. Ferling, *A Wilderness of Miseries: War and Warriors in Early America* (Westport, Conn.: Greenwood Press, 1980); and John Grenier, *The First Way of War: American War Making on the Frontier, 1607–1814* (Cambridge: Cambridge University Press, 2005).

57. Hubbard, *A Narrative of the Troubles*, 99.

58. Wheeler, *Thankefull Remembrance*, 56; Daniel Gookin, *An Historical Account of the Doings and Sufferings of the Christian Indians in New England, in the Years 1675, 1676, 1677* (1677), in American Antiquarian Society, *Archaeologia Americana: Transactions and Collections of the American Antiquarian Society*, 7 vols. (Cambridge, 1836), 2: 490.

59. Hubbard, *A Narrative of the Troubles*, 206.

60. Gookin, *Doings and Sufferings*, 441. Several sources mention how Native men used branches and brush to camouflage themselves. Cotton Mather's *Magnalia Christiana* described Indians "covering themselves with green boughs," so as to adopt the color of their surroundings like "cuttle fish," and to more easily slay the English from their cover behind "the thick under-woods" and "prodigious thicket." See Mather, *Magnalia*, 2: 564.

61. Thomas Stanton to Richard Smith, 13 September 1675, *Winthrop Papers* microfilm, Reel 11.

62. Gookin, *Doings and Sufferings*, 467.

63. John Allyn to Fitz-John Winthrop, 4 September 1675, *Winthrop Papers* microfilm, Reel 11.

64. Hubbard, *A Narrative of the Troubles*, 71 (Hubbard read the display as mocking, "bidding us Defiance."); Massachusetts Archives, vol. 67: 247.

65. On the display of "war trophies," including Philip's head and hand, see Lepore, *The Name of War*, 178–180. Importantly, notes Lepore, Algonquian and English customs of display differed in that "while the English displayed body parts in the commons of colonial towns, where they encouraged the public celebration

and commemoration of English victories, Indians placed their displays where English soldiers were likely to find them. Algonquians hoped to terrorize their enemies; the English hoped to cheer themselves" (180).

66. Hubbard, *A Narrative of the Troubles,* 111 ("cutting off"); Mather, *Brief History,* 80 ("much daunted").

67. Hubbard, *A Narrative of the Troubles,* 196.

68. Sam Quanohit and Kutquen with Peter Jethro as scribe to the Massachusetts Council, 12 April 1676, in Gookin, *Doings and Sufferings,* 508; James Printer to the Massachusetts Council, 27 April 1676, Massachusetts Archives, Hutchinson Papers, 2: 282. On literate Indians in King Philip's War, see Lepore, *The Name of War;* and Hilary E. Wyss, *Writing Indians: Literacy, Christianity, and Native Community in Early America* (Amherst: University of Massachusetts Press, 2000), 17–51.

69. Gookin, *Doings and Sufferings,* 494; Lepore, *The Name of War,* 94–96.

70. John Russell to [unknown], enclosure, John Allyn & Connecticut Council to Fitz-John Winthrop & Lt. John Mason, 5 September 1675, *Winthrop Papers* microfilm, Reel 11.

71. Willliam Harris, *A Rhode Islander Reports on King Philip's War; the second William Harris letter of August, 1676,* ed. Douglas Leach (Providence: Rhode Island Historical Society, 1963), 16, 18.

72. John Leverett to JWJ, 31 July 1675, *Winthrop Papers* microfilm, Reel 11.

73. Wheeler, *Thankefull Remembrance,* 57–58.

74. John Pynchon to JWJ, 7 August 1675, *Pynchon Papers,* 142; John Pynchon to John Winthrop, Jr., 12 August 1675, *Winthrop Papers* microfilm, Reel 11 ("ways").

75. RW to JWJ, 27 June 1675, *Winthrop Papers* microfilm, Reel 11 ("Sentinel," "InLands"); Mather, *Brief History,* 57–58 ("in their way"). Although the English frequently used sympathetic Natives as pilots during the war, Mather clarifies, on page 58, that this was an *"English Guide* slain" (emphasis his).

76. Wheeler, *Thankefull Remembrance,* 58, 62; John Russell to MBC, 8 October 1675, Massachusetts Archives, vol. 67: 288–289 ("hoops or watchwords").

77. Wheeler, *Thankefull Remembrance,* 64; James Quanapohit testimony, in Fiske, *Wheeler's Surprise,* 87; Hubbard, *A Narrative of the Troubles,* 167 ("Bridg"), 171 (burned bridge).

78. Hubbard, *A Narrative of the Troubles,* 112–113.

79. John Russell to MBC, 8 October 1675, Massachusetts Archives, vol. 67: 288–289.

80. John Pynchon to JWJ, 12 August 1675, *Pynchon Papers,* 143–144.

81. Stonington to Governor & Council of Connecticut, 30 June 1675, *Winthrop Papers* microfilm, Reel 11.

82. Nathaniel Brewster to JWJ, 12 July 1675, *Winthrop Papers* microfilm, Reel 11; Lepore, *The Name of War,* 60–63.

83. Joseph Eliot to JWJ, 16 August 1675, *MHSC,* 5th ser., 1 (Boston, 1871): 430–431.

84. N. S., *A New and Further Narrative of the State of New-England . . .* (London, 1676), reprinted in Lincoln, *Narratives of the Indian Wars,* 78. William Harris echoed: "Mesengers like Jobes came soone one after another" with news of "burneing houses, takeing cattell, killing men & women & Children: & carrying others captive." See Harris, *A Rhode Islander Reports,* 18.

85. Edmund Browne of Sudbury to Gov. Leverett, 26 September 1675, Massachusetts Archives, vol. 67: 268.

86. RW to Governor John Leverett, 14 January 1675/1676, in *Correspondence of Roger Williams,* 2: 714.

87. Roger Williams to John Winthrop, Jr., 27 June 1675, *Winthrop Papers* microfilm, Reel 11.

88. John Pynchon to Governor & Magistrates of Connecticut, 4 August 1675, *Pynchon Papers,* 139; John Pynchon to JWJ, 7 August 1675, *Pynchon Papers,* 142.

89. Few letters written during 1675–1676, unfortunately, offer up the identities of their couriers. Of the twenty surviving letters written by John Pynchon, for instance, none can be linked to any particular bearer. The case is much the same with Roger Williams's correspondence; only one of ten letters mentions its courier by name ("Mr. Scot"). Roughly thirty of the Winthrop letters (of 156 written between June 1675 and April 1676) identify their own couriers.

90. Giles Sylvester to Fitz-John Winthrop, 14 July 1676, *Winthrop Papers* microfilm, Reel 11.

91. Robert Chapman to Wait Winthrop, 5 July 1675, *Winthrop Papers* microfilm, Reel 11.

92. John Allyn & Connecticut Council to Fitz-John Winthrop & Lt. John Mason, 5 September 1675, *Winthrop Papers* microfilm, Reel 11 ("post sayth"); John Pynchon to Rev. John Russell of Hadley, 5 October 1675, *Pynchon Papers,* 157 ("send down"); Samuel Stow to JWJ, 29 October 1675, *Winthrop Papers* microfilm, Reel 11 (rubila).

93. Capt. Savage and Capt. Oliver were to "have charge" of these animals. Anonymous letter, reprinted in Bodge, *Soldiers in King Philip's War,* 46.

94. Gookin, *Doings and Sufferings,* 479.

95. Roger Williams to JWJ, 27 June 1675, *Winthrop Papers* microfilm, Reel 11.

96. Hubbard, *A Narrative of the Troubles,* 158.

97. Hubbard, *A Narrative of the Troubles,* 164, notes that on one occasion a party of Native travelers left "no less than sixty Horses Heads in one Place."

98. N. S., *A Continuation of the State of New-England; Being a Farther Account of the Indian Warr, And of the Engagement betwixt the Joynt Forces of the United English Collonies and the Indians . . .* (London, 1676), in Lincoln, *Narratives of the Indian Wars,* 67.

99. N. S., *New and Further Narrative,* 80.

100. At the outset of the war, small cavalry companies already existed within several of the colonies' militias. Massachusetts had five such regiments. When Swansea was attacked, the Bay Colony promptly raised one hundred foot soldiers and "50 horse" to relieve the town. Some of the colonies' foot companies were also subsequently "mounted as dragoons." Bodge, *Soldiers in King Philip's War*, 27, 46–47, 79. *Dragoons:* armed cavalry. For a concise history of mounted infantry ("dragoons"), see John Ellis, *Cavalry: The History of Mounted Warfare* (Edinburgh: Westbridge Books, 1978), esp. 99.

101. Edmund Browne of Sudbury to Governor John Leverett, 26 September 1675, Massachusetts Archives, vol. 67: 268.

102. Harris, *A Rhode Islander Reports,* 30; N. S., *New and Further Narrative,* 77.

103. *A True Account of the Most Considerable Occurrences,* 7 (Nahawton); Leach, *Flintlock and Tomahawk,* 242–243; Drake, *King Philip's War,* 140–167 ("ideologically coherent," 141). Drake and Leach agree on the importance of Indian allies in helping the English toward victory.

104. Harris, *A Rhode Islander Reports,* 18, 85–86.

105. John Pynchon to Governor John Leverett, 15 August 1676, *Pynchon Papers,* 167; Hubbard, *A Narrative of the Troubles,* 287.

106. She is called his "Squaw" in the court records. For lack of a better title, I describe this woman, who is unnamed, as Nuckquittaty's wife.

107. She and Nuckquittaty subsequently "left the path," though they still headed toward New London to offer information of the murder. The foregoing narrative is taken from Keweebhunt's testimony (6 June 1678) and Nuckquitatty's testimony (7 June 1678), both in Connecticut Archives, Crimes & Misdemeanors, Series I, Docs 105a and 106, Connecticut State Library, Hartford, Connecticut.

108. Mandell, *King Philip's War,* 134–135 (population estimates, quote). On Indian life and persistence after King Philip's War, see Colin Calloway, ed., *After King Philip's War: Presence and Persistence in Indian New England* (Hanover, NH: University Press of New England, 1997); Daniel R. Mandell, *Behind the Frontier: Indians in Eighteenth-Century Eastern Massachusetts* (Lincoln: University of Nebraska Press, 1996); and Laurie Weinstein, ed., *Enduring Traditions: The Native Peoples of New England* (Westport, CT.: Greenwood Press, 1994).

109. Roger Williams to John Winthrop, 14 August 1638, *Winthrop Papers,* 4: 52 ("be carefull"); Roger Williams to John Winthrop, Jr., 27 June 1675, *Winthrop Papers* microfilm, Reel 11 ("Common roade").

110. Stephen Saunders Webb, *1676: The End of American Independence* (Cambridge, Mass.: Harvard University Press, 1985). Quotes are from Webb's preface, xv.

111. Minor, *Diary,* 159.

112. Lepore, *The Name of War,* 51.

113. James D. Hart, *The Popular Book: A History of America's Literary Taste* (Westport, Conn.: Greenwood Press, 1976), 15.

114. Kesuckquunch testimony (6 June 1678), in Connecticut Archives, Crimes & Misdemeanors, Series I, Doc. 104, Connecticut State Library, Hartford, Connecticut.

115. Chachasiymes (Mohegan) and two unnamed Nipmuck women, testimony, in Connecticut Archives, Crimes & Misdemeanors, Series I, Doc. 107, Connecticut State Library, Hartford, Connecticut. On the "listed surrenderers" living in this part of Connecticut after King Philip's War, see Francis Manwaring Caulkins, *History of Norwich, Connecticut, from its Settlement in 1660 to January 1845* (Norwich, Conn.: T. Robinson, 1845), 66–67, and Trumbull, *CCR,* 3: 15, 44, and 225.

116. Connecticut Archives, Crimes & Misdemeanors, Series I, Docs 110 and 112, Connecticut State Library, Hartford, Connecticut.

117. Mendon to the Massachusetts General Court, [1681], in Metcalf, *Annals of the Town of Mendon,* 84.

6. TERROR UBIQUE TREMOR

1. Cotton Mather, *Humiliations Follow'd with Deliverances* (Boston: B. Green and J. Allen, 1697), 46–47 (quotes). On Hannah Dustan's story, see also Barbara Cutter, "The Female Indian Killer Memorialized: Hannah Duston and the Nineteenth-Century Feminization of American Violence," *Journal of Women's History,* 20:2 (Summer 2008): 10–33, and Laurel Thatcher Ulrich, *Good Wives: Image and Reality in the Lives of Women in Northern New England 1650–1750* (New York: Knopf, 1982), 167–183. On the gendered dimensions of captivity, as well as the rivalry with New France, see Ann M. Little, *Abraham in Arms: War and Gender in Colonial America* (Philadelphia: University of Pennsylvania Press, 2007).

2. Mather, *Humiliations,* 40 ("I think I see"), 42 ("Raging Dragons"), 50 ("After all").

3. Increase Mather, *An Essay for the Recording of Illustrious Providences* (Boston, 1684), 41.

4. Mather, *Humiliations,* 44 ("Prayers"); Samuel Sewall, *The Diary of Samuel Sewall 1674–1729,* ed. M. Halsey Thomas, 2 vols. (New York: Farrar, Straus and Giroux, 1973), 1: 372–373 ("master," "when he prayed").

5. Samuel Penhallow, *The History of the Wars of New-England, with the Eastern Indians* (Boston: T. Fleet, 1726), 10. As a political and military strategy, the use of terror depends on communication, to do its work. The news of the violence, and the fear, must spread well beyond those most immediately affected. That is what makes terror so powerful, particularly when used by those who are less numerous or less powerful: its leveraging of communication in order to multiply itself, in order to invade households well removed from the violence. Few studies of early America explore that pattern. But my thinking, in this chapter, is influenced especially by two recent studies: Mary Beth Norton, *In the Devil's Snare: The Salem Witchcraft*

Crisis of 1692 (New York: Vintage, 2002), which demonstrates how the Salem crisis emerged largely from terrors related to the Maine Indian wars, and Peter Silver, *Our Savage Neighbors: How Indian War Transformed Early America* (New York: W.W. Norton & Company, 2008), which details the fear, as well as its circulation and political uses, pervading the middle colonies during the later wars of the eighteenth century. On the use of terror, and its definitions, see Bruce Hoffman, *Inside Terrorism,* rev. ed. (New York: Columbia University Press, 2006), esp. 1–41.

6. Thomas Hutchinson, *The History of the Province of Massachusetts-Bay* (Boston: Thomas & John Fleet, 1767), 102; Cotton Mather, *Decennium Luctuosum: An History of Remarkable Occurrences in the Long War, which New-England Hath had with the Indian Salvages, from the Year 1688, to the Year 1698, Faithfully Composed and Improved* (Boston: B. Green and J. Allen, 1699), 138.

7. P. Schuyler, Dirck Wessell, and K. V. Rensselaer to the Massachusetts Governor and Council, 15 February 1689/1690, in *The Andros Tracts: Being a Collection of Pamphlets and Official Papers, Issued During the Period Between the Overthrow of the Andros Government and the Establishment of the Second Charter of Massachusetts,* 3 vols. (Boston: The Prince Society, 1868–1874), 3: 114.

8. Sir John Werden to Governor Dongan, 27 August 1684, in John Romeyn Brodhead, *Documents Relative to the Colonial History of the State of New-York,* 15 vols. (Albany: Weed, Parsons, and Company, 1853–1887), 3: 349–350 (quote); and Governor Dongan to Sir John Werden, 18 February 1684, in ibid., 355–356.

9. Edmund Andros to John Allyn, 23 November 1687, in John Hammond Trumbull, ed., *The Public Records of the Colony of Connecticut,* 15 vols. (Hartford, 1859), 3: 393; John Allyn to Edmund Andros, 5 December 1687, in ibid., 398. But, as of March 1688, the post wasn't settled (see ibid., 442).

10. Mary E. Woolley, *The Early History of the Colonial Post-Office* (Providence, 1894), 7–8.

11. Wayne R. Fuller, *The American Mail: Enlarger of the Common Life* (Chicago: University of Chicago Press, 1972), 20–21.

12. "An Act Encouraging a Post-Office" (1693), in *The Acts and Resolves, Public and Private, of the Province of the Massachusetts Bay,* 21 vols. (Boston: Wright & Potter, Printers to the State, 1869–1922), 1: 115–117.

13. Fuller, *The American Mail,* 21.

14. Samuel Sewall's diary includes several mentions of "the post" during the 1690s; see, for instance, Sewall, *Diary,* 1: 345 (11 January 1695/1696), 391 (23 March 1697/1698), and 398 (29 August 1698 and 16 September 1698). Wait and Fitz-John Winthrop's correspondence in the first decade of the 1700s also attests to the growing regularity of the post. The references become too numerous to list. See *MHSC,* 6th ser., 5 (Boston, 1892), passim. Mary E. Woolley posits that regular delivery of mail began around 1700. See Woolley, *The Early History of the Colonial Post-Office,* 23–24.

15. George Parker Winship, ed., *The Journal of Madam Knight* (Boston: Small, Maynard & Company, 1920), 9, 16.

16. Sewall, *Diary,* 1: 446 (15 and 22 March 1700/1701). He also learned "by the Post of my Lord's Interment" and, in 1702, of the arrival in New York of Bellomont's replacement. See Sewall, *Diary,* 1: 446 (7 April 1701), and 467 (9 May 1702).

17. Nathaniel B. Shurtleff, *Records of the Governor and Company of the Massachusetts Bay in New England,* 5 vols. (Boston: William White, 1853–1854), 5: 394.

18. Trumbull, *CCR,* 3: 157.

19. Trumbull, *CCR,* 3: 157 ("dirty"); ibid., 4: 246–247 ("great difficultie").

20. John Tulley, *An Almanack for the Year of Our Lord, MDCXCVIII* (Boston: Bartholomew Green and John Allen, 1697).

21. Robb Sagendorph, *America and Her Almanacs: Wit, Wisdom and Weather, 1639–1970* (Dublin, NH: Yankee, 1970); and Marion Barber Stowell, *Early American Almanacs: The Colonial Weekday Bible* (New York: Burt Franklin, 1977).

22. Daniel Leeds, *An Almanack for the Year of the Christian Account 1695* (New York: William Bradford, 1694). In 1699 Leeds did relate, for the first time, the route from Boston all the way to Jamestown in Virginia. See Leeds, *An Almanack for the Year of Christian Account 1700* (New York: William Bradford, 1699).

23. John Clapp, *An Almanack for the Year 1697* (New York: William Bradford, 1697). The other two 1697 almanacs were: John Tulley, *An Almanack for the Year of our Lord, MDCXCVIII,* and Daniel Leeds, *An Almanack for the Year of Christian Account 1697* (New York, 1697). John Tulley, one of the more prolific almanac makers of the period, lived in Saybrook, Connecticut, where the Boston post rider rendezvoused with the New York post to exchange letters. Tulley penned his drafts in Saybrook, then posted them to printer Benjamin Harris in Boston.

24. Samuel Clough, *The New-England Almanack for the Year of our Lord, MDCCII* (Boston: B. Green and J. Allen for N. Boone, 1701).

25. David Conroy, *In Public Houses: Drink and the Revolution of Authority in Colonial Massachusetts* (Chapel Hill: University of North Carolina Press, 1995); Sharon V. Salinger, *Taverns and Drinking in Early America* (Baltimore: Johns Hopkins University Press, 2002).

26. *Journal of Madam Knight,* 20.

27. Clapp, *An Almanack for the Year 1697* (1697). Clapp began offering his coach's service, which he counted "the first Hackney Coach . . . made and kept" in New York City, in 1696. See ibid.

28. The earliest mention of any coach or carriage that I have found is in 1683. In a diary entry for December 1683, Peter Thacher of Milton mentioned dining abroad with acquaintances, a "Coach-man" among them, and later that night, "thee Coach goeing home over set." See Peter Thacher Diary, 1682–1698/1699, Pre-Revolutionary

Diaries Collection, Massachusetts Historical Society, Reel 9. Another early reference dates to 1686, when a party of men came roaring through Boston one night "in a Coach from Roxbury," "singing as they come, being inflamed with Drink." See Sewall, *Diary*, 1: 121 (3 September 1686).

29. The first advertisement for a hackney coach (Jonathan Wardell's on Hanover Street in Boston) appeared in the October 6, 1712, edition of the *Boston News-letter*.

30. Sewall, *Diary*, 1: 143 ("Emms's"); 406–407 (Betty).

31. Sewall, *Diary*, 2: 931 ("Negro Charioteer"); SS to Rev. Samuel Treat, 10 August 1713, *MHSC* 6th ser., 2 (Boston, 1886): 23 ("want a Lad to drive").

32. Sewall, *Diary*, 1: 414.

33. Sewall, *Diary*, 2: 668.

34. See John Winthrop to Wait Winthrop, June 1711, *MHSC* 6th ser., 5 (Boston, 1892): 232–233 ("in the calash"); WW to John Winthrop, 19 July 1711, ibid., 234 ("find a coach-way"); Wait Winthrop to John Winthrop, 24 July 1711, ibid., 235 ("if anything," "see that the wheels"); Wait Winthrop to John Winthrop, 26 July 1711, ibid., 236–237; Wait Winthrop to John Winthrop, 1 August 1711, ibid., 238–239 ("greatly distressed"); John Winthrop to Wait Winthrop, 7 August 1711, ibid., 241.

35. *Journal of Madam Knight*, 13 (Narragansett), 26 (Stonington), 30.

36. See Sewall, *Diary*, 1: 256–258; and William Williams to John Winthrop, New York to Boston, 25 April 1709, *MHSC* 6th ser., 5 (Boston, 1892): 184–185 ("much better travelling upon ye island").

37. "Uring's Notices of New-England—1709," in *New Hampshire Historical Society Collections* (Concord, NH, 1824-), 3: 144.

38. Mark S. Shearer, "Bartholomew Green," in Benjamin Franklin V, ed., *Boston Printers, Publishers, and Booksellers: 1640–1800* (Boston: G.K. Hall & Co., 1980), 213–219 (quote, 213).

39. Increase Mather to John Cotton, 13 December 1676, Increase Mather Papers, Reel 16, Massachusetts Historical Society, Boston, Massachusetts.

40. George Parker Winship, *The Cambridge Press, 1638–1692* (Philadelphia: University of Pennsylvania Press, 1945), 165–166.

41. Samuel Eliot Morison, *Harvard College in the Seventeenth Century, Part 1* (Cambridge: Harvard University Press, 1936), 351–352.

42. Sewall, *Diary*, 1: 394.

43. William Kellaway, *The New England Company 1649–1776* (London: Longmans, 1961), 127–130 (Eliot quote, 127).

44. On Johnson, see George Emery Littlefield, *The Early Massachusetts Press, 1638–1711*, 2 vols. (Boston: The Club of Odd Volumes, 1907), 1: 209–269. The affair between Johnson and Green's daughter, Elizabeth, is detailed in Winship, *The Cambridge Press*, 225–232.

45. Michael G. Hall, *The Last American Puritan: the Life of Increase Mather, 1639–1723* (Middletown, CT.: Wesleyan University Press, 1988), 140.

46. Hugh Amory, "Printing and Bookselling in New England, 1638–1713," in Hugh Amory and David D. Hall, eds., *A History of the Book in America, Volume One: The Colonial Book in the Atlantic World* (Cambridge: Cambridge University Press, 2000), 83–116 (figures from 105, 108); David D. Hall, *Worlds of Wonder, Days of Judgment: Popular Religious Belief in Early New England* (Cambridge: Harvard University Press, 1989), 44–61.

47. Newsbooks—"in which remarkable providences, books of wonders, and execution sermons may be included"—comprised a category of print that colonists liked to read and, increasingly, they made up a major part of the output of American presses. The 1700 probate inventory of a Boston bookseller, Michael Perry, for instance, contained an array of newsbooks, "divided fairly equally between London and Boston printing." Amory, "Printing and Bookselling," 100.

48. William David Sloan and Julie Hedgepeth Williams, *The Early American Press, 1690–1783* (Westport, CT.: Greenwood Press, 1994), 1; John Tebbel, "Benjamin Harris," in Franklin, ed., *Boston Printers, Publishers, and Booksellers,* 277–281.

49. In 1690 England's Licensing Act, once lapsed, was back in effect. That meant license must be gotten, before printing anything. Licensing began in 1686 in Boston and Cambridge. This was the law under which Massachusetts suppressed *Publick Occurrences.* The suppression seems also to have been propelled by a faction displeased with Increase Mather. Harris had ties to the Mathers and had supported Increase Mather's charter negotiations in England. Sloan and Williams, *The Early American Press, 1690–1783,* 1–6; Sewall, *Diary,* 1: 267.

50. Carolyn Nelson and Matthew Seccombe, "The Creation of the Periodical Press, 1620–1695," in *The Cambridge History of the Book in Britain,* ed. J. Barnard and D. F. McKenzie (Cambridge: Cambridge University Press, 2002), 4: 535.

51. James Melvin Lee, *History of American Journalism* (Boston: Houghton Mifflin, 1917), 6.

52. Leona Rostenberg, "The Debut of English Journalism: Nathaniel Butter & Nicholas Bourne, First 'Masters of the Staple,'" in *Literary, Political, Scientific, Religious & Legal Publishing, Printing & Bookselling in England, 1551–1700: Twelve Studies* (New York: Burt Franklin, 1965), 1: 75–96; Nelson and Seccombe, "The Creation of the Periodical Press," 535.

53. Sloan and Williams *The Early American Press,* 10.

54. Sewall, *Diary,* 1: 251.

55. *Publick Occurrences, Both Foreign and Domestick,* September 25, 1690, 1 (suicide); 2 (smallpox, fires, "Trouble and Sorrow").

56. E. B. O'Callaghan, *The Documentary History of the State of New York,* 4 vols. (Albany: Weed, Parsons & Co., 1850–1851), 1: 303 ("shott threw his Thigh,"

"full of french and Indians," "being no Watch"); P. Schuyler, Dirck Wessell, and K. V. Rensselaer to the Massachusetts Governor and Council, 15 February 1689/1690, in *The Andros Tracts*, 3: 114 ("limbs frozen").

57. P. Schuyler, Dirck Wessell, and K. V. Rensselaer to the Massachusetts Governor and Council, 15 February 1689/1690, in *The Andros Tracts*, 3: 114–115.

58. O'Callaghan, *DHNY*, 1: 303–305.

59. Sewall, *Diary*, 1: 251. The "amazing news" took two weeks to reach Boston.

60. Sewall, *Diary*, 1: 254; Cotton Mather, *Decennium Luctuosum*, 46 ("best part").

61. Mather, *Decennium Luctuosum*, 46.

62. As many as fourteen hundred colonists may have been captured during the imperial wars of 1675–1713. Daniel Richter and Alden Vaughan, "Crossing the Cultural Divide: Indians and New Englanders, 1605–1763," *American Antiquarian Society Proceedings* 90:1 (April 1980): 23–99, and Richard Slotkin, *Regeneration through Violence: The Mythology of the American Frontier, 1600–1860* (Middletown, CT: Wesleyan University Press, 1973). Vaughan and Richter estimate about 700 were taken in the period 1675 to 1713; Slotkin thinks twice that. For reference works on captives taken during this period, see Charlotte Alice Baker, *True Stories of New England Captives Carried to Canada during the Old French and Indian Wars* (Greenfield, MA: Press of E.A. Hall & Co., 1897), and Emma Lewis Coleman, *New England Captives Carried to Canada between 1677 and 1760, During the French and Indian Wars* (Portland, ME: Southworth Press, 1925).

63. Mather, *Decennium Luctuosum*, 83.

64. SS to ___ Storke, 14 November 1698, *MHSC* 6th ser., 1 (Boston, 1886): 208. On King William's War, see Samuel Adams Drake, *The Border Wars of New England, Commonly Called King William's War and Queen Anne's Wars* (New York: C. Scribner's Sons, 1897); Evan Haefeli and Kevin Sweeney, *Captors and Captives: The 1704 French and Indian Raid on Deerfield* (Amherst: University of Massachusetts Press, 2003), 78–85; Norton, *In the Devil's Snare*, 82–111; Jenny Hale Pulsipher, "'Dark Cloud Rising from the East': Indian Sovereignty and the Coming of King William's War in New England," *New England Quarterly* 80:4 (Dec. 2007): 588–613; and Owen Stanwood, *The Empire Reformed: English America in the Age of the Glorious Revolution* (Philadelphia: University of Pennsylvania Press, 2011), 54–81.

65. James Axtell, "The White Indians of Colonial America," *WMQ* 32:1 (Jan. 1975): 55–88; Haefeli and Sweeney, *Captors and Captives;* Daniel K. Richter, *The Ordeal of the Longhouse: The Peoples of the Iroquois League in the Era of European Colonization* (Chapel Hill: University of North Carolina Press, 1992); Brett Rushforth, *Bonds of Alliance: Indigenous and Atlantic Slaveries in New France* (Chapel Hill: University of North Carolina Press, 2012).

66. Haefeli and Sweeney, *Captors and Captives*, 78–92; Kenneth M. Morrison, *The Embattled Northeast: The Elusive Ideal of Alliance in Abenaki-Euroamerican*

Relations (Berkeley: University of California Press, 1984); Norton, *In the Devil's Snare,* 82–111.

67. "Letter from Philippe de Rigaud de Vaudreuil to the Minister of the Marine, 1704," in Evan Haefeli and Kevin Sweeney, *Captive Histories: English, French, and Native Narratives of the 1704 Deerfield Raid* (Amherst: University of Massachusetts Press, 2006), 81.

68. Francis Parkman, *Count Frontenac and New France under Louis XIV* (Boston: Little, Brown and Company, 1880), 208–220; Haefeli and Sweeney, *Captors and Captives,* 34–54; Jon Parmenter, *The Edge of the Woods: Iroquoia, 1534–1701* (East Lansing: Michigan State University Press, 2010), 207–211.

69. Increase Mather diary, March 1693, in *IMP,* Reel 16 ("frownes"); ibid., 1 January 1703/1704 ("Is this the first day"); ibid., 11 July 1696 (Pascataway); ibid., 29 March 1696/1697 (Haverhill); ibid., 2 October 1697 (Lancaster).

70. Lawrence Hammond diary, 17 May 1690 (Casco); 25 January 1691/1692 (York); ibid., 2 September 1691 (Dunstable), Pre-Revolutionary Diaries Collection, Reel 5, Massachusetts Historical Society, Boston, Massachusetts.

71. "Journal of the Rev. John Pike," in *MHSP* 14 (Boston, 1875–1876): 121, 126, 127, 128 (Ursula Cutt), 130, and passim.

72. Lawrence Hammond diary, 21 March 1689/1690, in Pre-Revolutionary Diaries Collection, Reel 5.

73. SS to John Storke, 31 July 1696, *MHSC* 6th ser., 1 (Boston, 1886): 165 ("Rumors of War"); SS to John Ive, nd, in ibid., 169 ("hear of some slain").

74. John Marshall diary, Pre-Revolutionary Diaries Collection, Reel 6.

75. Increase Mather diary, 11 March 1703/1704., in *IMP,* Reel 16.

76. SS to John Ive, 19 February 1691/1692, *MHSC,* 6th ser., 1 (Boston, 1886): 129.

77. Mather quoted in *Collections of the New Hampshire Historical Society,* 3 (1832): 40 ("much beholden"); IM to Samuel Penhallow, 14 October 1706, *IMP,* Reel 16 ("post payed"); IM to Samuel Penhallow, 4 December 1704, ibid. ("Furr gloves").

78. "Copy of a Letter from the Hon. Samuel Penhallow, to Dr. Cotton Mather," Portsmouth, 27 February 1698/1699, in *Collections of the New Hampshire Historical Society,* 1 (1824): 133–135. Although this letter is labeled as having gone to Cotton Mather, Increase Mather answered it.

79. IM to Samuel Penhallow, 3 March 1698/1699, *IMP,* Reel 16.

80. Mather, *Decennium Luctuosum,* 15–16 (John Pike's letter) and 42–45 (Penhallow's letter); Mather, *Duodecennium Luctuosum. The History of a Long War with Indian Salvages, and Their Directors and Abettors; from the Year, 1702. To the Year, 1714* (Boston: B. Green for Samuel Gerrish, 1714), 27 ("Endebted").

81. Cotton Mather diary, *MHSC* 7th ser., 7 (1911): 528.

82. Cotton Mather diary, *MHSC* 7th ser., 7 (1911): 565.

83. Cotton Mather diary, *MHSC* 7th ser., 7 (1911): 566.

84. David Levin, *Cotton Mather: The Young Life of the Lord's Remembrancer, 1663–1703* (Cambridge: Harvard University Press, 1978); Robert Middlekauff, *The Mathers: Three Generations of Puritan Intellectuals, 1596–1728* (New York: Oxford University Press, 1971).

85. Cotton Mather diary, *MHSC* 7th ser., 7 (1911), 152 ("composed"), 155–156.

86. Cotton Mather diary, *MHSC* 7th ser., 7 (1911), 228.

87. Cotton Mather diary, *MHSC* 7th ser., 7 (1911), 210; Tulley, *An Almanack for the Year of Our Lord, MDCXCVII* (Boston: Bartholomew Green and John Allen, 1696), np. No composition entitled *Great Examples of Judgment and Mercy* ever seems to have been published, despite Tulley's advertisement and Mather's diary note. Probably the material that he planned to publish under that title ended up in 1697's *Humiliations Follow'd with Deliverances,* which detailed the experiences of Hannah Dustan and Hannah Swarton. See Thomas James Holmes, *Cotton Mather: A Bibliography of His Works,* 3 vols. (Cambridge: Harvard University Press, 1940), 1: 452–454.

88. Linda Colley, *Captives: Britain, Empire and the World, 1600–1850* (New York: Pantheon, 2002).

89. On this genre of early American literature, see Michelle Burnham, *Captivity and Sentiment: Cultural Exchange in American Literature, 1682–1861* (Hanover: University Press of New England, 1997); Gary L. Ebersole, *Captured by Texts: Puritan to Postmodern Images of Indian Captivity* (Charlottesville: University Press of Virginia, 1995); James D. Hartman, *Providence Tales and the Birth of American Literature* (Baltimore: Johns Hopkins University Press, 1999); June Namias, *White Captives: Gender and Ethnicity on the American Frontier* (Chapel Hill: University of North Carolina Press, 1993); Pauline Turner Strong, *Captive Selves, Captivating Others: The Politics and Poetics of Colonial American Captivity Narratives* (Boulder, CO: Westview Press, 1999); Richard VanDerBeets, *Held Captive by Indians: Selected Narratives 1642–1836* (Knoxville: University of Tennessee Press, 1994); Alden T. Vaughan and Edward W. Clark, *Puritans Among the Indians: Accounts of Captivity and Redemption 1676–1724* (Cambridge: The Belknap Press of Harvard University Press, 1981); Lisa Voigt, *Writing Captivity in the Early Modern Atlantic: Circulations of Knowledge and Authority in the Iberian and English Imperial Worlds* (Chapel Hill: University of North Carolina Press, 2009); and Kathryn Zabelle Derounian-Stodola and James Arthur Levernier, eds., *The Indian Captivity Narrative, 1550–1900* (New York: Twayne Publishers, 1993).

90. Derounian-Stodola and Levernier, *The Indian Captivity Narrative,* 14; on sales of captivity narratives, also see Hartman, *Providence Tales,* 16–17; Frank Luther Mott, *Golden Multitudes: The Story of Best Sellers in the United States* (New York: Bowker, 1960); and James D. Hart, *The Popular Book: A History of America's Literary Taste* (New York: Oxford University Press, 1950).

91. Cotton Mather diary, *MHSC* 7th ser., 7 (1911): 210.

92. See, for example, Hannah Parsons' tale, in Cotton Mather, *Good Fetch'd Out of Evil: A Collection of Memorables Relating to Our Captives* (Boston: B. Green, 1706), 34 ("Numberless").

93. Cotton Mather diary, *MHSC* 7th ser., 7 (1911): 210.

94. Mather, *Humiliations,* 12.

95. Mather, *Decennium Luctuosum,* 133–134.

96. Mather, *Humiliations,* 4–5.

97. Mather, *Decennium Luctuosum,* 72.

98. Mather, *Decennium Luctuosum,* 48–49. Roasting is a recurrent trope in tales of captivity, and seems to have carried special horror for English readers. See for example Mather, *Decennium Luctuosum,* 38; "Journal of the Rev. John Pike," 149 ("tis feared he & another English man were Roasted to Death"); and Penhallow, *History,* 23 (Joseph Ring "fastened to a stake and burnt alive").

99. See John Demos, *A Little Commonwealth: Family Life in Plymouth Colony* (New York: Oxford University Press, 1970); and Cotton Mather, *A Family Well-Ordered* (Boston: B. Green & J. Allen, 1699).

100. Mather, *Good Fetch'd Out of Evil,* 37.

101. Mather, *Decennium Luctuosum,* 53; also see ibid., 55–56; and Mather, *Good Fetch'd Out of Evil,* 40–42.

102. "If some of Mather's descriptions were gruesome, the raison d'etre for them was similar to that found in the *ars moriendi* of medieval Europe—to bring death and suffering before the eyes of the people so that a full awareness of the human condition would affect the conduct of their lives." See Ebersole, *Captured by Texts,* 70.

103. Cotton Mather diary, *MHSC* 7th ser., 7 (1911): 593.

104. Cotton Mather, *Frontiers Well-Defended* (Boston: T. Green, 1707), 4 ("Ever now"), 5 ("killing," "siezing"), 19 ("Countrey"), 46 ("O Hearts").

105. *Boston News-letter,* March 4–11, 1706.

106. Cotton Mather diary, *MHSC* 7th ser., 7 (1911): 520.

107. Cotton Mather diary, *MHSC* 7th ser., 7 (1911): 548.

108. Cotton Mather diary, *MHSC* 7th ser., 8 (1912): 242. In April 1705, the *Boston News-letter* memorialized James Gray, a man "*That used to go up and down the Country Selling of Books.*" See *BNL,* April 9–16, 1705.

109. Cotton Mather diary, *MHSC* 7th ser., 7 (1911): 568.

110. "Letter from William Whiting to Governor Fitz-John Winthrop, 1704," in Haefeli and Sweeney, *Captive Histories,* 68–69; John Williams, *The Redeemed Captive Returning to Zion* (1707), in ibid., 94–95; Samuel Partridge, "An Account of the Destruction of Deerfield, 1704," in ibid., 64–66; Jonathan Wells and Ebenezer Wright petition, in George Sheldon, *A History of Deerfield, Massachusetts,* 2 vols. (Greenfield, MA: Press of E.A. Hall & Co., 1895–1896), 1: 297 ("many dead bodies"). On the Deerfield raid, see John Demos, *The Unredeemed Captive:*

A Family Story from Early America (New York: Knopf, 1994); Haefeli and Sweeney, *Captors and Captives;* and Richard I. Melvoin, *New England Outpost: War and Society in Colonial Deerfield* (New York: W. W. Norton & Company, 1989).

111. John Pynchon to the Massachusetts Governor & Council, 2 December 1691, in Sheldon, *History of Deerfield,* 1: 223.

112. John Pynchon to William Stoughton, 13 September 1695, in Sheldon, *History of Deerfield,* 1: 250–251 ("dayly Infested," "in a sence"); JP to WS, 30 September 1695, in ibid., 252 ("feares").

113. For discussion of the anticipated raid, see Joseph Dudley to Fitz-John Winthrop, 27 May 1703, *MHSC* 6th ser., 3 (1889): 129; FJW to Joseph Dudley, 9 June 1703, in ibid., 131; Joseph Dudley to FJW, 31 July 1703, in ibid., 137; FJW to John Chester, 12 August 1703, in ibid., 138.

114. SS to Henry Newman, 6 March 1703/1704, *MHSC* 6th ser., 1 (1886): 299.

115. Sewall, *Diary,* 1: 498.

116. See Demos, *The Unredeemed Captive,* 40–42, for description of how the word initially spread (and Edwards' quote).

117. Col. Quary to the Council of Trade and Plantations, *Calendar of State Papers* (1704–1705), 139.

118. Samuel Partridge to FJW, 13 March 1703/1704, *MHSC* 6th ser., 3 (1889): 183 ("our people"); Samuel Partridge to FJW, 15 May 1704, in ibid., 200 ("awfull appearences").

119. *BNL,* May 8–15, 1704 *("French of Canada"); BNL,* June 12–19, 1704 ("We hear"); Increase Mather diary, 3 June 1704, in *IMP,* Reel 16 ("800"); *BNL,* Nov. 20–27, 1704 ("over the Ice"); Increase Mather diary, 17 June 1704, in *IMP,* Reel 16 ("dismal time").

120. Charles E. Clark, *The Public Prints: The Newspaper in Anglo-American Culture 1665–1740* (New York: Oxford University Press, 1994), 87.

121. Ten of Campbell's handwritten newsletters survive in the Winthrop Family Papers, several of them endorsed as "Publick Occurrences"; on the overleaf of one, he wrote, "On other Syde is what occurs, as I send your ho[nou]r Weekly." See John Campbell to FJW, 12 April 1703; 27 April 1703; 3 May 1703; 17 May 1703; 1 June 1703; 7 June 1703; 14 June 1703; 12 July 1703; 20 September 1703 ("I send your ho[nou]r Weekly"); [ ] October 1703, all in Marjorie F. Gutheim, ed., *Winthrop Family Papers* Microfilm, 53 reels (Boston, Mass.: Massachusetts Historical Society, 1976), Reel 16.

122. Lee, *History of Journalism,* 17. Campbell apparently inherited the postmaster position from his father, Duncan, a Boston bookseller who had become the Boston postmaster in 1693 (as the postal system was being launched). Duncan Campbell also penned handwritten newsletters; see *MHSP* 1st ser., 12 (Boston, 1871–1873): 423–424.

123. It was also, for a time, the colonies' *only* newspaper. Campbell did not face competition until 1719. On Campbell and his founding the *Boston News-letter,* see Clark, *The Public Prints,* 77–102.

124. Historians generally see the early BNL as a mouthpiece of the relatively unpopular Dudley government, about which Campbell did not publish unflattering news. See Sloan and Williams, *The Early American Press,* 21.

125. Campbell and Dudley were both Anglicans, and thus it is not surprising that a Puritan like Mather might have such an unflattering view of the paper. Sloan and Williams, *The Early American Press,* 21.

126. Clark, *The Public Prints,* 78; Richard D. Brown, *Knowledge Is Power: The Diffusion of Information in Early America, 1700–1865* (New York: Oxford University Press, 1989), 37.

127. See, for example, *BNL,* April 2–9, 1705.

128. John Winthrop to Wait Winthrop, [May 1709], *MHSC* 6th ser., 5 (1892): 188.

129. John Winthrop to WW, 18 May 1709, *MHSC* 6th ser., 5 (1892): 190.

130. *BNL,* April 23–30, 1705.

131. See *BNL,* April 23–30, 1705.

132. See, for example, *MHSC* 6th ser., 1 (1886): 330 (Sewall sends a copy to James Bayley at Roxbury in Sept. 1706); ibid., 358 (to "Cousin Moodey of York inclosing the News-Letter of the first of Decr" in February 1707/1708); ibid., 355 (to Samuel Shepard, at Woodbridge, [New Jersey], 29 Dec 1707); ibid., 372 ("To Mr. John Williams at Deerfield 7r 20 1708 inclosing . . . this days Newes-Letter"); ibid., 377 (to Thomas Cockerill, in New York, 10 Jan 1708/1709); ibid., 396 (sends three last newsletters to Edward Taylor, 27 June 1710); *MHSC* 6th ser., 2 (1886): 31 (to Mr. Seth Shove at Danbury, 14 July 1714: "News-Letter of July 5."); ibid., 48. John Campbell himself, of course, also distributed the *News-Letter* to other parts of New England, including Connecticut. "He sends me the News-Letter every post," Wait Winthrop noted, from New London, in 1710. See WW to his son John Winthrop, 26 October 1710, *MHSC* 6th ser., 5 (1892): 225.

133. Sewall, *Diary,* 2: 896 (passes on the "two last News-Letters" to Mrs. Denison in 1718).

134. Clark, *The Public Prints,* 79.

135. Clark, *The Public Prints,* 81; *BNL,* January 13–20, 1706/1707.

136. *BNL,* April 24–May 1, 1704; *BNL,* May 1–May 8, 1704. David Paul Nord notes that the girl's story "turned out to be a hoax, concocted and reported by the girl herself." See Nord, *Communities of Journalism: A History of American Newspapers and their Readers* (Urbana: University of Illinois Press, 2001), 52.

137. *BNL,* Nov 13–20, 1704.

138. *BNL,* June 3–10, 1706 ("Found"); *BNL,* June 2–9, 1712 ("stript"); *BNL,* August 25-Sept. 1, 1712 (Waldrons).

139. Sir William Phips' attempt to invade Quebec, early in King William's War, was ineffectual; an Albany expedition to invade New France also crumbled. Queen Anne's War, too, found the English colonies mounting humiliatingly unsuccessful expeditions. Emerson W. Baker and John G. Reid, *The New England Knight: Sir William Phips, 1651–1695* (Toronto: University of Toronto Press, 1998); Haefeli and Sweeney, *Captors and Captives*, 194, 204; Norton, *In the Devil's Snare*, 107.

140. "Letter From Claude de Ramezay to the Minister of the Marine, 1704," 14 November 1704, in Haefeli and Sweeney, *Captive Histories*, 86.

141. Haefeli and Sweeney, *Captors and Captives*, 92, 185, 192.

142. *BNL*, March 5–12, 1705. For Church's depredations on Native corn, cattle, and homes, see *BNL*, July 31–August 7, 1704.

143. *BNL*, July 31–August 7, 1704.

144. *BNL*, June 16–23, 1707.

145. Isaac Addington to FJW, 4 August 1704, *MHSC* 6th ser., 3 (1889): 252.

146. Joseph Dudley to FJW, 14 July 1707, *MHSC* 6th ser., 3 (1889): 392–393.

147. Penhallow, *History*, 44–45.

148. Penhallow, *History*, v.

149. *BNL*, July 21–28, 1707; Penhallow, *History*, 44.

150. Penhallow, *History*, 9, 10.

151. Caleb Stanley to FJW, 1 March 1699/1700, *MHSC* 6th ser., 3 (1889): 48 ("great fears," "out-places"); William Whiting to FJW, 27 January 1706/1707, in ibid., 365 ("much possess'd").

152. *BNL*, Feb 3–10, 1706/1707.

153. FJW to Joseph Dudley, 27 March 1707, *MHSC* 6th ser., 3 (1889): 373.

154. Robert Treat to FJW, 9 July 1700, *MHSC* 6th ser., 3 (1889): 53.

155. Cotton Mather diary, *MHSC* 7th ser., 7 (1911): 555 ("forgett"), 563 ("Our own").

156. Cotton Mather diary, *MHSC* 7th ser., 7 (1911): 575.

157. Hartman, *Providence Tales*, 16–17.

158. Cotton Mather, *Duodecennium Luctuosum*, 13.

159. Timothy Harrington, *A Century-SERMON, Preach'd at the First-Parish in Lancaster* (Boston: S. Kneeland, 1753), 17.

160. Daniel Neal, *The History of New-England*, 2 vols. (London: J. Clark, R. Ford, and R. Cruttenden, 1720), 2: 579.

161. Increase Mather diary, 1 September 1721, in *IMP*, Reel 16.

162. WW to John Winthrop, 13 July 1713, *MHSC* 6th ser., 5 (1892): 269.

163. CM to John Winthrop, 4 September 1718, *MHSC* 4th ser., 8 (Boston, 1868): 430 ("Don't send packets"); CM to JW, 10 January 1722/1723, in ibid., 453 ("very chargeable"); CM to JW, 11 January 1719/1720, in ibid., 437 ("My Ink-glass").

164. It moved temporarily to Milk Street and was back on Cornhill, its old home, by July 1713. See *BNL*, Oct. 1–8, 1711.

MILESTONES

1. Trudy Tynan, "Boston Post Road Lined with Historic Milestones," *Lawrence Journal-World*, Sept. 12, 2004, 7E. The purported odometer, made of iron and brass, is housed in the Frankliniana Collection at the Franklin Institute in Philadelphia, Pennsylvania. A picture of it can be seen in E. Philip Krider, "Benjamin Franklin's Science," in Page Talbott, ed., *Benjamin Franklin: In Search of a Better World* (New Haven: Yale University Press, 2005), 179.

2. Ms Record, Boston Births, 5: 113, City Registry, Boston, quoted in Leonard W. Labaree et al., eds., *The Papers of Benjamin Franklin*, 37 vols. (New Haven: Yale University Press, 1959-), 1: 3.

3. Benjamin Franklin, *Autobiography* (1793), accessed at franklinpapers.org, 15 October 2013.

4. Ibid.

5. Charles E. Clark, *The Public Prints: The Newspaper in American Culture, 1665–1740* (New York: Oxford University Press, 1994), 104, 132.

6. Clark, *The Public Prints*, 132.

7. Franklin, *Papers*, 1: 194–199.

8. Benjamin Franklin, *Autobiography* (1793), accessed at <franklinpapers.org>, 15 October 2013.

9. Joanna Brooks, ed., *The Collected Writings of Samson Occom, Mohegan* (New York: Oxford University Press, 2006), 8 (Brooks's description of Occom); 51–52 (quotes from his own "Autobiographical Narrative, First Draft," Nov. 28, 1765).

10. Samson Occom, "Autobiographical Narrative, Second Draft," Sept. 17, 1768, in Brooks, ed., *Collected Writings*, 53.

11. "Occom believed," writes Joanna Brooks, "that English-language literacy and New Light Christianity could potentially serve to bolster Native peoples' political autonomy and spiritual well-being." Brooks, ed., *Collected Writings*, 3–4.

12. Hilary Wyss, *Writing Indians: Literacy, Christianity, and Native Community in Early America* (Amherst: University of Massachusetts Press, 2000), 2 (Josiah Attaunitt quote).

13. Brooks, ed., *Collected Writings*, 20, 52 (Occom quote).

14. Daniel R. Mandell, *Behind the Frontier: Indians in Eighteenth-Century Eastern Massachusetts* (Lincoln: University of Nebraska Press, 1996), esp. 66, 78.

15. Mandell, *Behind the Frontier*, 59, 160–163 (quotes); Linford D. Fisher, *The Indian Great Awakening: Religion and the Shaping of Native Cultures in Early America* (New York: Oxford University Press, 2012); David J. Silverman, *Faith and Boundaries: Colonists, Christianity, and Community among the Wampanoag Indians of Martha's Vineyard, 1600-1871* (Cambridge: Cambridge University Press, 2005). For the hidden numbers of "non-reservation" Indians in the New England of these years, see Jason Mancini, "'in contempt and oblivion': Censuses, Ethnogeography,

and Hidden Indian Histories in Eighteenth-Century Southern New England"
(forthcoming, *Ethnohistory*, 2015).

16. *The New England Courant*, January 28-February 4, 1723, 2.

17. Ruth Lapham Butler, *Doctor Franklin, Postmaster General* (Garden City,
NY: Doubleday, Doran & Co., 1928), 36; John Franklin to Benjamin Franklin, 26
November 1753, in Franklin, *Papers*, 5: 118 ("Bring and Carry").

18. Butler, *Doctor Franklin;* Eric Jaffe, *The King's Best Highway: The Lost History
of the Boston Post Road, the Route that Made America* (New York: Scribner, 2010), 39–43.

19. Franklin, *Papers*, 1: 4.

20. Fred Anderson, *The War that Made America: A Short History of the French
and Indian War* (New York: Viking, 2005); Colin G. Calloway, *The Scratch of a Pen:
1763 and the Transformation of North America* (New York: Oxford University Press,
2006); Peter Silver, *Our Savage Neighbors: How Indian War Transformed Early
America* (New York: W.W. Norton, 2008).

21. Brooks, ed., *Collected Writings;* Brad D. E. Jarvis, *The Brothertown Nation of
Indians: Land Ownership and Nationalism in Early America, 1740–1840* (Lincoln:
University of Nebraska Press, 2010); David J. Silverman, *Red Brethren: The
Brothertown and Stockbridge Indians and the Problem of Race in Early America*
(Ithaca: Cornell University Press, 2010).

22. Quoted in Brooks, ed., *Collected Writings*, 6.

23. Williams, *Key*, 61–62.

24. On the role that domesticated animals played in driving English-Native
relations, see especially Virginia DeJohn Anderson, *Creatures of Empire: How
Domestic Animals Transformed Early America* (New York: Oxford University
Press, 2004).

25. Jean M. O'Brien, *Firsting and Lasting: Writing Indians Out of Existence in
New England* (Minneapolis: University of Minnesota Press, 2010).

A NOTE ON METHOD

1. The letters of John Pynchon and Roger Williams, for example, rely so completely on the Winthrop collection, in this period, that to include them would have
added relatively little quantitative evidence.

2. The book's narrative reaches beyond 1675. But the Winthrop collection
changes considerably after the death of John Winthrop, Jr., in 1676. It becomes
spottier and less reliable. The database, therefore, ends at the 1670s.

3. A further note on this source base: Some—but not all—of the Winthrop
Papers that fall within these dates, 1635–1675, have been published. The first two
decades are covered, largely, in the six-volume collection *Winthrop Papers, 1498–
1654*, ed. Allyn B. Forbes et al., 6 vols. (Boston: Massachusetts Historical Society,
1929–1992). Roughly a third of the letters in my database are drawn from these

volumes. But for the years 1655–1675 (where the vast bulk of letters fall, in fact), I turn principally to the published microfilms of the Winthrops' manuscripts, Marjorie F. Gutheim, ed., *Winthrop Family Papers* Microfilm, 53 reels (Boston, Mass.: Massachusetts Historical Society, 1976). Although many of these later letters have appeared in print, they have not been published in chronological order. Because I aimed to be as exhaustive as possible, within the collection, I have relied on the filmed collection—in which the letters do appear, roughly, according to date.

To a much lesser degree, I have also made use, here and there, of letters appearing in the published *Collections of the Massachusetts Historical Society* and the Winthrop Family Papers transcripts, housed at the Massachusetts Historical Society, sometimes to confirm my own readings of seventeenth-century script. The transcripts are cited as follows: Winthrop Family, Winthrop Family Papers [transcripts], 1630–1741, 10 boxes, Massachusetts Historical Society, Boston, Massachusetts.

Acknowledgments

Many guides helped me through the writing of this book. At Harvard I had the very good fortune to work with Laurel Thatcher Ulrich, Joyce Chaplin, and Jill Lepore. I cannot imagine three more stellar mentors. I thank all of them, deeply. Many other colleagues and friends also commented on my writing over the years. For reading generously and critically, I thank especially Konstantin Dierks, Julie Fisher, Lin Fisher, Alison Games, Andrew Lipman, Sean Harvey, Jason Mancini, Daniel Richter, David Silverman, and several anonymous readers. Others who offered comments and questions that steered my work in important ways include Adam Beaver, Rick Bell, Akeia Benard, Vince Brown, Sarah Anne Carter, David Hall, Rebecca Goetz, Mark Hanna, Judy Kertész, Steve Marini, Kevin McBride, Phil Mead, Mark Meuwese, Margot Minardi, Jay Turner, Cynthia van Zandt, Dan Wewers, and Conrad Wright. Very generously, Julie Fisher and David Silverman shared with me their then-unpublished biography of Ninigret. Toward the end of the book's writing, Jill Lepore, Jenny Hale Pulsipher, Laurel Ulrich, and Walt Woodward all read, very kindly, the whole manuscript.

Early stages of my research were funded by the American Philosophical Society's Phillips Fund for Native American Research, the Charles Warren Center for Studies in American History, Harvard Law School's Mark DeWolfe Howe Fund, and an Artemus Ward Fund Grant from the History Department at Harvard. An Andrew W. Mellon postdoctoral fellowship at the College of the Holy Cross gave me time to rethink the project, as well as fantastic colleagues with whom to talk. Much of the first chapter was written there. Later, a Malcolm and Mildred Freiberg fellowship allowed me to spend a summer at the Massachusetts Historical Society, working on the book's final chapter. With a Michael Kraus Research Grant from the American Historical Association and a faculty research grant from Wellesley, I went to London, where I plumbed materials at the National Postal Museum & Archive, as well as the British Library.

I spent the final year of revision as a resident fellow at Wellesley's Susan and Donald Newhouse Center for the Humanities, where my fellow visiting scholars have been terrific friends and critical readers. Marié Abe, Beth DeSombre, Carol Dougherty, Carla Kaplan, Eugene Marshall, Alex Orquiza, Yasmine Ramadan, Sonia Sabnis, Duncan White, and Kristin Williams, thank you. My colleagues in the History department have also been immensely supportive. I am particularly indebted to the three who have chaired the department during my early years, Lidwien Kapteijns, Guy Rogers, and Nina Tumarkin. But warm thanks, also, to Pat Giersch, Brenna Greer, Simon Grote, Fran Malino, Tak Matsusaka, Alejandra Osorio, Ryan Quintana, Nikhil Rao, Valerie Ramseyer, and Quinn Slobodian.

I have also had wonderful support, in digging through dusty volumes and old papers. In particular, I am grateful to the librarians, archivists, and staff at the American Antiquarian Society; the Connecticut Historical Society; the Connecticut State Library; the John Carter Brown Library; the Massachusetts Historical Society; the Massachusetts State Archives; the Mashantucket Pequot Museum and Research Center; the New England Historic Genealogical Society; the Rhode Island Historical Society; and Wellesley College Special Collections (where Ruth Rogers has offered unfailing enthusiasm and aid). My gratitude also goes to Katherine Ruffin, Book Arts Program Director at Wellesley, from whom I learned intimately the processes of early modern letterpress printing and papermaking. Setting type, it turns out, is more difficult than I had imagined. Making a decent woodcut is even harder.

I shared many of the ideas in this book at various conferences, workshops, and other venues. Members of the Boston Area Early American History Seminar at the Massachusetts Historical Society, of Harvard's Early American History Workshop, and of the Newberry Library Seminar in Early American History and Culture, allowed me to test arguments and to gather important insights. The spring 2010 fellows at the McNeil Center for Early American Studies gamely engaged with my thoughts about King Philip's War. I am also grateful to audiences at meetings of the American Historical Association; the Dublin Seminar for New England Folklife; the Forum on European Expansion and Global Interaction; the Omohundro Institute of Early American History and Culture; the Society of Early Americanists; and the Society for the History of Authorship, Reading and Publishing. Portions of Chapter 1 previously appeared as Katherine A. Grandjean, "New World Tempests: Environment, Scarcity, and the Coming of the Pequot War," *William and Mary Quarterly*, vol. 68, no. 1 (January 2011): 75–100. Brief portions of Chapters 2, 4, and 5 include material from Katherine A. Grandjean, "A Trail in Paper: Thomas Minor's Diary and the Evolution of Travel in New England, 1653–1684," in *In Our Own Worlds: New England Diaries, 1600 to Present,* Peter Benes, ed., Dublin Seminar for New England Folklife *Annual Proceedings* (Boston: Boston University, 2009): 73–84. I am grateful to the reviewers and editors of each publication for their astute guidance.

This project has found a warm reception at Harvard University Press, whose editors and staff deserve many thanks. Andrew Kinney has been an enthusiastic, generous, and careful editor, and I am thankful for his steady guidance. I also owe a great debt to Bill Keegan, who created the book's maps (in large part from his own knowledge and research on New England's early roads, paths, and settlements). The story herein is the richer for his expertise.

This book is for my parents, who, when I could barely spell or hold a pen, watched me begin to write books. This is the first one to be published. I could not have done it without their years of support and encouragement. Thank you, Mom and Dad. It is also, in many ways, for my daughter Laura, whose story is just beginning. Finally, my deepest love and gratitude to Zachary Gragen. He has been a paragon of support—a tireless listener, a one-man focus group for the wildest of my ideas, the fixer of many a computer problem, a mapmaker, an editor, and my compass through many of New England's woods. He impelled me, always, to do my best work. Thank you, Zack.

Index